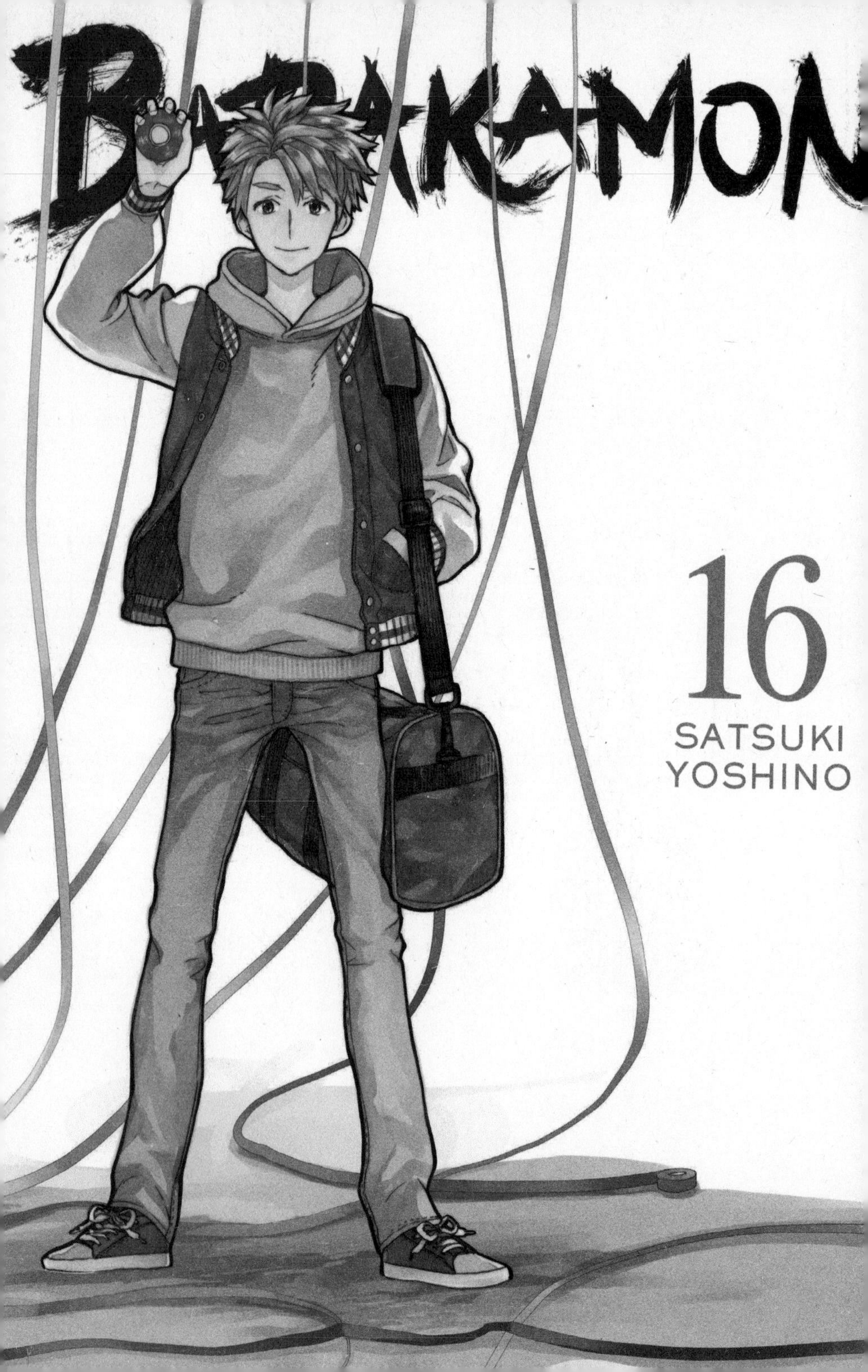
BARAKAMON
16
SATSUKI
YOSHINO

Contents

Act.115   Hiroshi Graduates   003

Act.116   Toretaeta   043

Act.117   Komakuroshika   059

Act.118   Totodon   069

Act.119   Yattattotta   107

Act.120   Un ni Orabu   137

Act.121   Itekoi Hiroshi   173

Bonus   Danpo the 16th   209

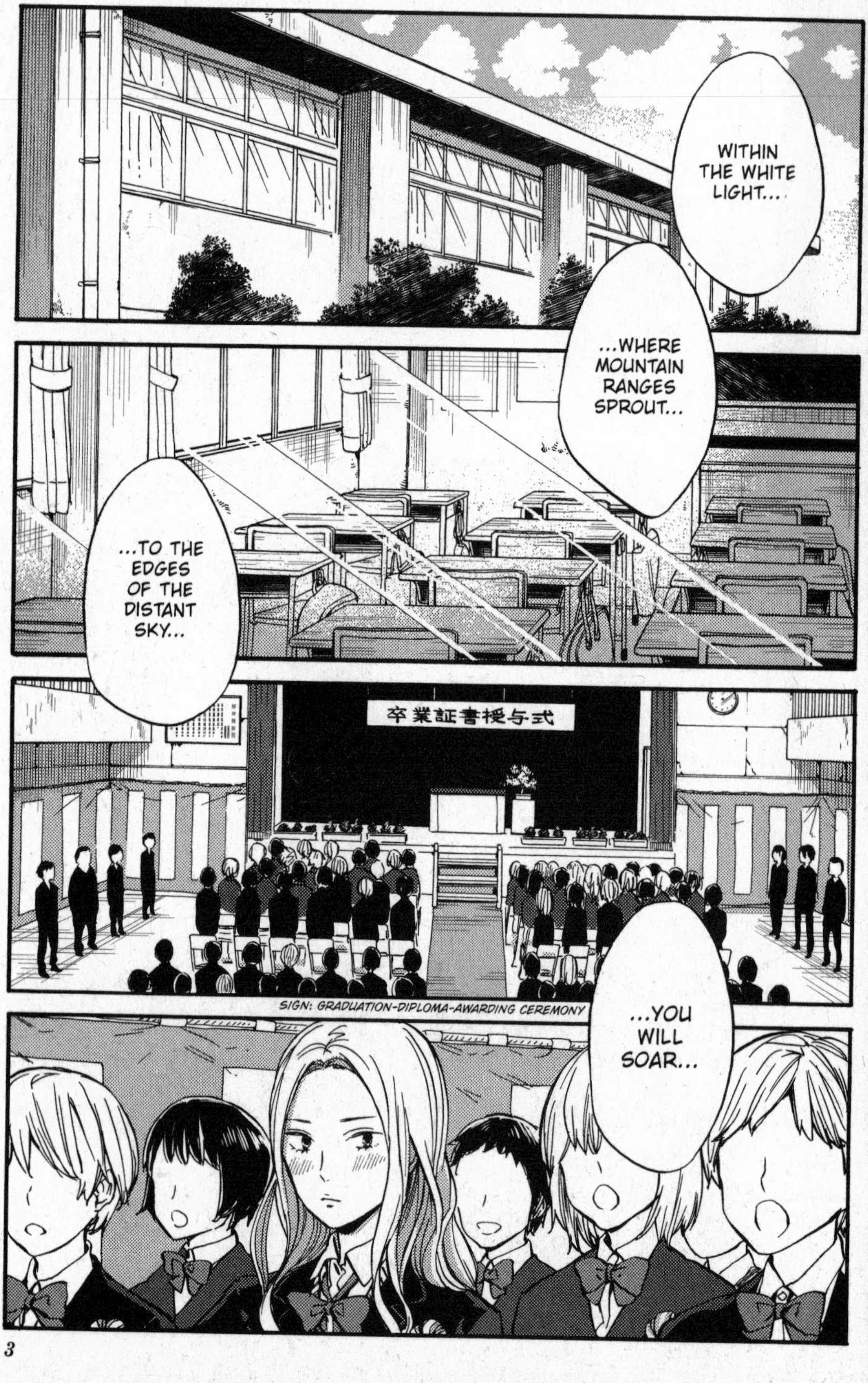
WITHIN THE WHITE LIGHT...
...WHERE MOUNTAIN RANGES SPROUT...
...TO THE EDGES OF THE DISTANT SKY...
卒業証書授与式
SIGN: GRADUATION-DIPLOMA-AWARDING CEREMONY
...YOU WILL SOAR...

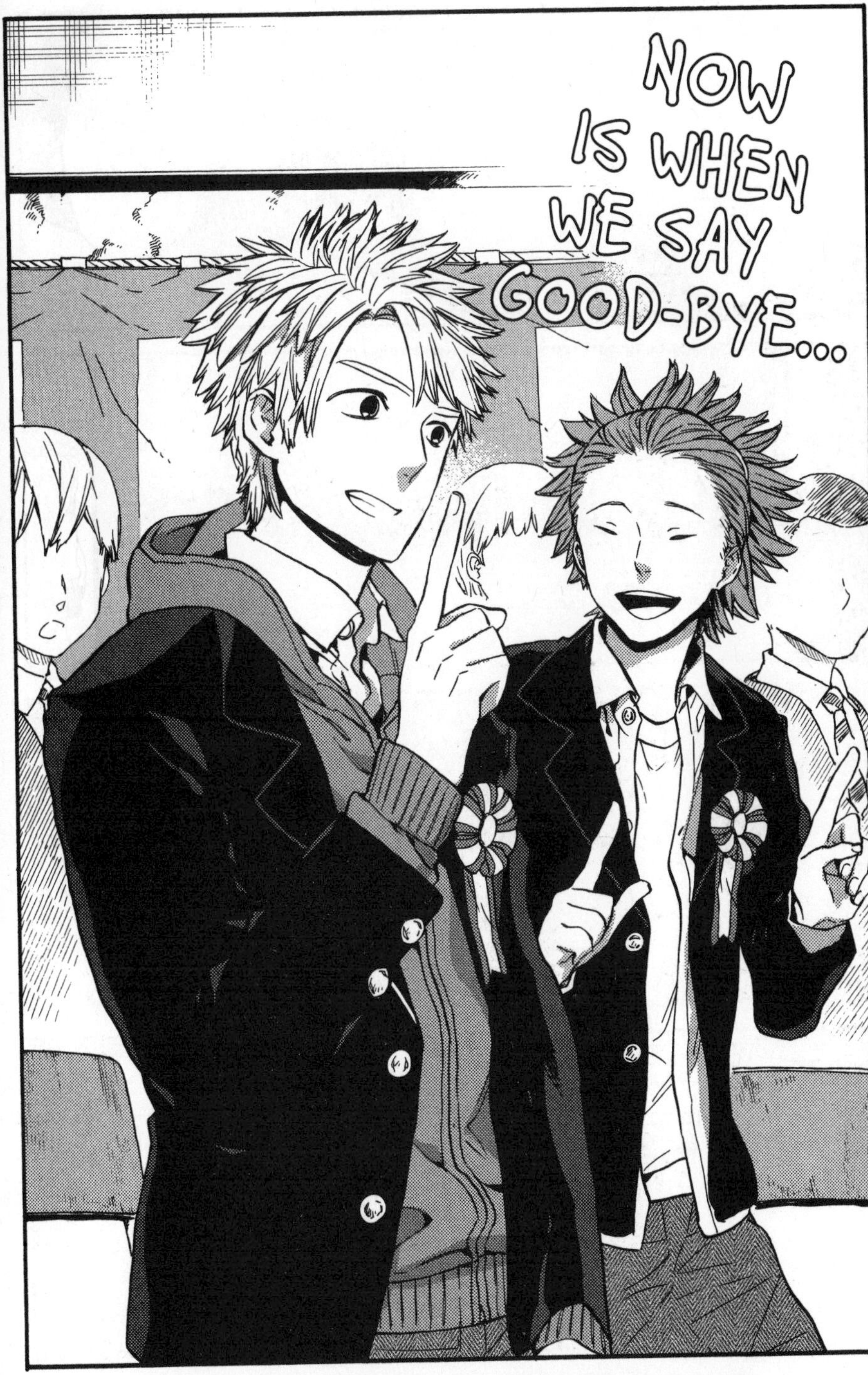
NOW IS WHEN WE SAY GOOD-BYE...

Act.115 HIROSHI GRADUATES

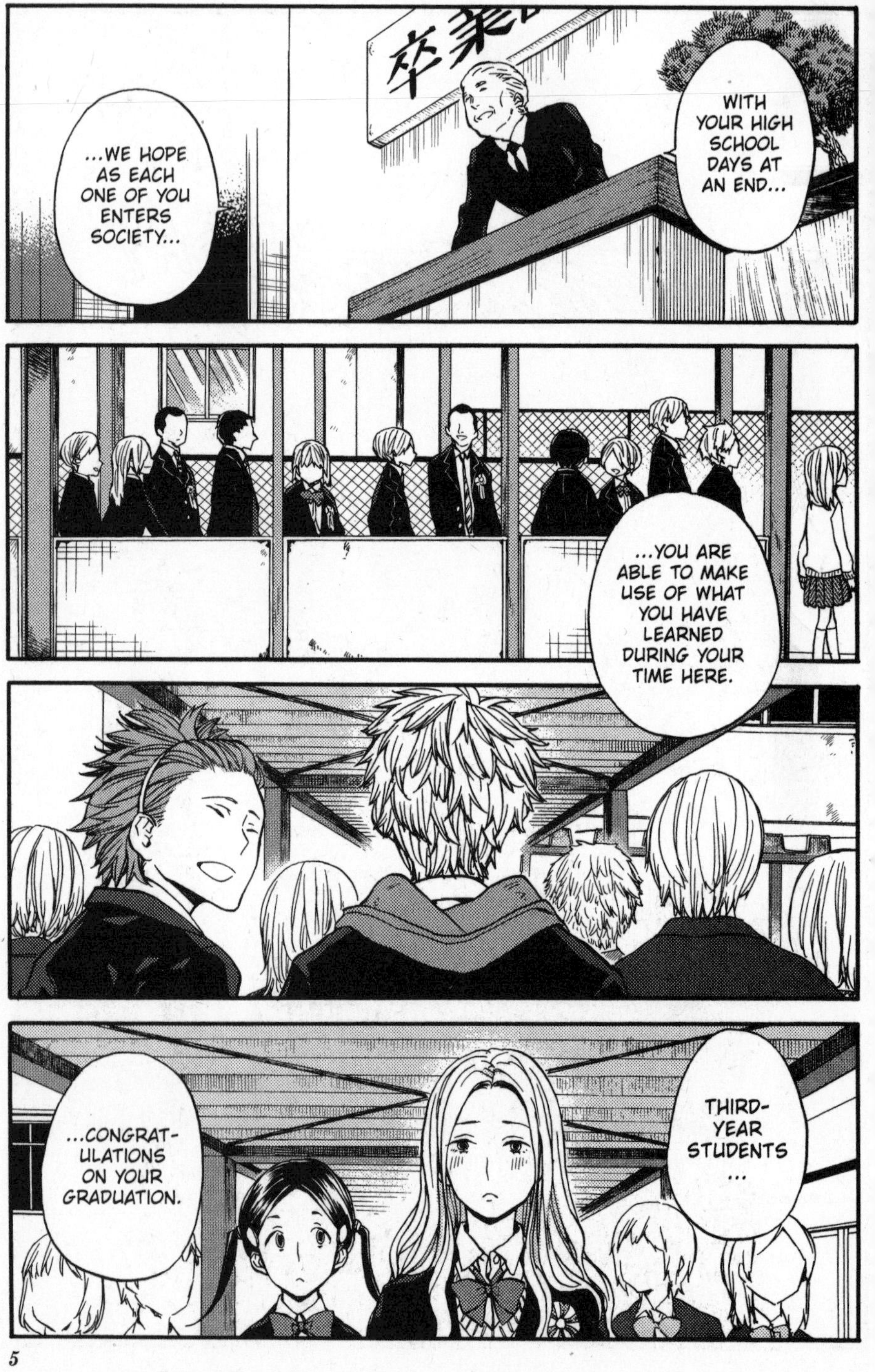
WITH YOUR HIGH SCHOOL DAYS AT AN END...
...WE HOPE AS EACH ONE OF YOU ENTERS SOCIETY...
...YOU ARE ABLE TO MAKE USE OF WHAT YOU HAVE LEARNED DURING YOUR TIME HERE.
THIRD-YEAR STUDENTS...
...CONGRATULATIONS ON YOUR GRADUATION.

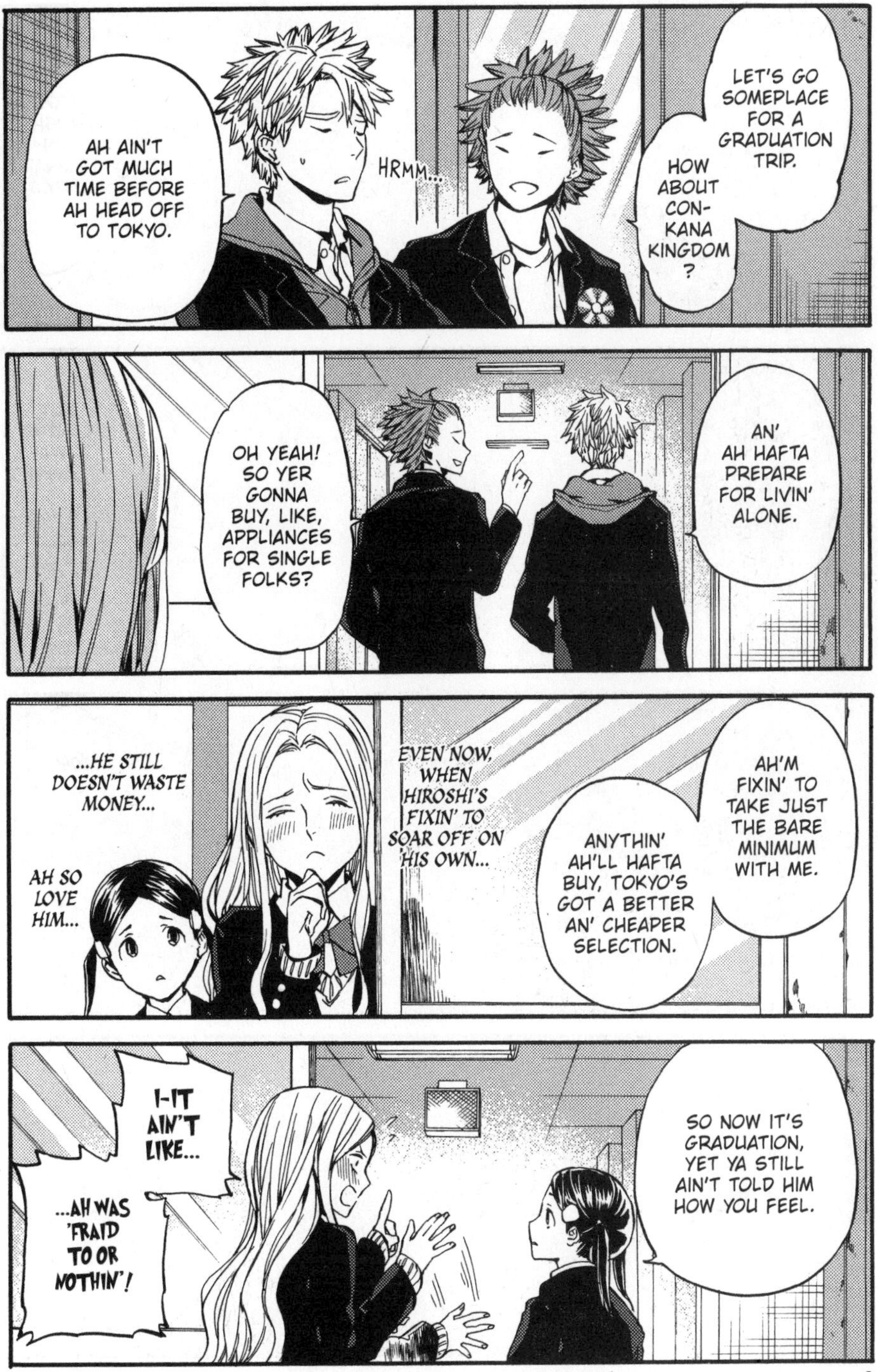
LET'S GO SOMEPLACE FOR A GRADUATION TRIP.
HOW ABOUT CON-KANA KINGDOM?
HRMM...
AH AIN'T GOT MUCH TIME BEFORE AH HEAD OFF TO TOKYO.
AN' AH HAFTA PREPARE FOR LIVIN' ALONE.
OH YEAH! SO YER GONNA BUY, LIKE, APPLIANCES FOR SINGLE FOLKS?
AH'M FIXIN' TO TAKE JUST THE BARE MINIMUM WITH ME.
ANYTHIN' AH'LL HAFTA BUY, TOKYO'S GOT A BETTER AN' CHEAPER SELECTION.
EVEN NOW, WHEN HIROSHI'S FIXIN' TO SOAR OFF ON HIS OWN...
...HE STILL DOESN'T WASTE MONEY...
AH SO LOVE HIM...
SO NOW IT'S GRADUATION, YET YA STILL AIN'T TOLD HIM HOW YOU FEEL.
I-IT AIN'T LIKE...
...AH WAS 'FRAID TO OR NOTHIN'!

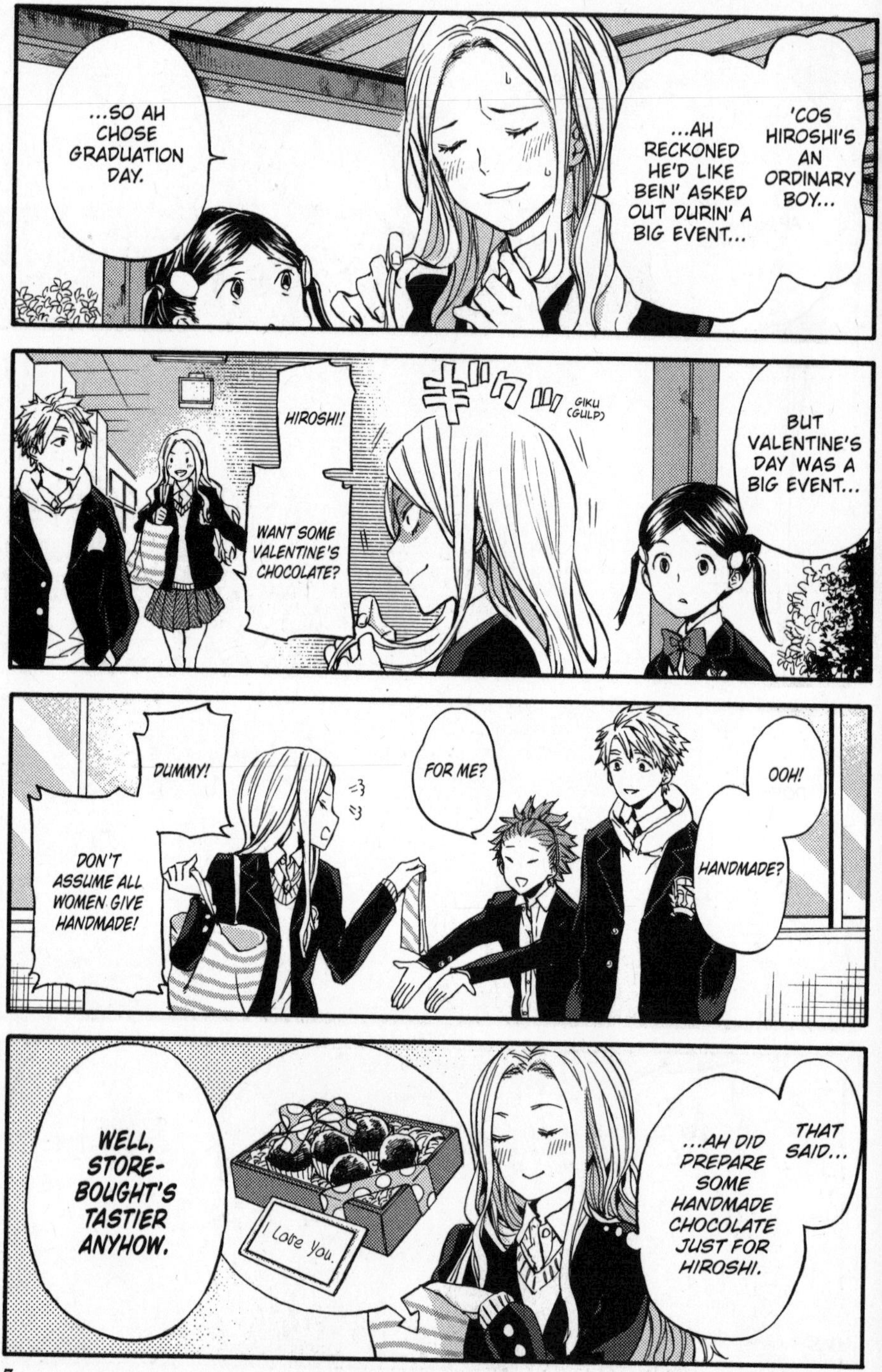
'COS HIROSHI'S AN ORDINARY BOY...
...AH RECKONED HE'D LIKE BEIN' ASKED OUT DURIN' A BIG EVENT...
...SO AH CHOSE GRADUATION DAY.
BUT VALENTINE'S DAY WAS A BIG EVENT...
GIKU (GULP)
HIROSHI!
WANT SOME VALENTINE'S CHOCOLATE?
OOH! HANDMADE?
FOR ME?
DUMMY!
DON'T ASSUME ALL WOMEN GIVE HANDMADE!
THAT SAID...
...AH DID PREPARE SOME HANDMADE CHOCOLATE JUST FOR HIROSHI.
I Love You.
WELL, STORE-BOUGHT'S TASTIER ANYHOW.

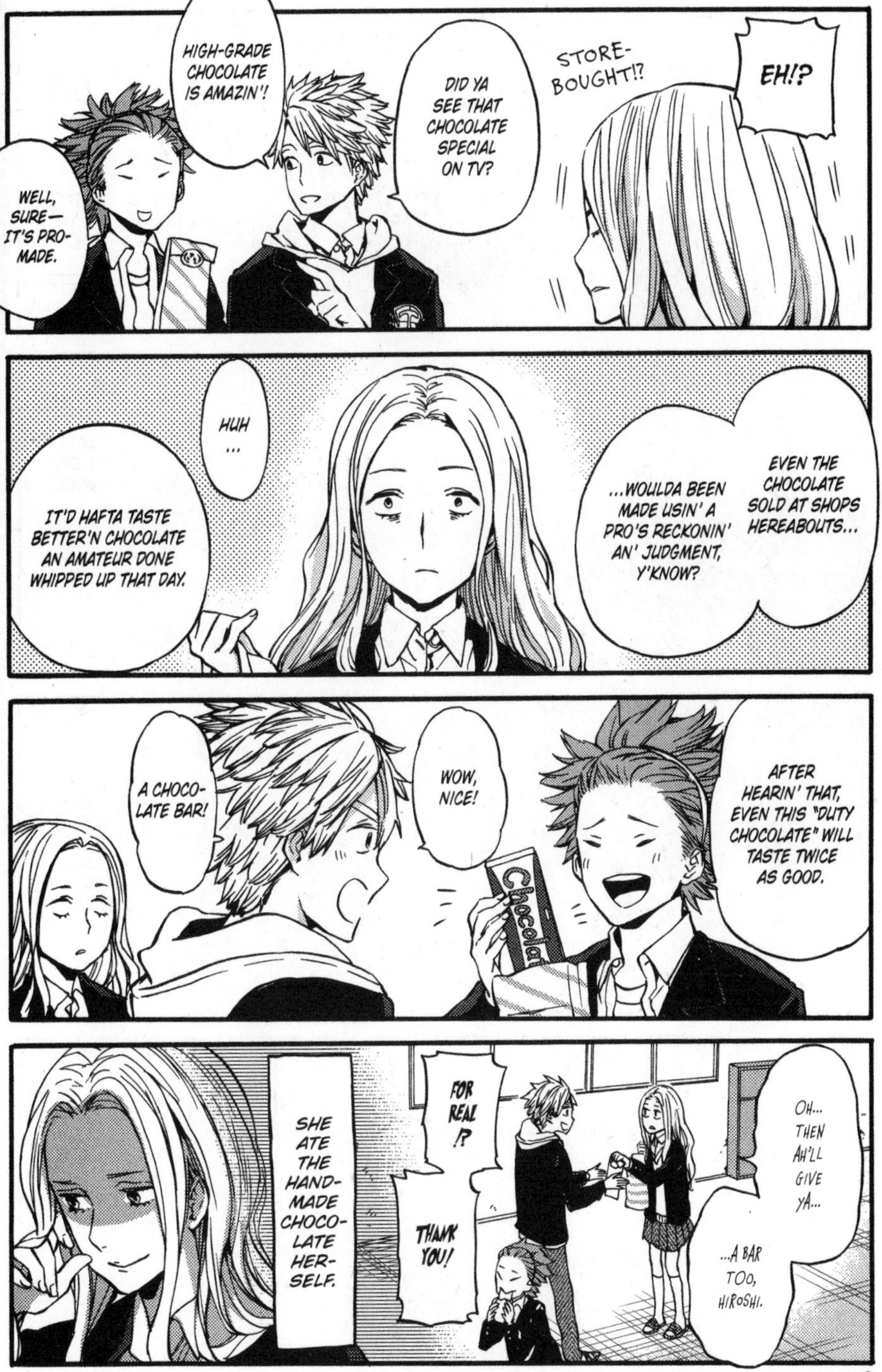
EH!?
STORE-BOUGHT!?
DID YA SEE THAT CHOCOLATE SPECIAL ON TV?
HIGH-GRADE CHOCOLATE IS AMAZIN'!
WELL, SURE— IT'S PRO-MADE.
EVEN THE CHOCOLATE SOLD AT SHOPS HEREABOUTS...
...WOULDA BEEN MADE USIN' A PRO'S RECKONIN' AN' JUDGMENT, Y'KNOW?
HUH ...
IT'D HAFTA TASTE BETTER'N CHOCOLATE AN AMATEUR DONE WHIPPED UP THAT DAY.
AFTER HEARIN' THAT, EVEN THIS "DUTY CHOCOLATE" WILL TASTE TWICE AS GOOD.
WOW, NICE!
A CHOCO-LATE BAR!
OH... THEN AH'LL GIVE YA...
...A BAR TOO, HIROSHI.
FOR REAL!?
THANK YOU!
SHE ATE THE HAND-MADE CHOCO-LATE HER-SELF.

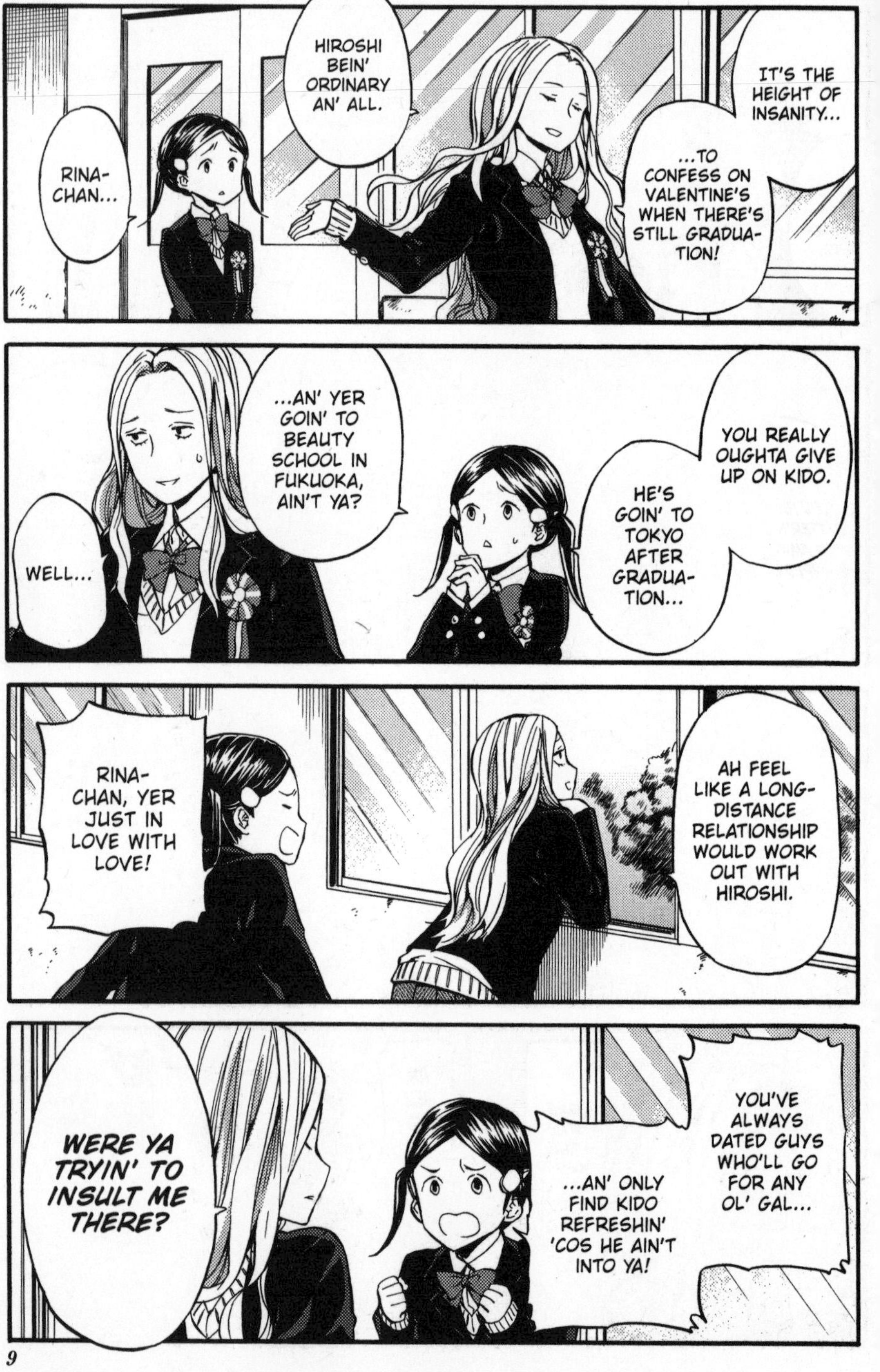
IT'S THE HEIGHT OF INSANITY...
...TO CONFESS ON VALENTINE'S WHEN THERE'S STILL GRADUATION!
HIROSHI BEIN' ORDINARY AN' ALL.
RINA-CHAN...
YOU REALLY OUGHTA GIVE UP ON KIDO.
HE'S GOIN' TO TOKYO AFTER GRADUATION...
...AN' YER GOIN' TO BEAUTY SCHOOL IN FUKUOKA, AIN'T YA?
WELL...
AH FEEL LIKE A LONG-DISTANCE RELATIONSHIP WOULD WORK OUT WITH HIROSHI.
RINA-CHAN, YER JUST IN LOVE WITH LOVE!
YOU'VE ALWAYS DATED GUYS WHO'LL GO FOR ANY OL' GAL...
...AN' ONLY FIND KIDO REFRESHIN' 'COS HE AIN'T INTO YA!
WERE YA TRYIN' TO INSULT ME THERE?

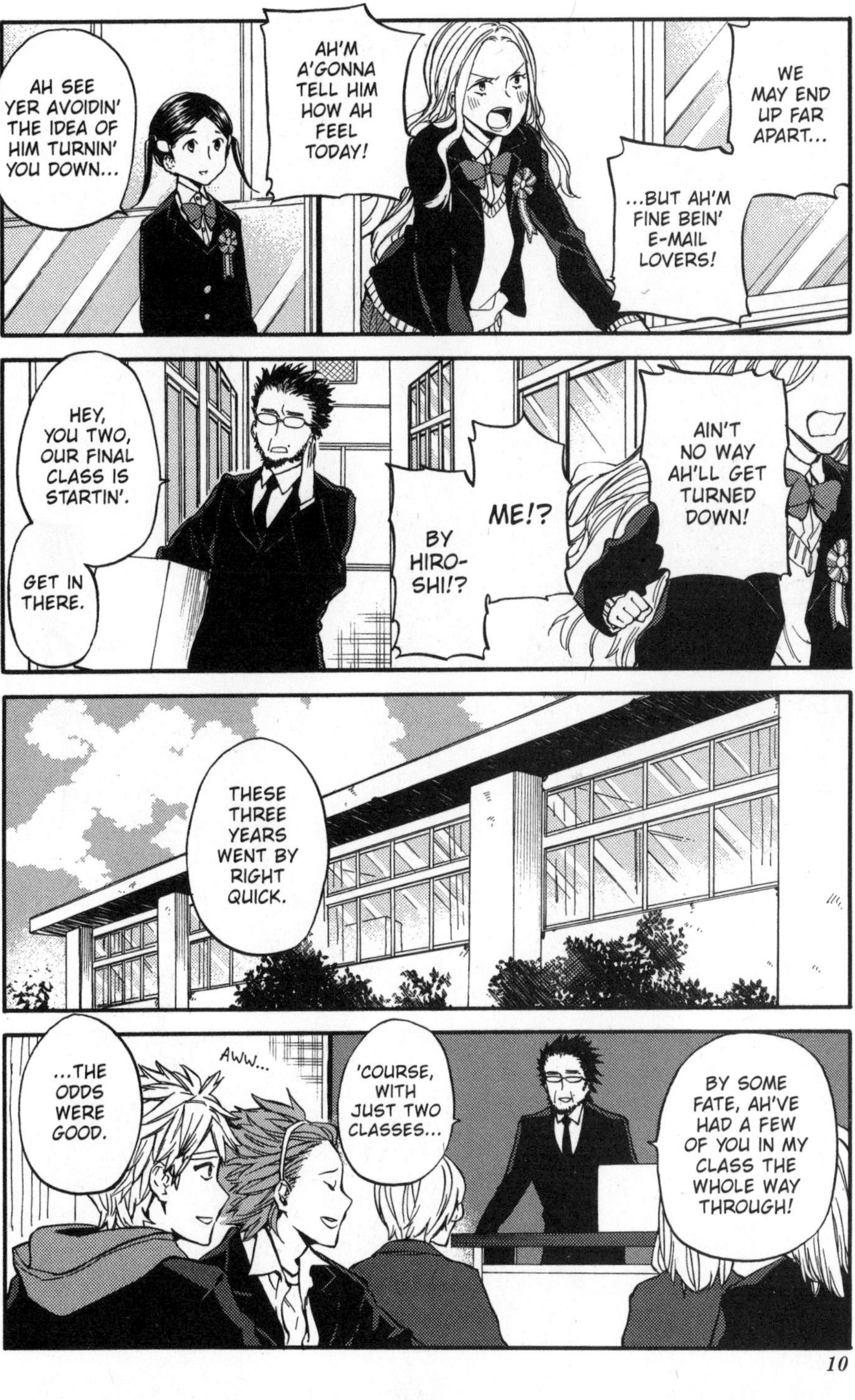
WE MAY END UP FAR APART...
...BUT AH'M FINE BEIN' E-MAIL LOVERS!
AH'M A'GONNA TELL HIM HOW AH FEEL TODAY!
AH SEE YER AVOIDIN' THE IDEA OF HIM TURNIN' YOU DOWN...
AIN'T NO WAY AH'LL GET TURNED DOWN!
ME!?
BY HIRO-SHI!?
HEY, YOU TWO, OUR FINAL CLASS IS STARTIN'.
GET IN THERE.
THESE THREE YEARS WENT BY RIGHT QUICK.
BY SOME FATE, AH'VE HAD A FEW OF YOU IN MY CLASS THE WHOLE WAY THROUGH!
'COURSE, WITH JUST TWO CLASSES...
AWW...
...THE ODDS WERE GOOD.

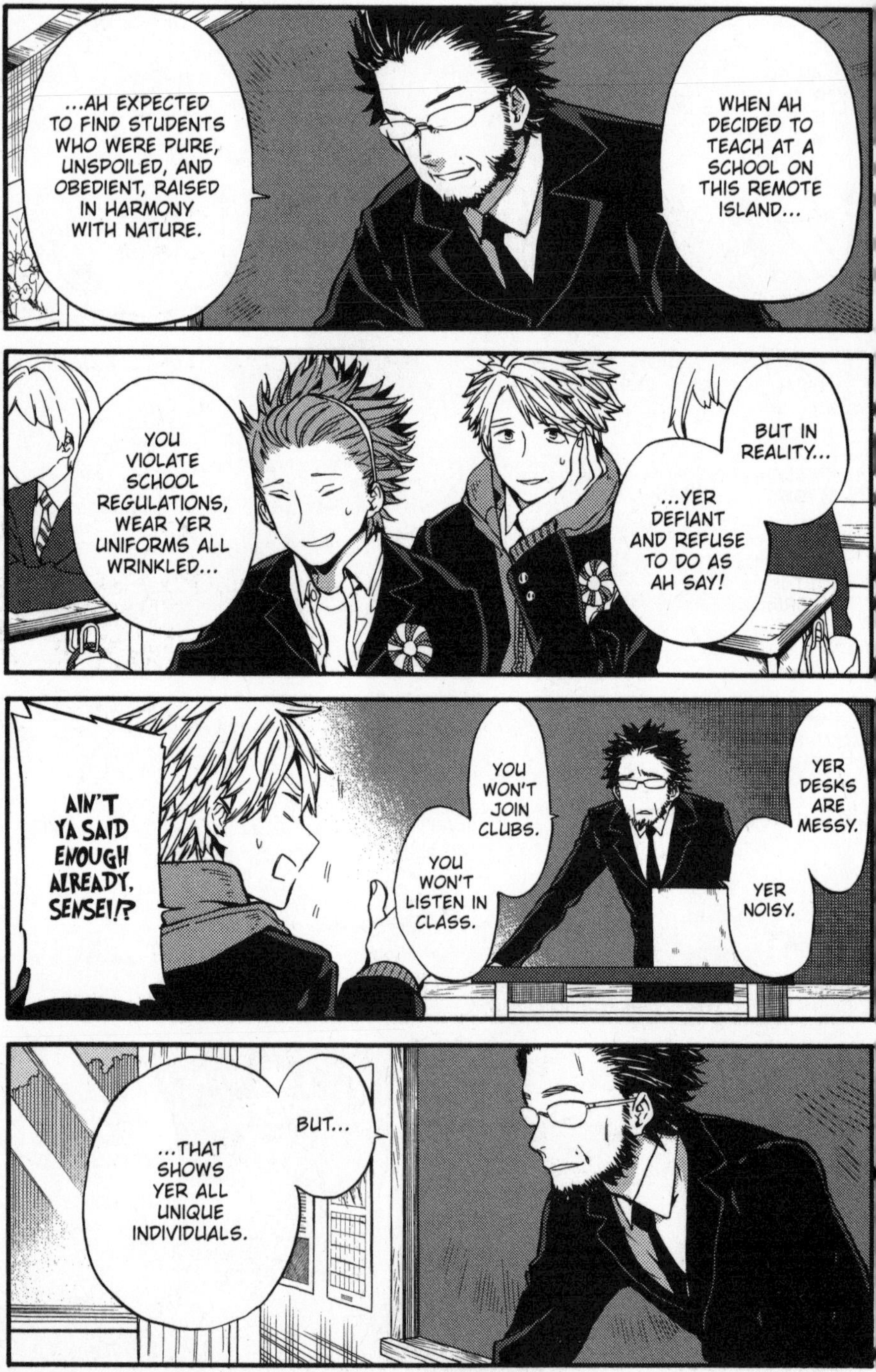
WHEN AH DECIDED TO TEACH AT A SCHOOL ON THIS REMOTE ISLAND...
...AH EXPECTED TO FIND STUDENTS WHO WERE PURE, UNSPOILED, AND OBEDIENT, RAISED IN HARMONY WITH NATURE.
BUT IN REALITY...
...YER DEFIANT AND REFUSE TO DO AS AH SAY!
YOU VIOLATE SCHOOL REGULATIONS, WEAR YER UNIFORMS ALL WRINKLED...
YER DESKS ARE MESSY.
YER NOISY.
YOU WON'T JOIN CLUBS.
YOU WON'T LISTEN IN CLASS.
AIN'T YA SAID ENOUGH ALREADY, SENSEI!?
BUT...
...THAT SHOWS YER ALL UNIQUE INDIVIDUALS.

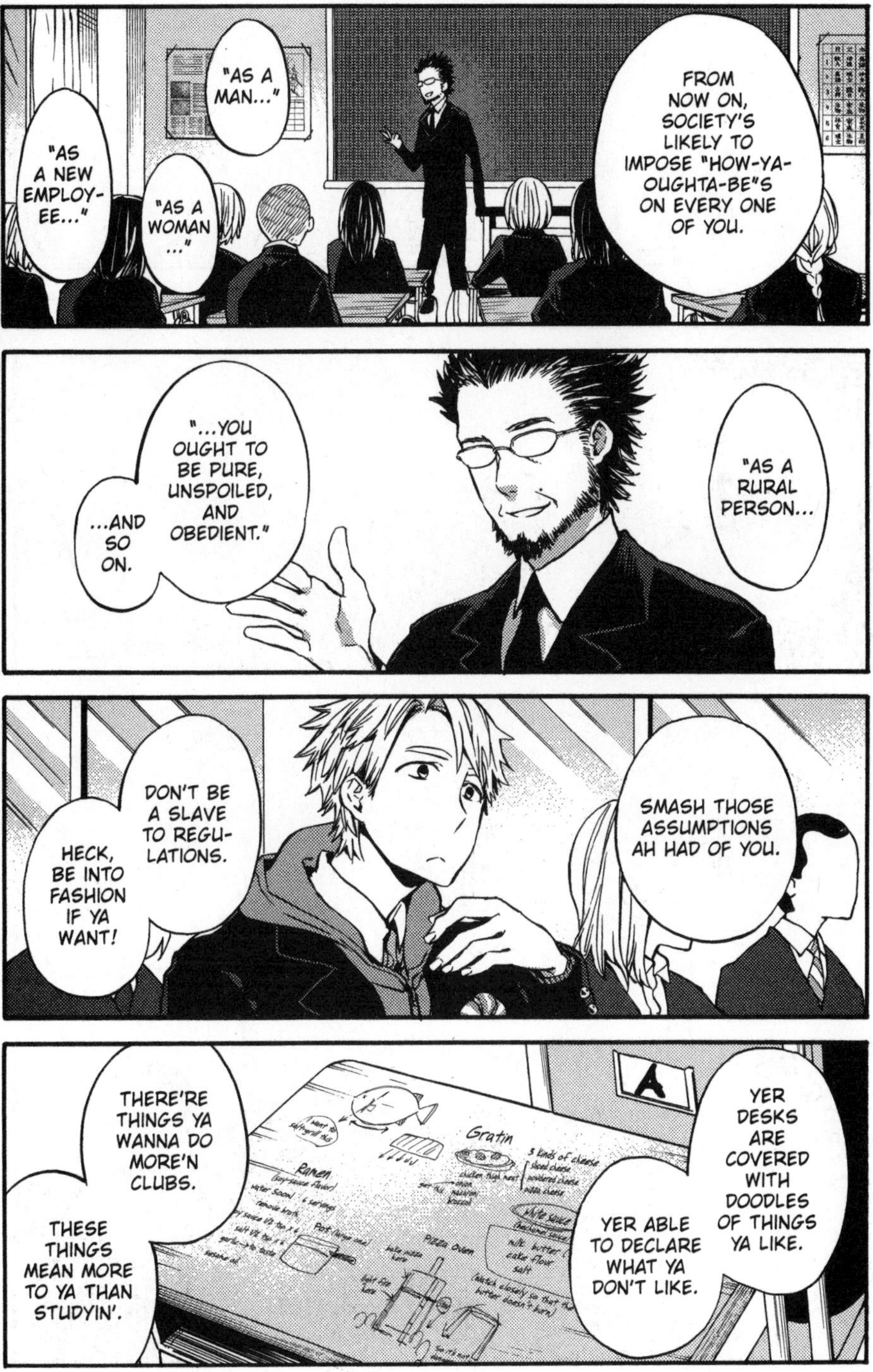
FROM NOW ON, SOCIETY'S LIKELY TO IMPOSE "HOW-YA-OUGHTA-BE"S ON EVERY ONE OF YOU.
"AS A MAN..."
"AS A WOMAN..."
"AS A NEW EMPLOYEE..."
"AS A RURAL PERSON...
"...YOU OUGHT TO BE PURE, UNSPOILED, AND OBEDIENT."
...AND SO ON.
SMASH THOSE ASSUMPTIONS AH HAD OF YOU.
DON'T BE A SLAVE TO REGULATIONS.
HECK, BE INTO FASHION IF YA WANT!
YER DESKS ARE COVERED WITH DOODLES OF THINGS YA LIKE.
YER ABLE TO DECLARE WHAT YA DON'T LIKE.
Gratin
Ramen
THERE'RE THINGS YA WANNA DO MORE'N CLUBS.
THESE THINGS MEAN MORE TO YA THAN STUDYIN'.

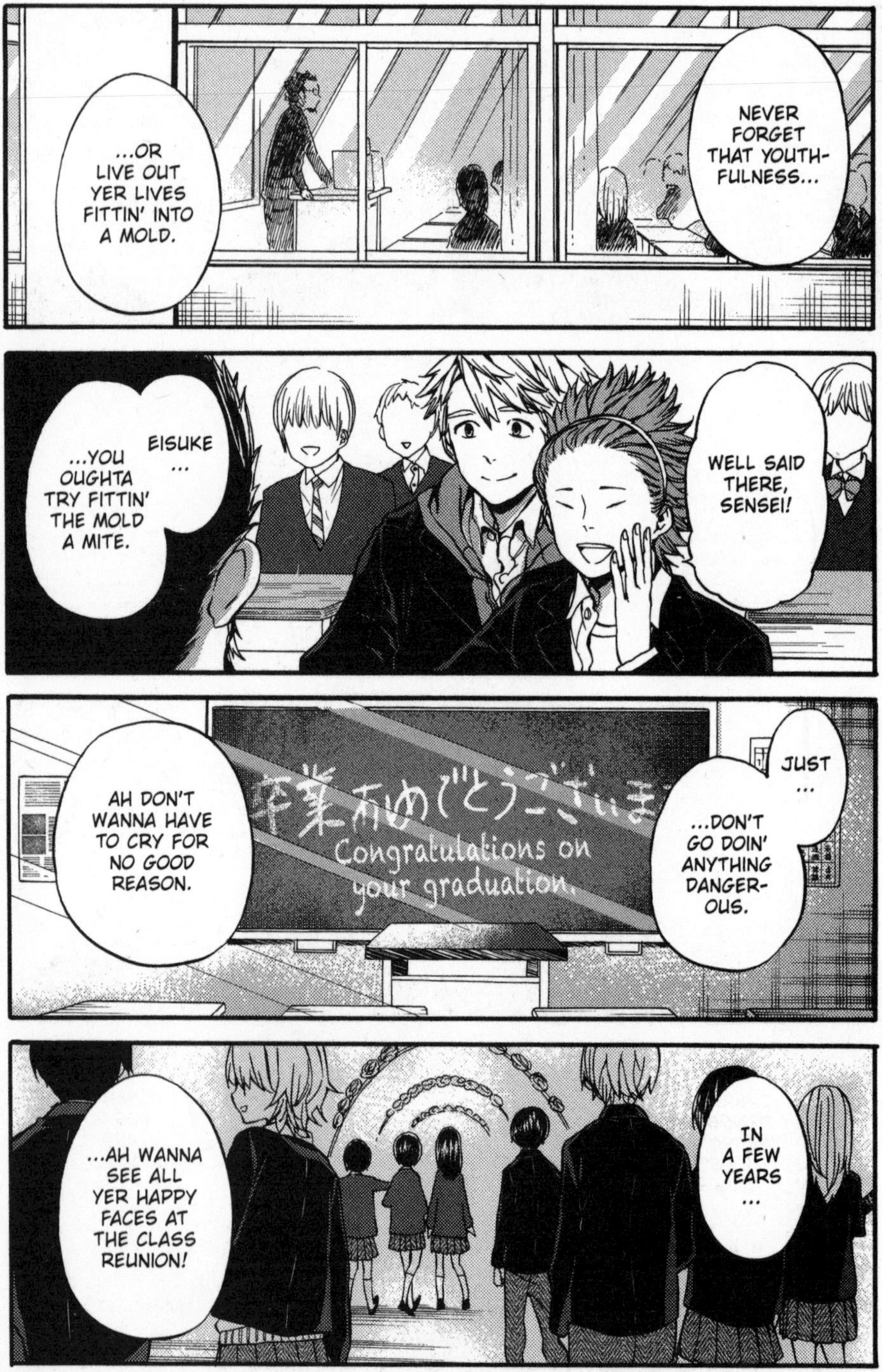
NEVER FORGET THAT YOUTH-FULNESS...
...OR LIVE OUT YER LIVES FITTIN' INTO A MOLD.
WELL SAID THERE, SENSEI!
EISUKE ...
...YOU OUGHTA TRY FITTIN' THE MOLD A MITE.
JUST ...
...DON'T GO DOIN' ANYTHING DANGER-OUS.
Congratulations on your graduation.
AH DON'T WANNA HAVE TO CRY FOR NO GOOD REASON.
IN A FEW YEARS ...
...AH WANNA SEE ALL YER HAPPY FACES AT THE CLASS REUNION!

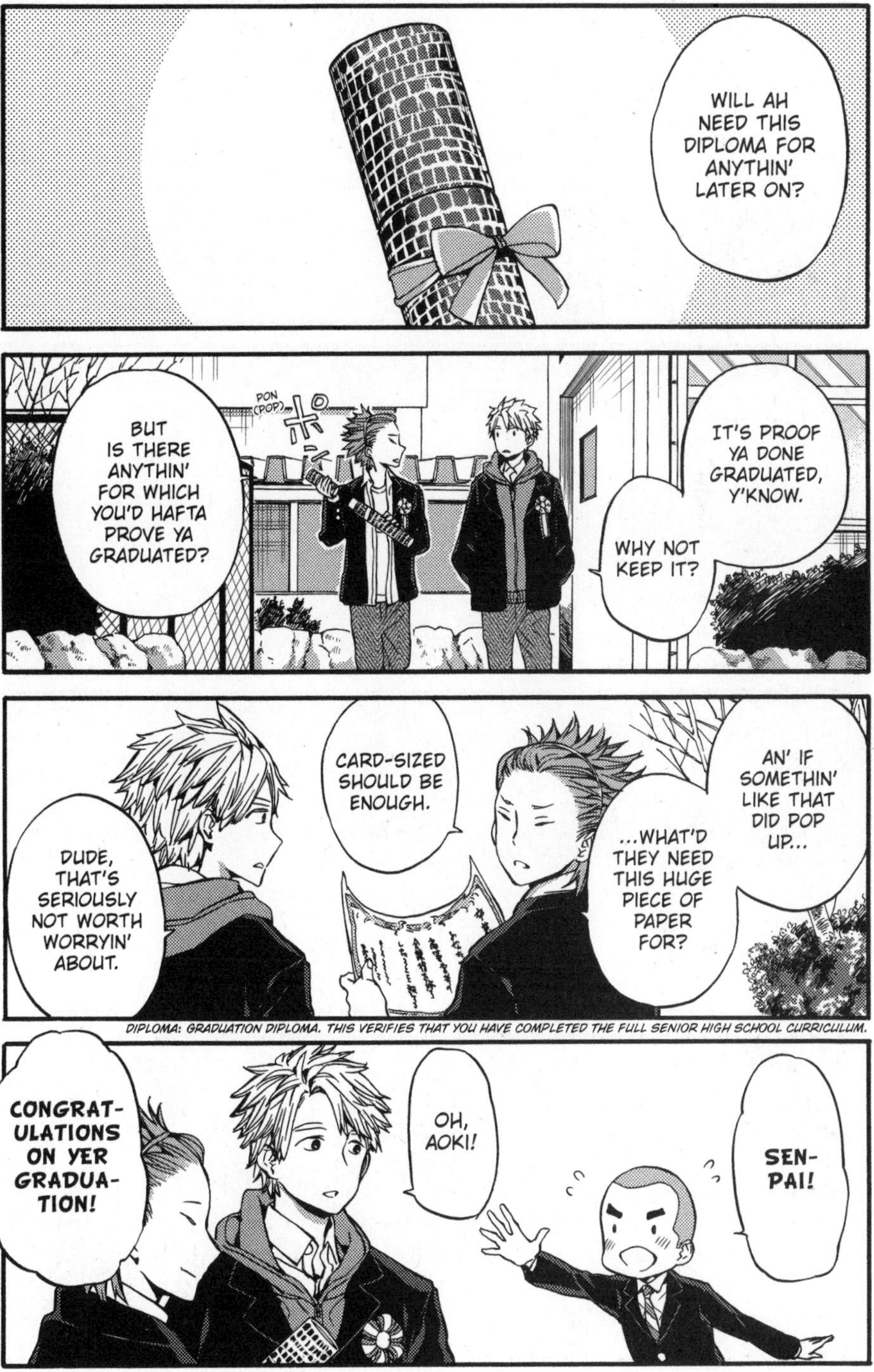
WILL AH NEED THIS DIPLOMA FOR ANYTHIN' LATER ON?
IT'S PROOF YA DONE GRADUATED, Y'KNOW.
WHY NOT KEEP IT?
PON (POP)
BUT IS THERE ANYTHIN' FOR WHICH YOU'D HAFTA PROVE YA GRADUATED?
AN' IF SOMETHIN' LIKE THAT DID POP UP...
...WHAT'D THEY NEED THIS HUGE PIECE OF PAPER FOR?
CARD-SIZED SHOULD BE ENOUGH.
DUDE, THAT'S SERIOUSLY NOT WORTH WORRYIN' ABOUT.
SEN-PAI!
OH, AOKI!
CONGRAT-ULATIONS ON YER GRADUA-TION!

DIPLOMA: GRADUATION DIPLOMA. THIS VERIFIES THAT YOU HAVE COMPLETED THE FULL SENIOR HIGH SCHOOL CURRICULUM.

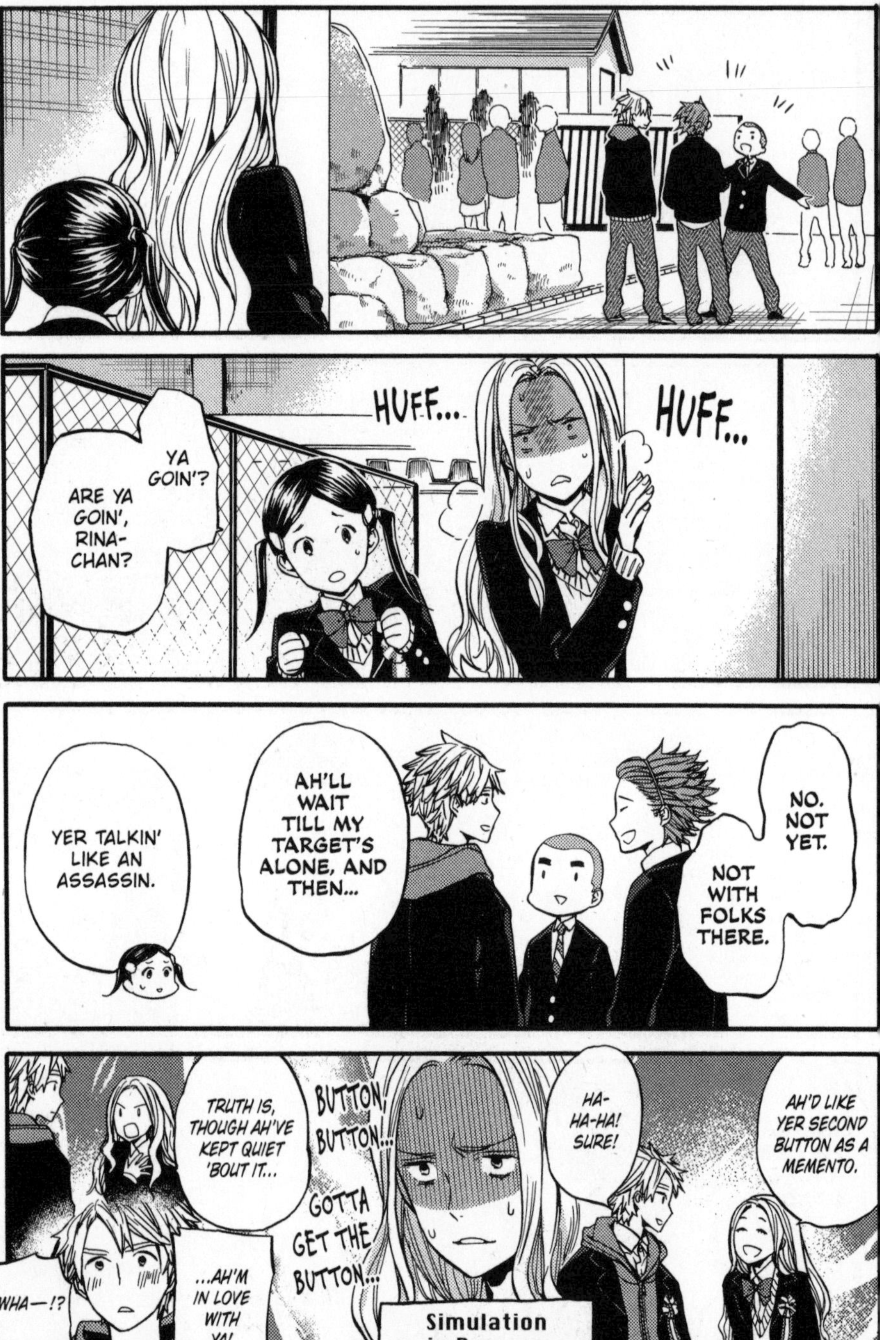
HUFF...
HUFF...
YA GOIN'?
ARE YA GOIN', RINA-CHAN?
NO. NOT YET.
NOT WITH FOLKS THERE.
AH'LL WAIT TILL MY TARGET'S ALONE, AND THEN...
YER TALKIN' LIKE AN ASSASSIN.
AH'D LIKE YER SECOND BUTTON AS A MEMENTO.
HA-HA-HA! SURE!
BUTTON, BUTTON...
GOTTA GET THE BUTTON...
Simulation in Process
TRUTH IS, THOUGH AH'VE KEPT QUIET 'BOUT IT...
...AH'M IN LOVE WITH YA!
WHA—!?

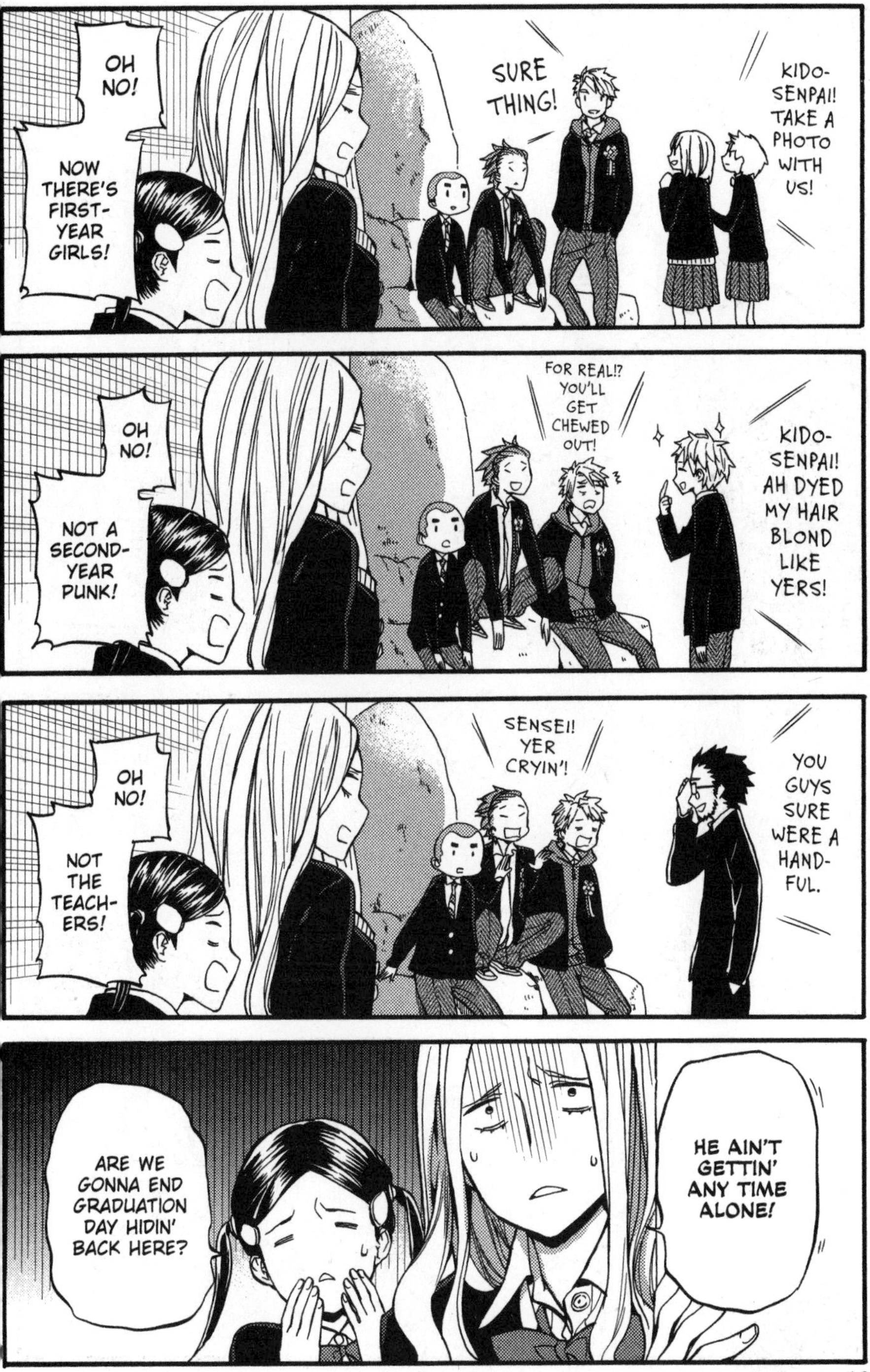
KIDO-SENPAI! TAKE A PHOTO WITH US!
SURE THING!
OH NO!
NOW THERE'S FIRST-YEAR GIRLS!
KIDO-SENPAI! AH DYED MY HAIR BLOND LIKE YERS!
FOR REAL!? YOU'LL GET CHEWED OUT!
OH NO!
NOT A SECOND-YEAR PUNK!
YOU GUYS SURE WERE A HANDFUL.
SENSEI! YER CRYIN'!
OH NO!
NOT THE TEACHERS!
HE AIN'T GETTIN' ANY TIME ALONE!
ARE WE GONNA END GRADUATION DAY HIDIN' BACK HERE?

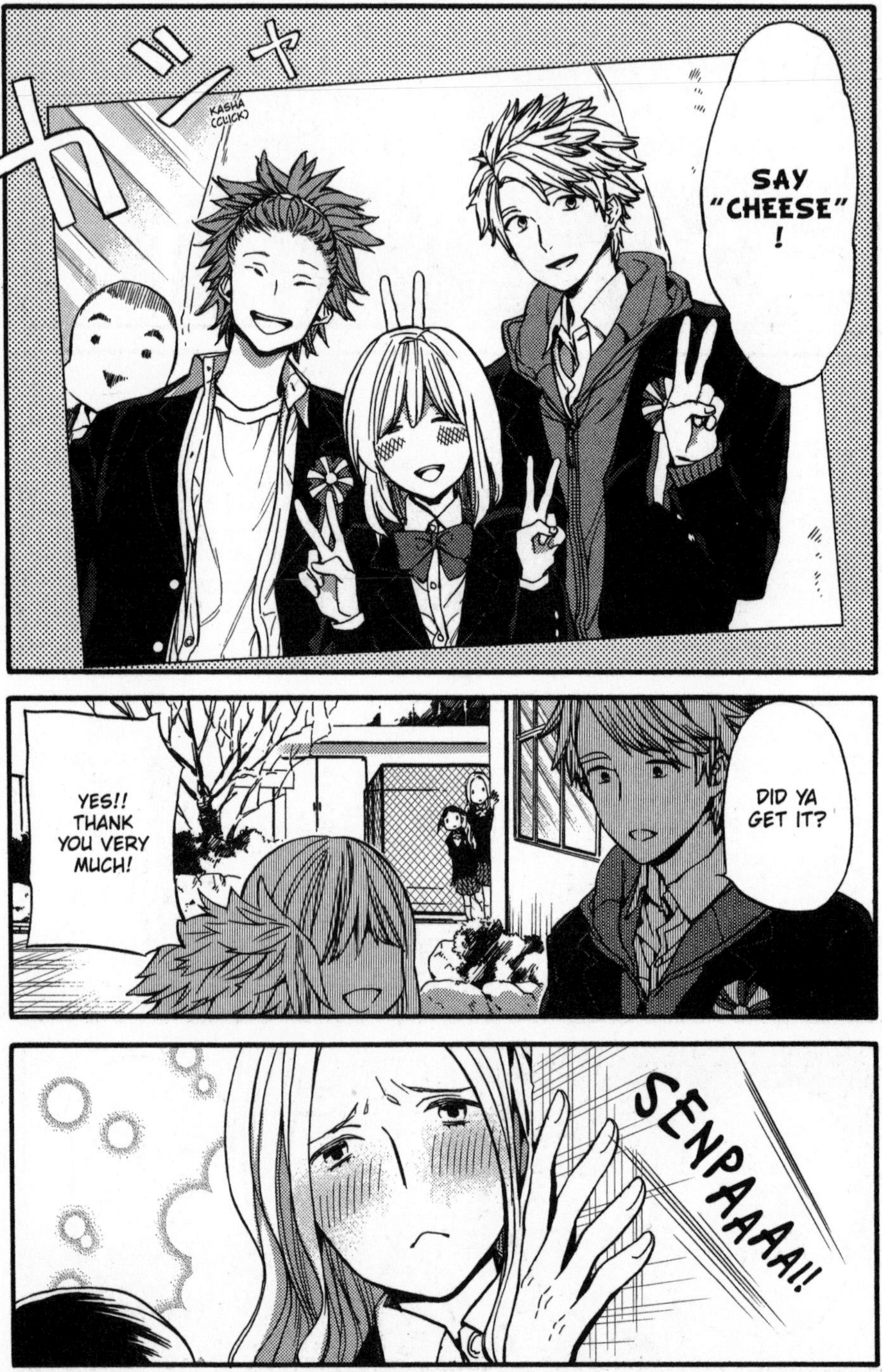
SAY "CHEESE"!
カシャ
KASHA (CLICK)
DID YA GET IT?
YES!! THANK YOU VERY MUCH!
SENPAAAAI!!

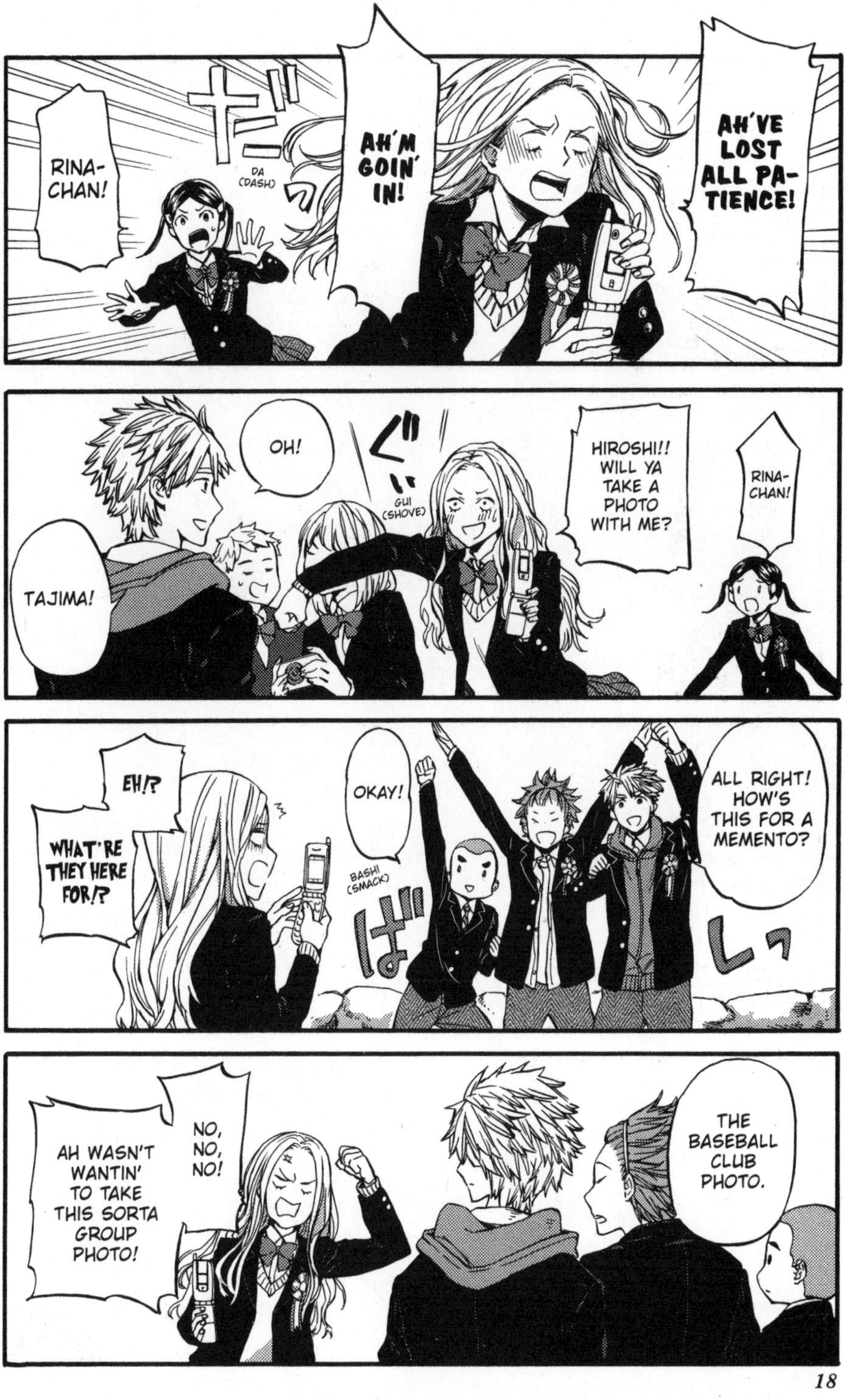
AH'VE LOST ALL PATIENCE!
AH'M GOIN' IN!
DA (DASH)
RINA-CHAN!
RINA-CHAN!
HIROSHI!! WILL YA TAKE A PHOTO WITH ME?
GUI (SHOVE)
OH!
TAJIMA!
ALL RIGHT! HOW'S THIS FOR A MEMENTO?
BASHI (SMACK)
OKAY!
EH!?
WHAT'RE THEY HERE FOR!?
THE BASEBALL CLUB PHOTO.
NO, NO, NO!
AH WASN'T WANTIN' TO TAKE THIS SORTA GROUP PHOTO!

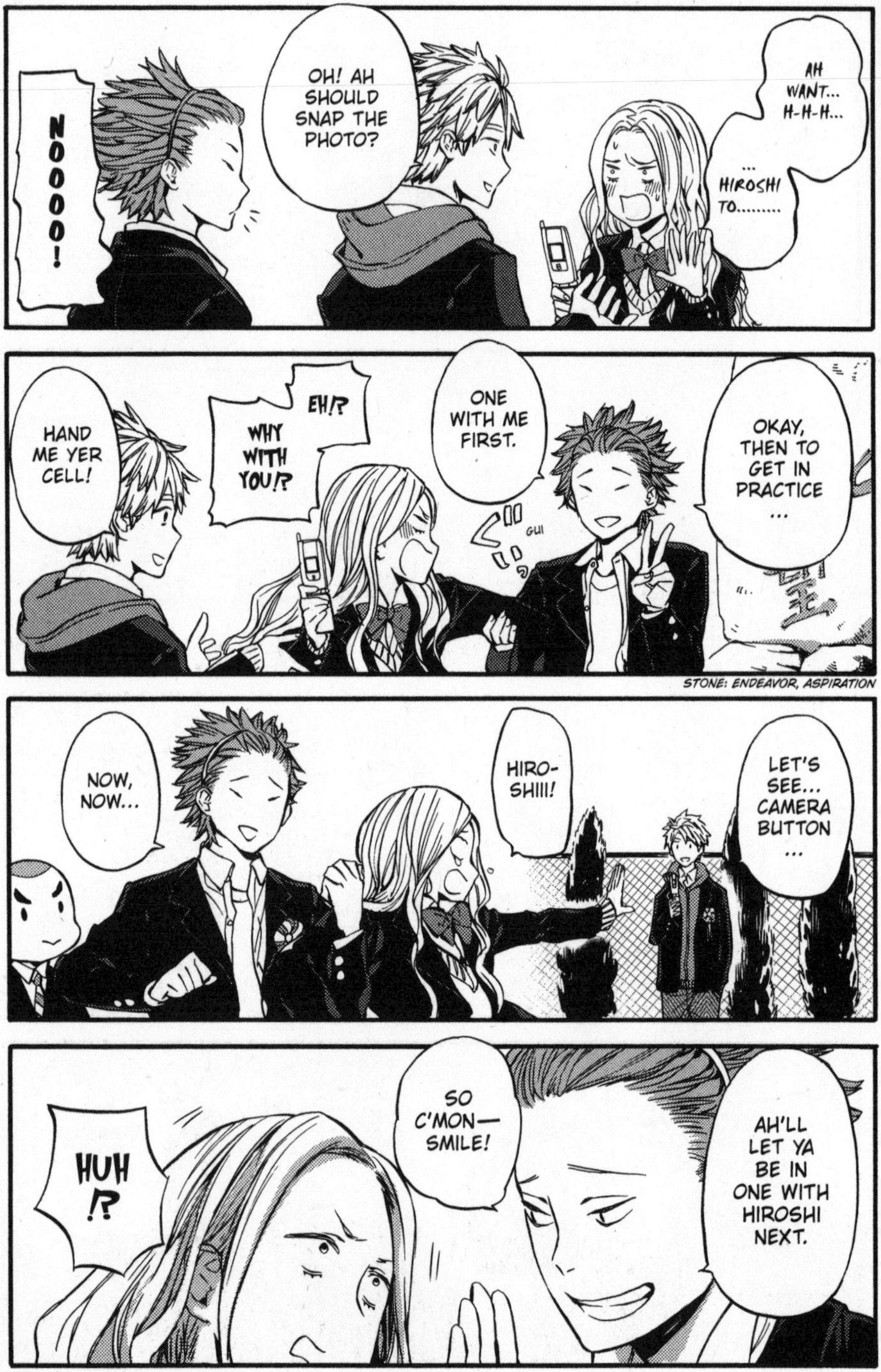
AH WANT... H-H-H...
... HIROSHI TO.........
OH! AH SHOULD SNAP THE PHOTO?
NOOOOO!
OKAY, THEN TO GET IN PRACTICE ...
ONE WITH ME FIRST.
GUI
EH!? WHY WITH YOU!?
HAND ME YER CELL!
LET'S SEE... CAMERA BUTTON ...
HIRO-SHIII!
NOW, NOW...
AH'LL LET YA BE IN ONE WITH HIROSHI NEXT.
SO C'MON— SMILE!
HUH !?

STONE: ENDEAVOR, ASPIRATION

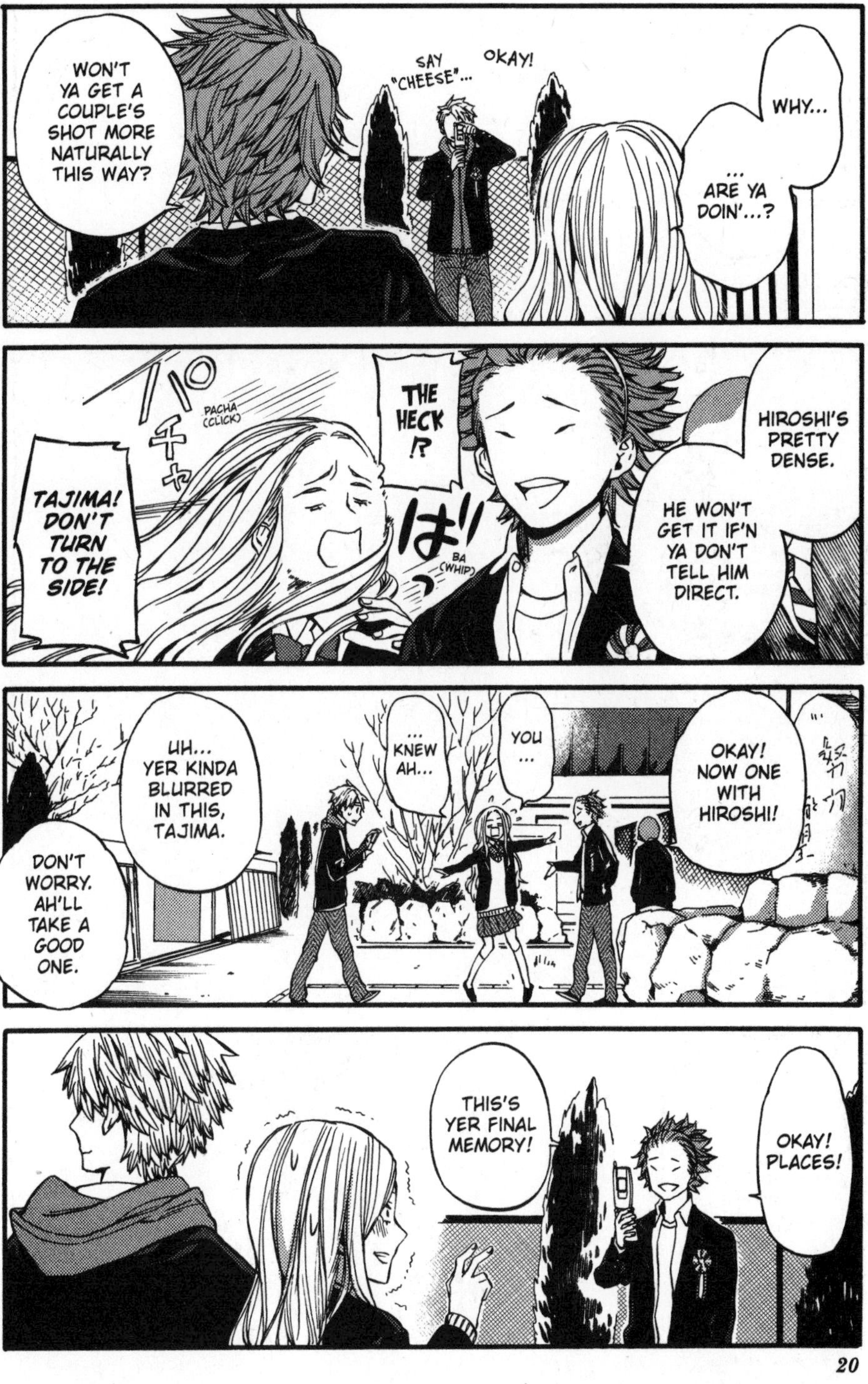
WHY...
... ARE YA DOIN'...?
OKAY!
SAY "CHEESE"...
WON'T YA GET A COUPLE'S SHOT MORE NATURALLY THIS WAY?
HIROSHI'S PRETTY DENSE.
HE WON'T GET IT IF'N YA DON'T TELL HIM DIRECT.
THE HECK!?
パチャ
PACHA (CLICK)
ばッ
BA (WHIP)
TAJIMA! DON'T TURN TO THE SIDE!
OKAY! NOW ONE WITH HIROSHI!
YOU...
... KNEW AH...
UH... YER KINDA BLURRED IN THIS, TAJIMA.
DON'T WORRY. AH'LL TAKE A GOOD ONE.
OKAY! PLACES!
THIS'S YER FINAL MEMORY!

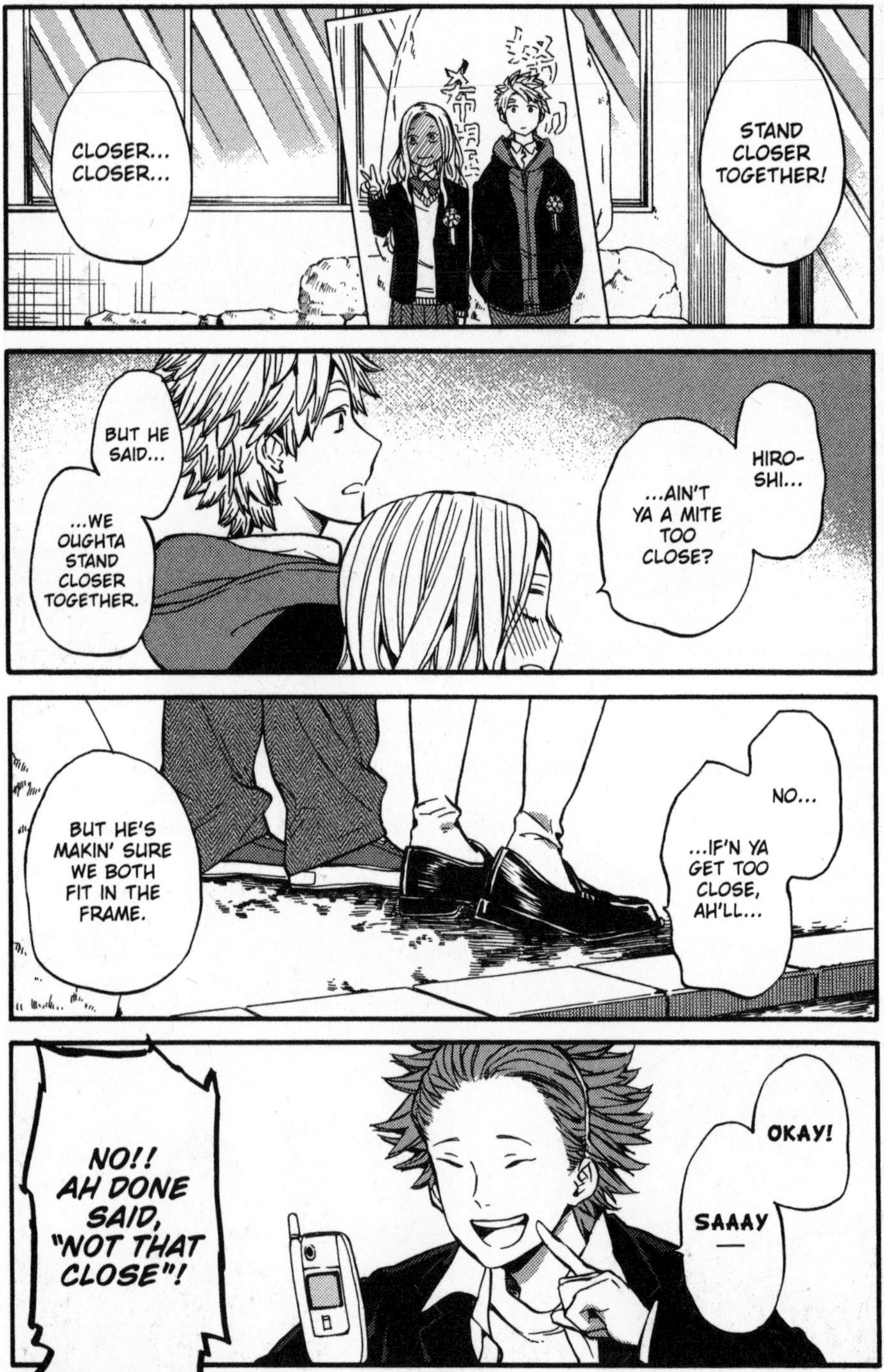
STAND CLOSER TOGETHER!
CLOSER... CLOSER...
HIRO-SHI...
...AIN'T YA A MITE TOO CLOSE?
BUT HE SAID...
...WE OUGHTA STAND CLOSER TOGETHER.
NO...
...IF'N YA GET TOO CLOSE, AH'LL...
BUT HE'S MAKIN' SURE WE BOTH FIT IN THE FRAME.
OKAY!
SAAAY—
NO!! AH DONE SAID, "NOT THAT CLOSE"!

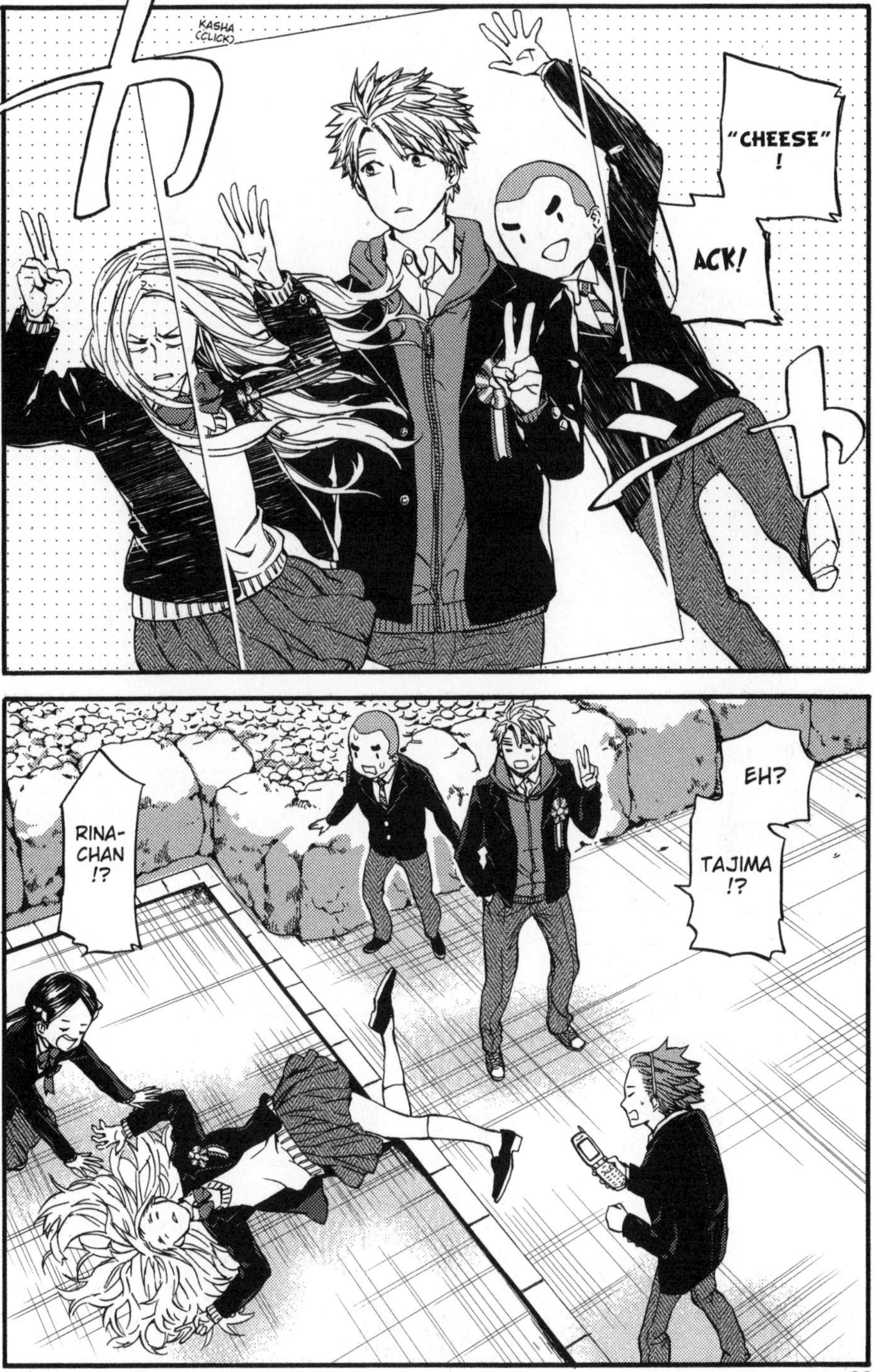
"CHEESE"!
ACK!
KASHA (CLICK)
EH?
TAJIMA!?
RINA-CHAN!?

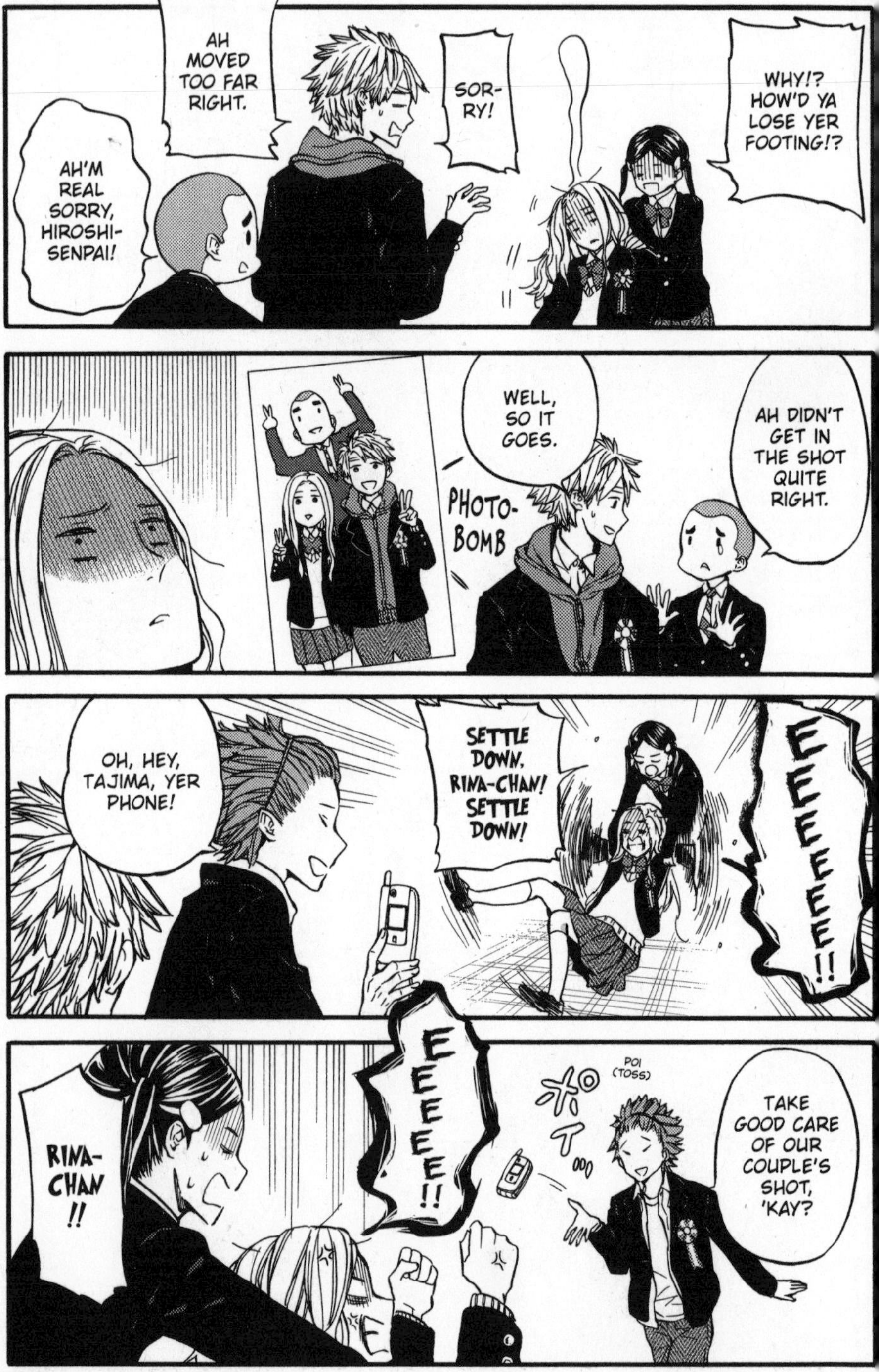
WHY!? HOW'D YA LOSE YER FOOTING!?
SOR-RY!
AH MOVED TOO FAR RIGHT.
AH'M REAL SORRY, HIROSHI-SENPAI!
AH DIDN'T GET IN THE SHOT QUITE RIGHT.
WELL, SO IT GOES.
PHOTO-BOMB
EEEEEEE!!
SETTLE DOWN, RINA-CHAN! SETTLE DOWN!
OH, HEY, TAJIMA, YER PHONE!
TAKE GOOD CARE OF OUR COUPLE'S SHOT, 'KAY?
POI (TOSS)
EEEEEE!!
RINA-CHAN!!

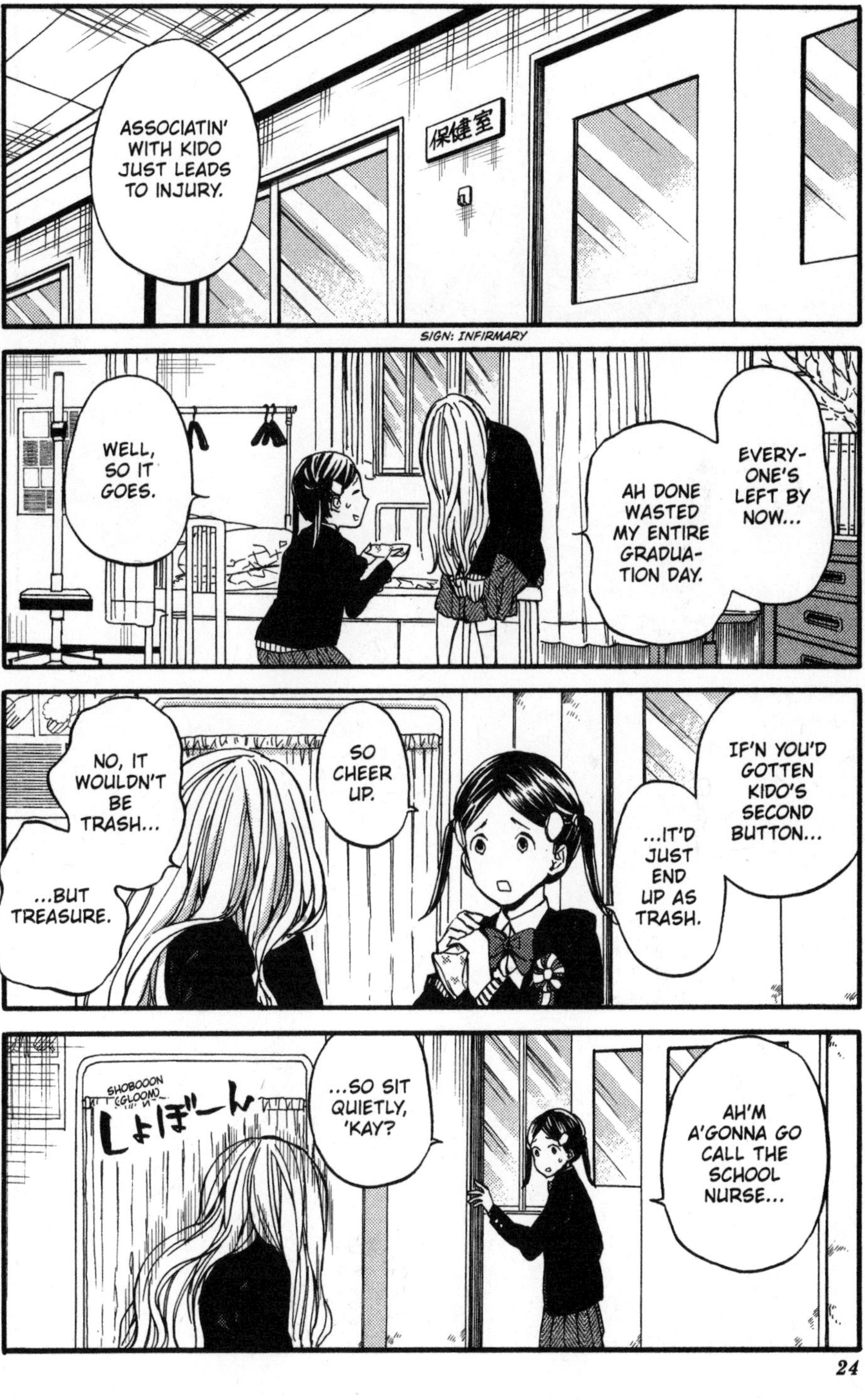
ASSOCIATIN' WITH KIDO JUST LEADS TO INJURY.
保健室
SIGN: INFIRMARY
EVERY-ONE'S LEFT BY NOW...
AH DONE WASTED MY ENTIRE GRADUA-TION DAY.
WELL, SO IT GOES.
IF'N YOU'D GOTTEN KIDO'S SECOND BUTTON...
...IT'D JUST END UP AS TRASH.
SO CHEER UP.
NO, IT WOULDN'T BE TRASH...
...BUT TREASURE.
AH'M A'GONNA GO CALL THE SCHOOL NURSE...
...SO SIT QUIETLY, 'KAY?
しょぼーん
SHOBOOON (GLOOM)

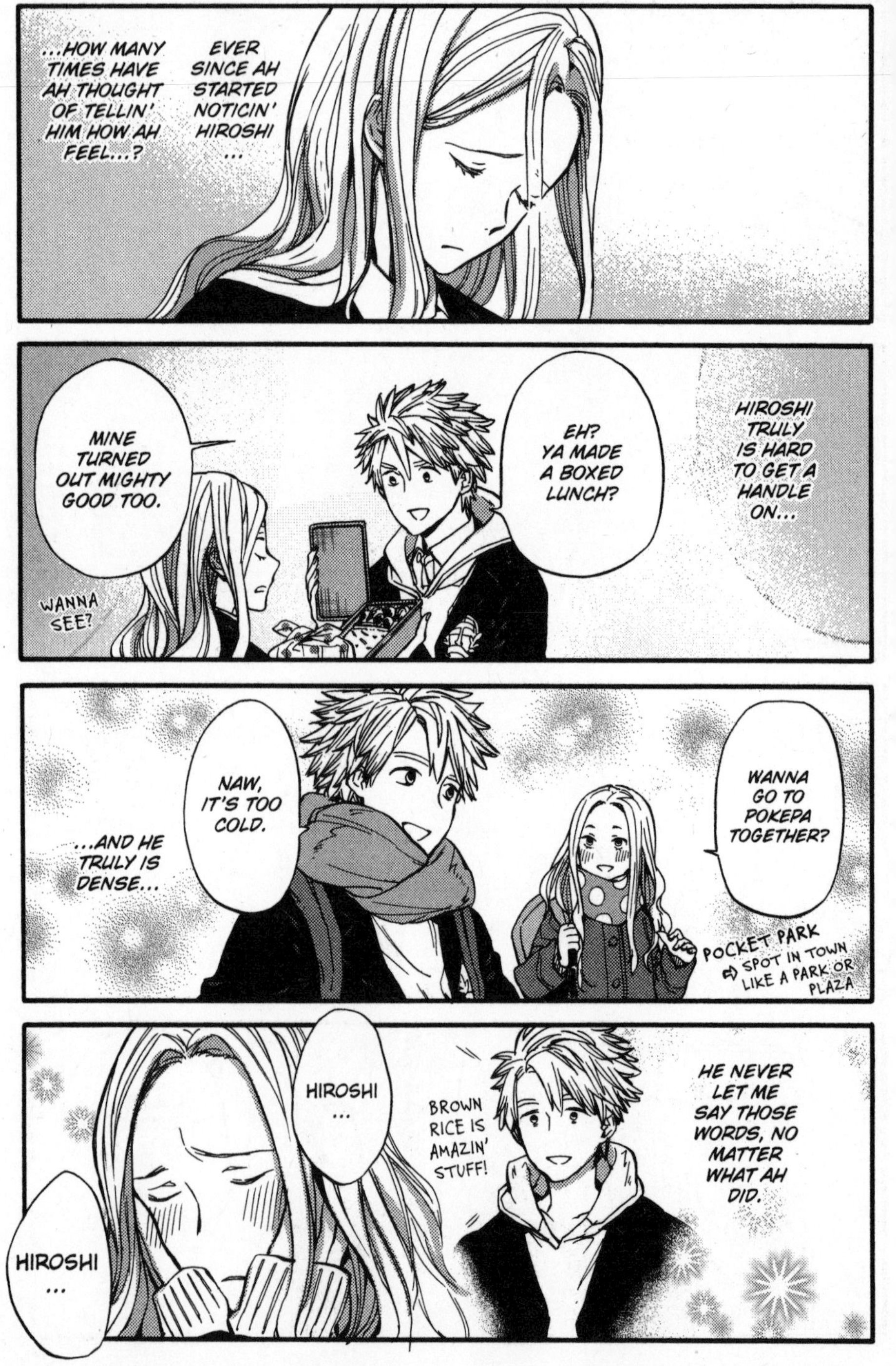
EVER SINCE AH STARTED NOTICIN' HIROSHI...
...HOW MANY TIMES HAVE AH THOUGHT OF TELLIN' HIM HOW AH FEEL...?
HIROSHI TRULY IS HARD TO GET A HANDLE ON...
EH? YA MADE A BOXED LUNCH?
MINE TURNED OUT MIGHTY GOOD TOO.
WANNA SEE?
WANNA GO TO POKEPA TOGETHER?
POCKET PARK ⇨ SPOT IN TOWN LIKE A PARK OR PLAZA
NAW, IT'S TOO COLD.
...AND HE TRULY IS DENSE...
HE NEVER LET ME SAY THOSE WORDS, NO MATTER WHAT AH DID.
BROWN RICE IS AMAZIN' STUFF!
HIROSHI...
HIROSHI...

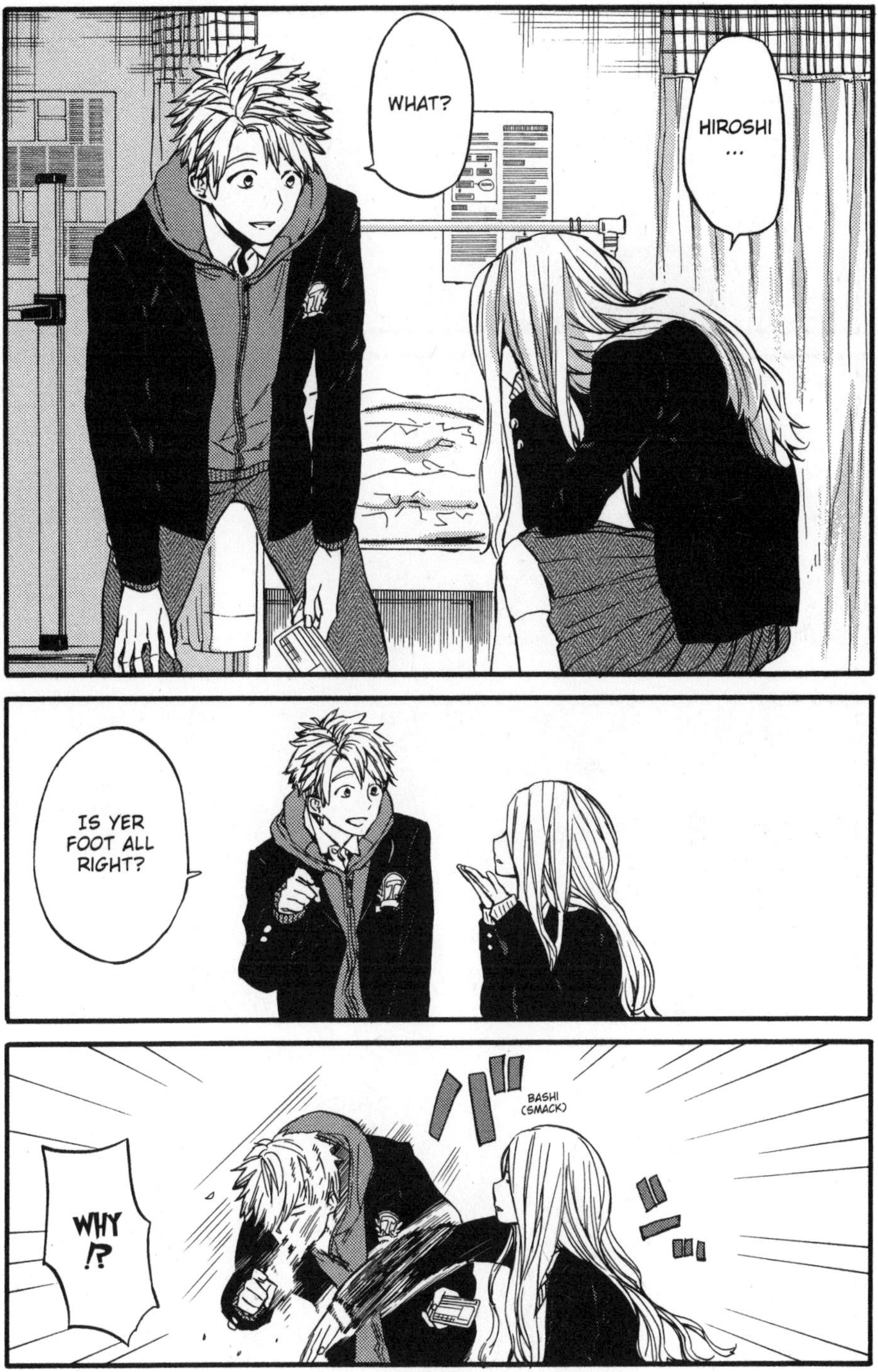
HIROSHI ...
WHAT?
IS YER FOOT ALL RIGHT?
BASHI (SMACK)
WHY !?

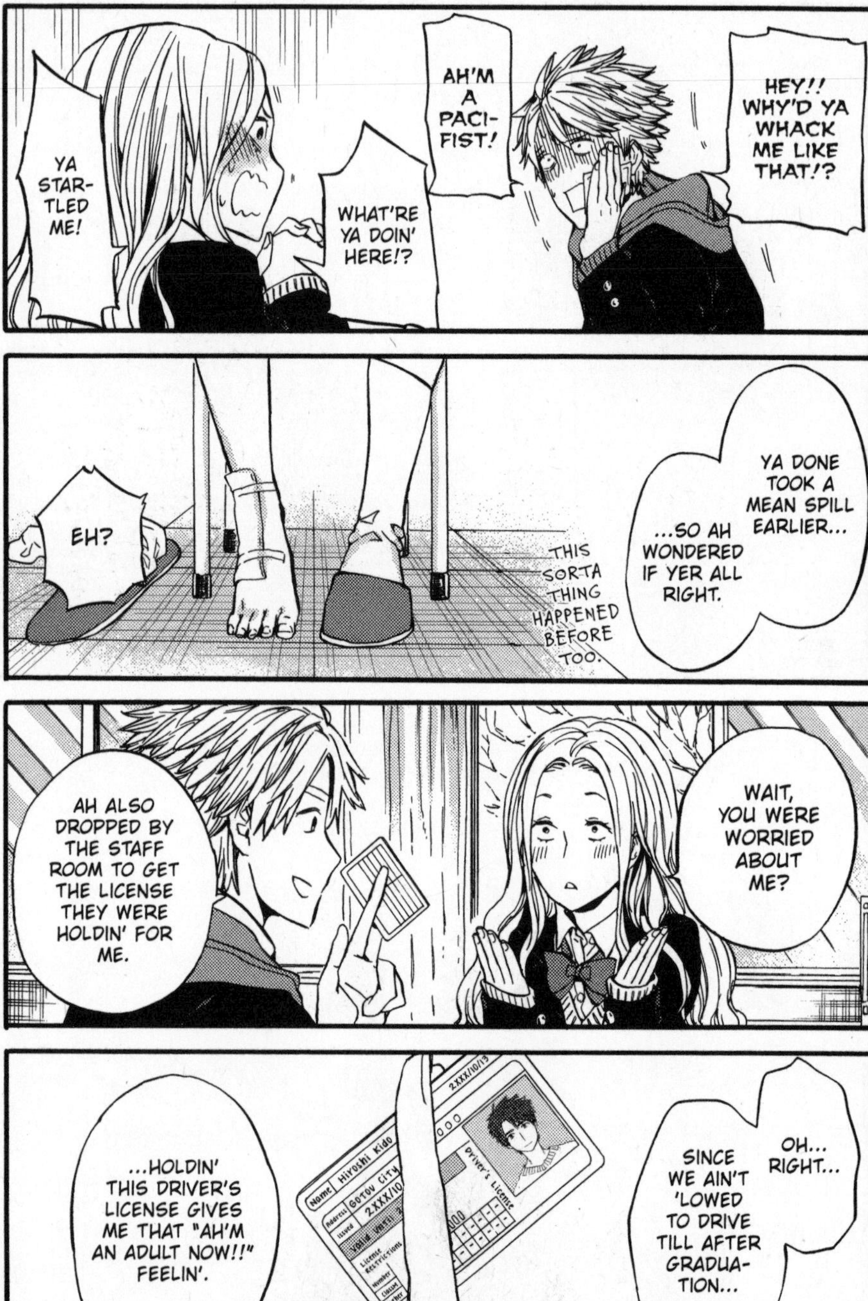
HEY!! WHY'D YA WHACK ME LIKE THAT!?
AH'M A PACI-FIST!
WHAT'RE YA DOIN' HERE!?
YA STAR-TLED ME!
YA DONE TOOK A MEAN SPILL EARLIER...
...SO AH WONDERED IF YER ALL RIGHT.
THIS SORTA THING HAPPENED BEFORE TOO.
EH?
WAIT, YOU WERE WORRIED ABOUT ME?
AH ALSO DROPPED BY THE STAFF ROOM TO GET THE LICENSE THEY WERE HOLDIN' FOR ME.
OH... RIGHT...
SINCE WE AIN'T 'LOWED TO DRIVE TILL AFTER GRADUA-TION...
...HOLDIN' THIS DRIVER'S LICENSE GIVES ME THAT "AH'M AN ADULT NOW!!" FEELIN'.

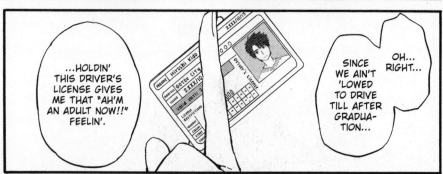

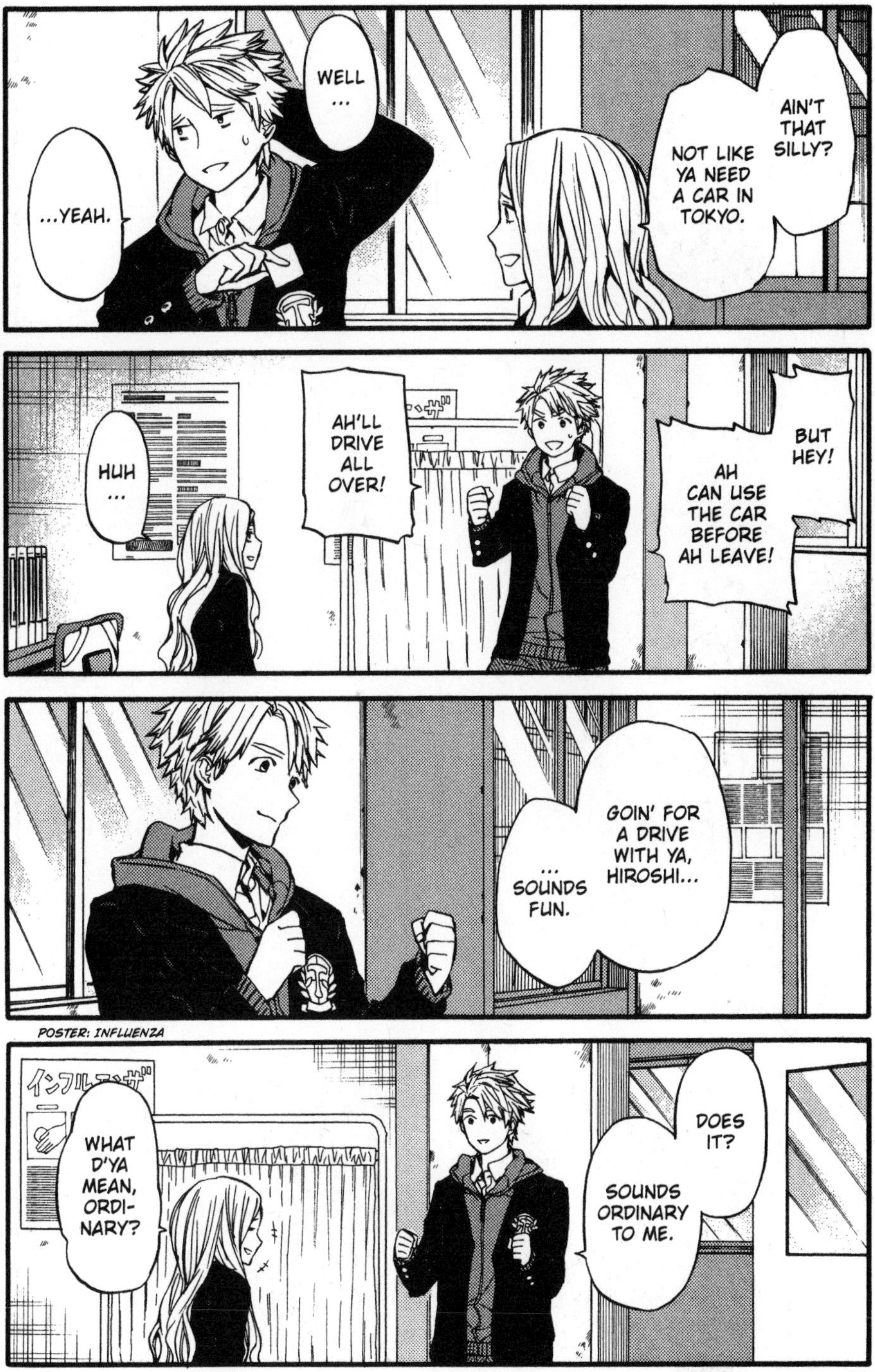
AIN'T THAT SILLY?
NOT LIKE YA NEED A CAR IN TOKYO.
WELL ...
...YEAH.
BUT HEY!
AH CAN USE THE CAR BEFORE AH LEAVE!
AH'LL DRIVE ALL OVER!
HUH ...
GOIN' FOR A DRIVE WITH YA, HIROSHI...
... SOUNDS FUN.
POSTER: INFLUENZA
DOES IT?
SOUNDS ORDINARY TO ME.
WHAT D'YA MEAN, ORDI-NARY?

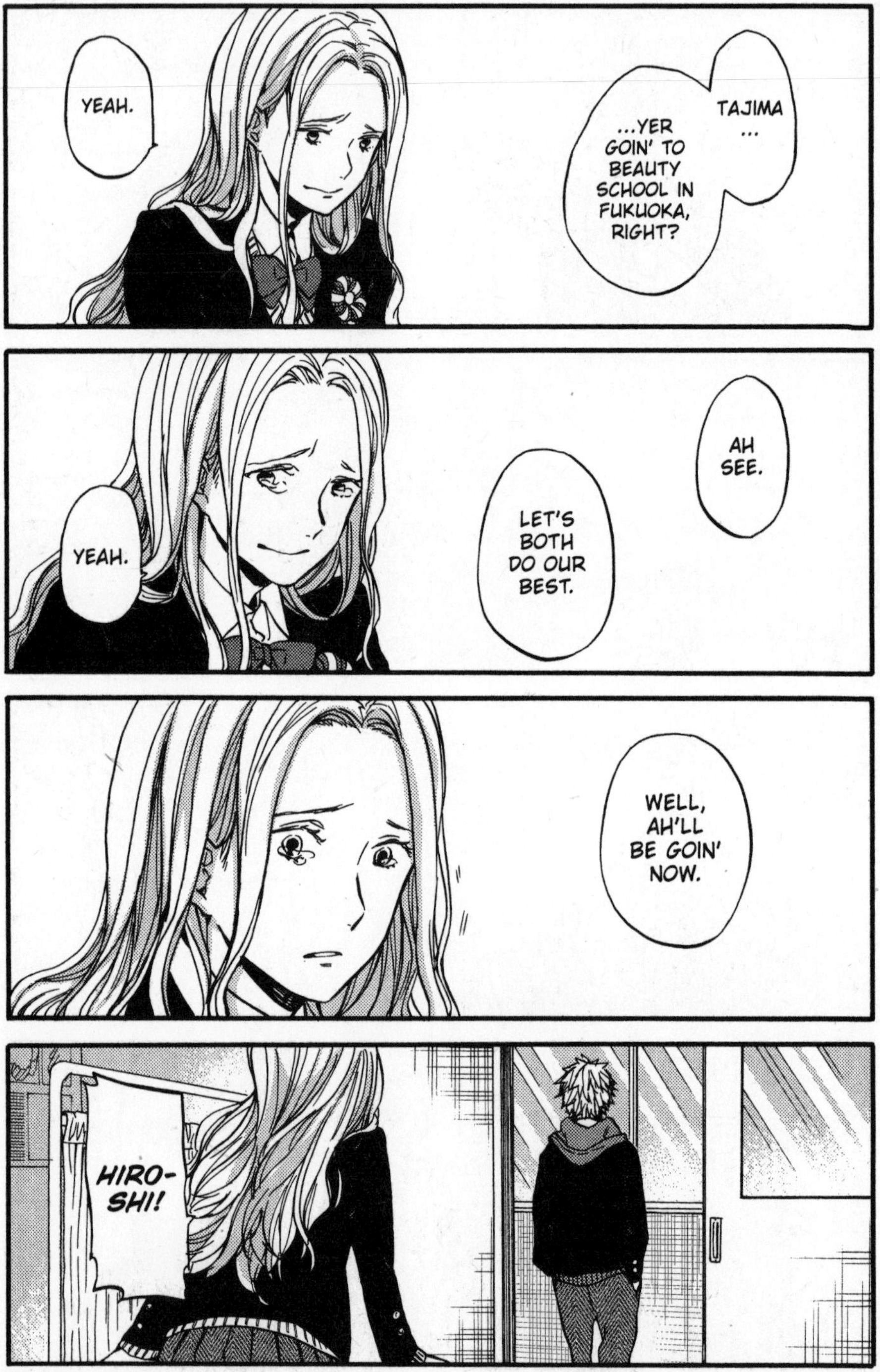
TAJIMA ...
...YER GOIN' TO BEAUTY SCHOOL IN FUKUOKA, RIGHT?
YEAH.
AH SEE.
LET'S BOTH DO OUR BEST.
YEAH.
WELL, AH'LL BE GOIN' NOW.
HIRO-SHI!

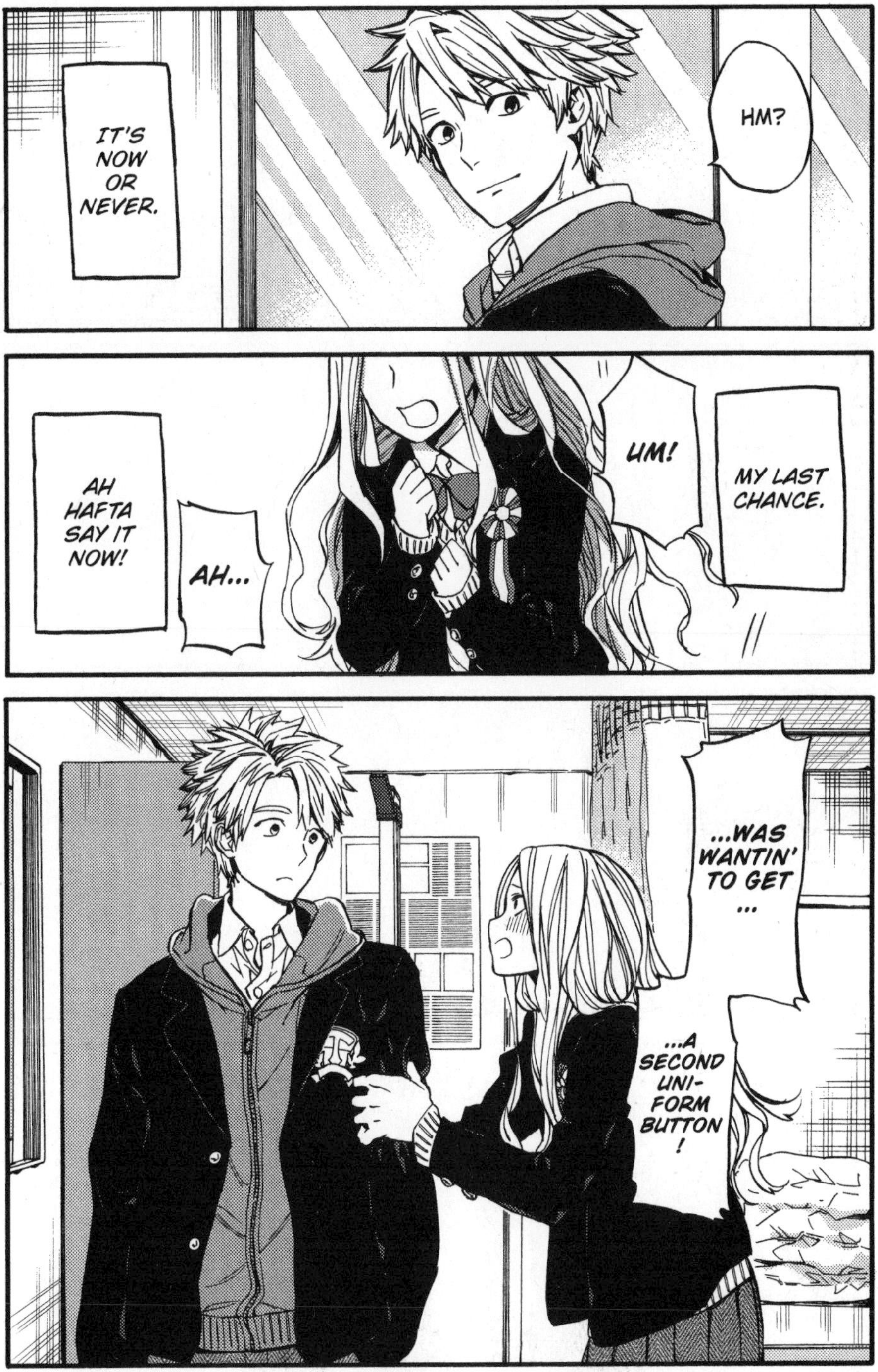
HM?
IT'S NOW OR NEVER.
MY LAST CHANCE.
UM!
AH...
AH HAFTA SAY IT NOW!
...WAS WANTIN' TO GET ...
...A SECOND UNI-FORM BUTTON!

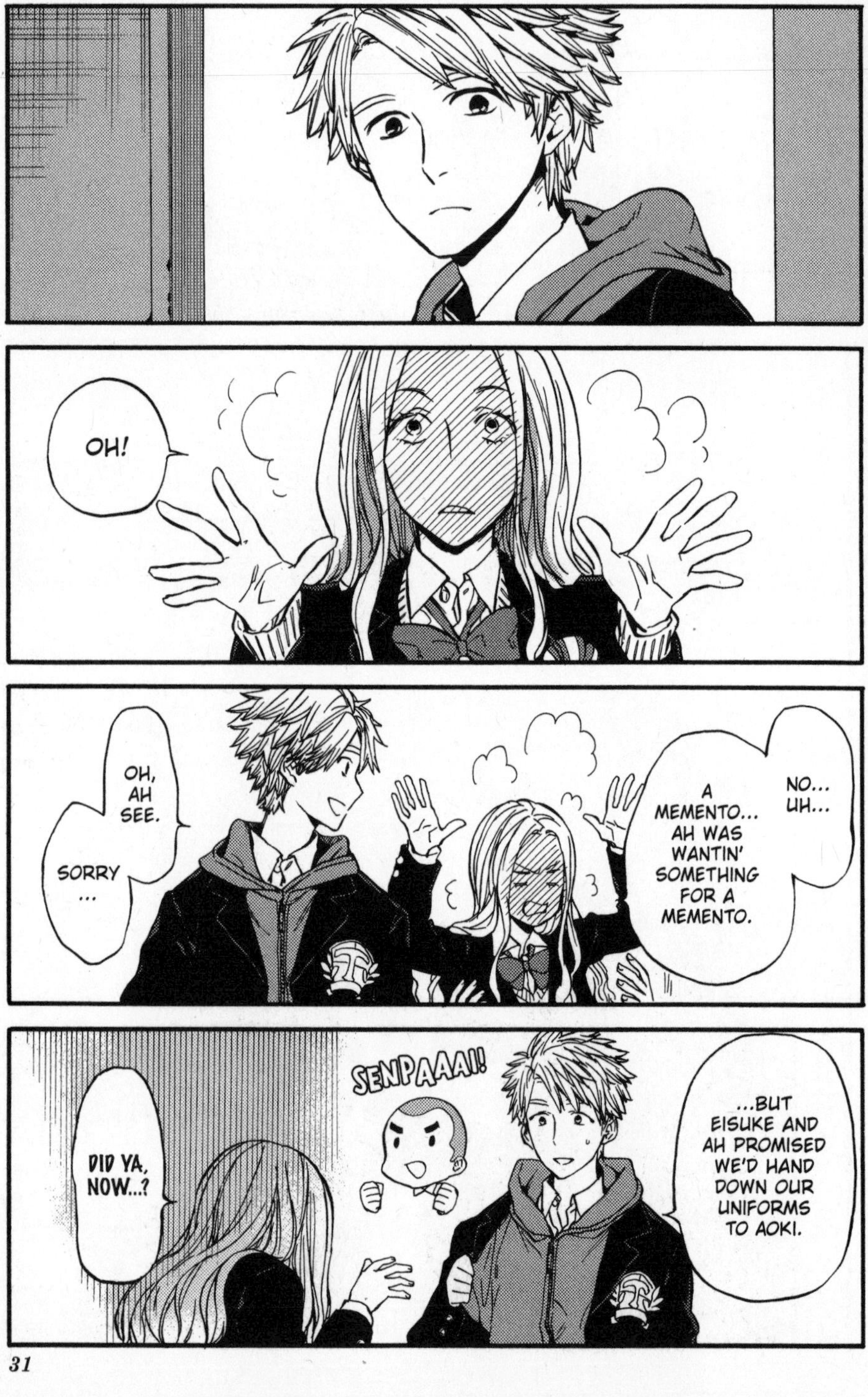
OH!
NO... UH...
A MEMENTO... AH WAS WANTIN' SOMETHING FOR A MEMENTO.
OH, AH SEE.
SORRY...
...BUT EISUKE AND AH PROMISED WE'D HAND DOWN OUR UNIFORMS TO AOKI.
SENPAAAI!
DID YA, NOW...?

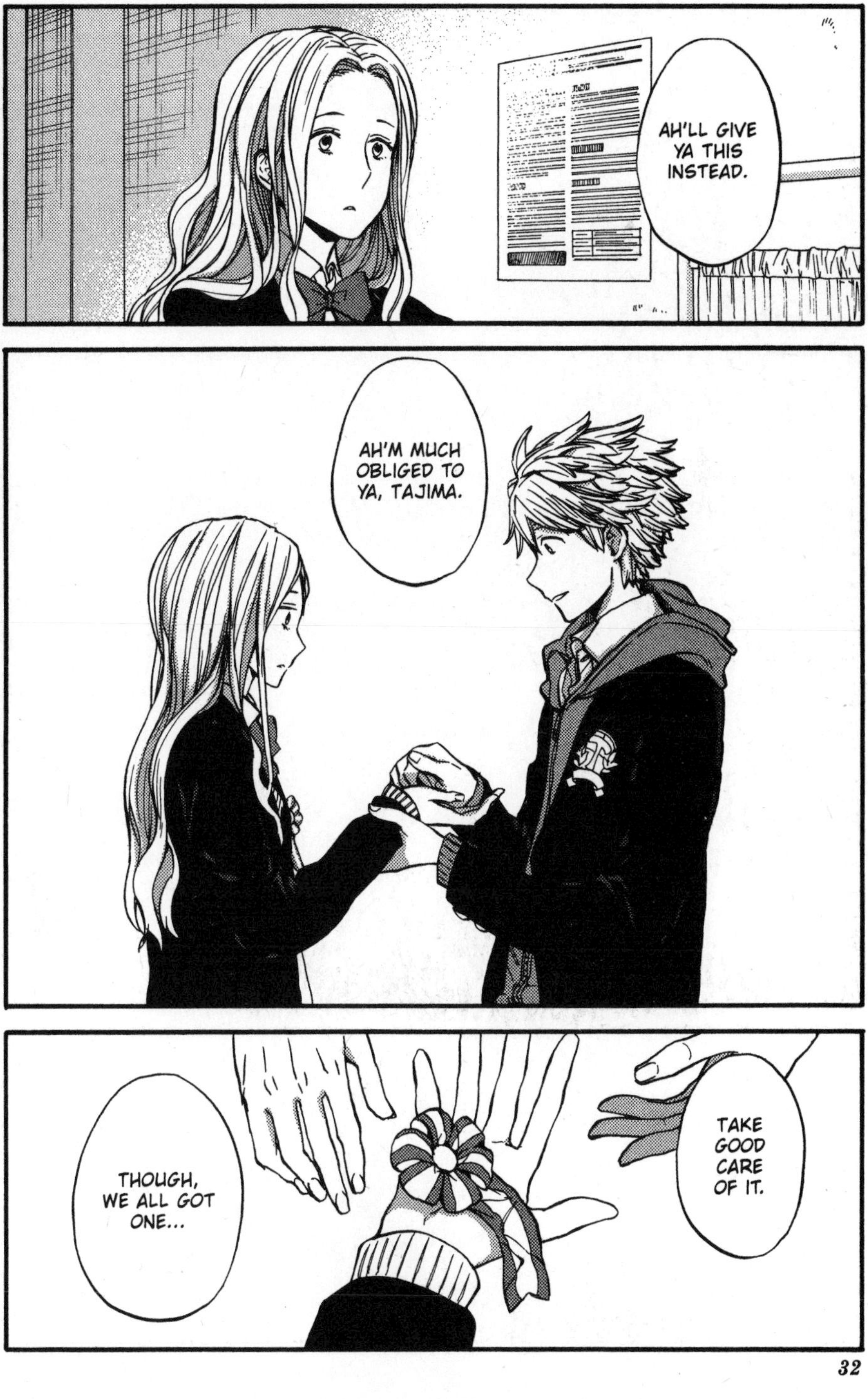
AH'LL GIVE YA THIS INSTEAD.
AH'M MUCH OBLIGED TO YA, TAJIMA.
TAKE GOOD CARE OF IT.
THOUGH, WE ALL GOT ONE...

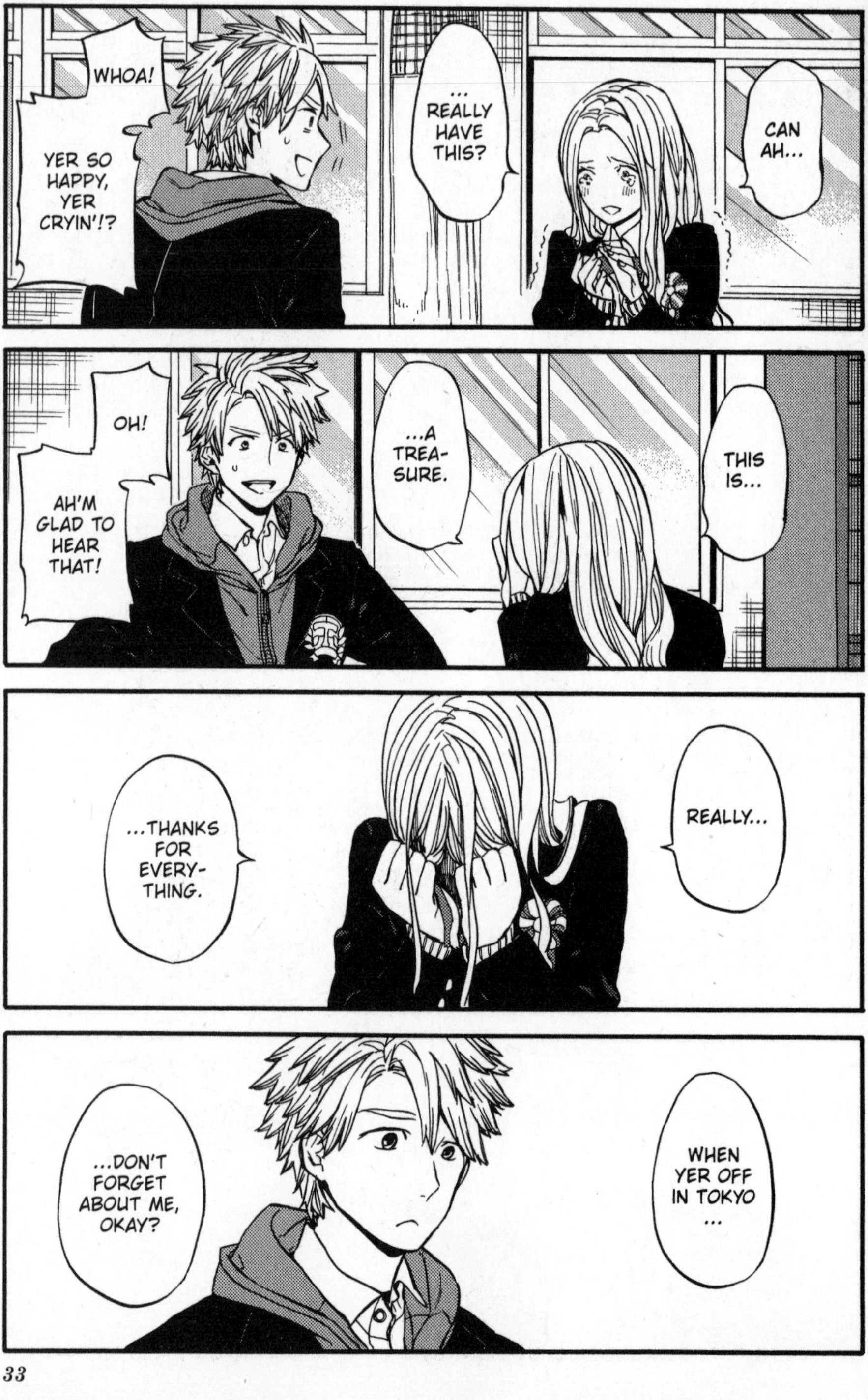
CAN AH...
...REALLY HAVE THIS?
WHOA!
YER SO HAPPY, YER CRYIN'!?
THIS IS...
...A TREA-SURE.
OH!
AH'M GLAD TO HEAR THAT!
REALLY...
...THANKS FOR EVERY-THING.
WHEN YER OFF IN TOKYO ...
...DON'T FORGET ABOUT ME, OKAY?

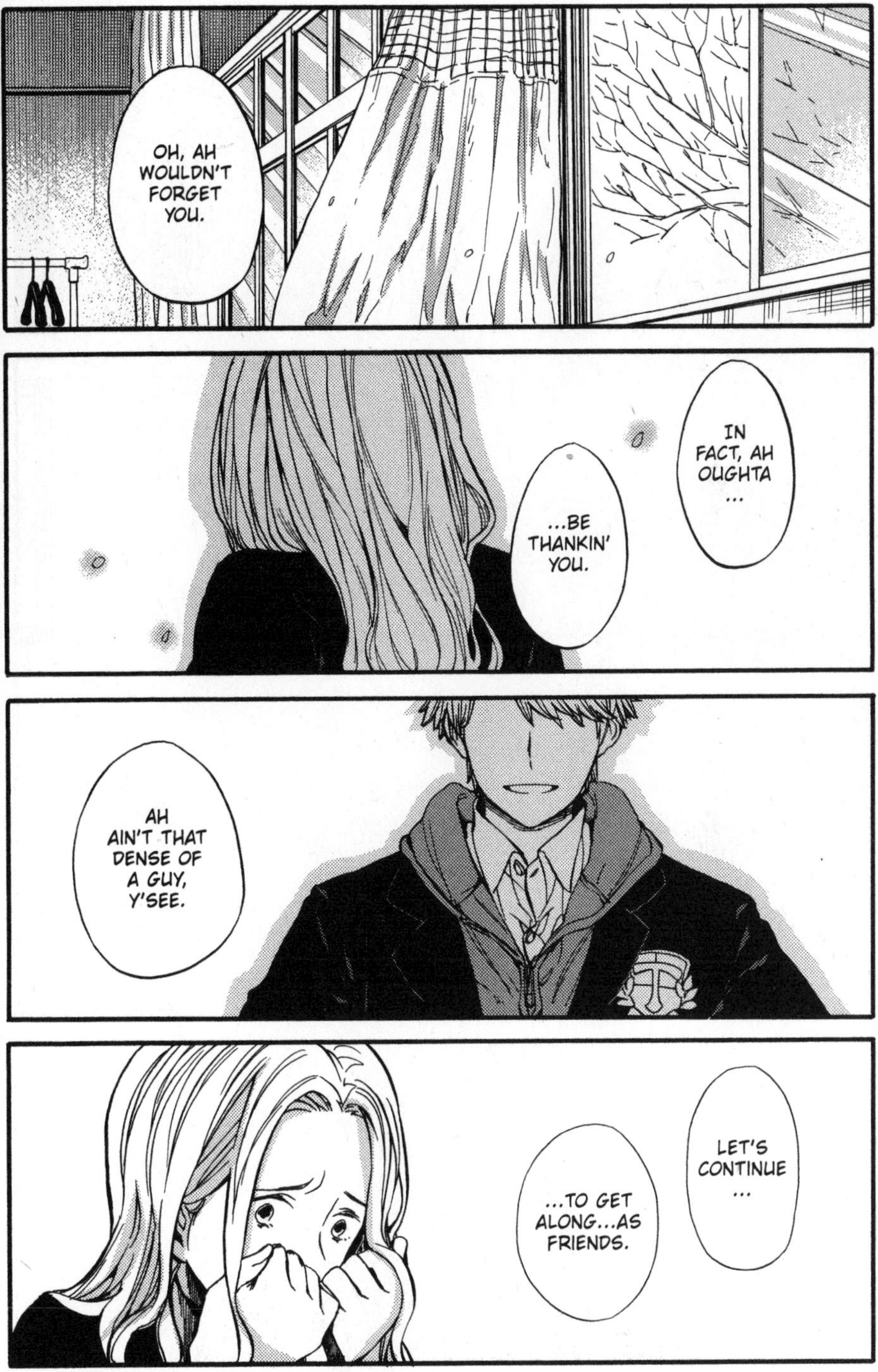
OH, AH WOULDN'T FORGET YOU.
IN FACT, AH OUGHTA ...
...BE THANKIN' YOU.
AH AIN'T THAT DENSE OF A GUY, Y'SEE.
LET'S CONTINUE ...
...TO GET ALONG...AS FRIENDS.

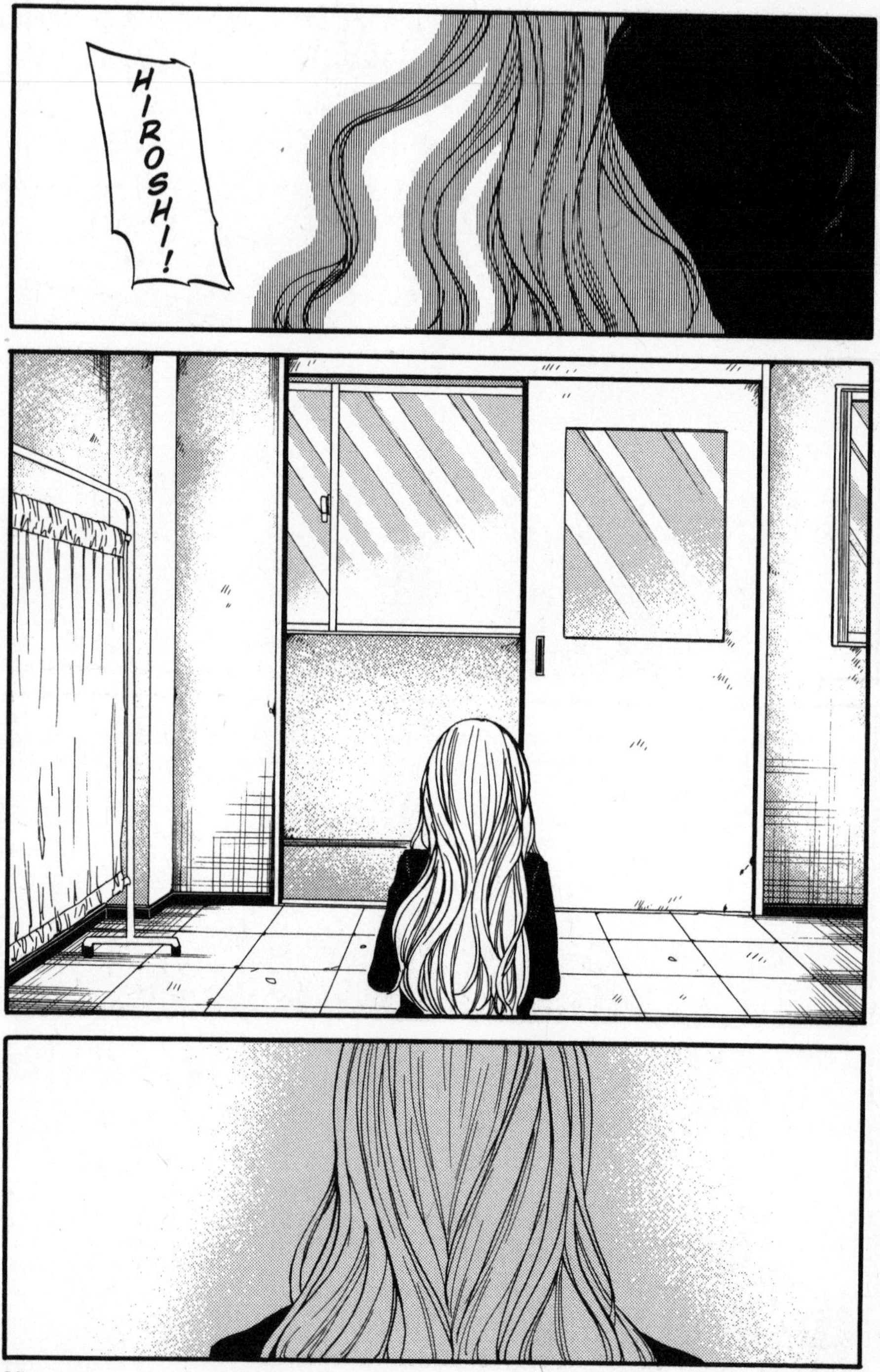
HIROSHI!

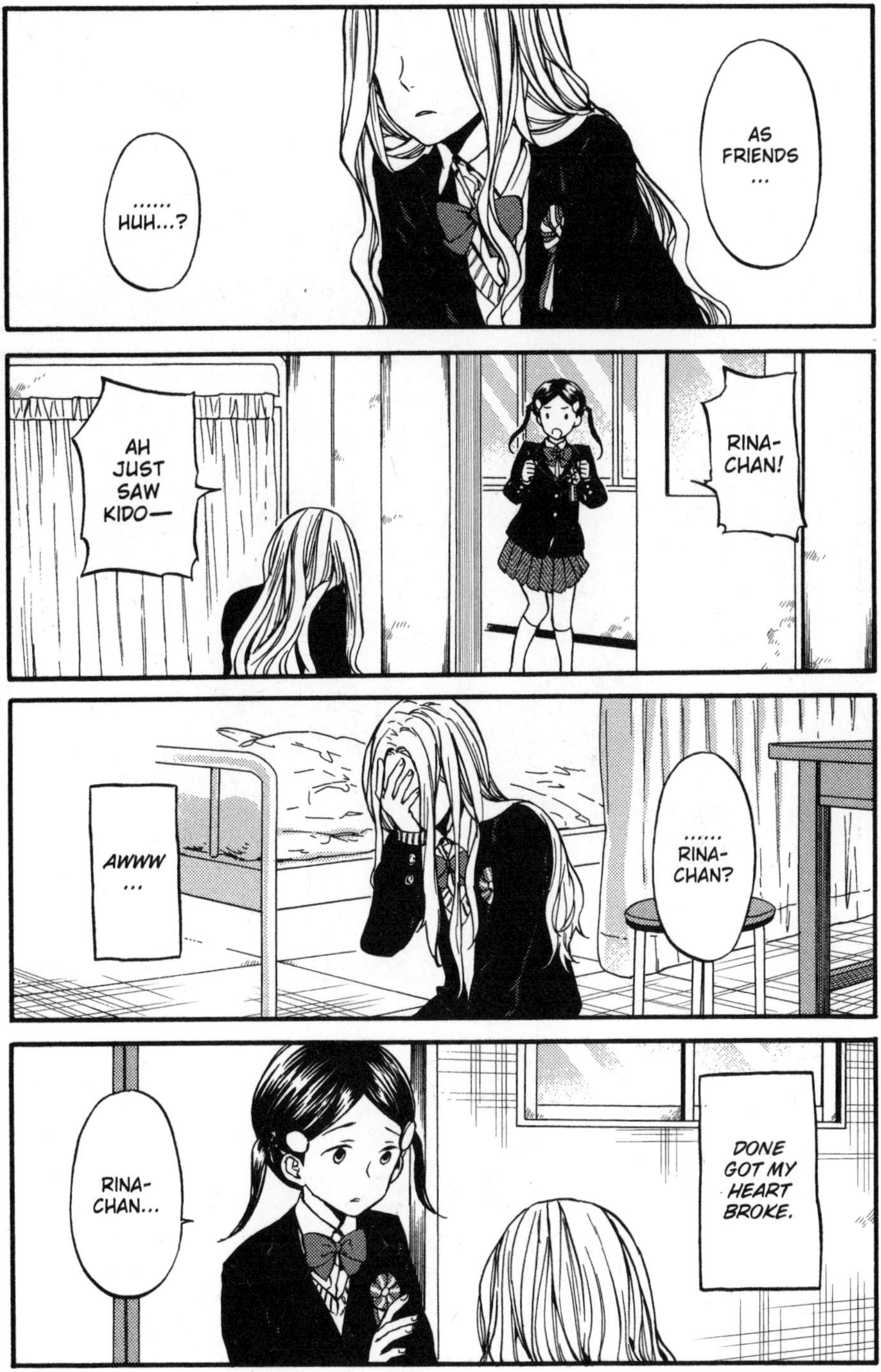
AS FRIENDS …
…… HUH…?
RINA-CHAN!
AH JUST SAW KIDO—
…… RINA-CHAN?
AWWW …
DONE GOT MY HEART BROKE.
RINA-CHAN…

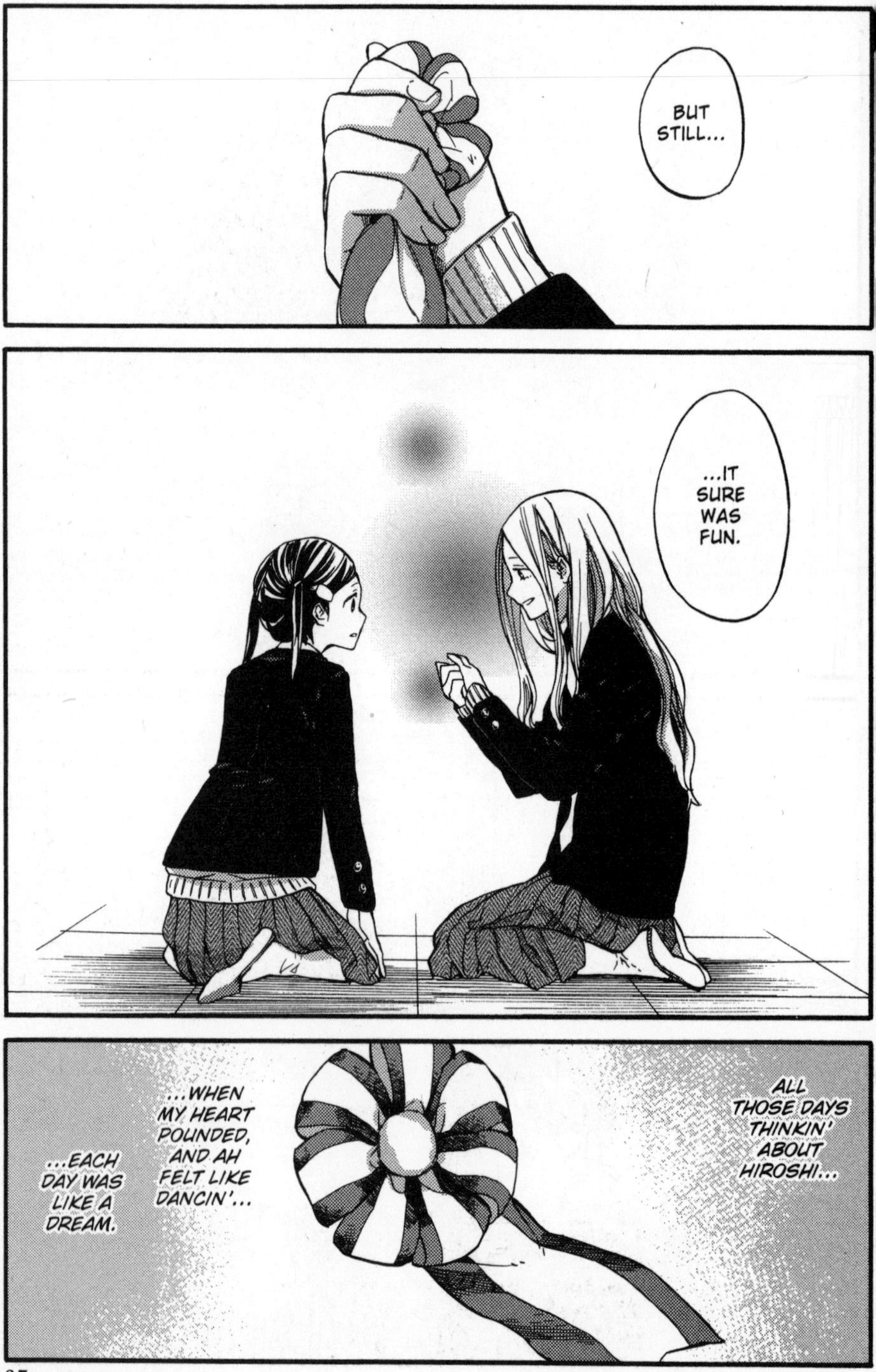
BUT STILL...
...IT SURE WAS FUN.
ALL THOSE DAYS THINKIN' ABOUT HIROSHI...
...WHEN MY HEART POUNDED, AND AH FELT LIKE DANCIN'...
...EACH DAY WAS LIKE A DREAM.

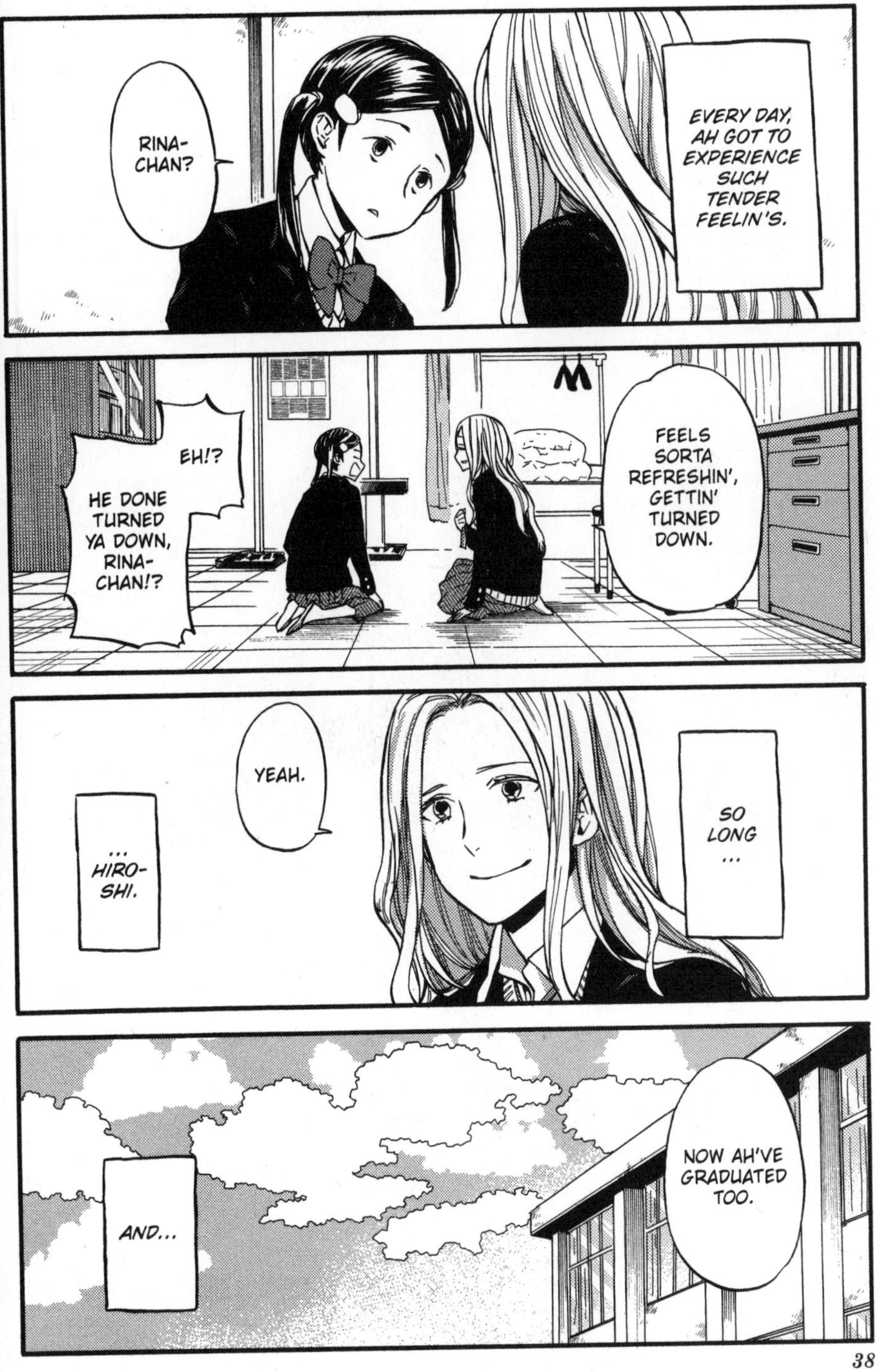
EVERY DAY, AH GOT TO EXPERIENCE SUCH TENDER FEELIN'S.
RINA-CHAN?
FEELS SORTA REFRESHIN', GETTIN' TURNED DOWN.
EH!? HE DONE TURNED YA DOWN, RINA-CHAN!?
SO LONG ...
YEAH.
... HIRO-SHI.
NOW AH'VE GRADUATED TOO.
AND...

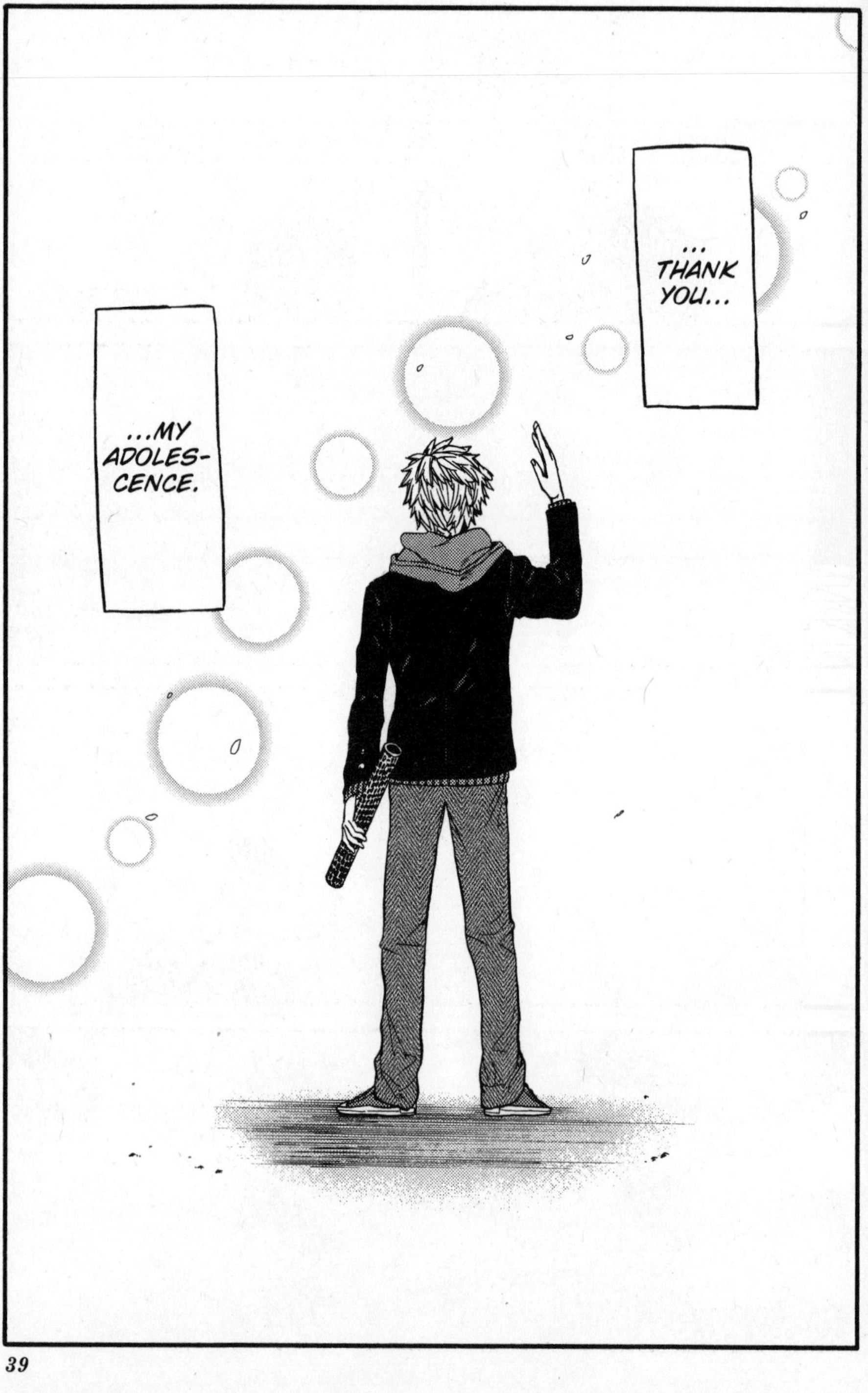
...THANK YOU...
...MY ADOLES-CENCE.

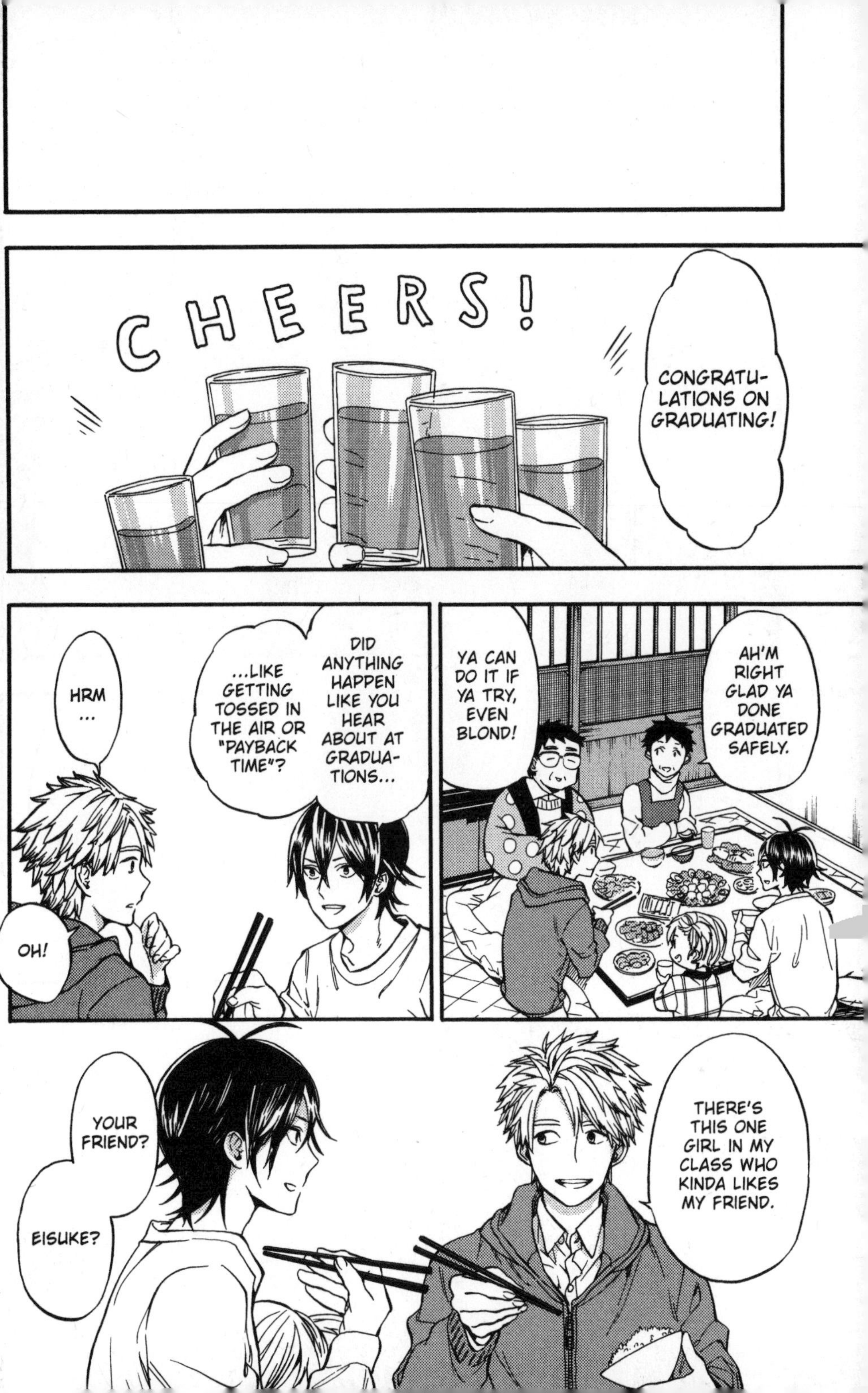
CONGRATULATIONS ON GRADUATING!
CHEERS!
AH'M RIGHT GLAD YA DONE GRADUATED SAFELY.
YA CAN DO IT IF YA TRY, EVEN BLOND!
DID ANYTHING HAPPEN LIKE YOU HEAR ABOUT AT GRADUATIONS...
...LIKE GETTING TOSSED IN THE AIR OR "PAYBACK TIME"?
HRM...
OH!
THERE'S THIS ONE GIRL IN MY CLASS WHO KINDA LIKES MY FRIEND.
YOUR FRIEND?
EISUKE?

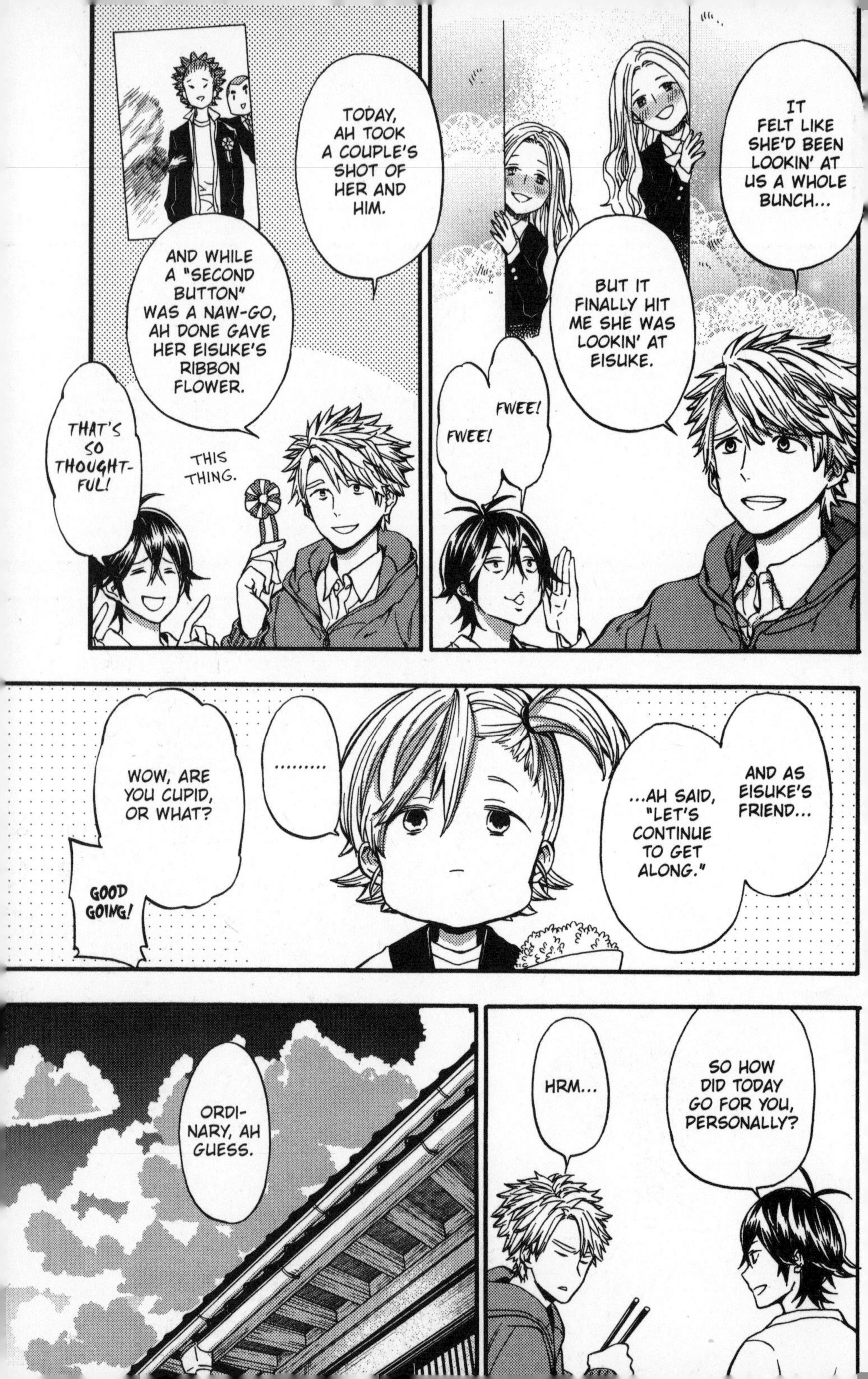
IT FELT LIKE SHE'D BEEN LOOKIN' AT US A WHOLE BUNCH...
BUT IT FINALLY HIT ME SHE WAS LOOKIN' AT EISUKE.
FWEE! FWEE!
TODAY, AH TOOK A COUPLE'S SHOT OF HER AND HIM.
AND WHILE A "SECOND BUTTON" WAS A NAW-GO, AH DONE GAVE HER EISUKE'S RIBBON FLOWER.
THIS THING.
THAT'S SO THOUGHT-FUL!
AND AS EISUKE'S FRIEND...
...AH SAID, "LET'S CONTINUE TO GET ALONG."
....
WOW, ARE YOU CUPID, OR WHAT?
GOOD GOING!
SO HOW DID TODAY GO FOR YOU, PERSONALLY?
HRM...
ORDI-NARY, AH GUESS.

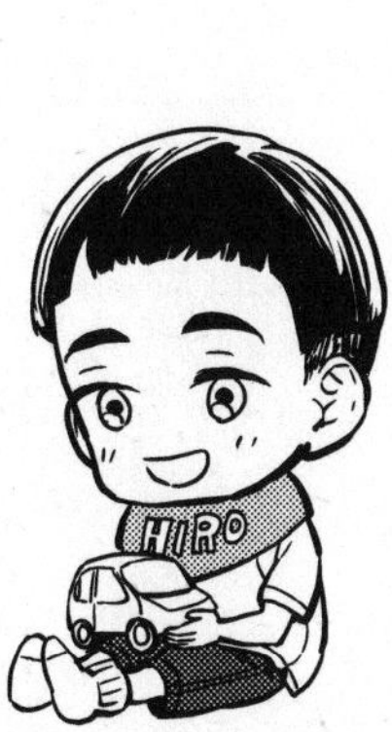
HIRO

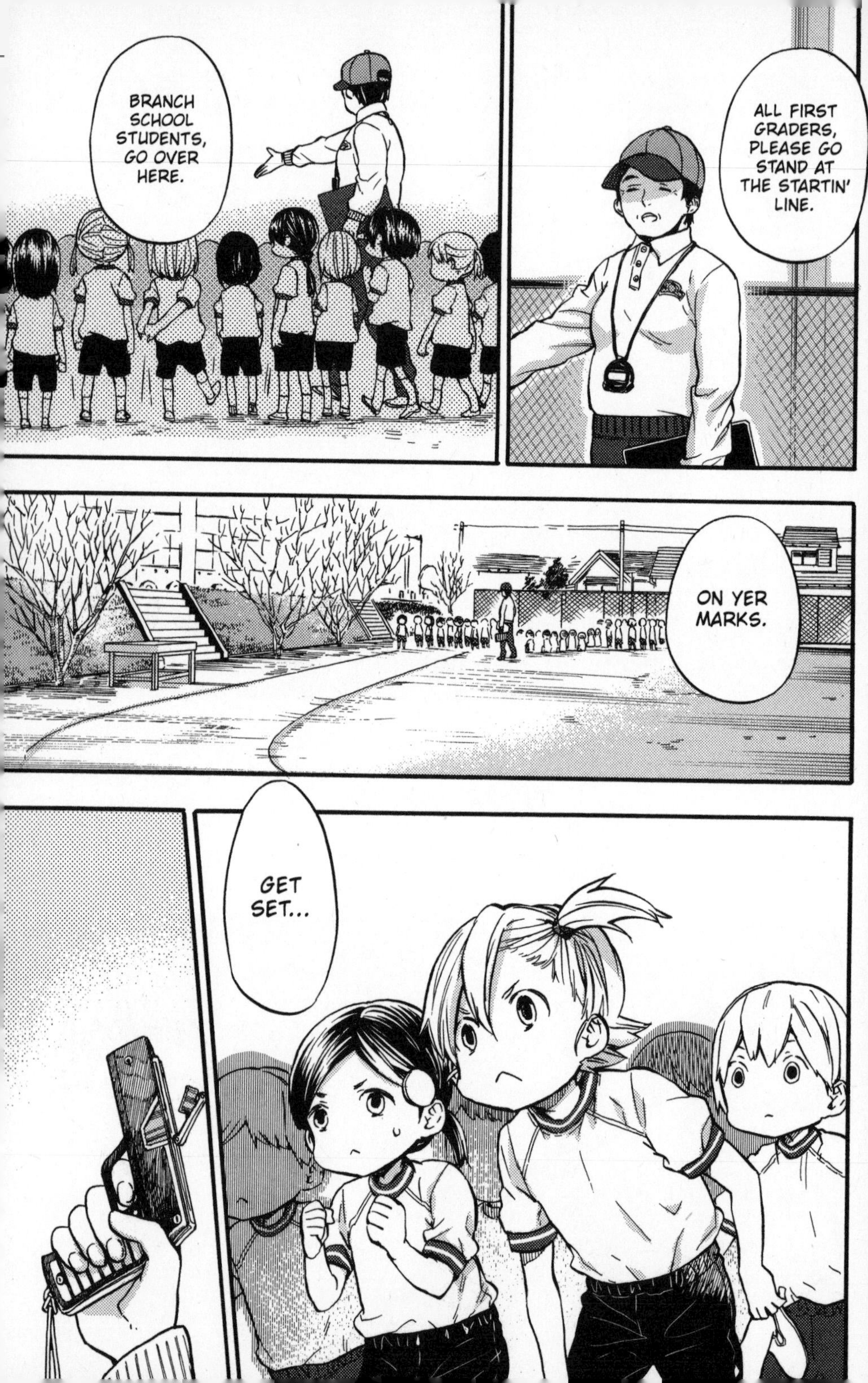
ALL FIRST GRADERS, PLEASE GO STAND AT THE STARTIN' LINE.
BRANCH SCHOOL STUDENTS, GO OVER HERE.
ON YER MARKS.
GET SET...

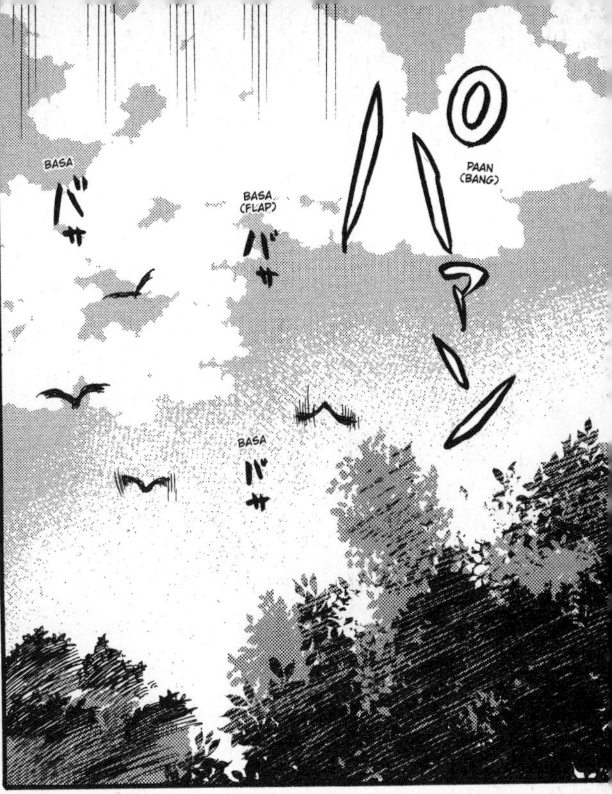
PAAN (BANG)
BASA (FLAP)
BASA
BASA
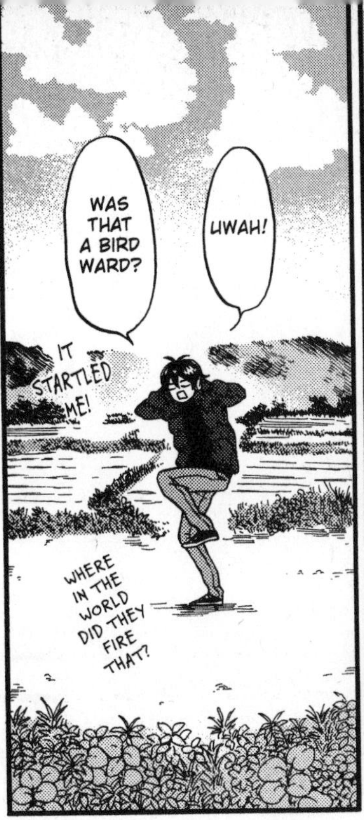
UWAH!
WAS THAT A BIRD WARD?
IT STARTLED ME!
WHERE IN THE WORLD DID THEY FIRE THAT?

Act.116
TORETAETA
(Translation: Fell Down)

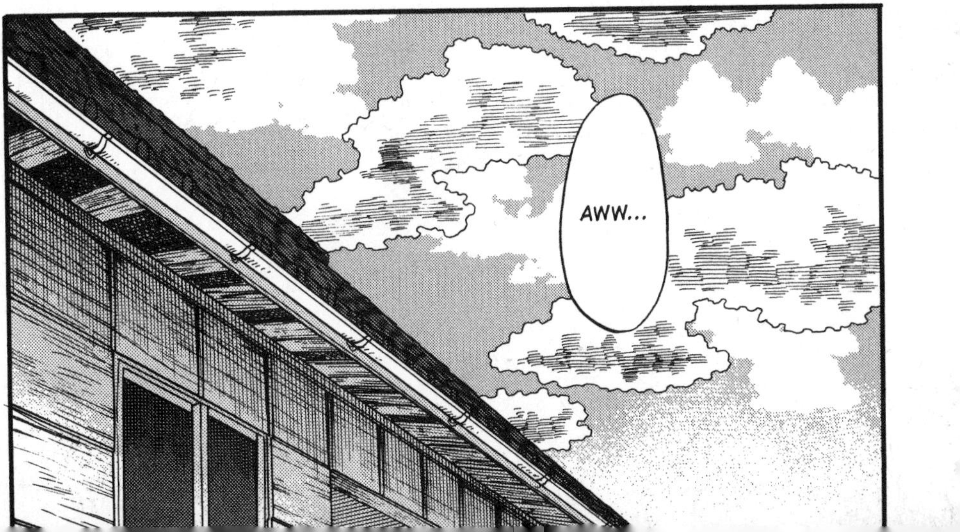
AWW...

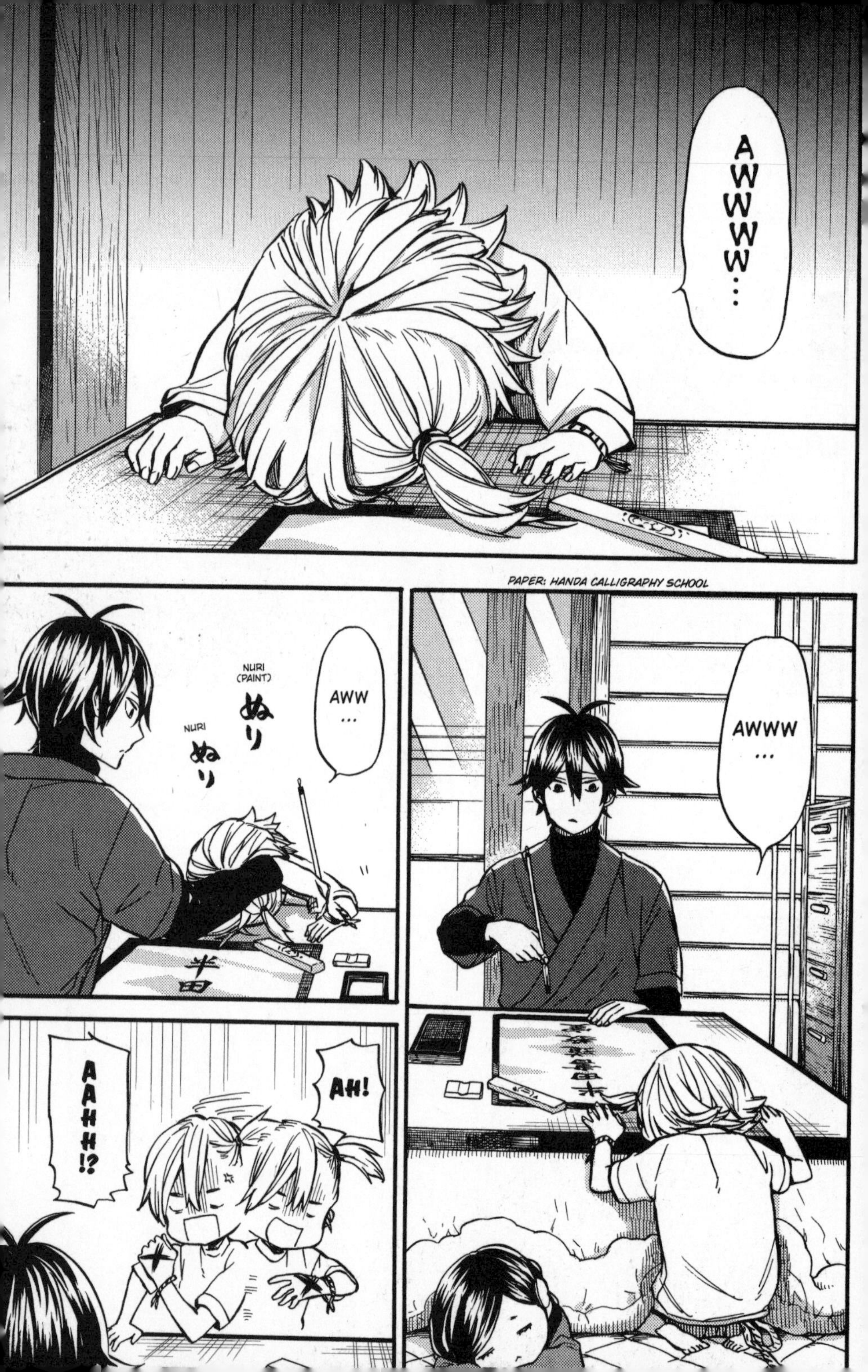
AWWWW...
PAPER: HANDA CALLIGRAPHY SCHOOL
AWWW...
AWW...
NURI (PAINT)
ぬり
NURI
ぬり
AH!
AAHH!?

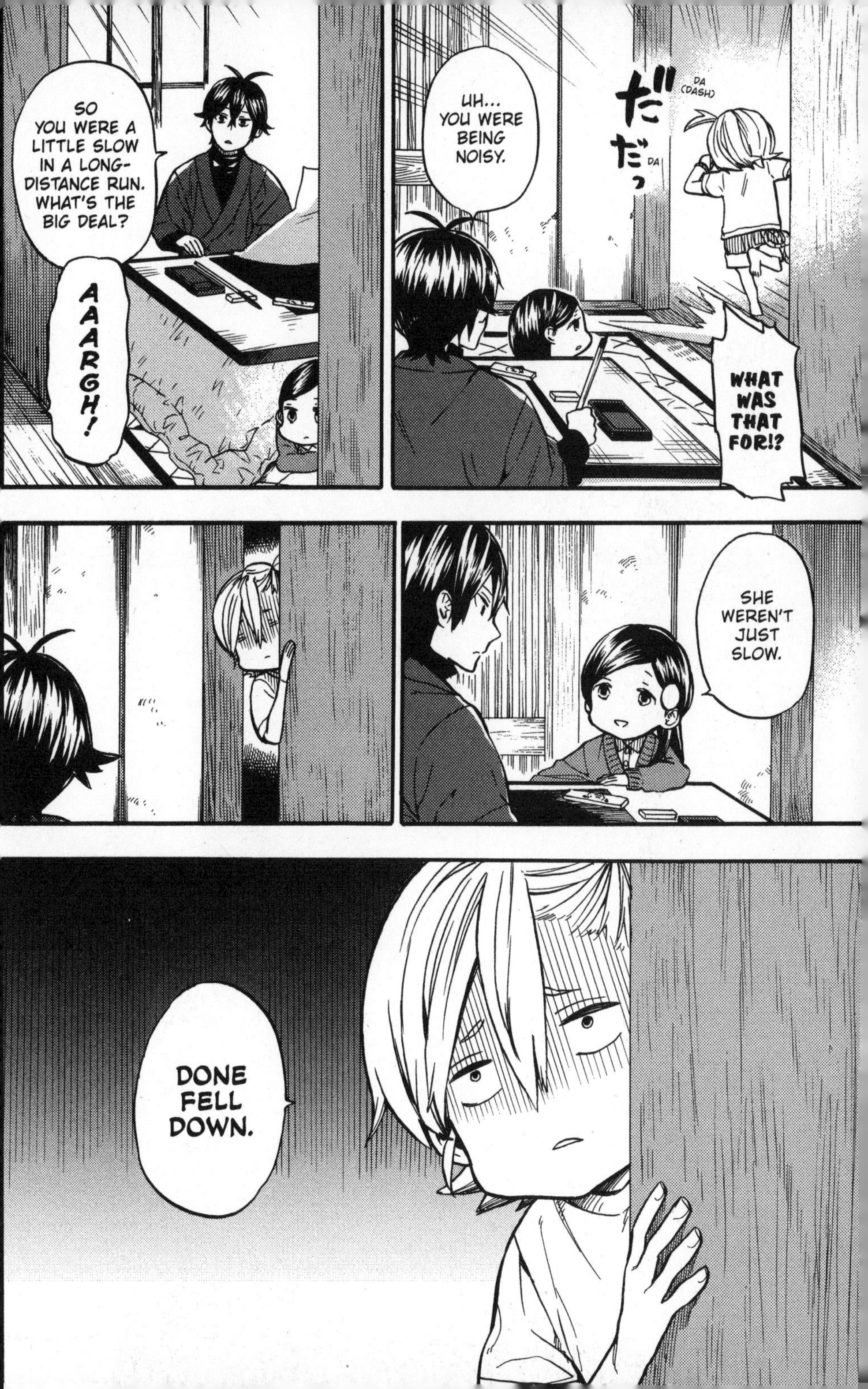
だ
DA (DASH)
だっ
DA
WHAT WAS THAT FOR!?
UH... YOU WERE BEING NOISY.
SO YOU WERE A LITTLE SLOW IN A LONG-DISTANCE RUN. WHAT'S THE BIG DEAL?
AAAARGH!
SHE WEREN'T JUST SLOW.
DONE FELL DOWN.

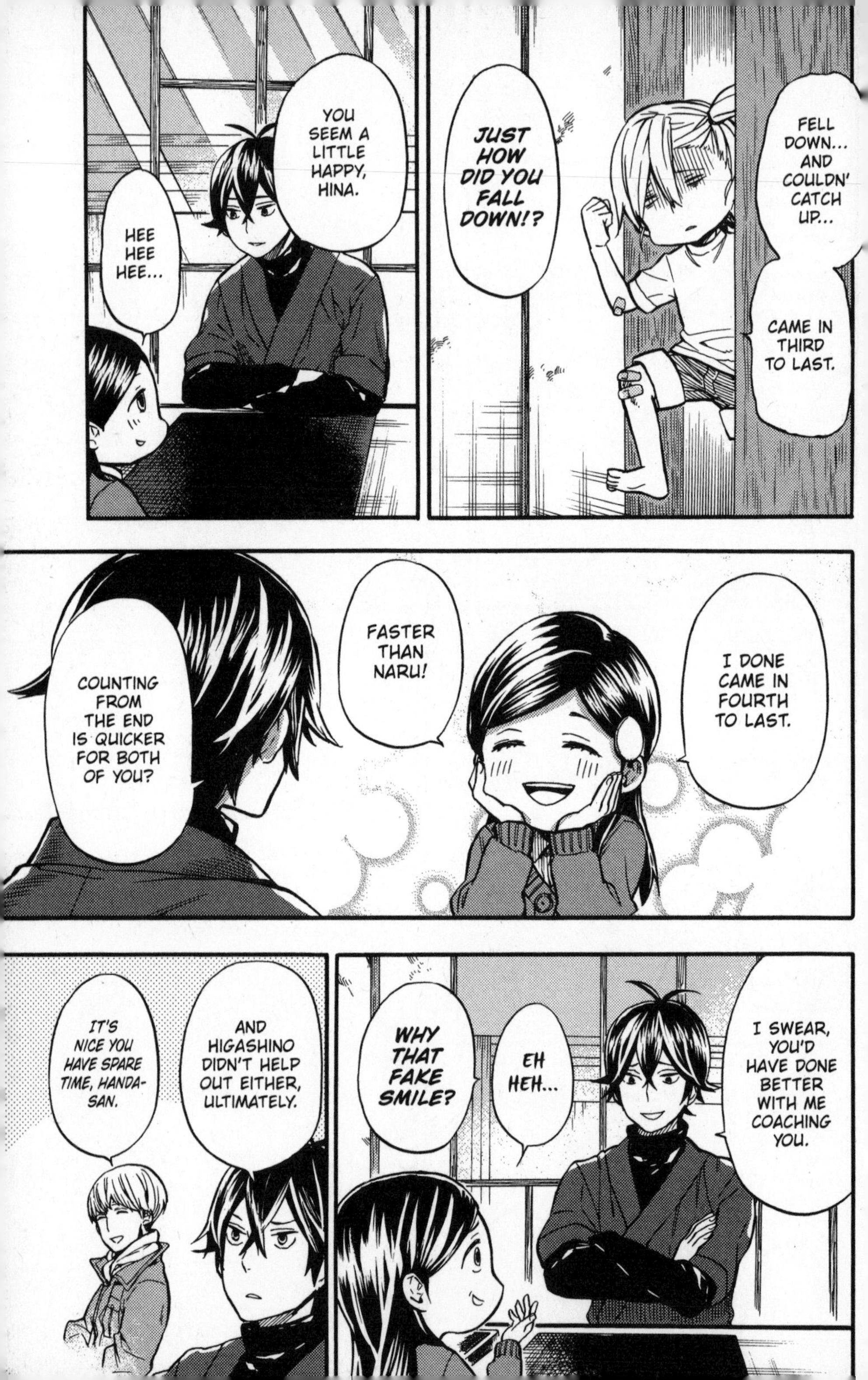
FELL DOWN... AND COULDN' CATCH UP...
CAME IN THIRD TO LAST.
JUST HOW DID YOU FALL DOWN!?
YOU SEEM A LITTLE HAPPY, HINA.
HEE HEE HEE...
I DONE CAME IN FOURTH TO LAST.
FASTER THAN NARU!
COUNTING FROM THE END IS QUICKER FOR BOTH OF YOU?
I SWEAR, YOU'D HAVE DONE BETTER WITH ME COACHING YOU.
EH HEH...
WHY THAT FAKE SMILE?
AND HIGASHINO DIDN'T HELP OUT EITHER, ULTIMATELY.
IT'S NICE YOU HAVE SPARE TIME, HANDA-SAN.

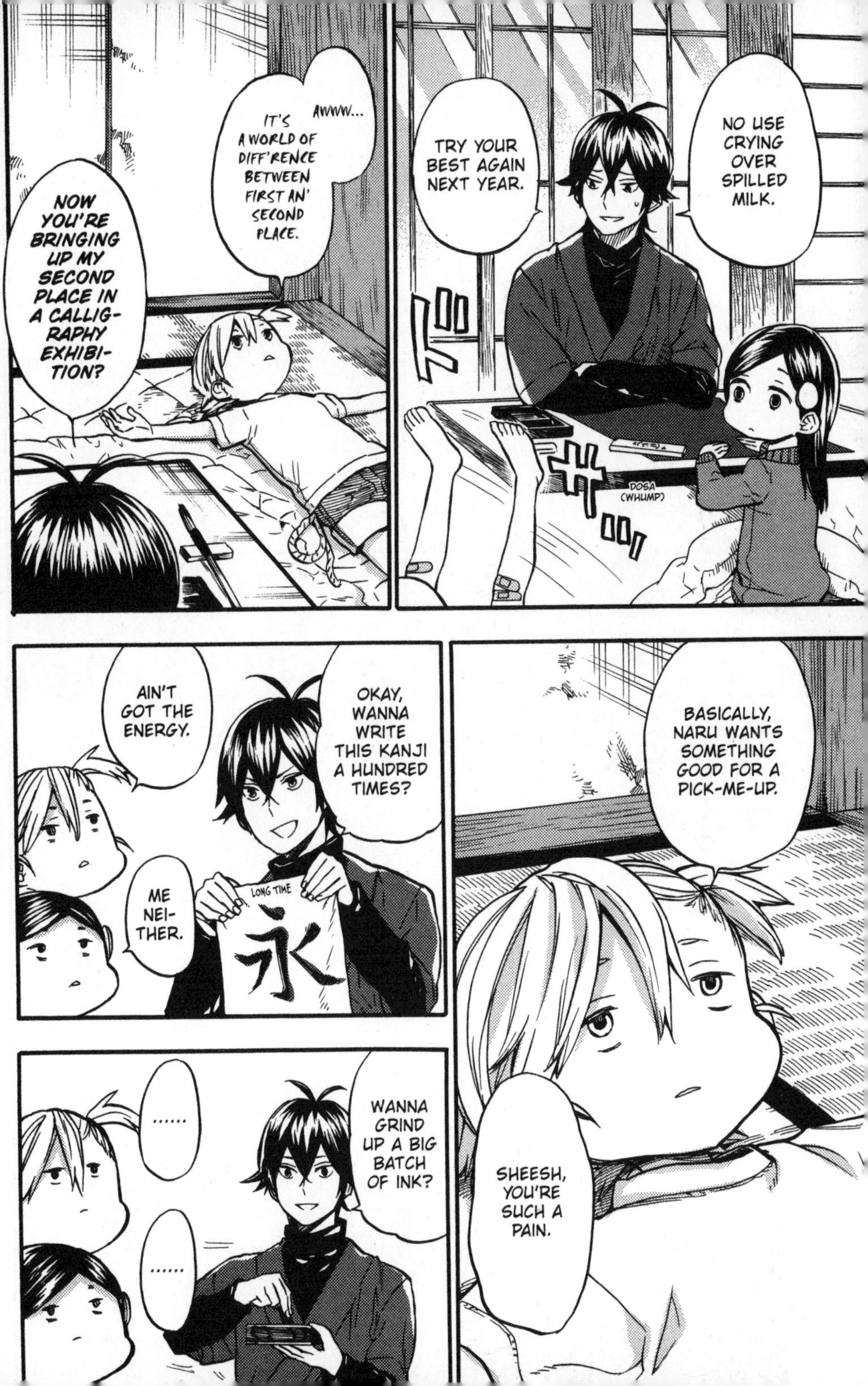
NO USE CRYING OVER SPILLED MILK.
TRY YOUR BEST AGAIN NEXT YEAR.
DOSA (WHUMP)
AWWW...
IT'S A WORLD OF DIFF'RENCE BETWEEN FIRST AN' SECOND PLACE.
NOW YOU'RE BRINGING UP MY SECOND PLACE IN A CALLIGRAPHY EXHIBITION?
BASICALLY, NARU WANTS SOMETHING GOOD FOR A PICK-ME-UP.
SHEESH, YOU'RE SUCH A PAIN.
OKAY, WANNA WRITE THIS KANJI A HUNDRED TIMES?
LONG TIME
AIN'T GOT THE ENERGY.
ME NEITHER.
WANNA GRIND UP A BIG BATCH OF INK?
......
......

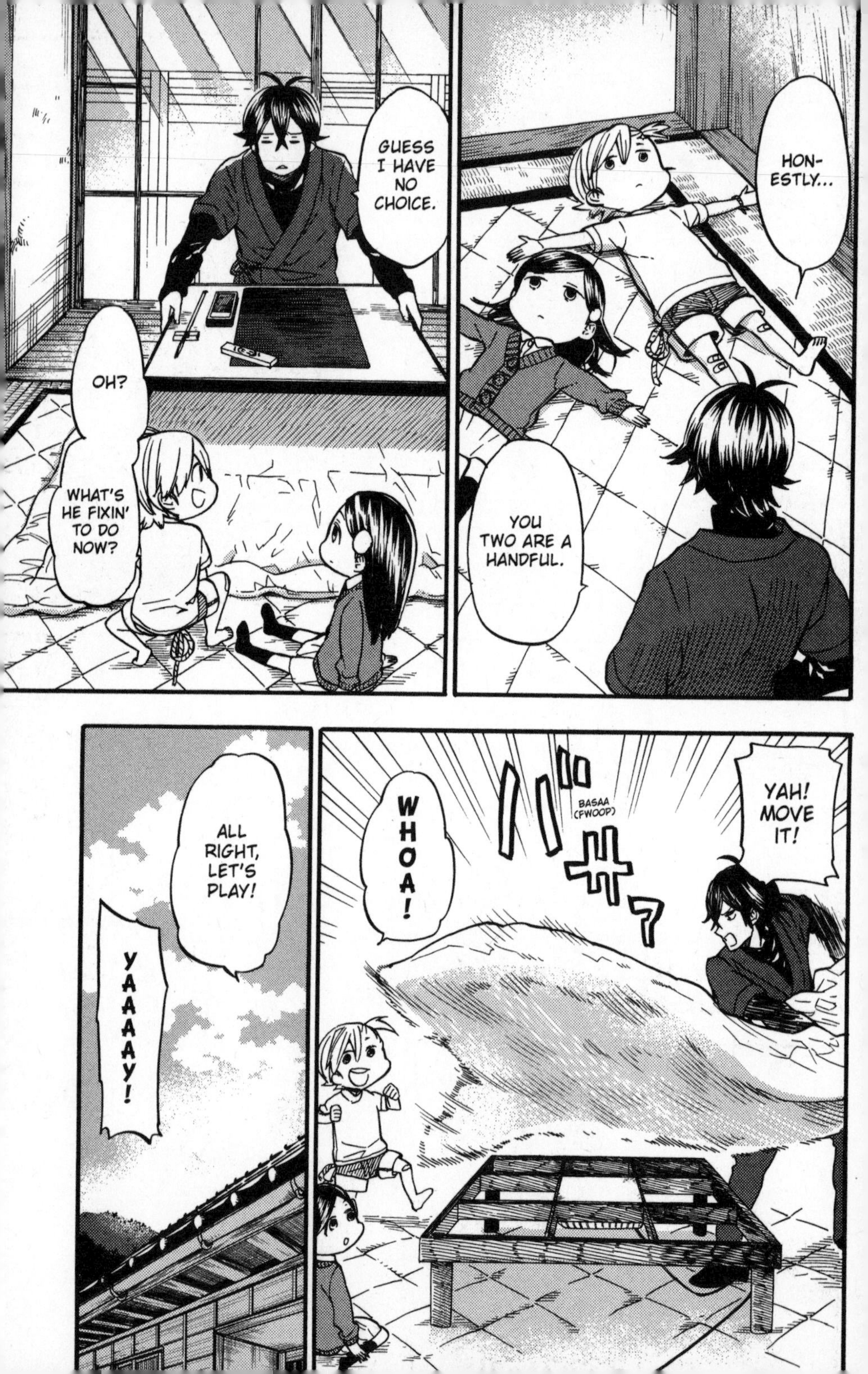
HON-ESTLY...
YOU TWO ARE A HANDFUL.
GUESS I HAVE NO CHOICE.
OH?
WHAT'S HE FIXIN' TO DO NOW?
YAH! MOVE IT!
BASAA (FWOOP)
WHOA!
ALL RIGHT, LET'S PLAY!
YAAAAAY!

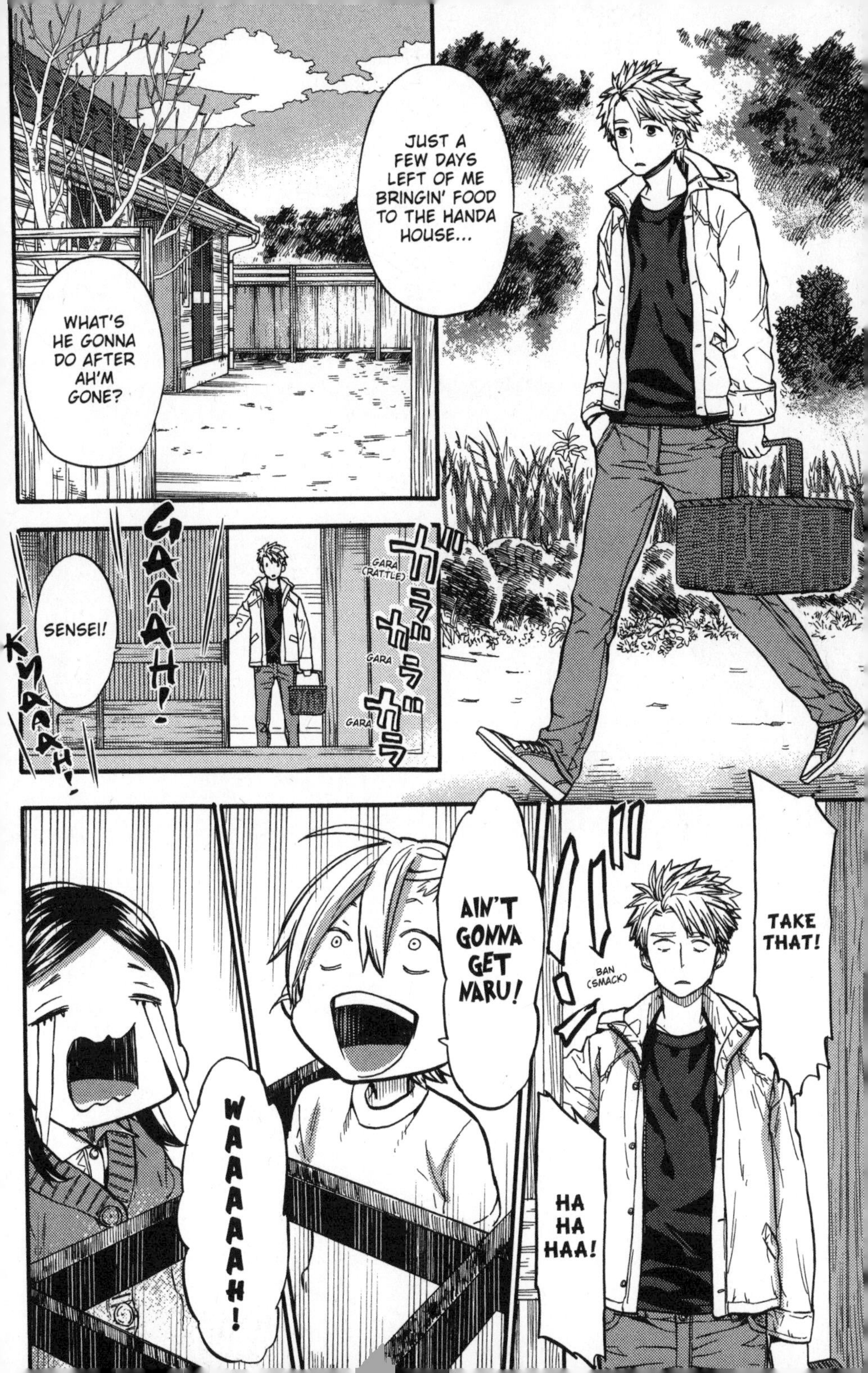

JUST A FEW DAYS LEFT OF ME BRINGIN' FOOD TO THE HANDA HOUSE...
WHAT'S HE GONNA DO AFTER AH'M GONE?
GARA (RATTLE)
GARA
GARA
SENSEI!
GAAAH!
KYAAAAH!
TAKE THAT!
BAN (SMACK)
AIN'T GONNA GET NARU!
HA HA HAA!
WAAAAAAH!

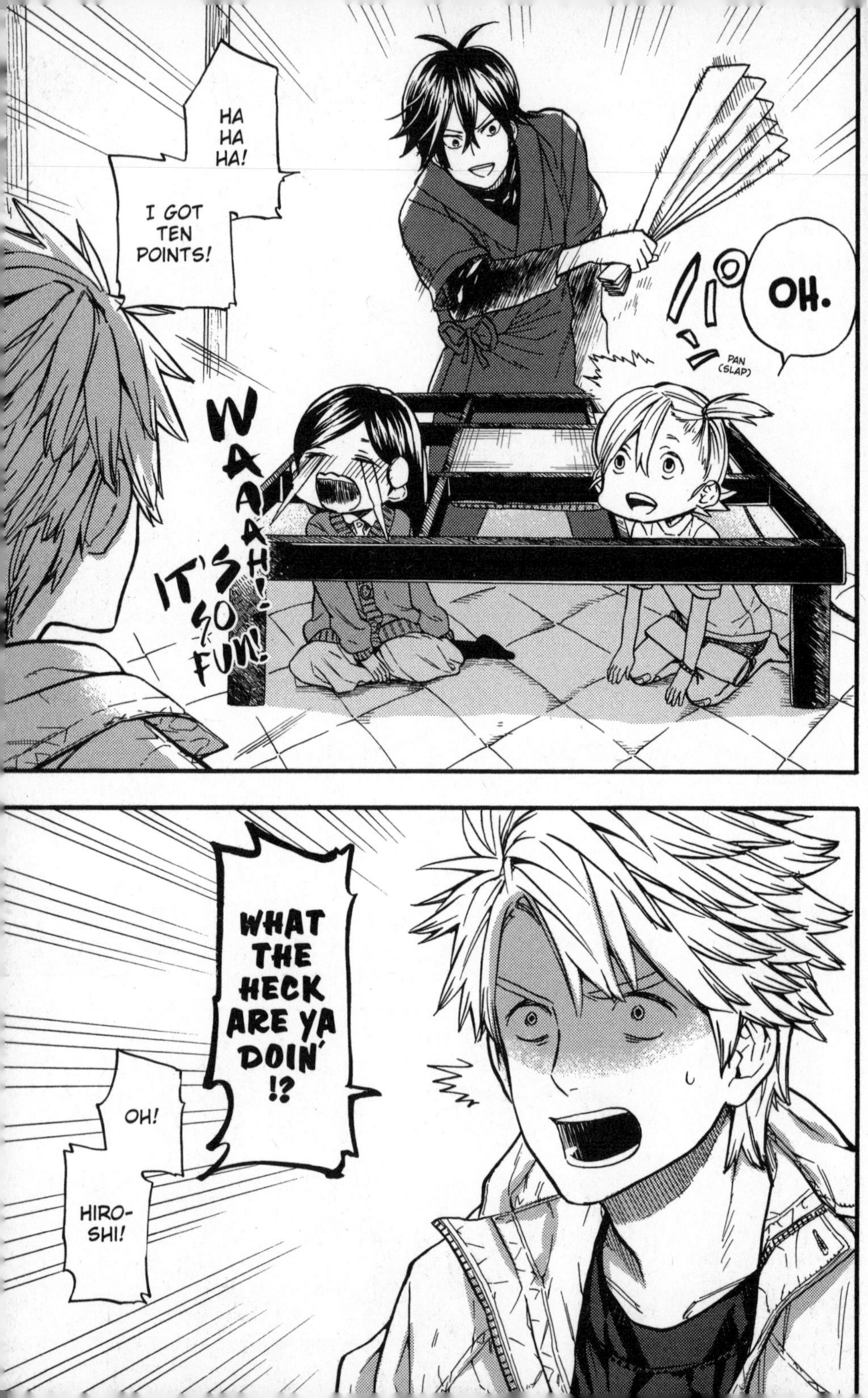
OH.
PAN (SLAP)
HA HA HA!
I GOT TEN POINTS!
WAAAAH!
IT'S SO FUN!
WHAT THE HECK ARE YA DOIN'!?
OH!
HIRO-SHI!

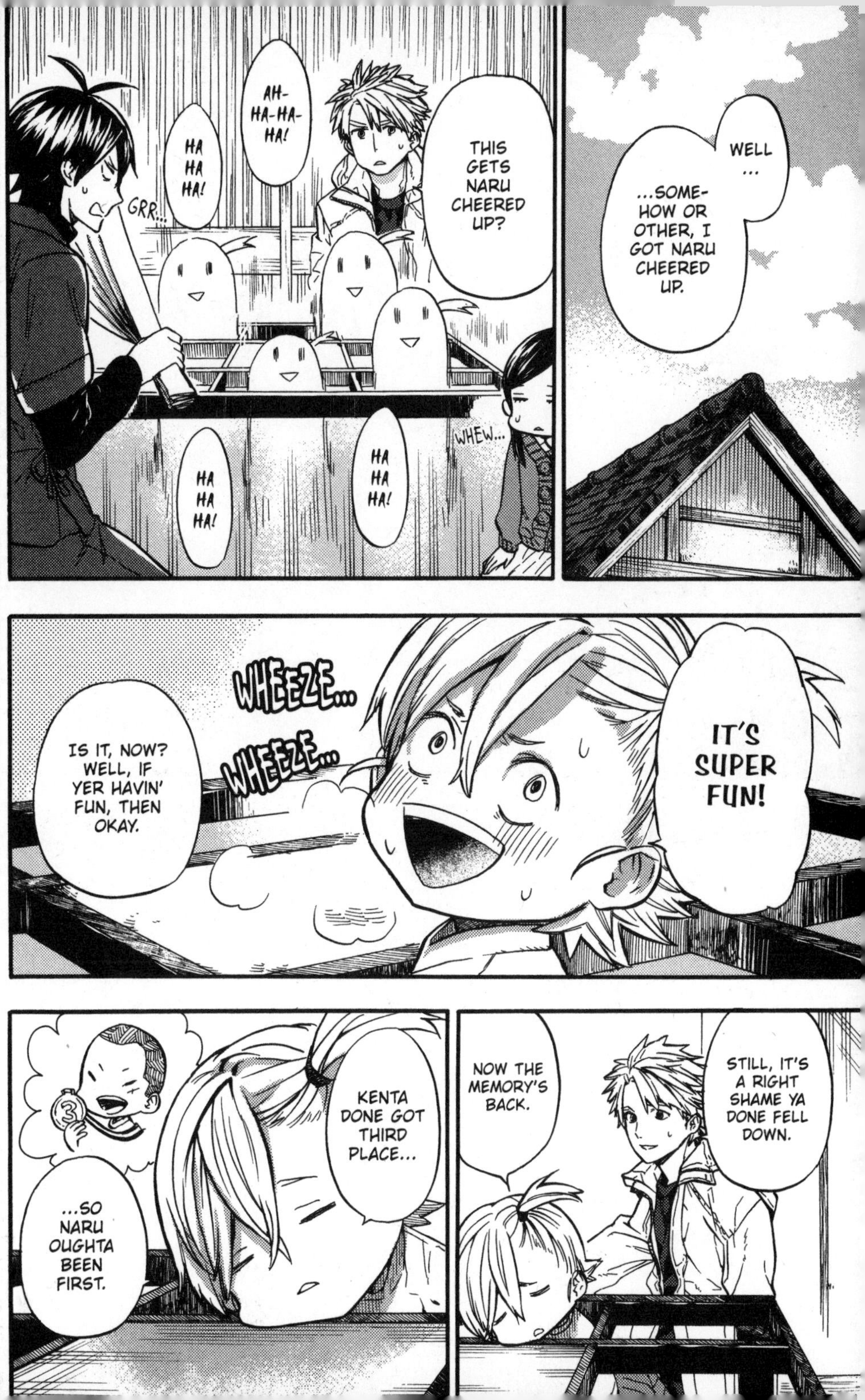
WELL...
...SOME-HOW OR OTHER, I GOT NARU CHEERED UP.
THIS GETS NARU CHEERED UP?
AH-HA-HA-HA!
HA HA HA!
GRR...
WHEW...
HA HA HA!
HA HA HA!
IT'S SUPER FUN!
WHEEZE...
WHEEZE...
IS IT, NOW? WELL, IF YER HAVIN' FUN, THEN OKAY.
STILL, IT'S A RIGHT SHAME YA DONE FELL DOWN.
NOW THE MEMORY'S BACK.
KENTA DONE GOT THIRD PLACE...
3
...SO NARU OUGHTA BEEN FIRST.

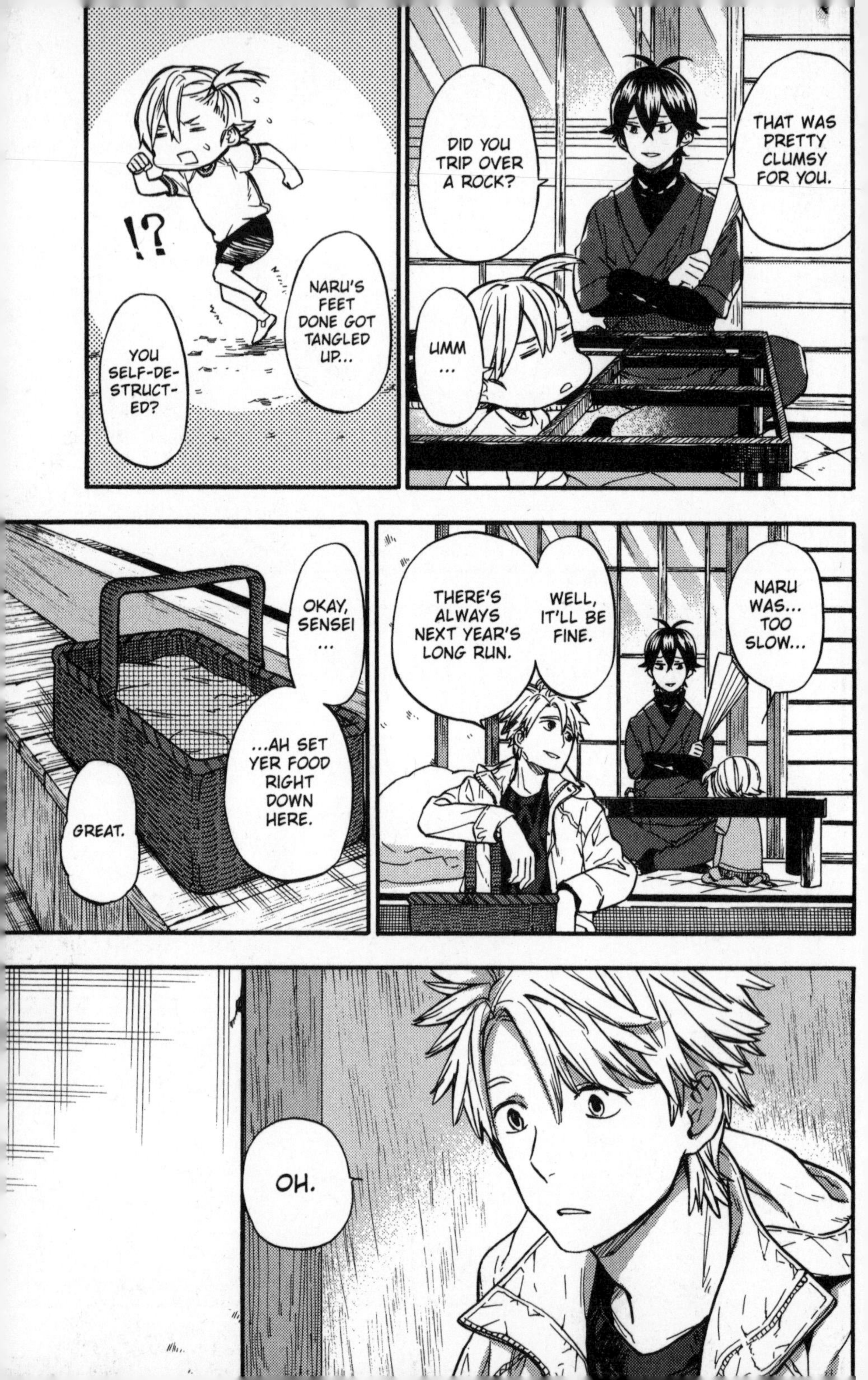
THAT WAS PRETTY CLUMSY FOR YOU.
DID YOU TRIP OVER A ROCK?
UMM ...
NARU'S FEET DONE GOT TANGLED UP...
YOU SELF-DESTRUCTED?
!?
NARU WAS... TOO SLOW...
WELL, IT'LL BE FINE.
THERE'S ALWAYS NEXT YEAR'S LONG RUN.
OKAY, SENSEI ...
...AH SET YER FOOD RIGHT DOWN HERE.
GREAT.
OH.

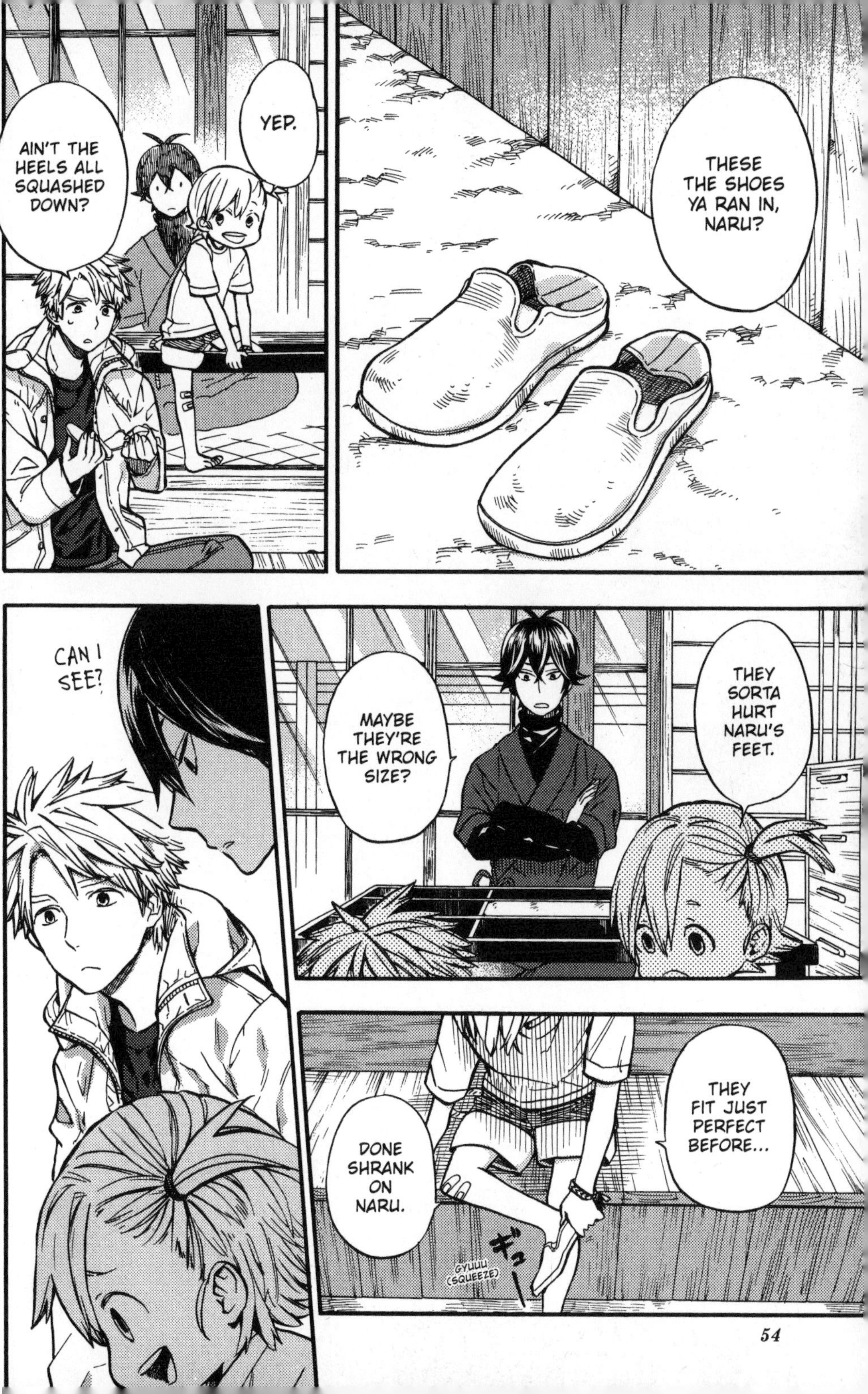
THESE THE SHOES YA RAN IN, NARU?
YEP.
AIN'T THE HEELS ALL SQUASHED DOWN?
THEY SORTA HURT NARU'S FEET.
MAYBE THEY'RE THE WRONG SIZE?
THEY FIT JUST PERFECT BEFORE...
DONE SHRANK ON NARU.
ギュー
GYUUU (SQUEEZE)
CAN I SEE?

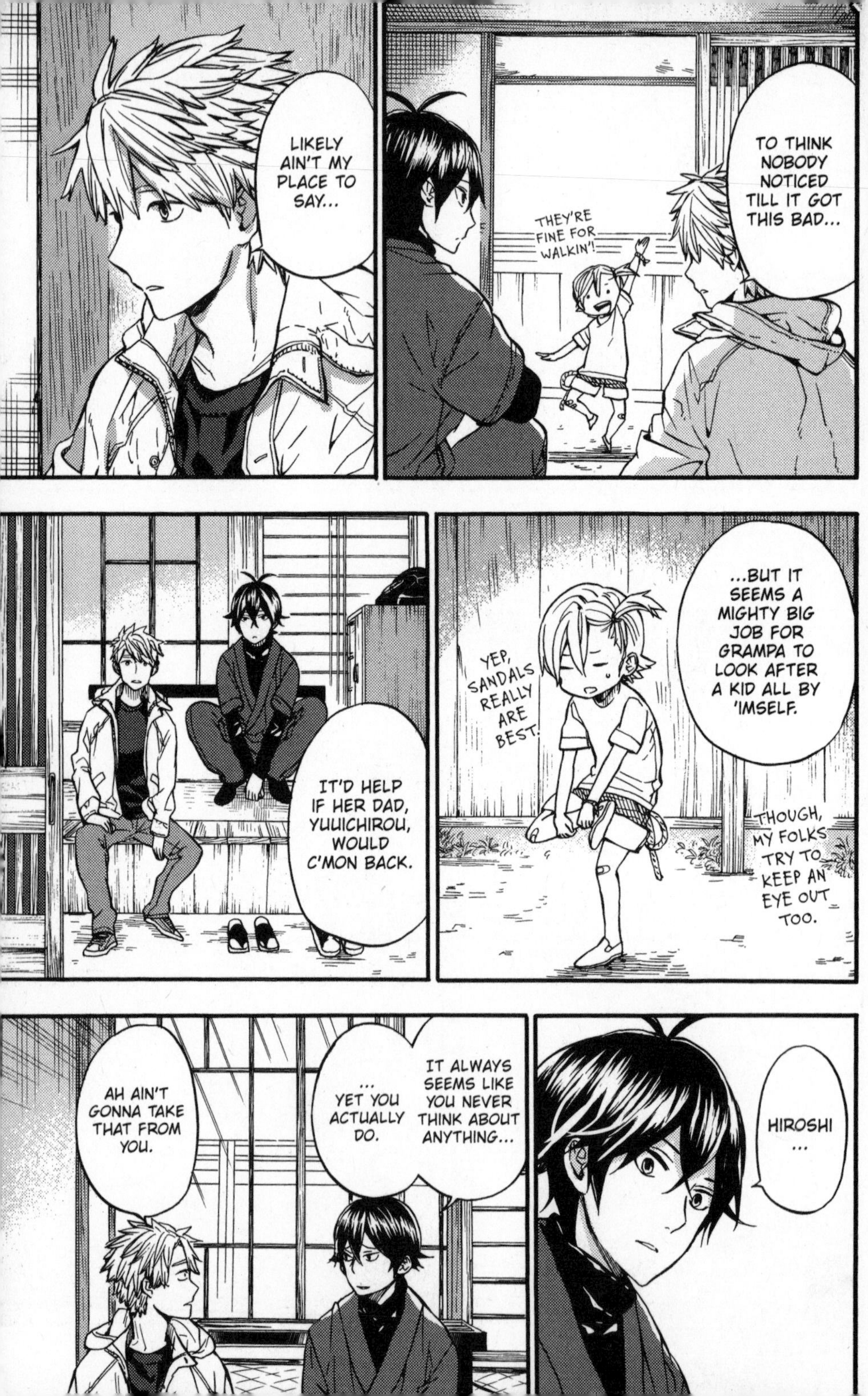
TO THINK NOBODY NOTICED TILL IT GOT THIS BAD...
THEY'RE FINE FOR WALKIN'!
LIKELY AIN'T MY PLACE TO SAY...
...BUT IT SEEMS A MIGHTY BIG JOB FOR GRAMPA TO LOOK AFTER A KID ALL BY 'IMSELF.
YEP, SANDALS REALLY ARE BEST.
THOUGH, MY FOLKS TRY TO KEEP AN EYE OUT TOO.
IT'D HELP IF HER DAD, YUUICHIROU, WOULD C'MON BACK.
HIROSHI...
IT ALWAYS SEEMS LIKE YOU NEVER THINK ABOUT ANYTHING...
...YET YOU ACTUALLY DO.
AH AIN'T GONNA TAKE THAT FROM YOU.

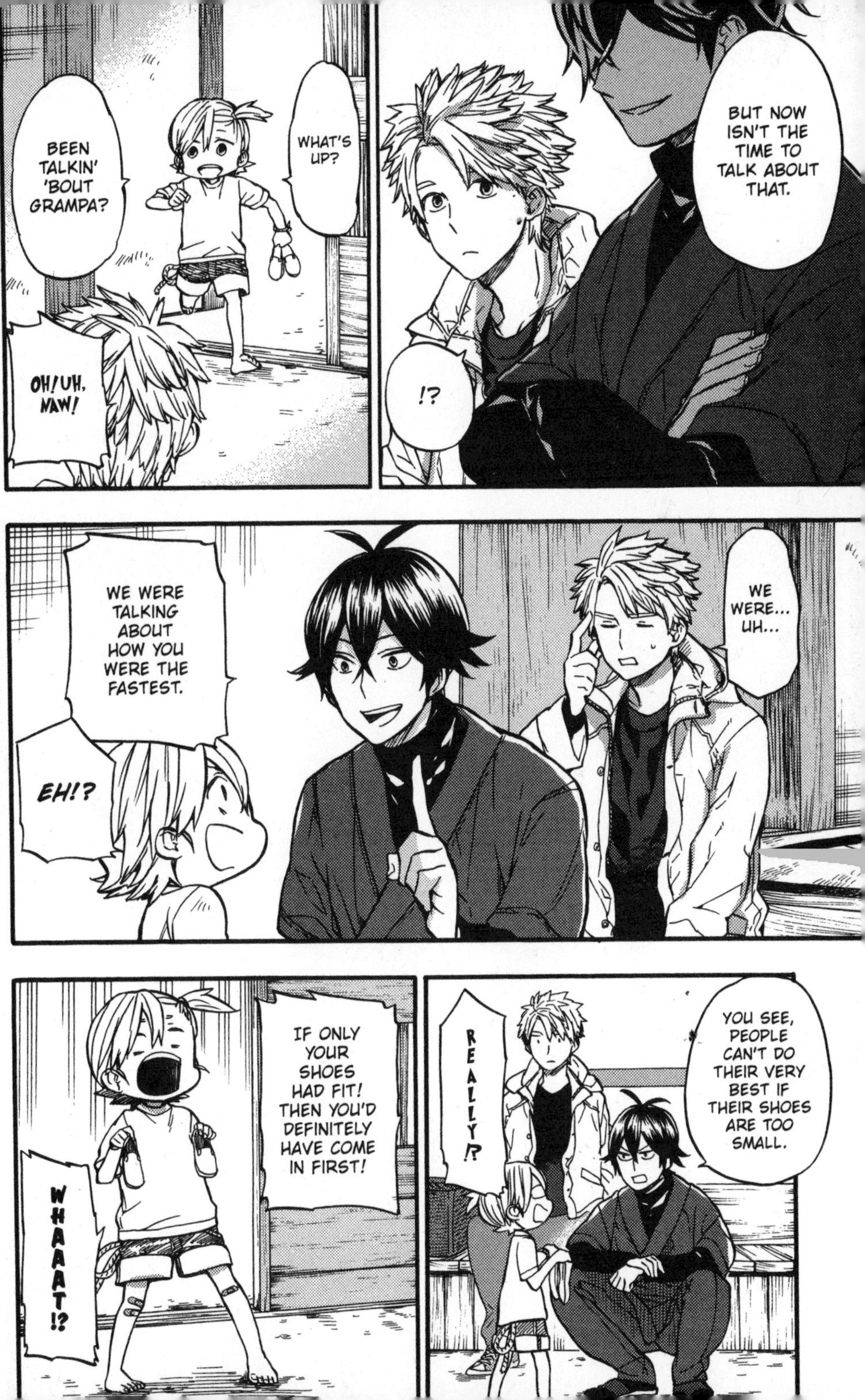
BUT NOW ISN'T THE TIME TO TALK ABOUT THAT.
!?
WHAT'S UP?
BEEN TALKIN' 'BOUT GRAMPA?
OH! UH, NAW!
WE WERE... UH...
WE WERE TALKING ABOUT HOW YOU WERE THE FASTEST.
EH!?
YOU SEE, PEOPLE CAN'T DO THEIR VERY BEST IF THEIR SHOES ARE TOO SMALL.
REALLY!?
IF ONLY YOUR SHOES HAD FIT! THEN YOU'D DEFINITELY HAVE COME IN FIRST!
WHAAAAT!?

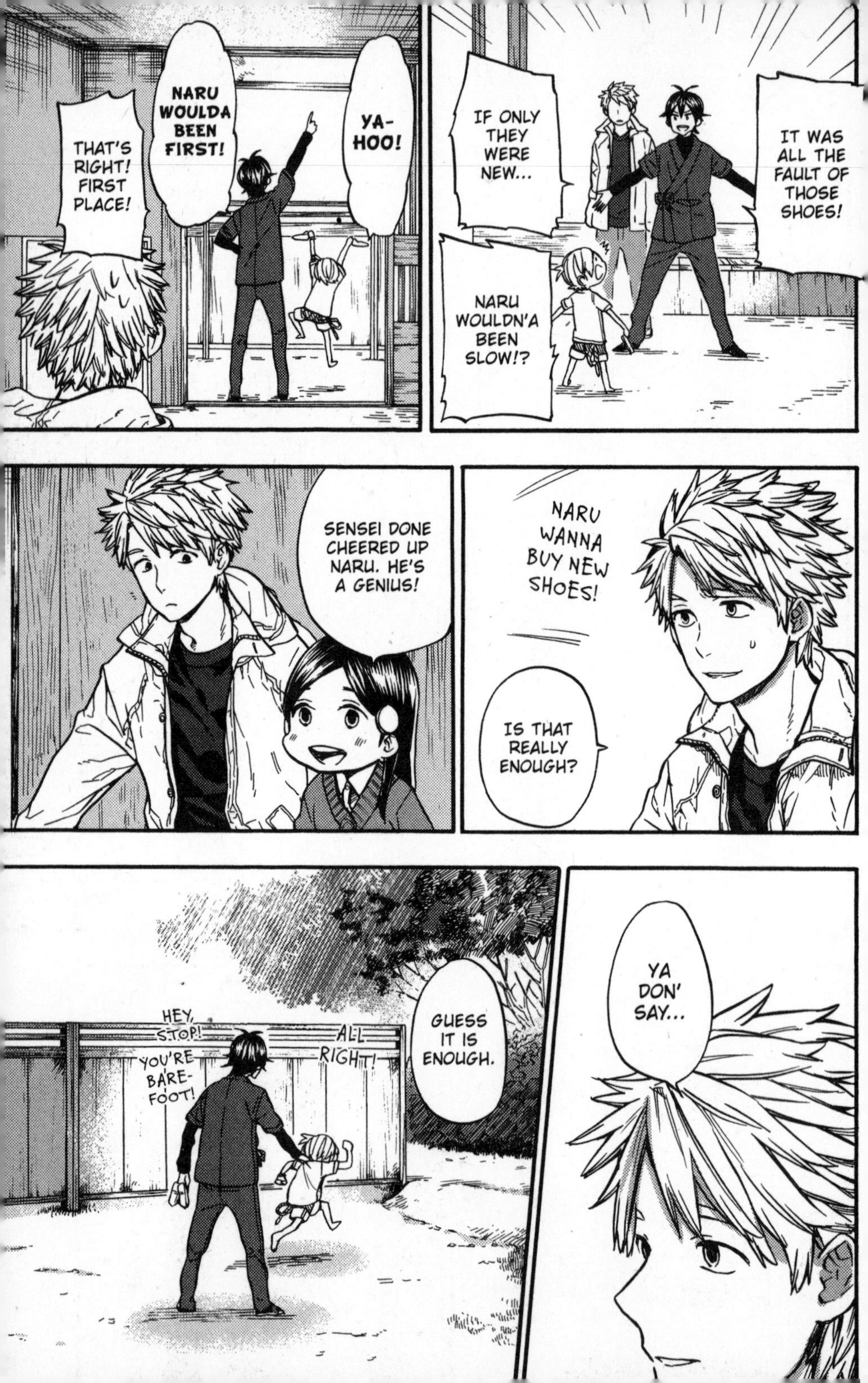
IT WAS ALL THE FAULT OF THOSE SHOES!
IF ONLY THEY WERE NEW...
NARU WOULDN'A BEEN SLOW!?
YA-HOO!
NARU WOULDA BEEN FIRST!
THAT'S RIGHT! FIRST PLACE!
NARU WANNA BUY NEW SHOES!
IS THAT REALLY ENOUGH?
SENSEI DONE CHEERED UP NARU. HE'S A GENIUS!
YA DON' SAY...
GUESS IT IS ENOUGH.
ALL RIGHT!
HEY, STOP!
YOU'RE BARE-FOOT!

Act.117
KOMAKUROSHIKA
(Translation: Hard to Handle)

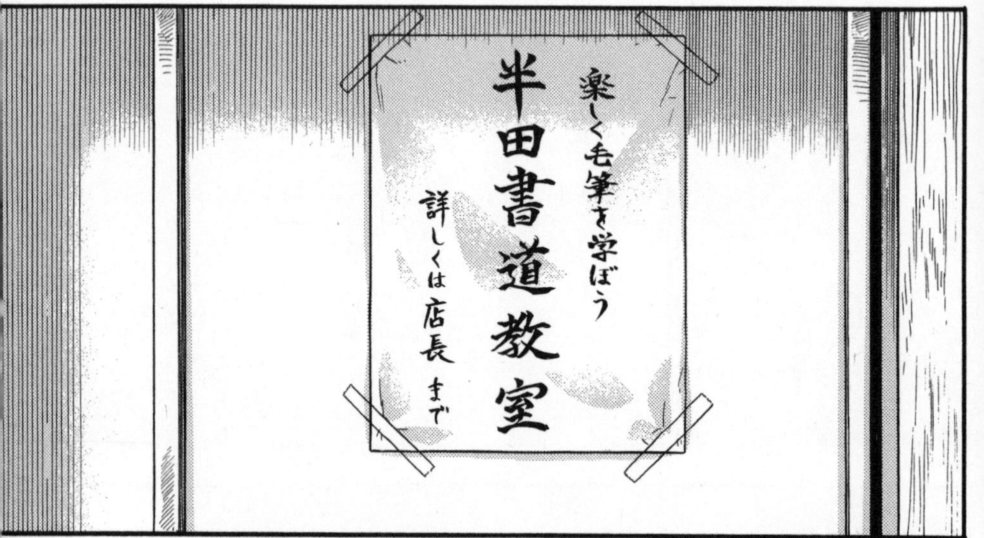
楽しく毛筆を学ぼう
半田書道教室
詳しくは店長まで

SIGN: LET'S HAVE FUN LEARNING BRUSH-WRITING. HANDA CALLIGRAPHY SCHOOL. ASK THE MANAGER FOR DETAILS.

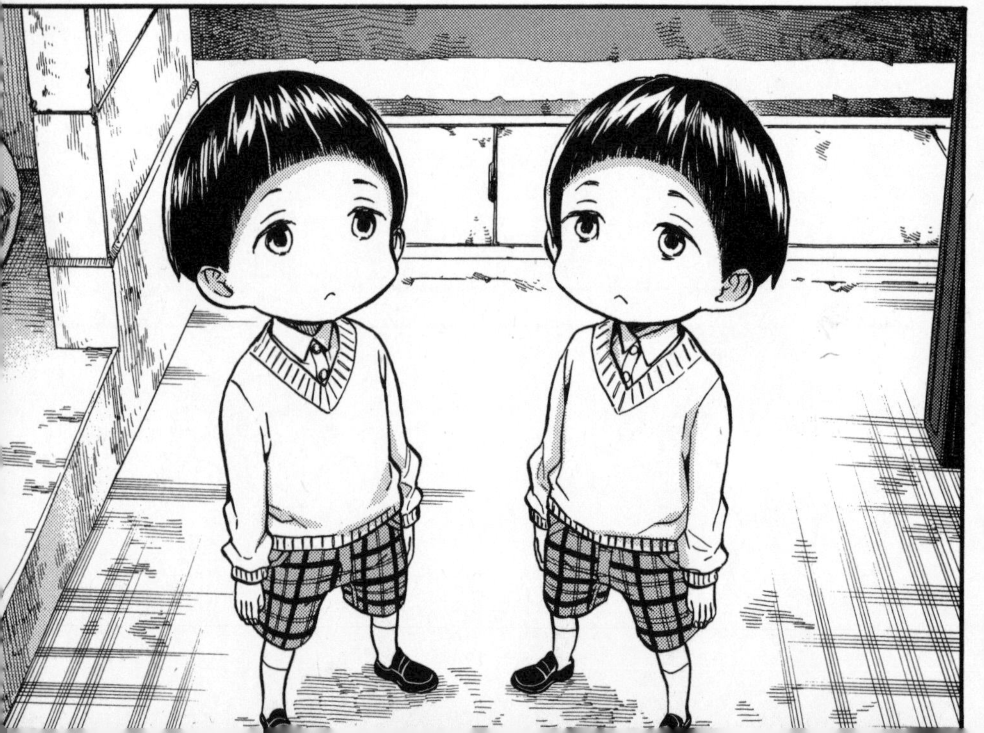

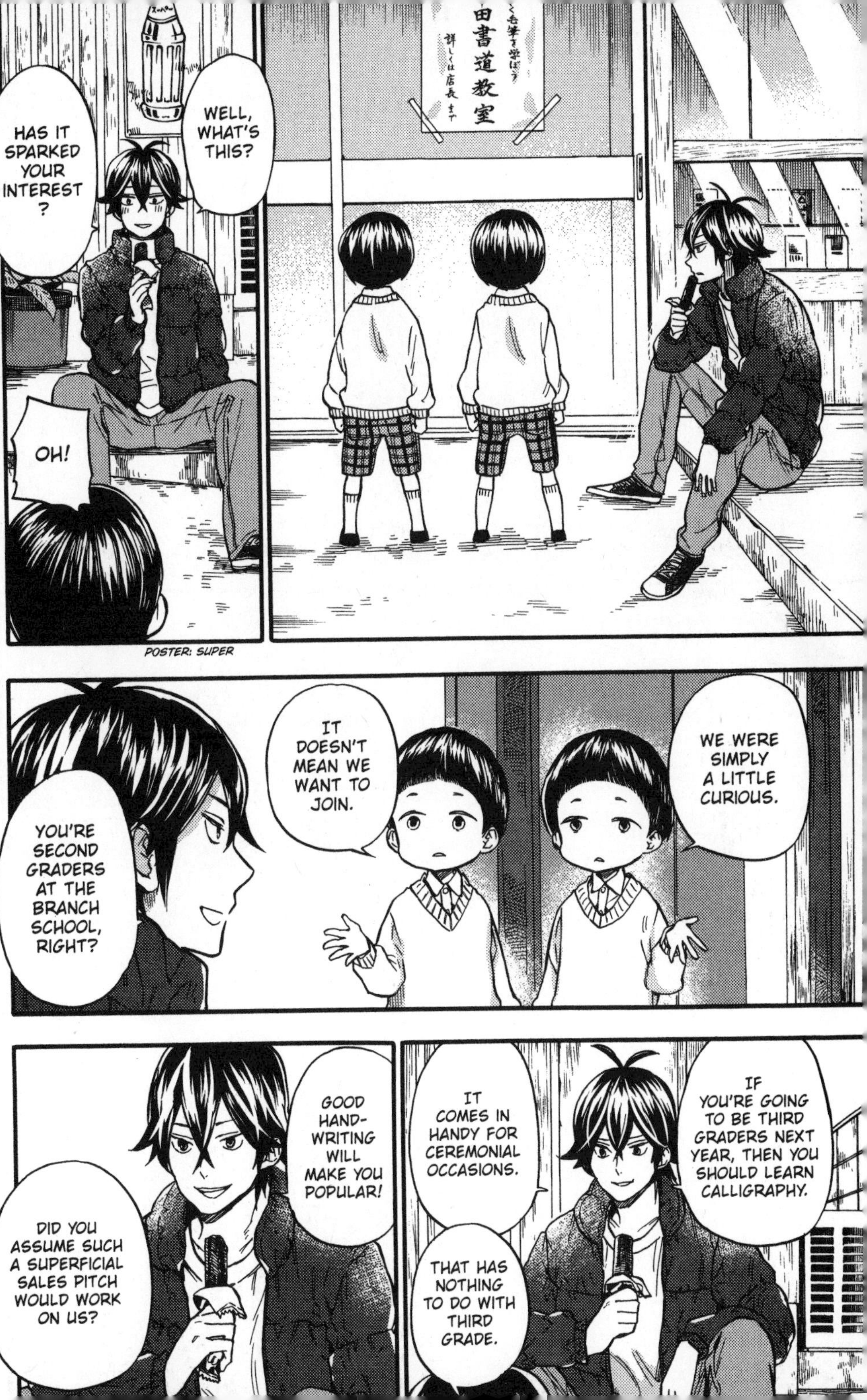

く毛筆を学ぼう
田書道教室
詳しくは店長まで
WELL, WHAT'S THIS?
HAS IT SPARKED YOUR INTEREST?
OH!
POSTER: SUPER
WE WERE SIMPLY A LITTLE CURIOUS.
IT DOESN'T MEAN WE WANT TO JOIN.
YOU'RE SECOND GRADERS AT THE BRANCH SCHOOL, RIGHT?
IF YOU'RE GOING TO BE THIRD GRADERS NEXT YEAR, THEN YOU SHOULD LEARN CALLIGRAPHY.
IT COMES IN HANDY FOR CEREMONIAL OCCASIONS.
THAT HAS NOTHING TO DO WITH THIRD GRADE.
GOOD HAND-WRITING WILL MAKE YOU POPULAR!
DID YOU ASSUME SUCH A SUPERFICIAL SALES PITCH WOULD WORK ON US?

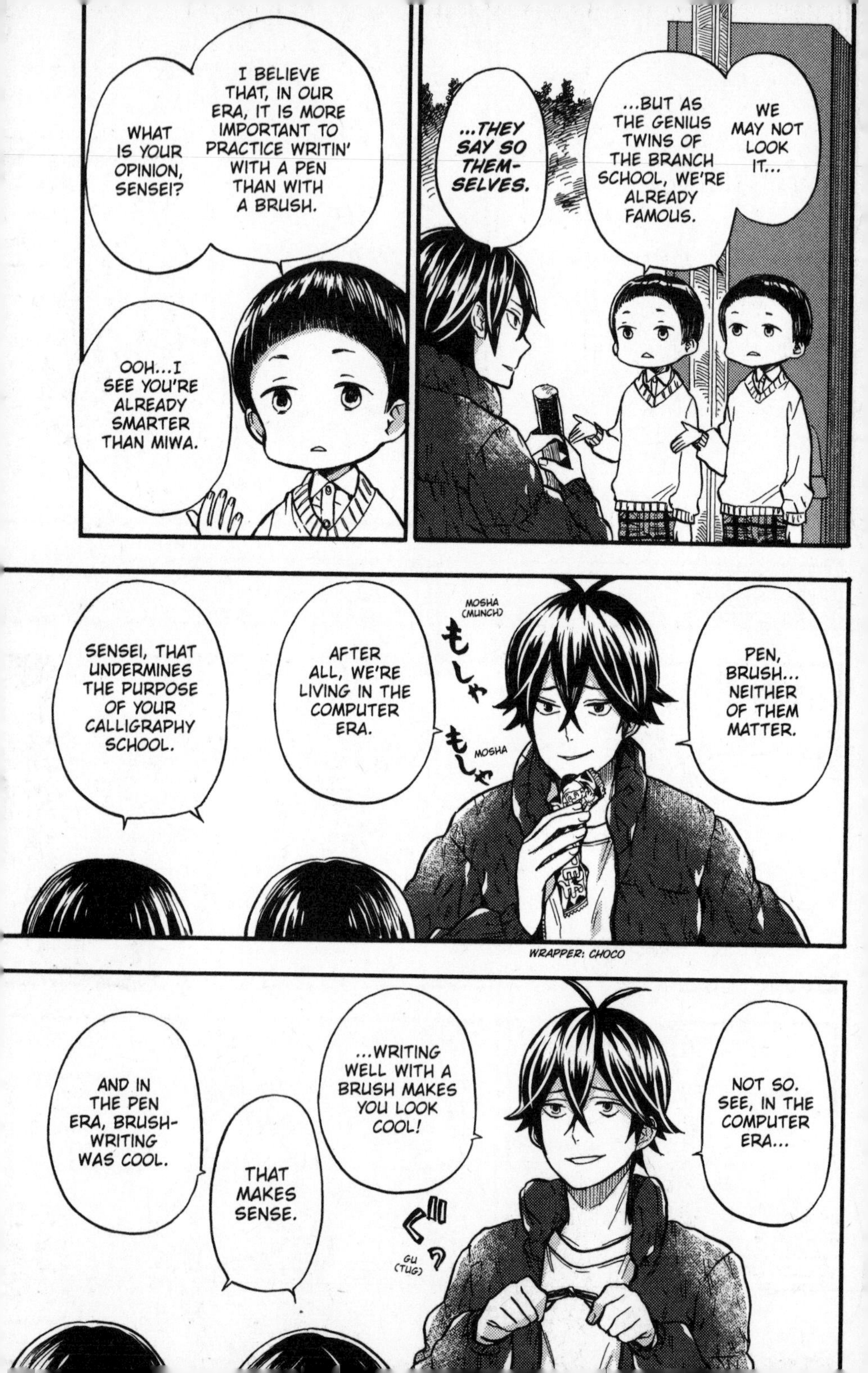
WE MAY NOT LOOK IT...
...BUT AS THE GENIUS TWINS OF THE BRANCH SCHOOL, WE'RE ALREADY FAMOUS.
...THEY SAY SO THEMSELVES.
I BELIEVE THAT, IN OUR ERA, IT IS MORE IMPORTANT TO PRACTICE WRITIN' WITH A PEN THAN WITH A BRUSH.
WHAT IS YOUR OPINION, SENSEI?
OOH...I SEE YOU'RE ALREADY SMARTER THAN MIWA.
PEN, BRUSH... NEITHER OF THEM MATTER.
もしゃ
MOSHA (MUNCH)
もしゃ
MOSHA
AFTER ALL, WE'RE LIVING IN THE COMPUTER ERA.
SENSEI, THAT UNDERMINES THE PURPOSE OF YOUR CALLIGRAPHY SCHOOL.
WRAPPER: CHOCO
NOT SO. SEE, IN THE COMPUTER ERA...
...WRITING WELL WITH A BRUSH MAKES YOU LOOK COOL!
ぐっ
GU (TUG)
AND IN THE PEN ERA, BRUSH-WRITING WAS COOL.
THAT MAKES SENSE.

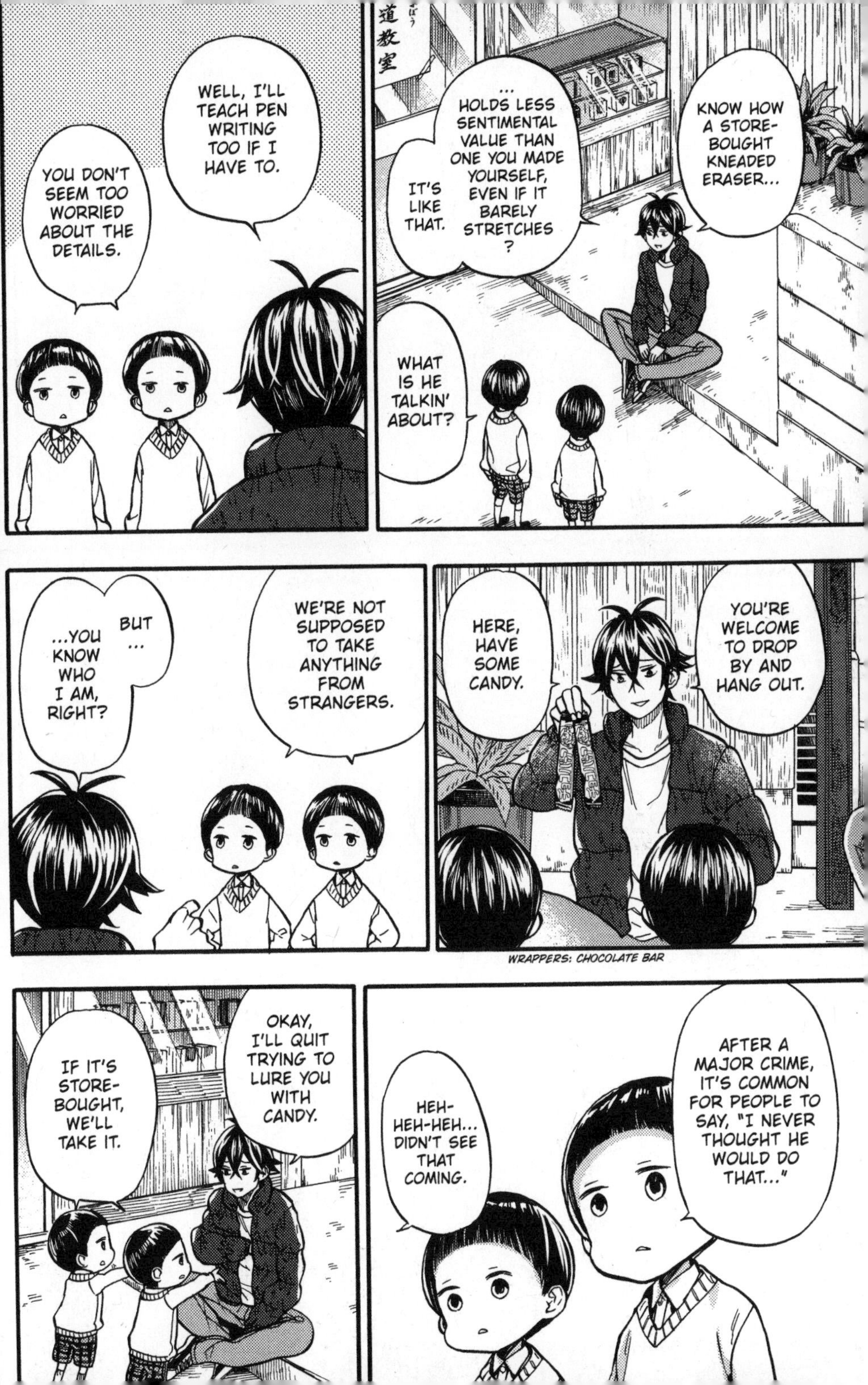
道教室
KNOW HOW A STORE-BOUGHT KNEADED ERASER...
... HOLDS LESS SENTIMENTAL VALUE THAN ONE YOU MADE YOURSELF, EVEN IF IT BARELY STRETCHES ?
IT'S LIKE THAT.
WHAT IS HE TALKIN' ABOUT?
WELL, I'LL TEACH PEN WRITING TOO IF I HAVE TO.
YOU DON'T SEEM TOO WORRIED ABOUT THE DETAILS.
YOU'RE WELCOME TO DROP BY AND HANG OUT.
HERE, HAVE SOME CANDY.
WRAPPERS: CHOCOLATE BAR
WE'RE NOT SUPPOSED TO TAKE ANYTHING FROM STRANGERS.
BUT ...
...YOU KNOW WHO I AM, RIGHT?
AFTER A MAJOR CRIME, IT'S COMMON FOR PEOPLE TO SAY, "I NEVER THOUGHT HE WOULD DO THAT..."
HEH-HEH-HEH... DIDN'T SEE THAT COMING.
OKAY, I'LL QUIT TRYING TO LURE YOU WITH CANDY.
IF IT'S STORE-BOUGHT, WE'LL TAKE IT.

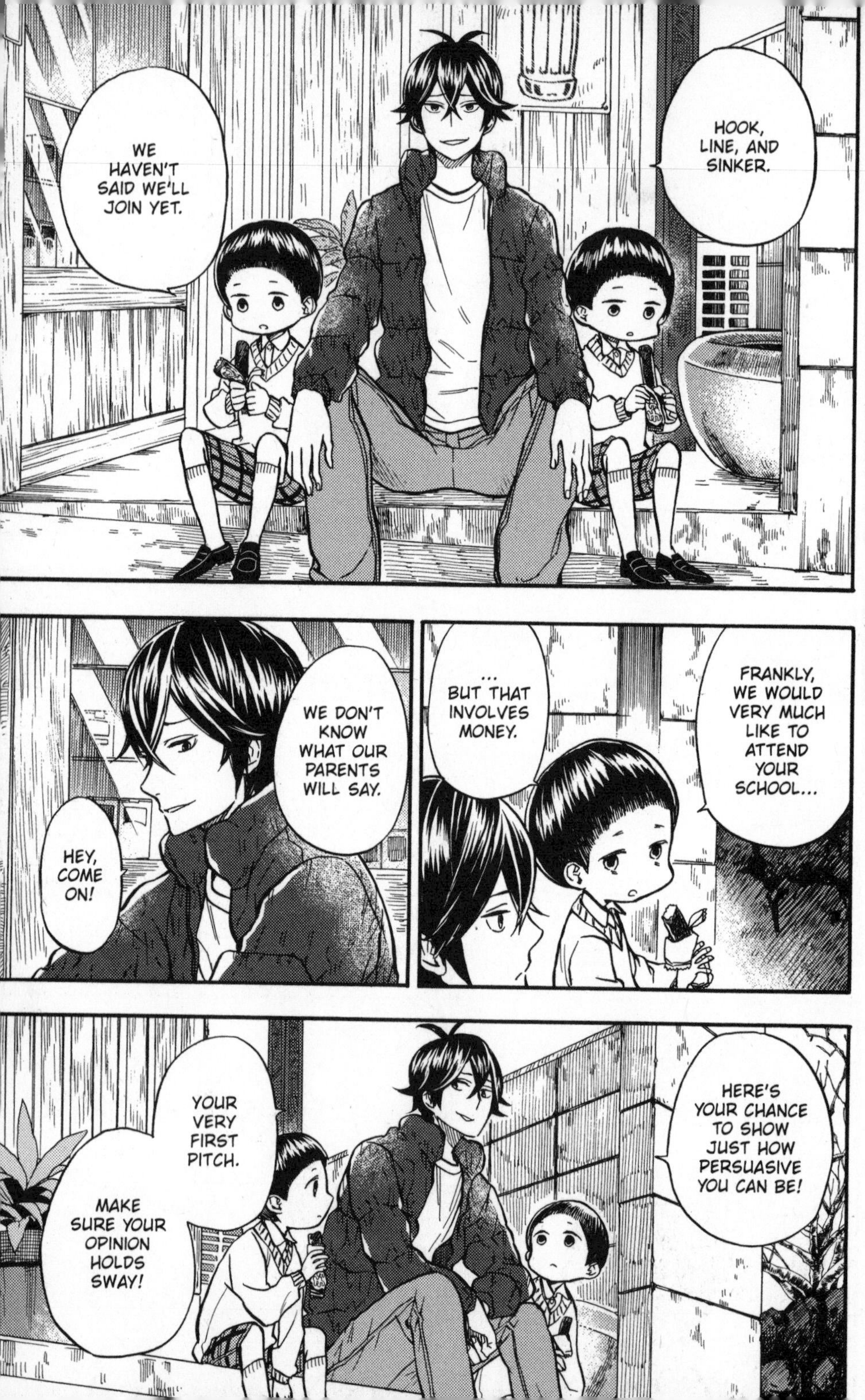
HOOK, LINE, AND SINKER.
WE HAVEN'T SAID WE'LL JOIN YET.
FRANKLY, WE WOULD VERY MUCH LIKE TO ATTEND YOUR SCHOOL...
... BUT THAT INVOLVES MONEY.
WE DON'T KNOW WHAT OUR PARENTS WILL SAY.
HEY, COME ON!
HERE'S YOUR CHANCE TO SHOW JUST HOW PERSUASIVE YOU CAN BE!
YOUR VERY FIRST PITCH.
MAKE SURE YOUR OPINION HOLDS SWAY!

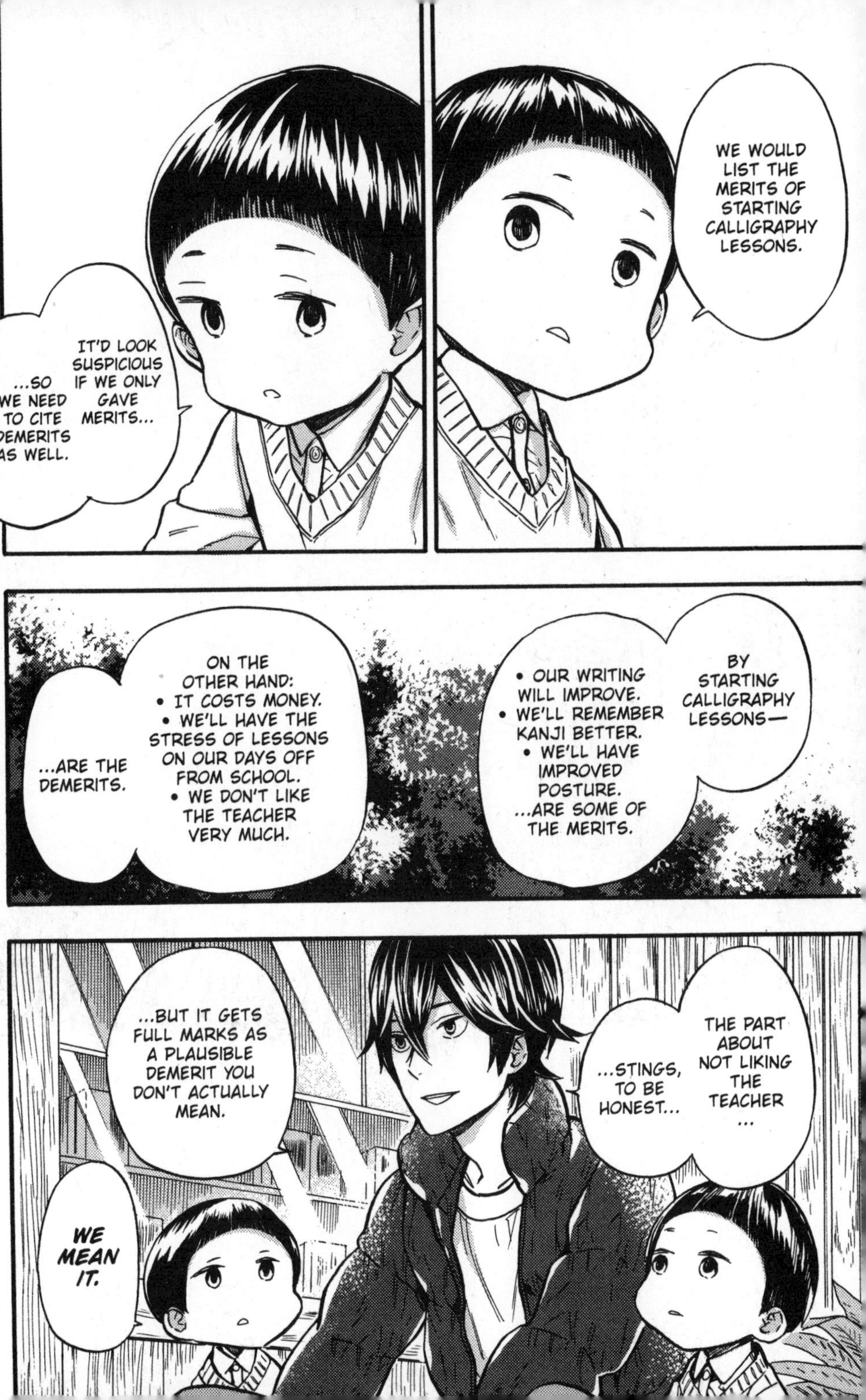
WE WOULD LIST THE MERITS OF STARTING CALLIGRAPHY LESSONS.
IT'D LOOK SUSPICIOUS IF WE ONLY GAVE MERITS...
...SO WE NEED TO CITE DEMERITS AS WELL.
BY STARTING CALLIGRAPHY LESSONS—
• OUR WRITING WILL IMPROVE. • WE'LL REMEMBER KANJI BETTER. • WE'LL HAVE IMPROVED POSTURE. ...ARE SOME OF THE MERITS.
ON THE OTHER HAND: • IT COSTS MONEY. • WE'LL HAVE THE STRESS OF LESSONS ON OUR DAYS OFF FROM SCHOOL. • WE DON'T LIKE THE TEACHER VERY MUCH.
...ARE THE DEMERITS.
THE PART ABOUT NOT LIKING THE TEACHER ...
...STINGS, TO BE HONEST...
...BUT IT GETS FULL MARKS AS A PLAUSIBLE DEMERIT YOU DON'T ACTUALLY MEAN.
WE MEAN IT.

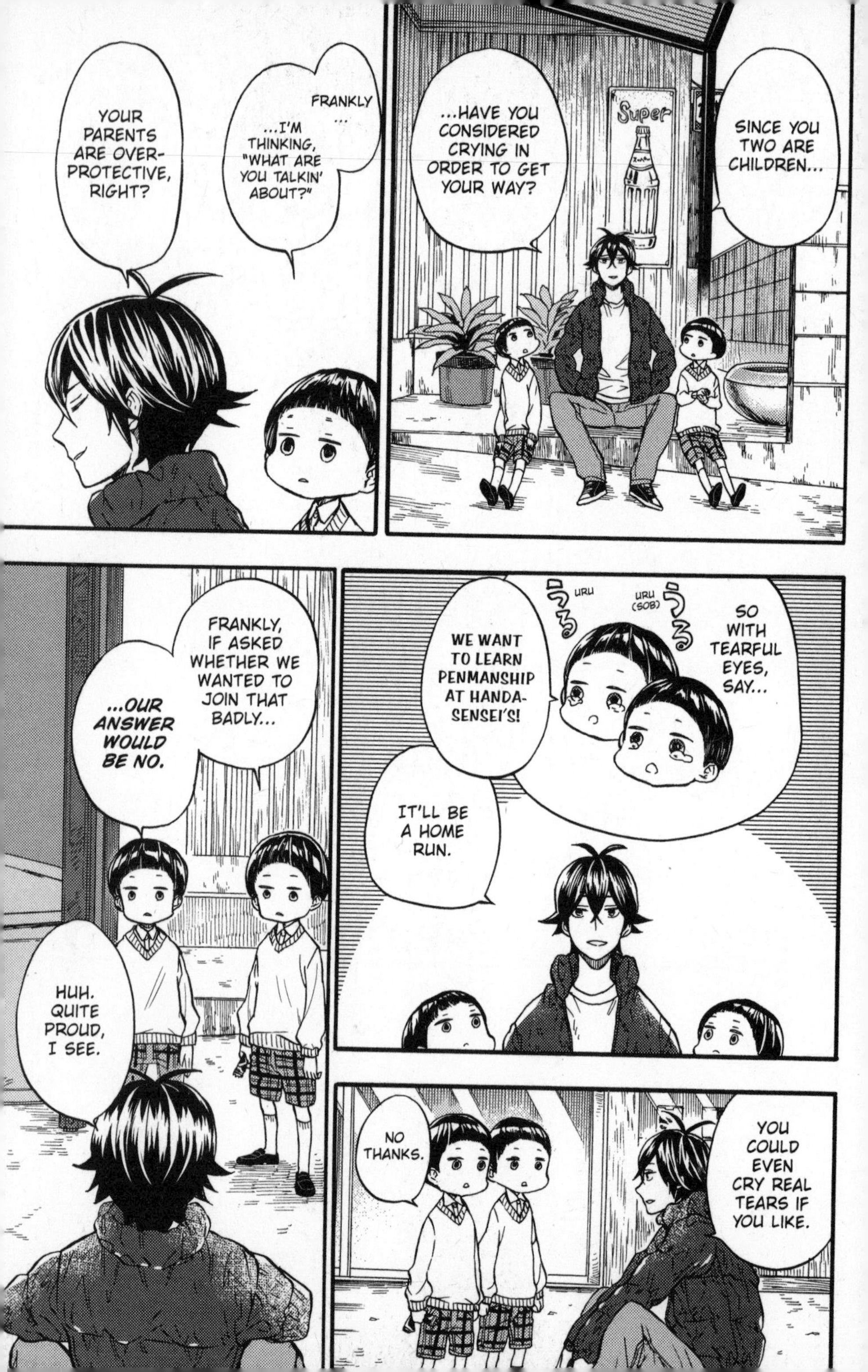
SINCE YOU TWO ARE CHILDREN...
...HAVE YOU CONSIDERED CRYING IN ORDER TO GET YOUR WAY?
FRANKLY...
...I'M THINKING, "WHAT ARE YOU TALKIN' ABOUT?"
YOUR PARENTS ARE OVER-PROTECTIVE, RIGHT?
SO WITH TEARFUL EYES, SAY...
うる URU (SOB)
うる URU
WE WANT TO LEARN PENMANSHIP AT HANDA-SENSEI'S!
IT'LL BE A HOME RUN.
YOU COULD EVEN CRY REAL TEARS IF YOU LIKE.
NO THANKS.
FRANKLY, IF ASKED WHETHER WE WANTED TO JOIN THAT BADLY...
...OUR ANSWER WOULD BE NO.
HUH. QUITE PROUD, I SEE.

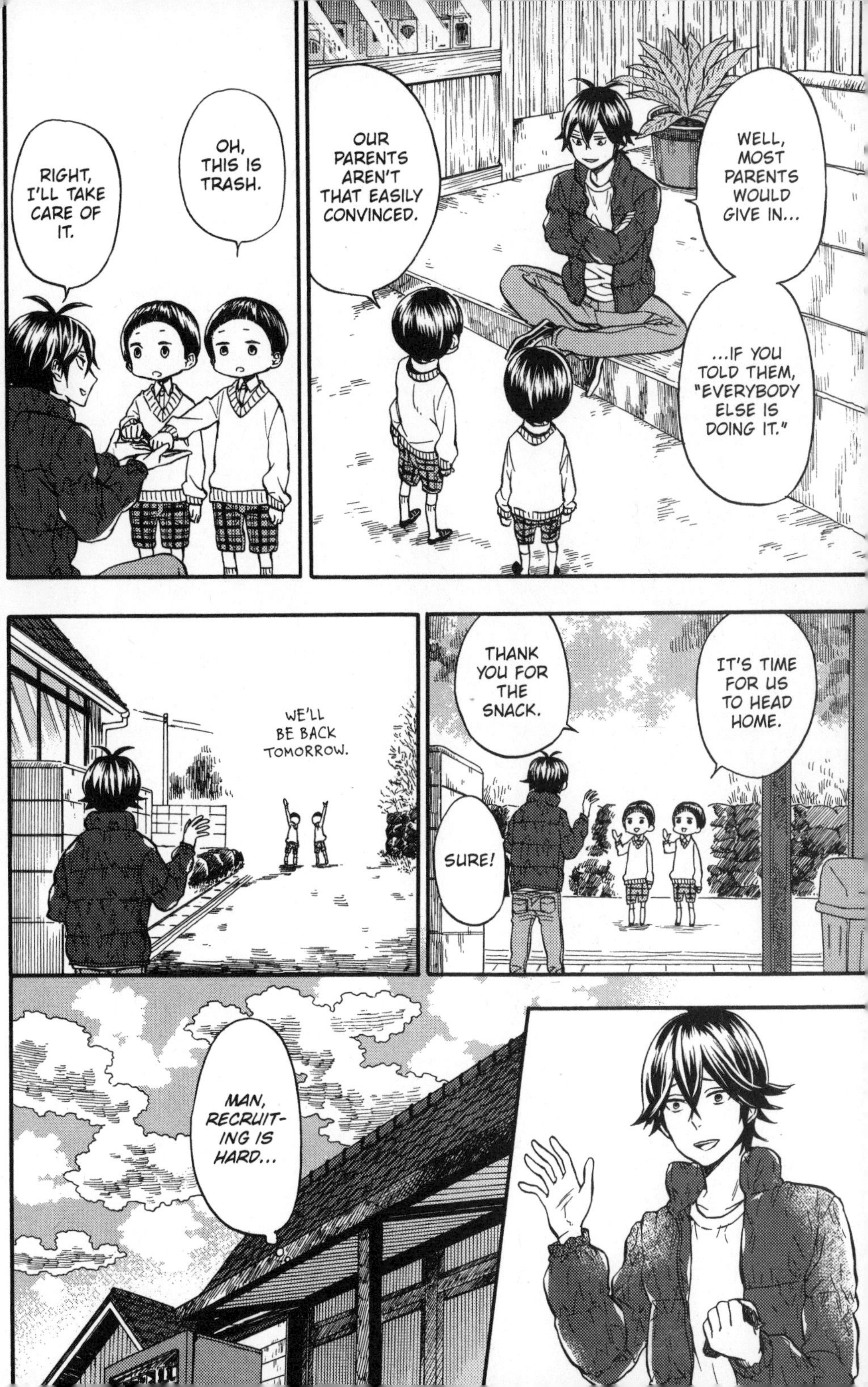
WELL, MOST PARENTS WOULD GIVE IN...
...IF YOU TOLD THEM, "EVERYBODY ELSE IS DOING IT."
OUR PARENTS AREN'T THAT EASILY CONVINCED.
OH, THIS IS TRASH.
RIGHT, I'LL TAKE CARE OF IT.
IT'S TIME FOR US TO HEAD HOME.
THANK YOU FOR THE SNACK.
SURE!
WE'LL BE BACK TOMORROW.
MAN, RECRUIT-ING IS HARD...

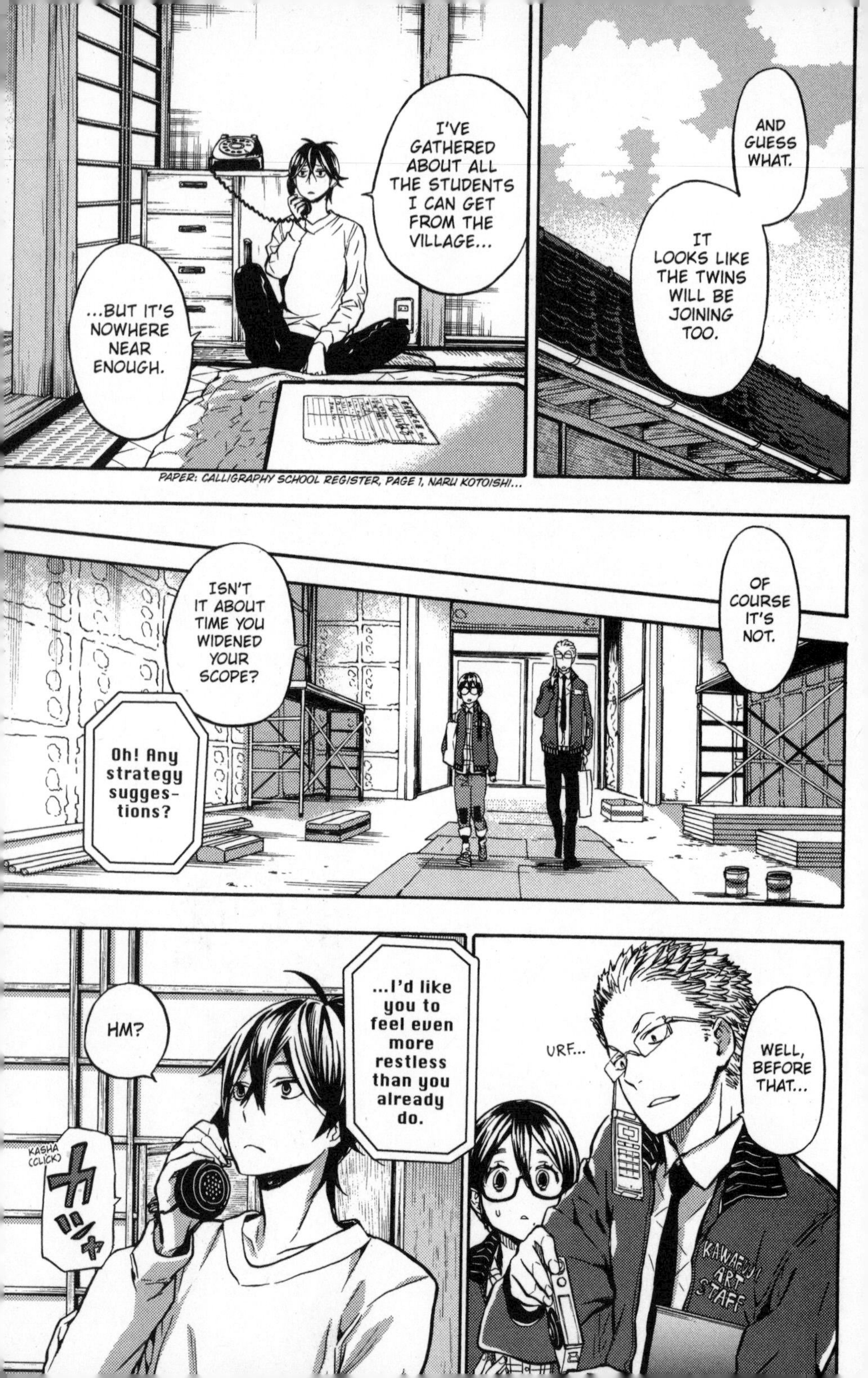
AND GUESS WHAT.
IT LOOKS LIKE THE TWINS WILL BE JOINING TOO.
I'VE GATHERED ABOUT ALL THE STUDENTS I CAN GET FROM THE VILLAGE...
...BUT IT'S NOWHERE NEAR ENOUGH.
PAPER: CALLIGRAPHY SCHOOL REGISTER, PAGE 1, NARU KOTOISHI...
OF COURSE IT'S NOT.
ISN'T IT ABOUT TIME YOU WIDENED YOUR SCOPE?
Oh! Any strategy suggestions?
WELL, BEFORE THAT...
URF...
KAWAFUJI ART STAFF
...I'd like you to feel even more restless than you already do.
HM?
KASHA (CLICK)

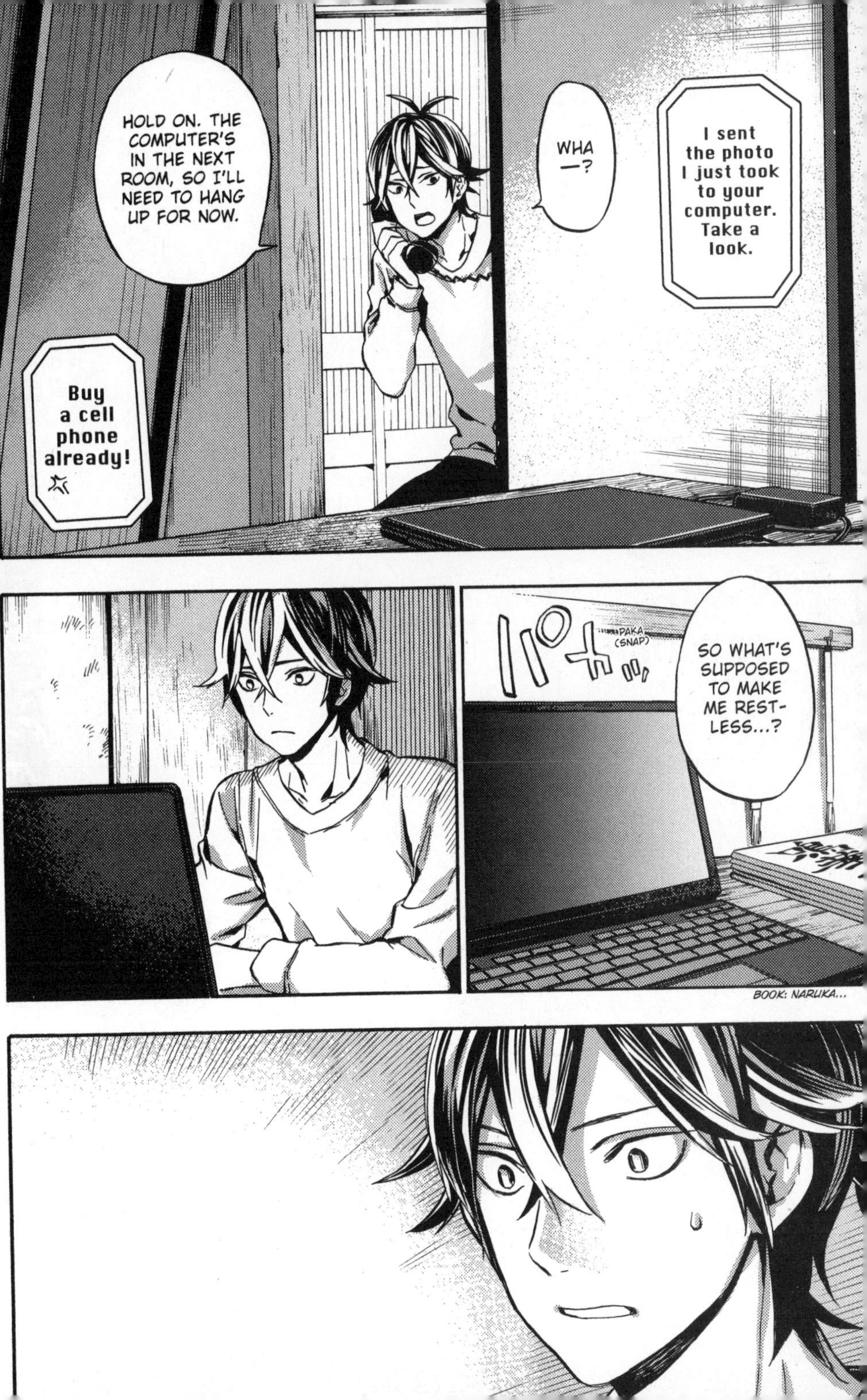
I sent the photo I just took to your computer. Take a look.
WHA—?
HOLD ON. THE COMPUTER'S IN THE NEXT ROOM, SO I'LL NEED TO HANG UP FOR NOW.
Buy a cell phone already!
パカッ
PAKA (SNAP)
SO WHAT'S SUPPOSED TO MAKE ME REST-LESS...?
BOOK: NARUKA...

Act.118 TOTODON

(Translation: Dads)

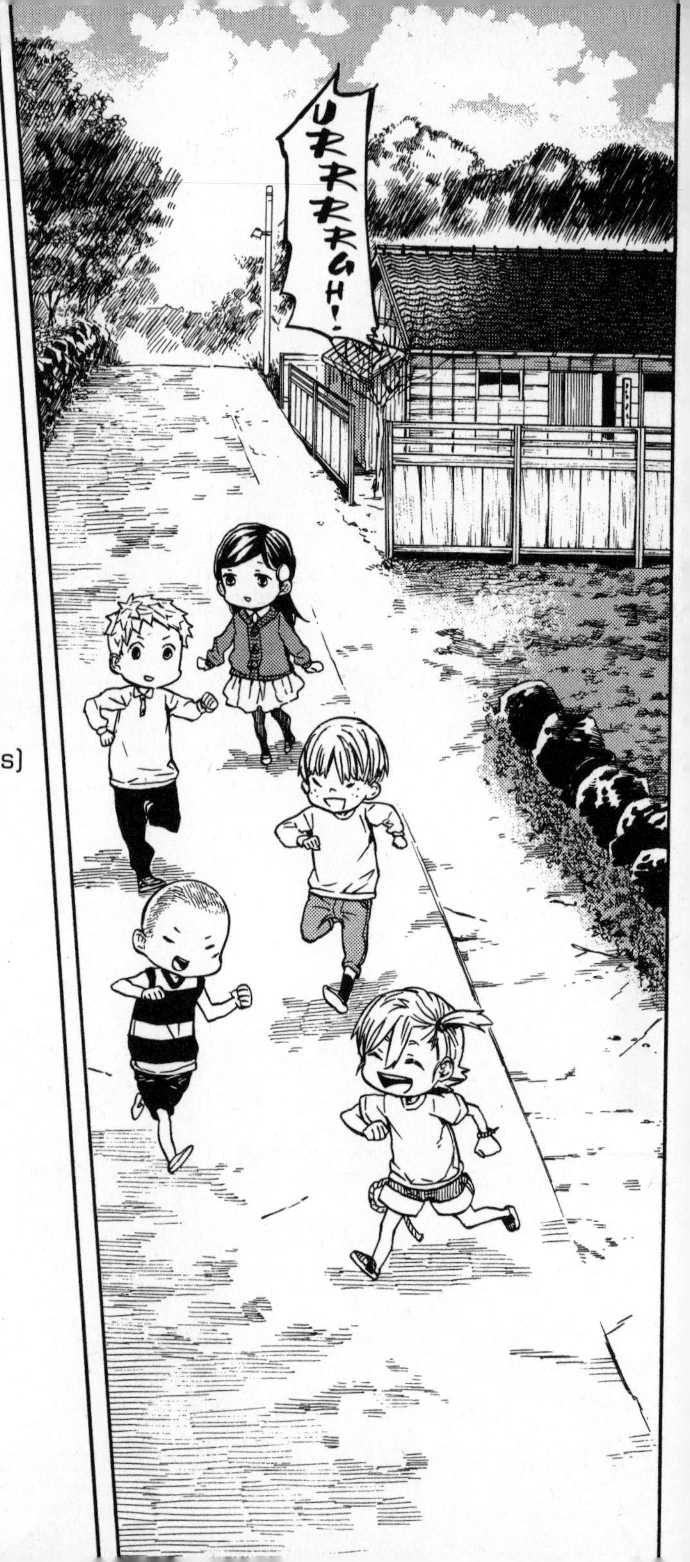
URRRRGH!

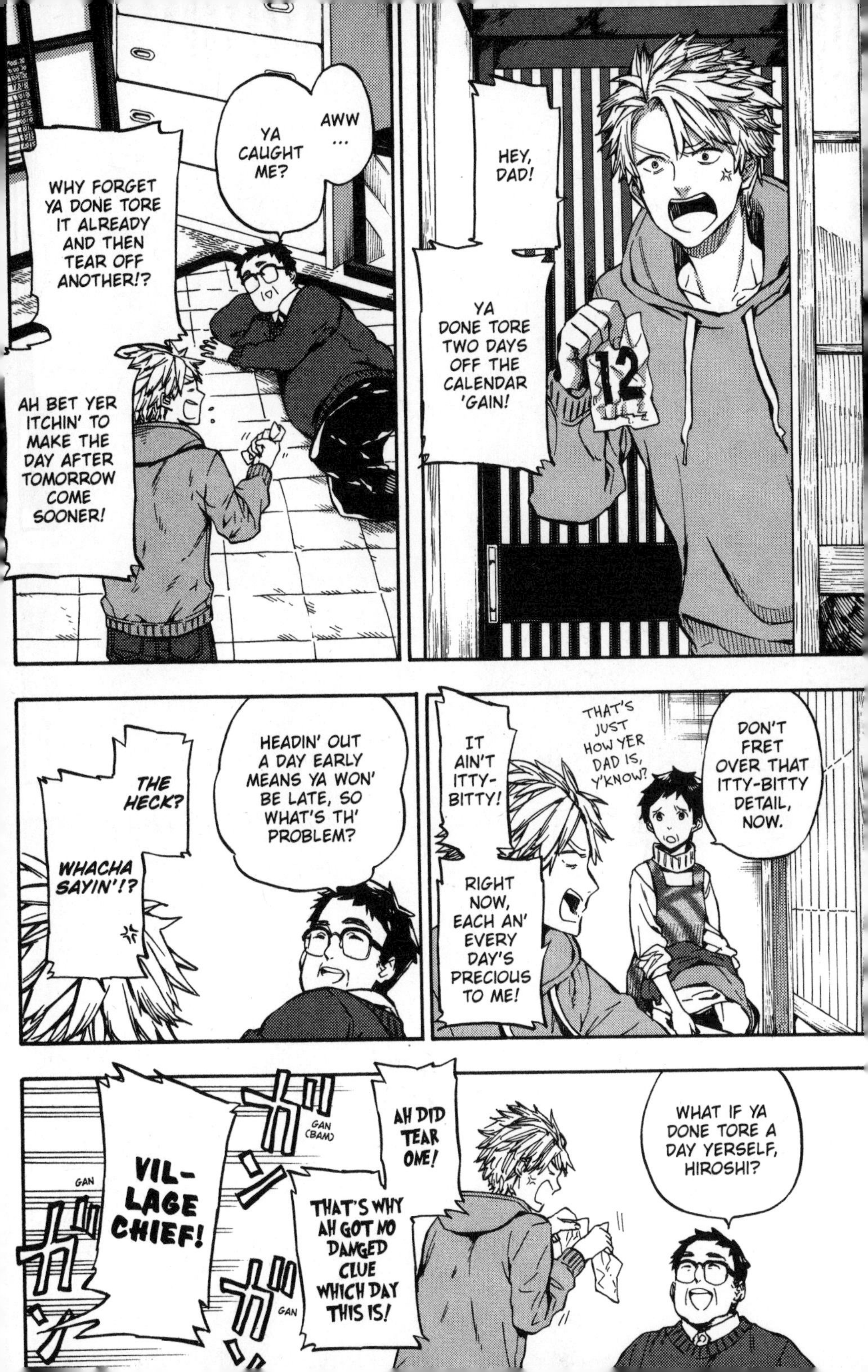
HEY, DAD!
YA DONE TORE TWO DAYS OFF THE CALENDAR 'GAIN!
12
AWW ...
YA CAUGHT ME?
WHY FORGET YA DONE TORE IT ALREADY AND THEN TEAR OFF ANOTHER!?
AH BET YER ITCHIN' TO MAKE THE DAY AFTER TOMORROW COME SOONER!
DON'T FRET OVER THAT ITTY-BITTY DETAIL, NOW.
THAT'S JUST HOW YER DAD IS, Y'KNOW?
IT AIN'T ITTY-BITTY!
RIGHT NOW, EACH AN' EVERY DAY'S PRECIOUS TO ME!
HEADIN' OUT A DAY EARLY MEANS YA WON' BE LATE, SO WHAT'S TH' PROBLEM?
THE HECK?
WHACHA SAYIN'!?
WHAT IF YA DONE TORE A DAY YERSELF, HIROSHI?
AH DID TEAR ONE!
THAT'S WHY AH GOT NO DANGED CLUE WHICH DAY THIS IS!
GAN (BAM)
VIL-LAGE CHIEF!
GAN
GAN

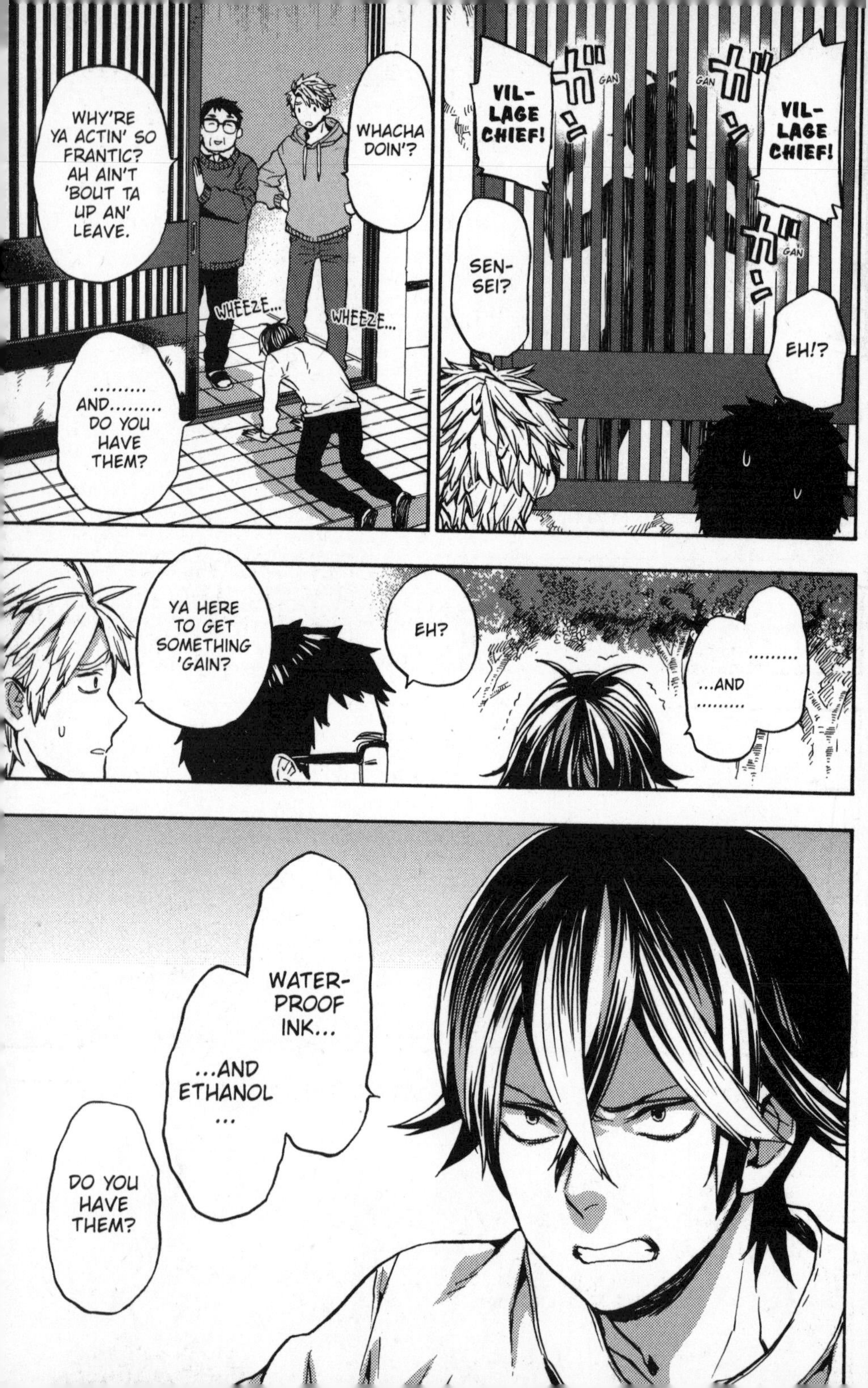
VIL-LAGE CHIEF!
GAN
GAN
VIL-LAGE CHIEF!
GAN
EH!?
SEN-SEI?
WHACHA DOIN'?
WHY'RE YA ACTIN' SO FRANTIC? AH AIN'T 'BOUT TA UP AN' LEAVE.
WHEEZE...
WHEEZE...
.... AND......... DO YOU HAVE THEM?
....AND ....
EH?
YA HERE TO GET SOMETHING 'GAIN?
WATER-PROOF INK... ...AND ETHANOL ...
DO YOU HAVE THEM?

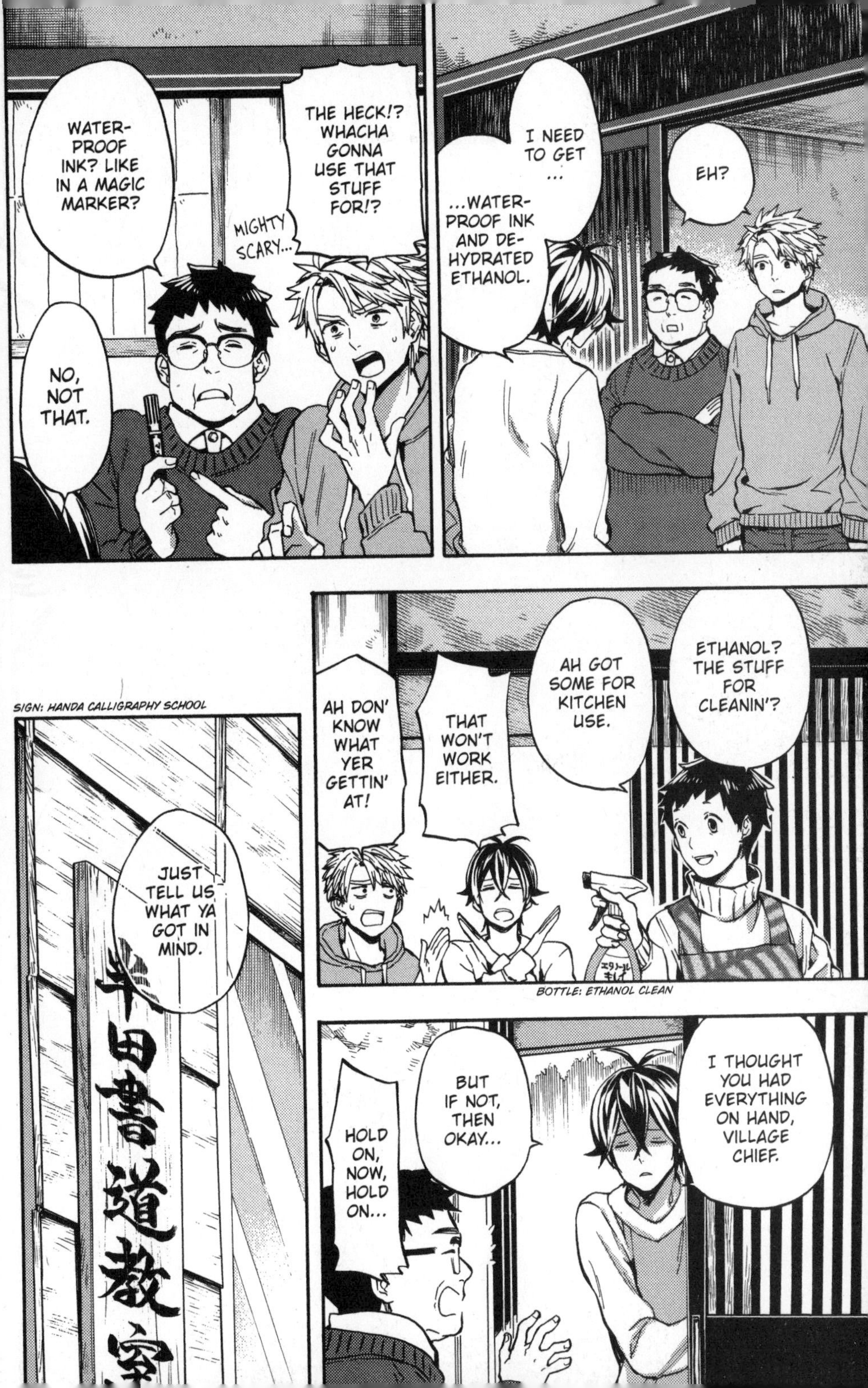
I NEED TO GET ...
...WATER-PROOF INK AND DE-HYDRATED ETHANOL.
EH?
THE HECK!? WHACHA GONNA USE THAT STUFF FOR!?
MIGHTY SCARY...
WATER-PROOF INK? LIKE IN A MAGIC MARKER?
NO, NOT THAT.
ETHANOL? THE STUFF FOR CLEANIN'?
AH GOT SOME FOR KITCHEN USE.
THAT WON'T WORK EITHER.
AH DON' KNOW WHAT YER GETTIN' AT!
BOTTLE: ETHANOL CLEAN
I THOUGHT YOU HAD EVERYTHING ON HAND, VILLAGE CHIEF.
BUT IF NOT, THEN OKAY...
HOLD ON, NOW, HOLD ON...
SIGN: HANDA CALLIGRAPHY SCHOOL
JUST TELL US WHAT YA GOT IN MIND.
半田書道教

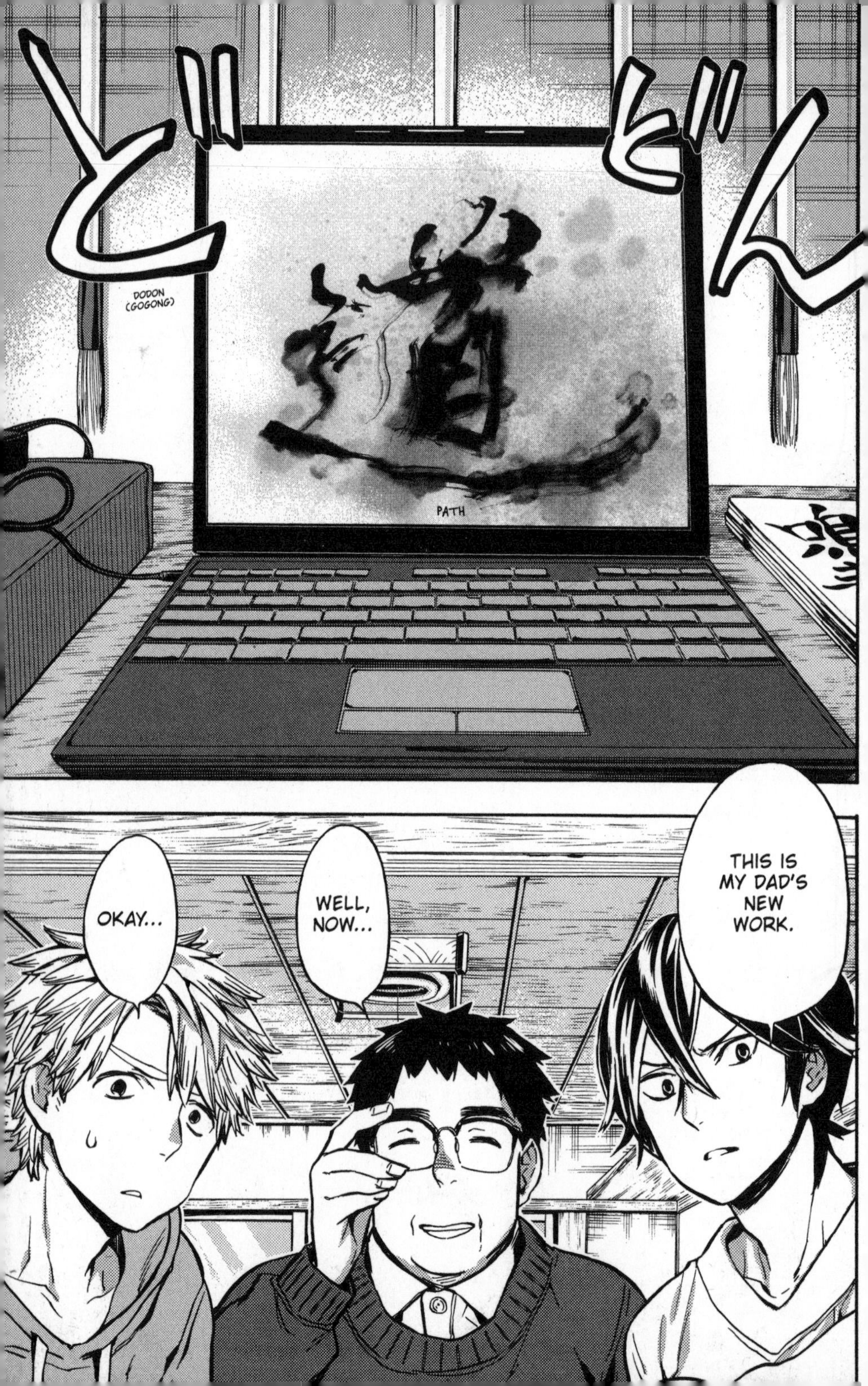
どどん
DODON (GOGONG)
道
PATH
THIS IS MY DAD'S NEW WORK.
WELL, NOW...
OKAY...

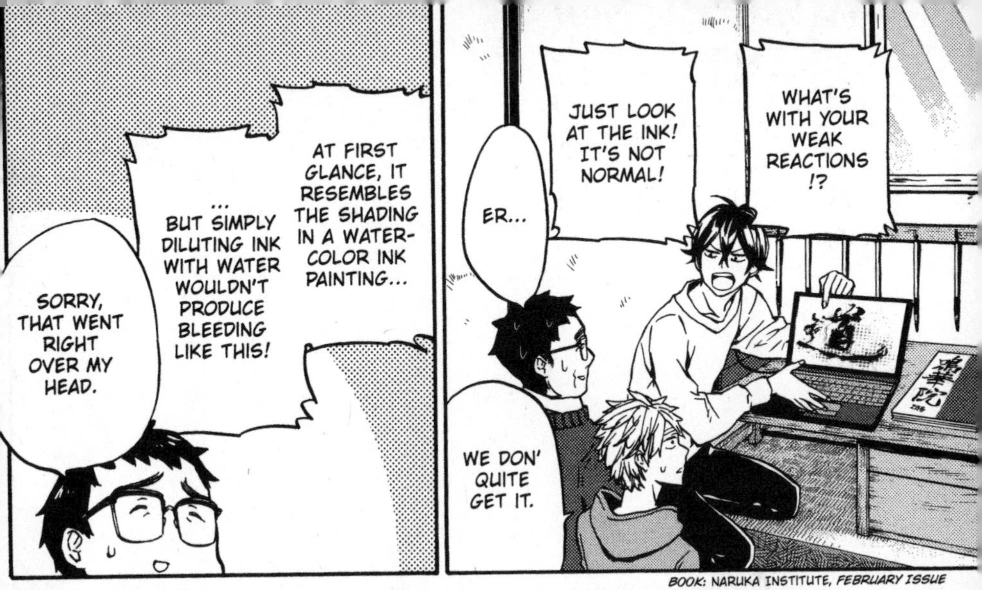
WHAT'S WITH YOUR WEAK REACTIONS !?
JUST LOOK AT THE INK! IT'S NOT NORMAL!
ER...
WE DON' QUITE GET IT.
AT FIRST GLANCE, IT RESEMBLES THE SHADING IN A WATER-COLOR INK PAINTING...
... BUT SIMPLY DILUTING INK WITH WATER WOULDN'T PRODUCE BLEEDING LIKE THIS!
SORRY, THAT WENT RIGHT OVER MY HEAD.

BOOK: NARUKA INSTITUTE, *FEBRUARY ISSUE*

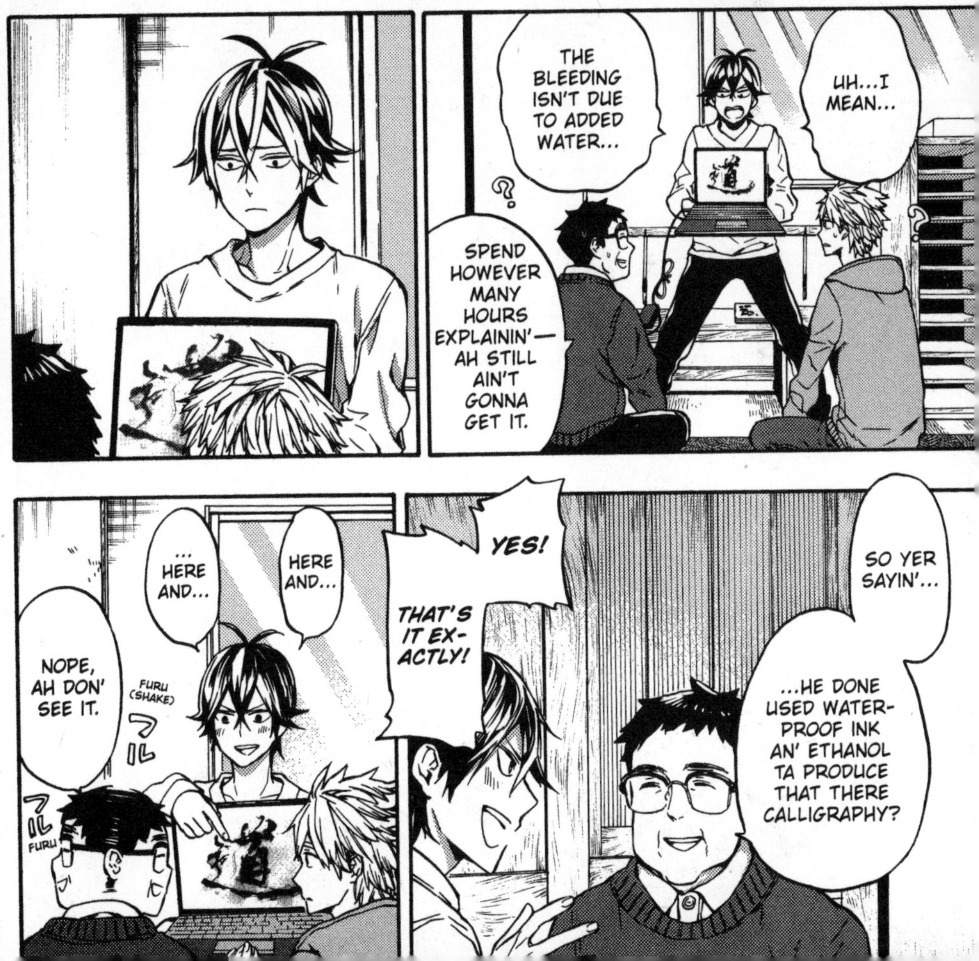
UH...I MEAN...
THE BLEEDING ISN'T DUE TO ADDED WATER...
?
SPEND HOWEVER MANY HOURS EXPLAININ'— AH STILL AIN'T GONNA GET IT.
SO YER SAYIN'...
...HE DONE USED WATER-PROOF INK AN' ETHANOL TA PRODUCE THAT THERE CALLIGRAPHY?
YES!
THAT'S IT EX-ACTLY!
HERE AND...
... HERE AND...
NOPE, AH DON' SEE IT.
FURU (SHAKE)
FURU

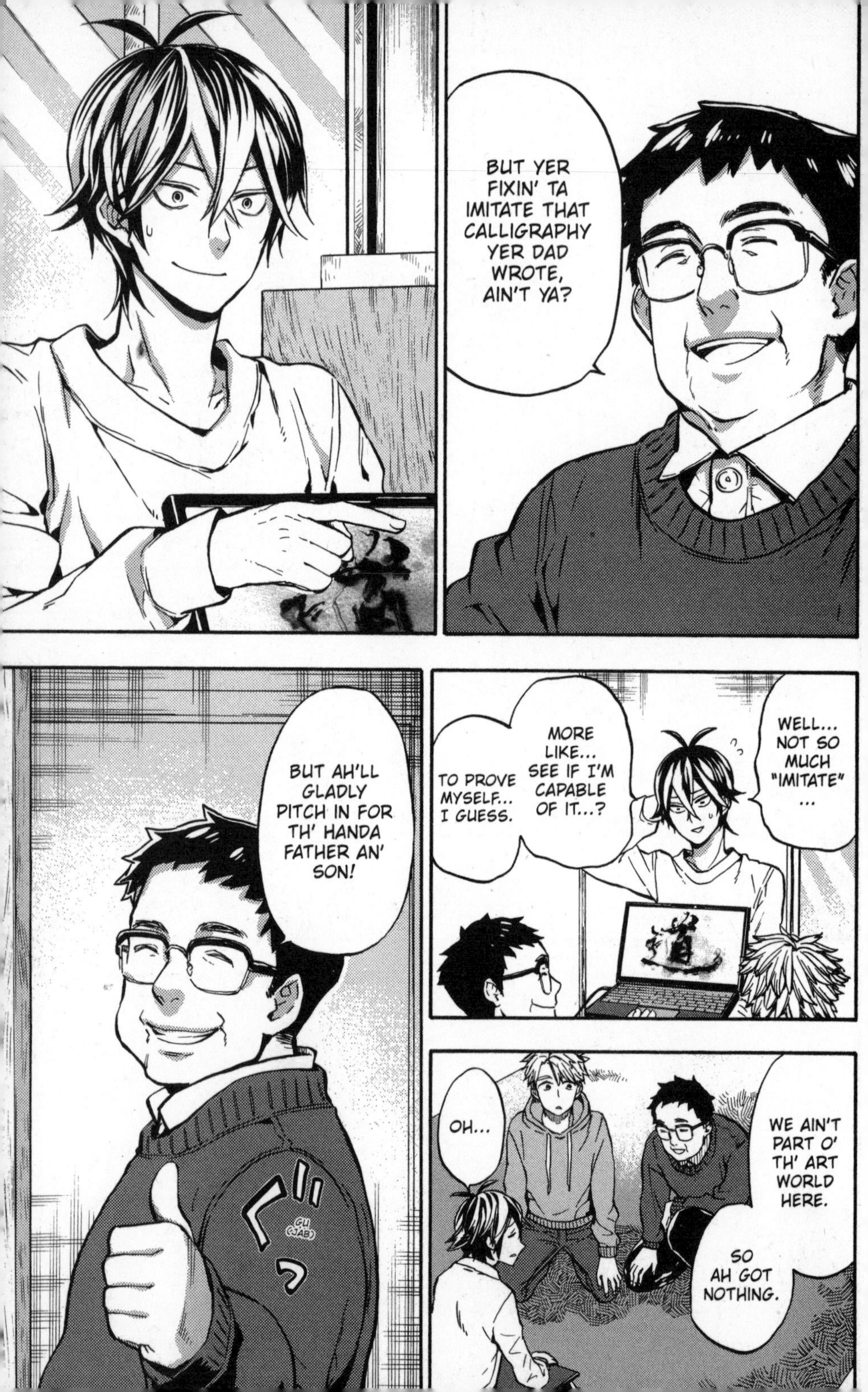
BUT YER FIXIN' TA IMITATE THAT CALLIGRAPHY YER DAD WROTE, AIN'T YA?
WELL... NOT SO MUCH "IMITATE" ...
MORE LIKE... SEE IF I'M CAPABLE OF IT...?
TO PROVE MYSELF... I GUESS.
WE AIN'T PART O' TH' ART WORLD HERE.
SO AH GOT NOTHING.
OH...
BUT AH'LL GLADLY PITCH IN FOR TH' HANDA FATHER AN' SON!
GU! (JAB)

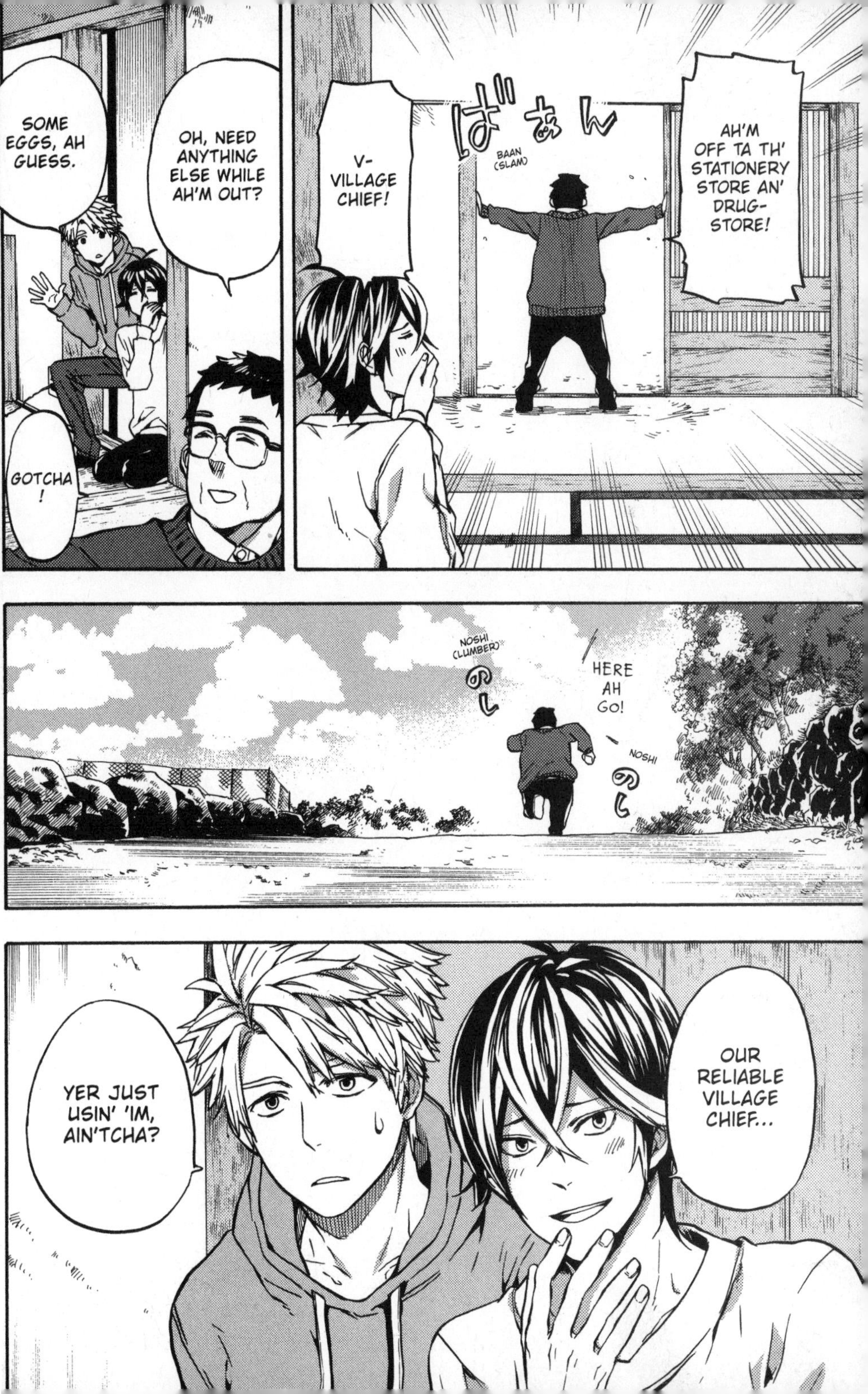
AH'M OFF TA TH' STATIONERY STORE AN' DRUG-STORE!
ばぁん
BAAN (SLAM)
V-VILLAGE CHIEF!
OH, NEED ANYTHING ELSE WHILE AH'M OUT?
SOME EGGS, AH GUESS.
GOTCHA!
HERE AH GO!
のし
NOSHI
のし
NOSHI (LUMBER)
OUR RELIABLE VILLAGE CHIEF...
YER JUST USIN' 'IM, AIN'TCHA?

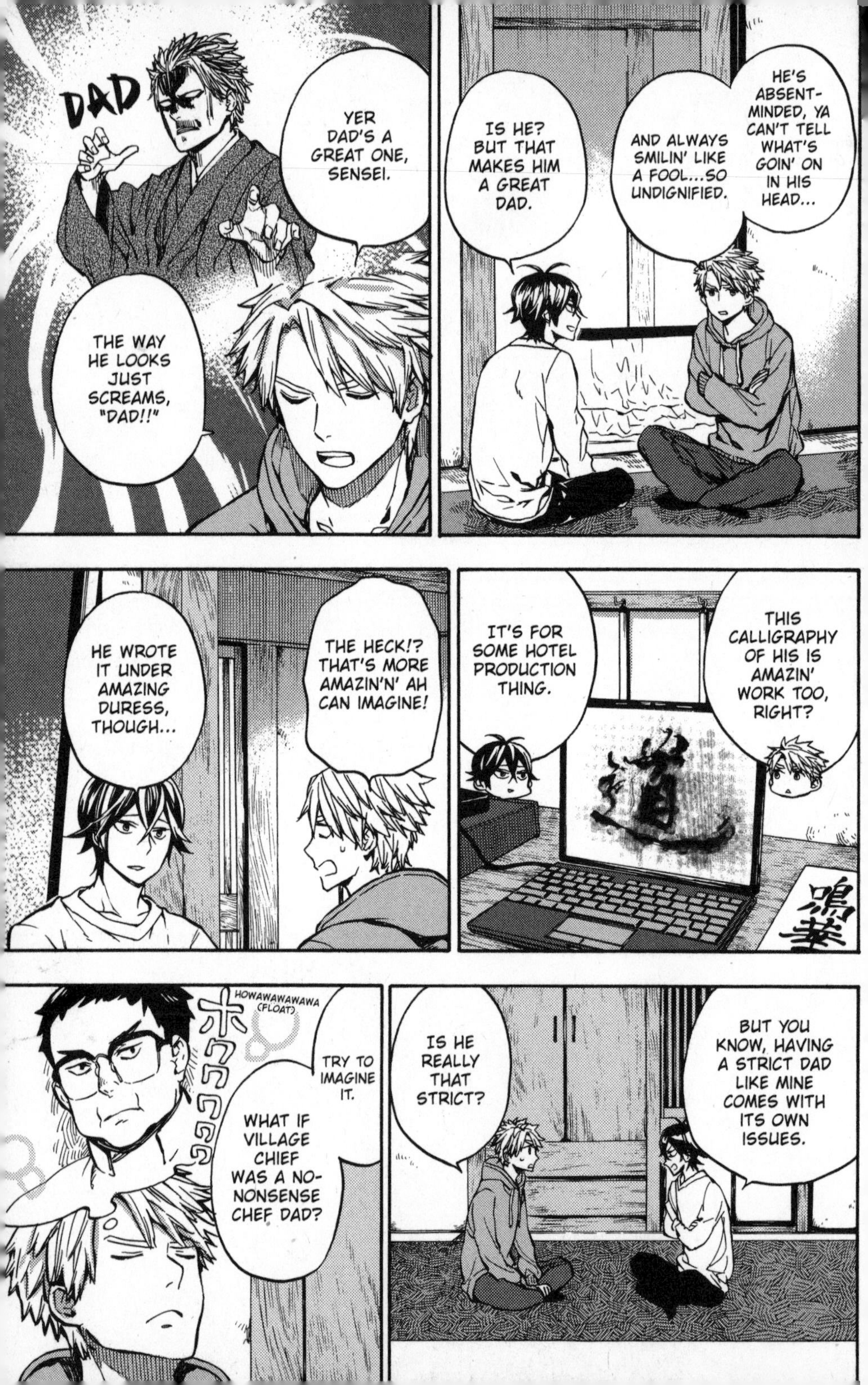
HE'S ABSENT-MINDED, YA CAN'T TELL WHAT'S GOIN' ON IN HIS HEAD...
AND ALWAYS SMILIN' LIKE A FOOL...SO UNDIGNIFIED.
IS HE? BUT THAT MAKES HIM A GREAT DAD.
YER DAD'S A GREAT ONE, SENSEI.
DAD
THE WAY HE LOOKS JUST SCREAMS, "DAD!!"
THIS CALLIGRAPHY OF HIS IS AMAZIN' WORK TOO, RIGHT?
IT'S FOR SOME HOTEL PRODUCTION THING.
THE HECK!? THAT'S MORE AMAZIN'N' AH CAN IMAGINE!
HE WROTE IT UNDER AMAZING DURESS, THOUGH...
BUT YOU KNOW, HAVING A STRICT DAD LIKE MINE COMES WITH ITS OWN ISSUES.
IS HE REALLY THAT STRICT?
TRY TO IMAGINE IT.
WHAT IF VILLAGE CHIEF WAS A NO-NONSENSE CHEF DAD?
HOWAWAWAWAWA (FLOAT)

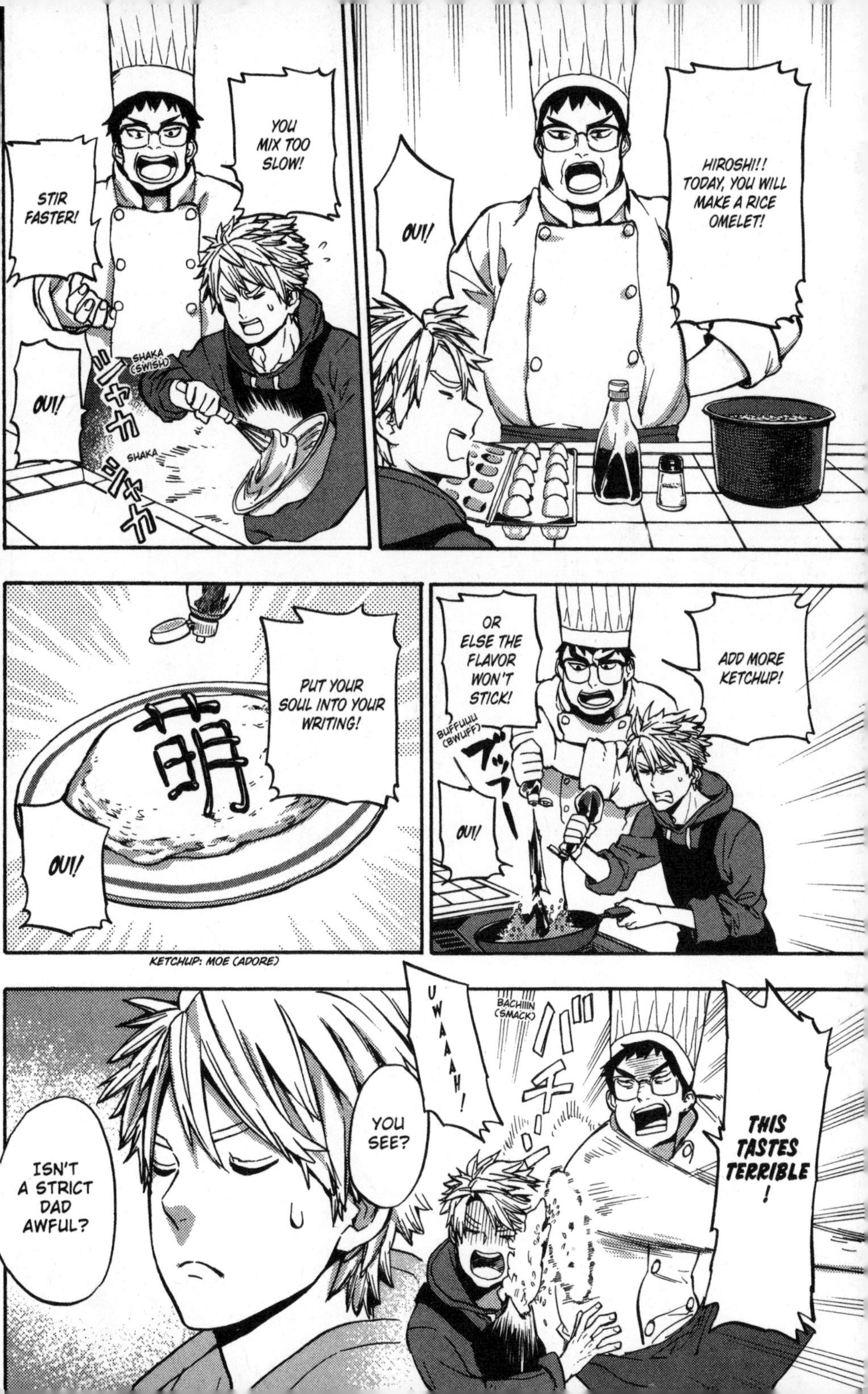
HIROSHI!! TODAY, YOU WILL MAKE A RICE OMELET!
OUI!
YOU MIX TOO SLOW!
STIR FASTER!
SHAKA (SWISH)
SHAKA
OUI!
ADD MORE KETCHUP!
OR ELSE THE FLAVOR WON'T STICK!
BUFFUUU (BWUFF)
OUI!
PUT YOUR SOUL INTO YOUR WRITING!
OUI!
KETCHUP: MOE (ADORE)
THIS TASTES TERRIBLE!
BACHIIIN (SMACK)
UWAAAH!
YOU SEE?
ISN'T A STRICT DAD AWFUL?

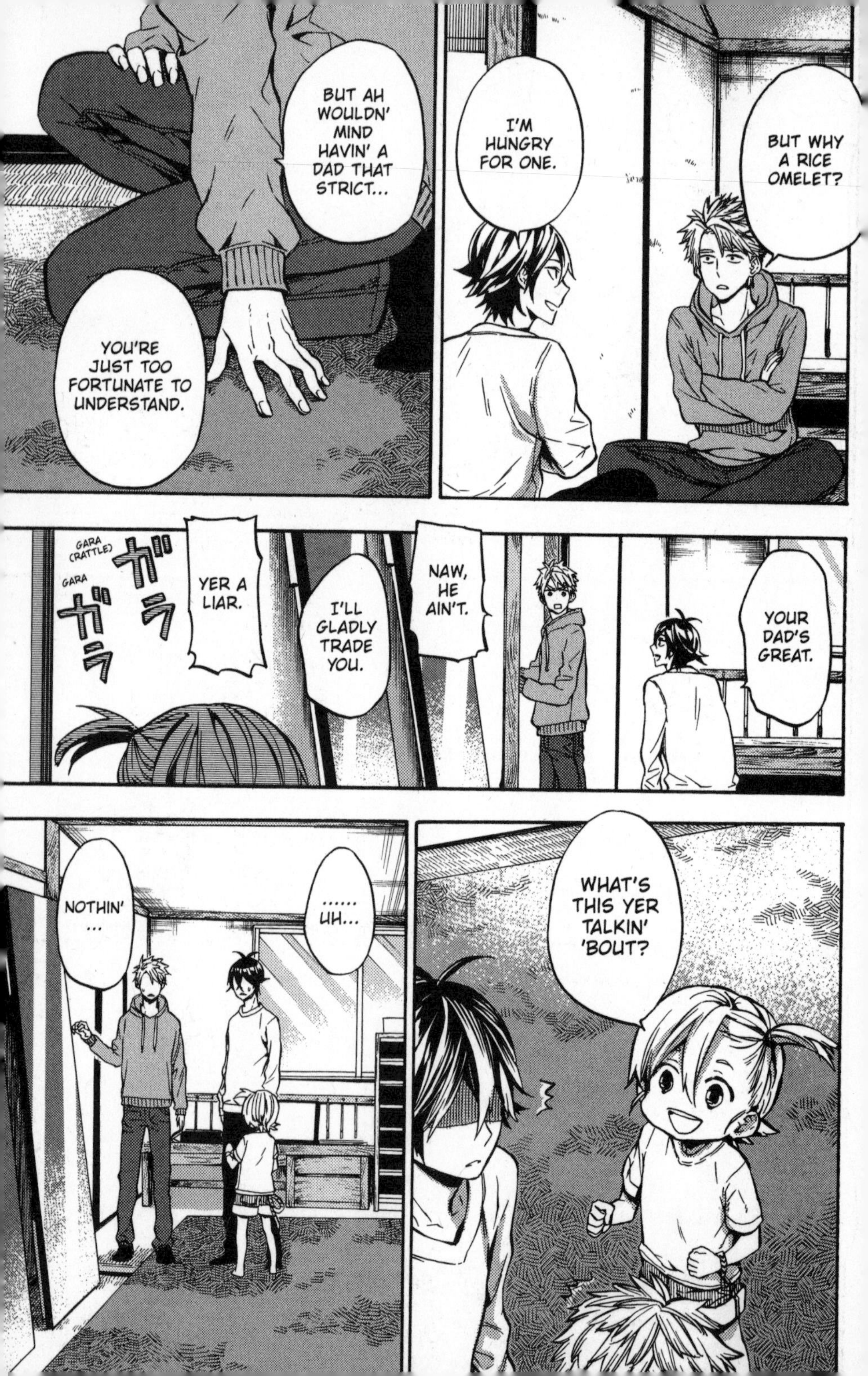
BUT WHY A RICE OMELET?
I'M HUNGRY FOR ONE.
BUT AH WOULDN' MIND HAVIN' A DAD THAT STRICT...
YOU'RE JUST TOO FORTUNATE TO UNDERSTAND.
YOUR DAD'S GREAT.
NAW, HE AIN'T.
I'LL GLADLY TRADE YOU.
YER A LIAR.
GARA (RATTLE)
GARA
ガラ
ガラ
WHAT'S THIS YER TALKIN' 'BOUT?
......UH...
NOTHIN'...

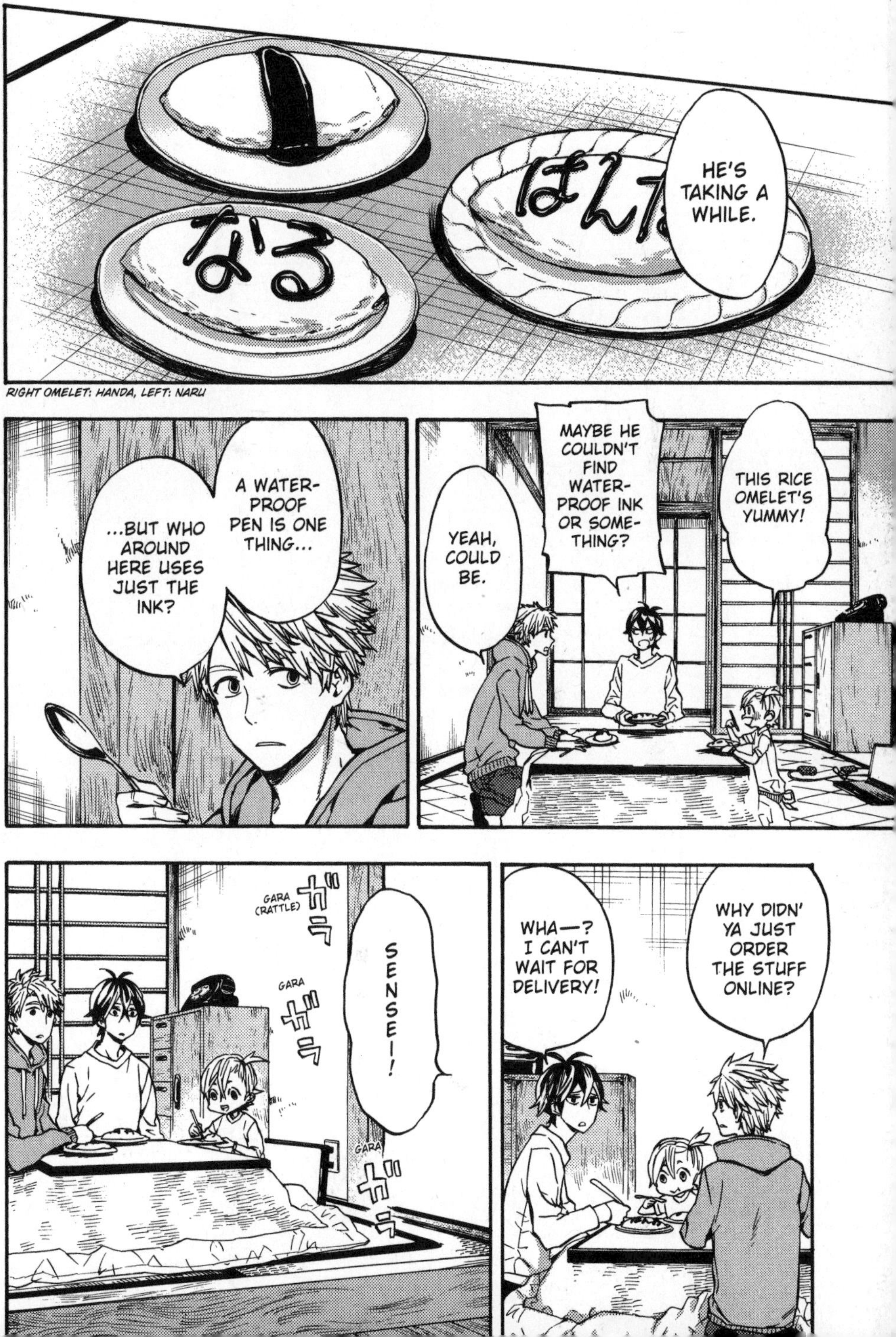
はん
なる
HE'S TAKING A WHILE.
THIS RICE OMELET'S YUMMY!
MAYBE HE COULDN'T FIND WATERPROOF INK OR SOMETHING?
YEAH, COULD BE.
A WATERPROOF PEN IS ONE THING...
...BUT WHO AROUND HERE USES JUST THE INK?
WHY DIDN' YA JUST ORDER THE STUFF ONLINE?
WHA—? I CAN'T WAIT FOR DELIVERY!
GARA (RATTLE)
ガラ
GARA
ガラ
SENSE-!
GARA
ガラ

RIGHT OMELET: HANDA, LEFT: NARU

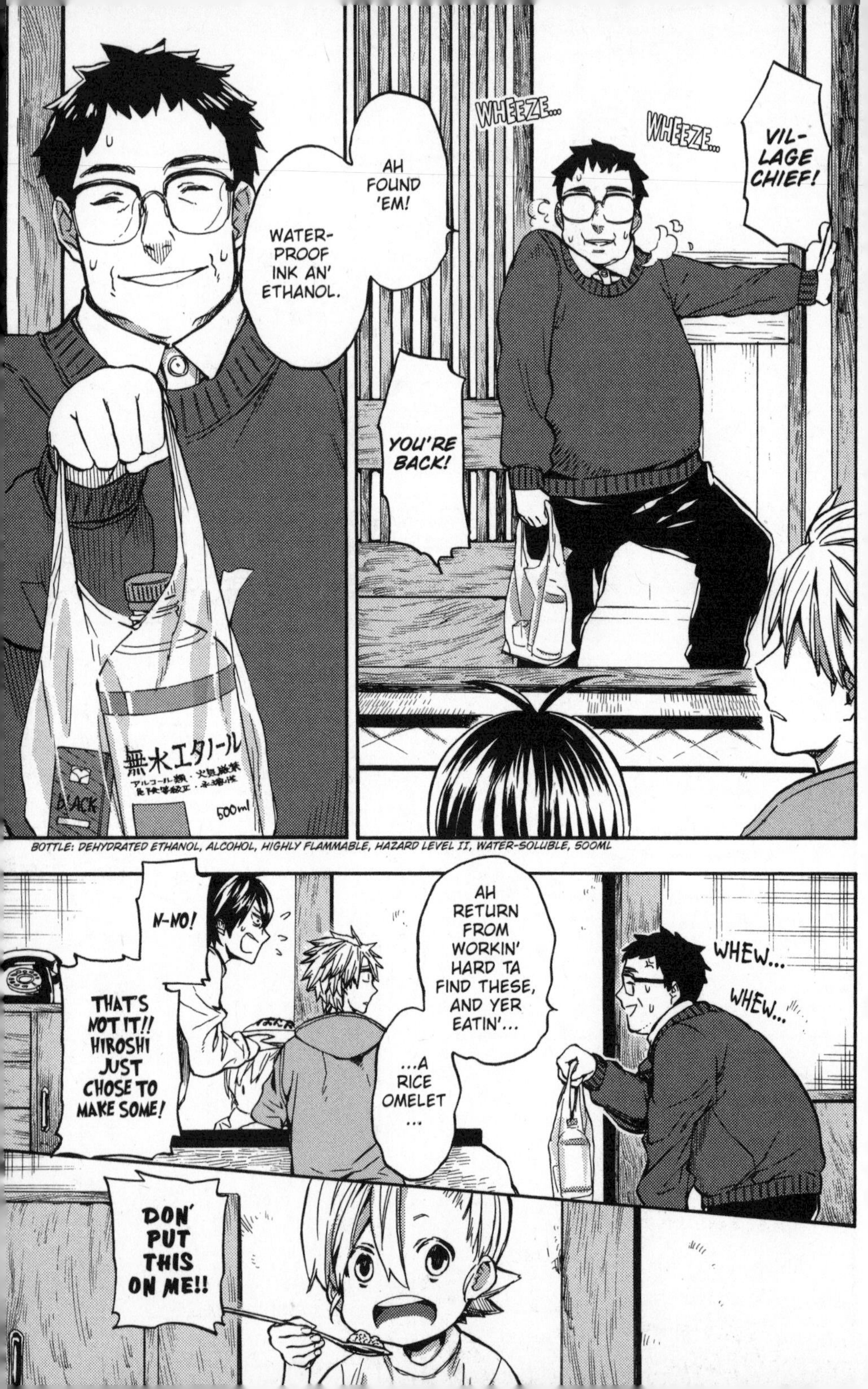
VIL-
LAGE
CHIEF!
WHEEZE...
WHEEZE...
YOU'RE BACK!
AH FOUND 'EM!
WATER-PROOF INK AN' ETHANOL.
無水エタノール
アルコール類・火気厳禁
500ml
BLACK
BOTTLE: DEHYDRATED ETHANOL, ALCOHOL, HIGHLY FLAMMABLE, HAZARD LEVEL II, WATER-SOLUBLE, 500ML
WHEW...
WHEW...
AH RETURN FROM WORKIN' HARD TA FIND THESE, AND YER EATIN'...
...A RICE OMELET...
N-NO!
THAT'S NOT IT!! HIROSHI JUST CHOSE TO MAKE SOME!
DON' PUT THIS ON ME!!

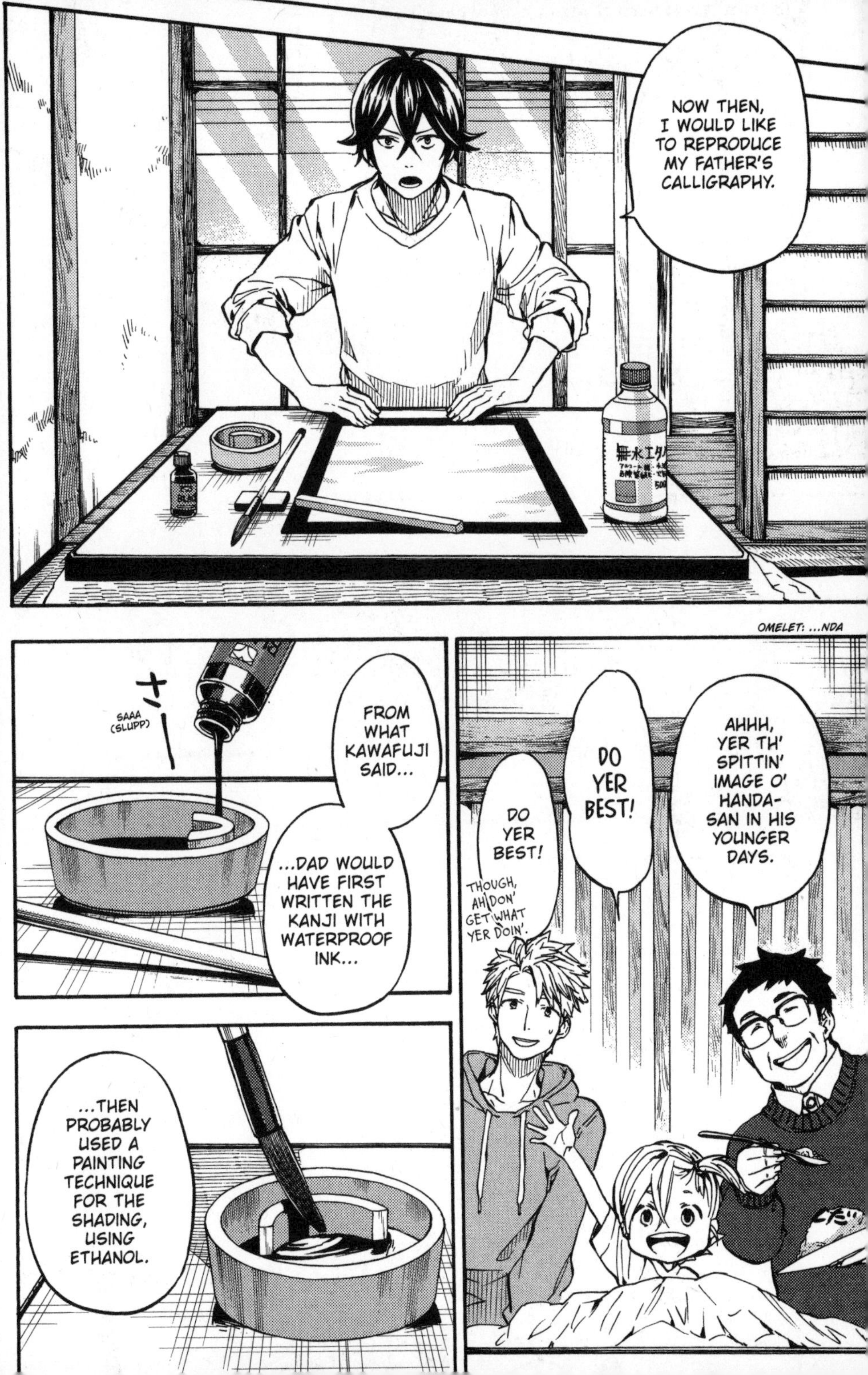
NOW THEN, I WOULD LIKE TO REPRODUCE MY FATHER'S CALLIGRAPHY.
OMELET: ...NDA
AHHH, YER TH' SPITTIN' IMAGE O' HANDA-SAN IN HIS YOUNGER DAYS.
DO YER BEST!
DO YER BEST!
THOUGH, AH DON' GET WHAT YER DOIN'.
さー
SAAA (SLUPP)
FROM WHAT KAWAFUJI SAID...
...DAD WOULD HAVE FIRST WRITTEN THE KANJI WITH WATERPROOF INK...
...THEN PROBABLY USED A PAINTING TECHNIQUE FOR THE SHADING, USING ETHANOL.

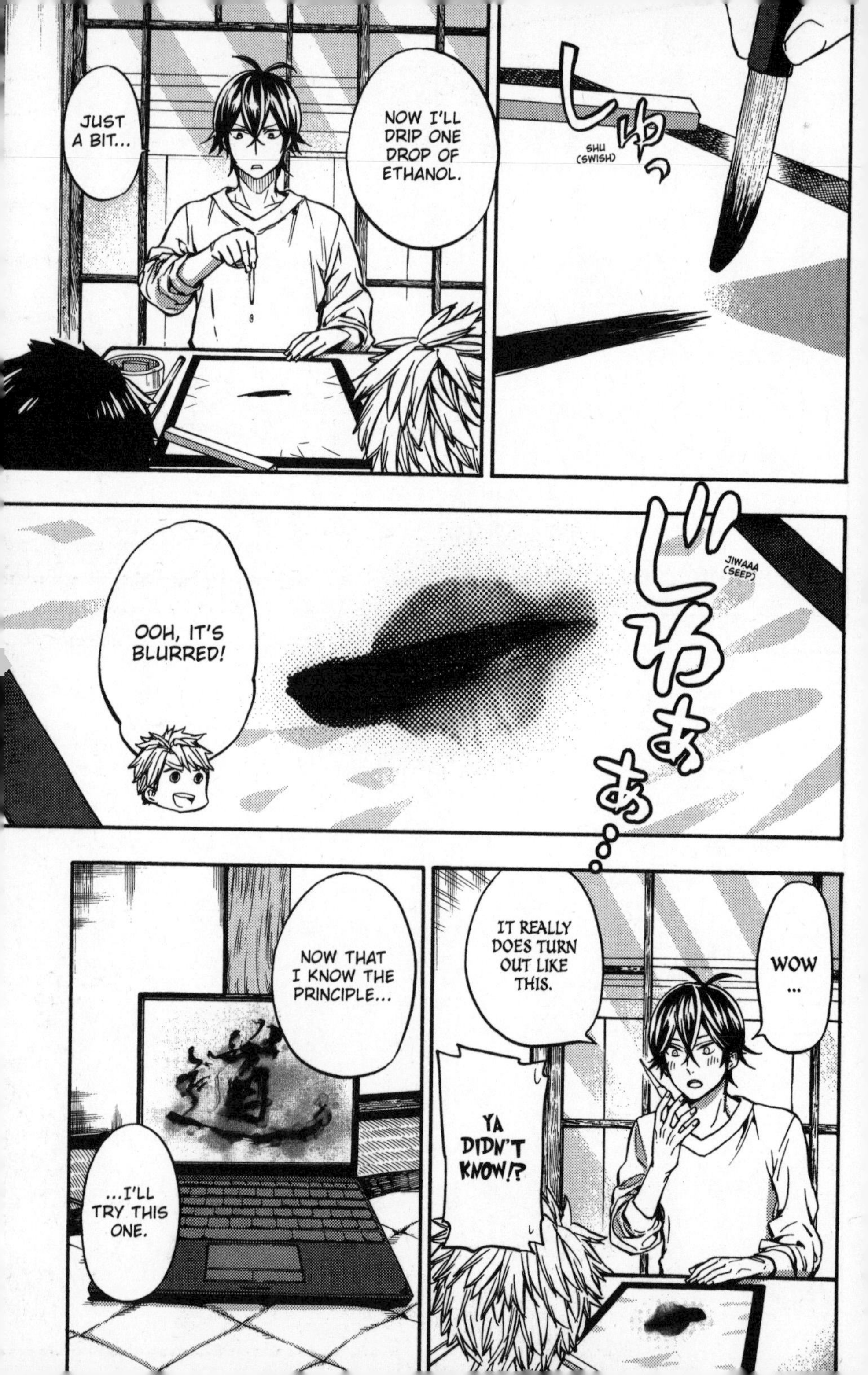
しゅっ
SHU (SWISH)
NOW I'LL DRIP ONE DROP OF ETHANOL.
JUST A BIT...
じわぁあ…
JIWAAA (SEEP)
OOH, IT'S BLURRED!
WOW ...
IT REALLY DOES TURN OUT LIKE THIS.
YA DIDN'T KNOW!?
NOW THAT I KNOW THE PRINCIPLE...
...I'LL TRY THIS ONE.

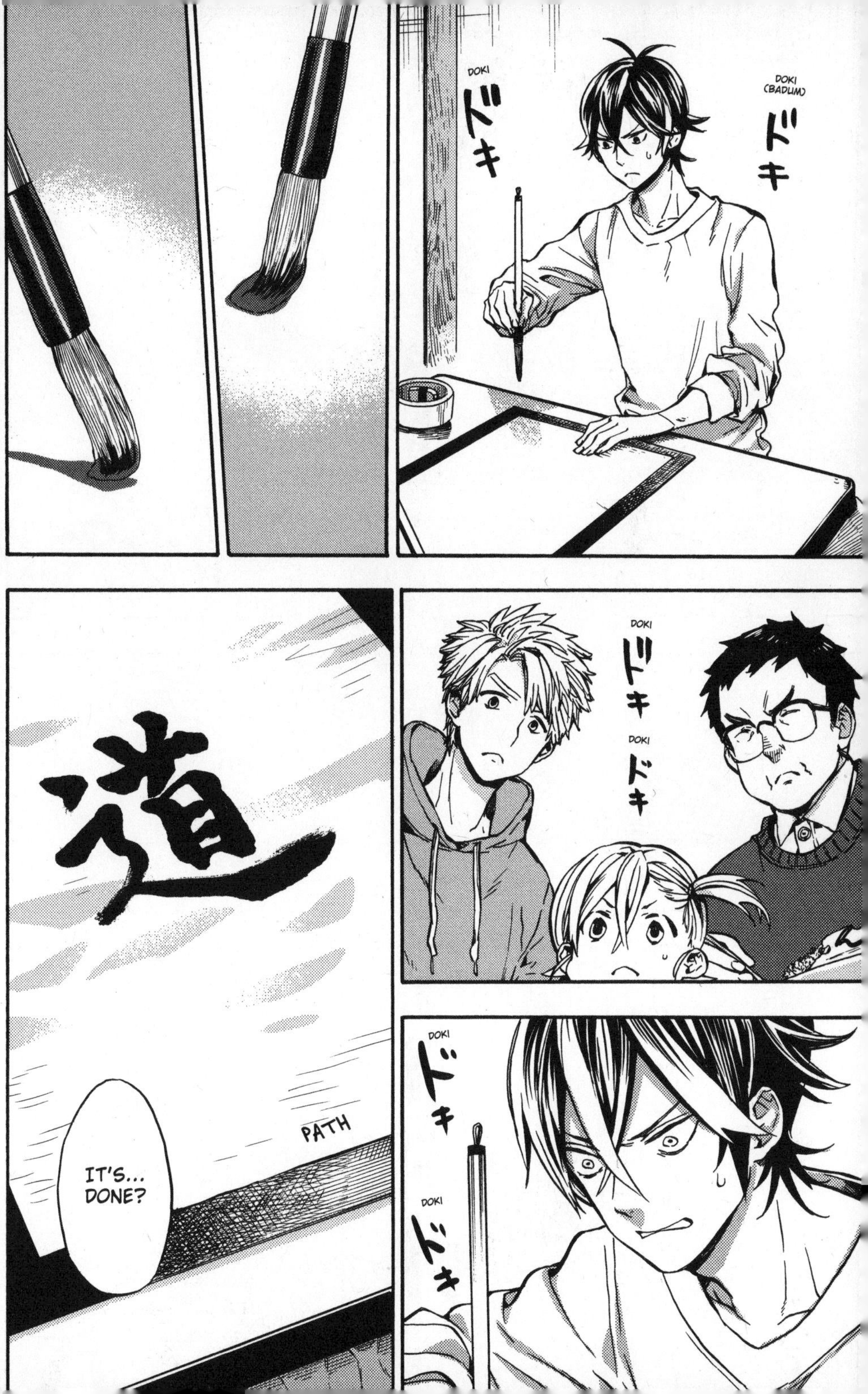
DOKI (BADUM)
ドキ
DOKI
ドキ
DOKI
ドキ
DOKI
ドキ
DOKI
ドキ
DOKI
ドキ
道
PATH
IT'S... DONE?

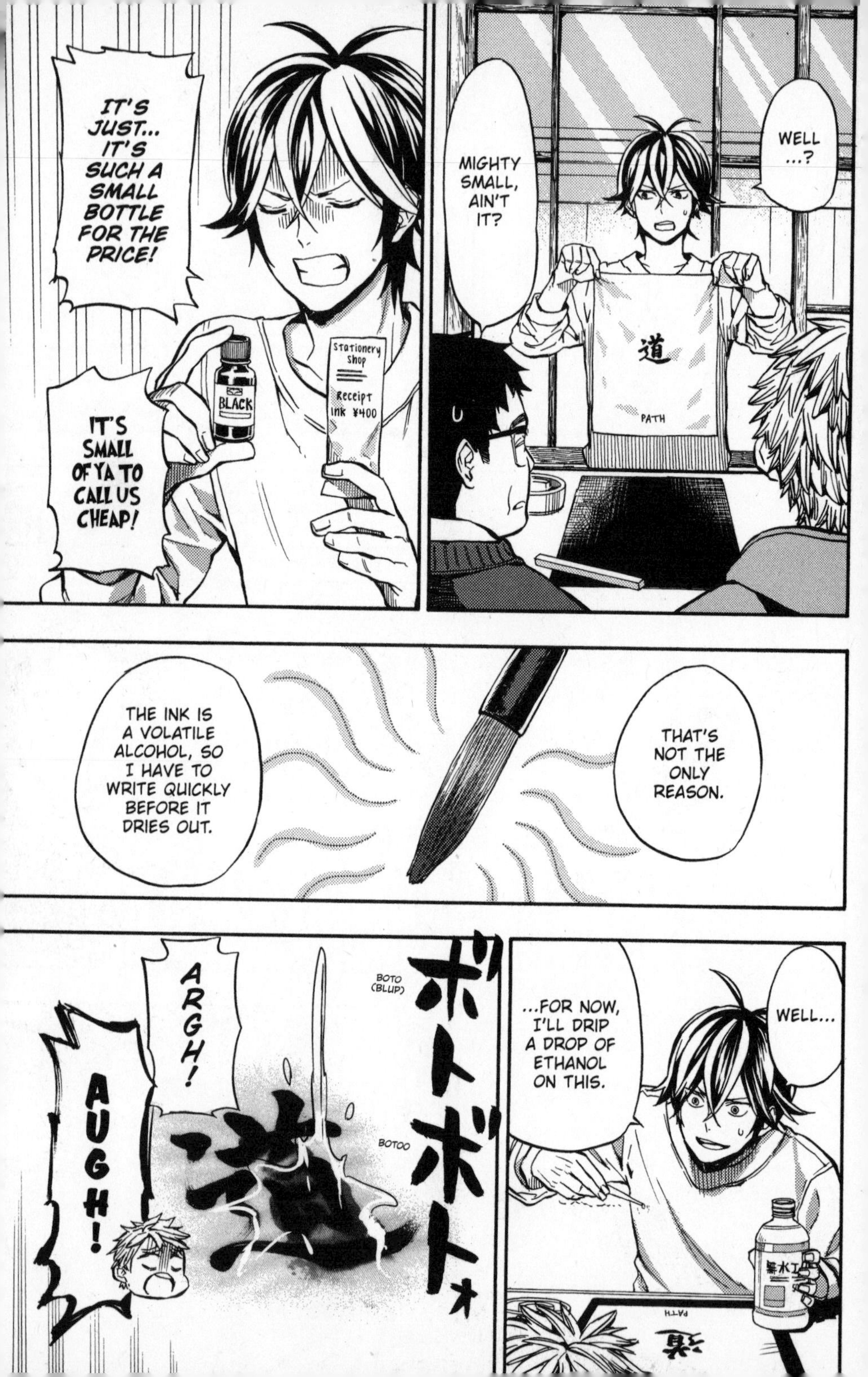
WELL ...?
MIGHTY SMALL, AIN'T IT?
道
PATH
IT'S JUST... IT'S SUCH A SMALL BOTTLE FOR THE PRICE!
BLACK
Stationery Shop
Receipt
ink ¥400
IT'S SMALL OF YA TO CALL US CHEAP!
THAT'S NOT THE ONLY REASON.
THE INK IS A VOLATILE ALCOHOL, SO I HAVE TO WRITE QUICKLY BEFORE IT DRIES OUT.
WELL...
...FOR NOW, I'LL DRIP A DROP OF ETHANOL ON THIS.
PATH
BOTO (BLUP)
BOTOO
ARGH!
AUGH!

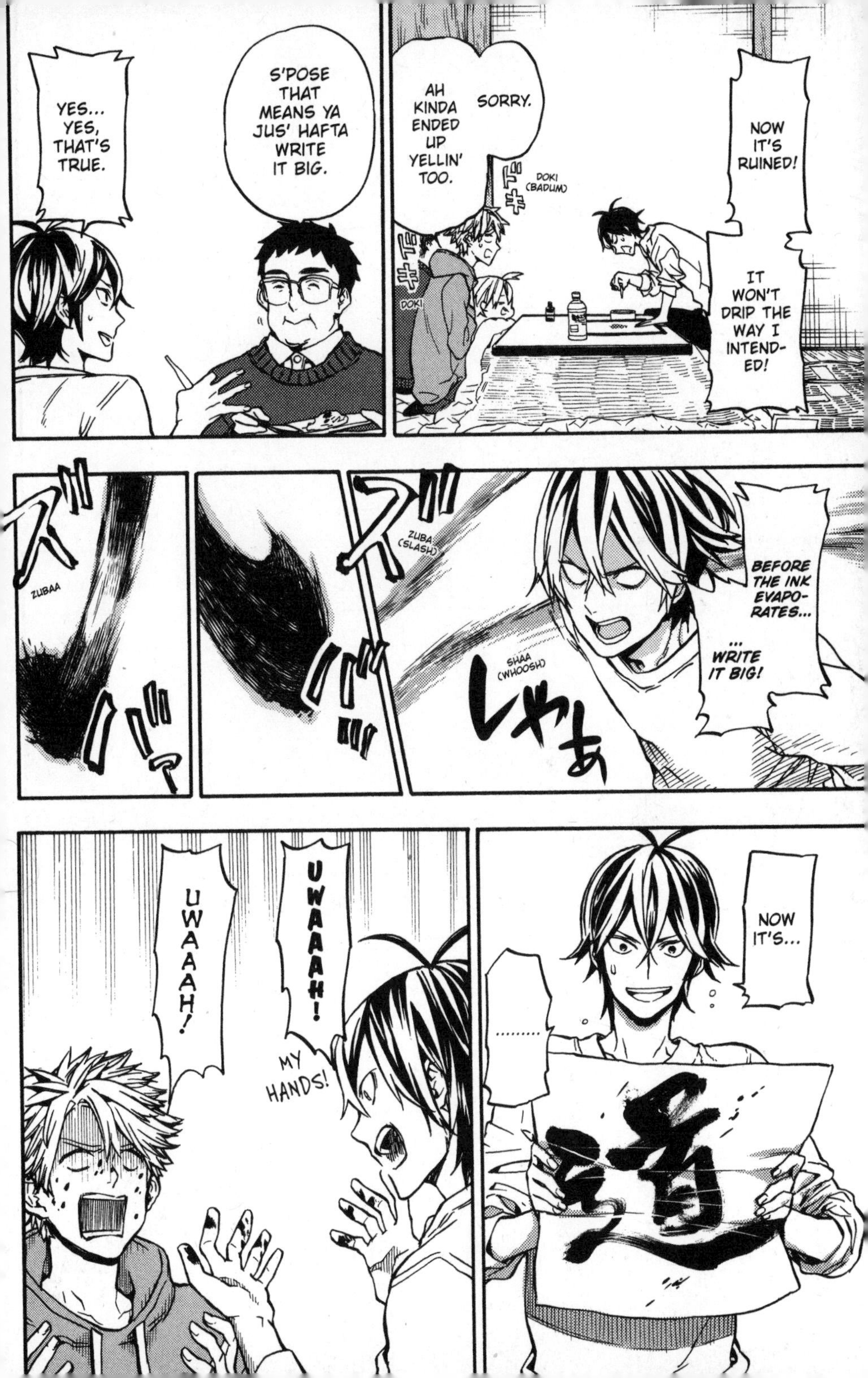
NOW IT'S RUINED!
IT WON'T DRIP THE WAY I INTENDED!
DOKI (BADUM)
SORRY.
AH KINDA ENDED UP YELLIN' TOO.
DOKI
S'POSE THAT MEANS YA JUS' HAFTA WRITE IT BIG.
YES... YES, THAT'S TRUE.
BEFORE THE INK EVAPORATES...
...WRITE IT BIG!
ZUBA (SLASH)
SHAA (WHOOSH)
ZUBAA
NOW IT'S...
....
UWAAAAH!
MY HANDS!
UWAAAAH!

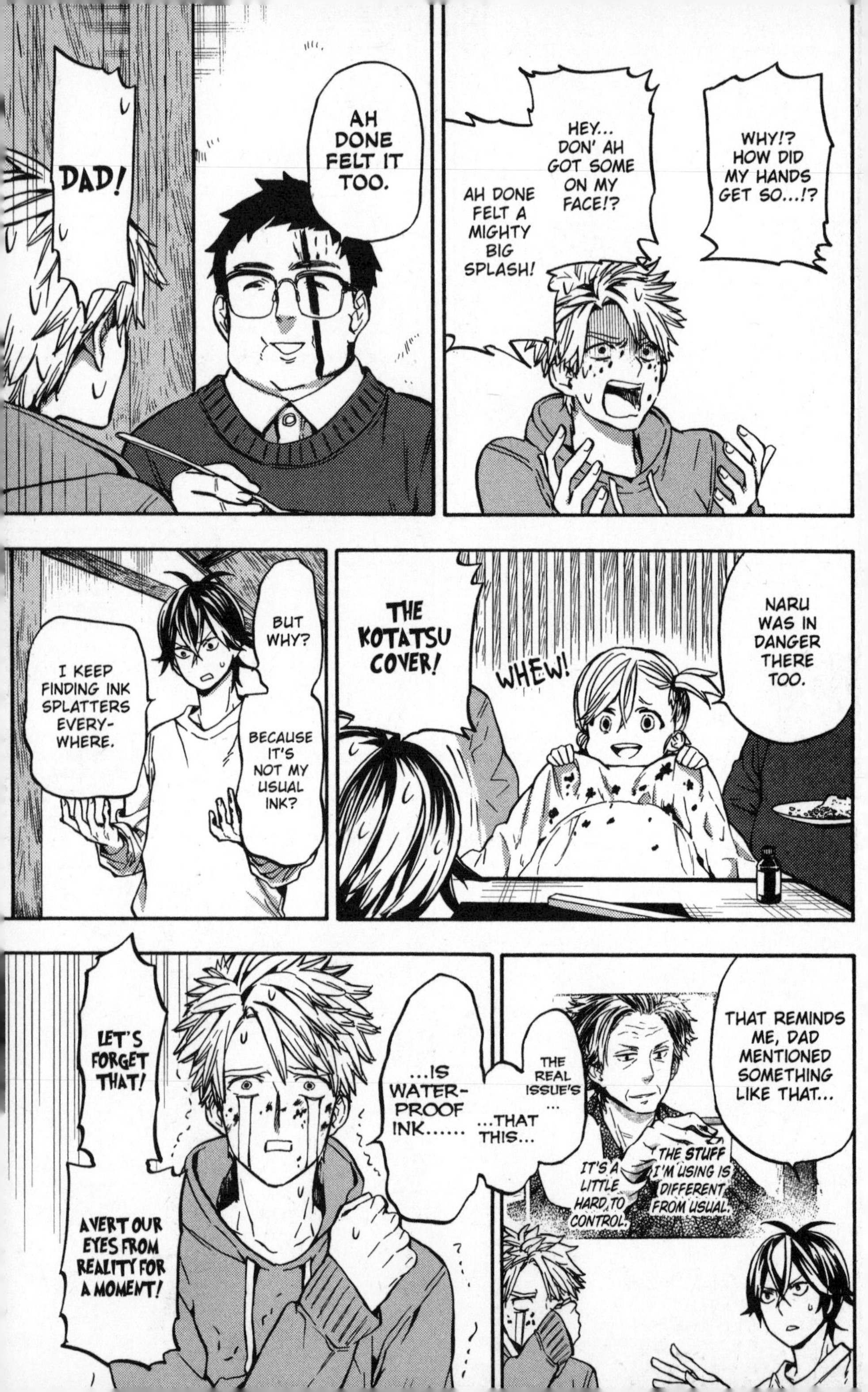
WHY!? HOW DID MY HANDS GET SO...!?
HEY... DON' AH GOT SOME ON MY FACE!?
AH DONE FELT A MIGHTY BIG SPLASH!
AH DONE FELT IT TOO.
DAD!
NARU WAS IN DANGER THERE TOO.
WHEW!
THE KOTATSU COVER!
BUT WHY?
BECAUSE IT'S NOT MY USUAL INK?
I KEEP FINDING INK SPLATTERS EVERY-WHERE.
THAT REMINDS ME, DAD MENTIONED SOMETHING LIKE THAT...
THE STUFF I'M USING IS DIFFERENT FROM USUAL.
IT'S A LITTLE HARD TO CONTROL.
THE REAL ISSUE'S ...
...THAT THIS...
...IS WATER-PROOF INK......
LET'S FORGET THAT!
AVERT OUR EYES FROM REALITY FOR A MOMENT!

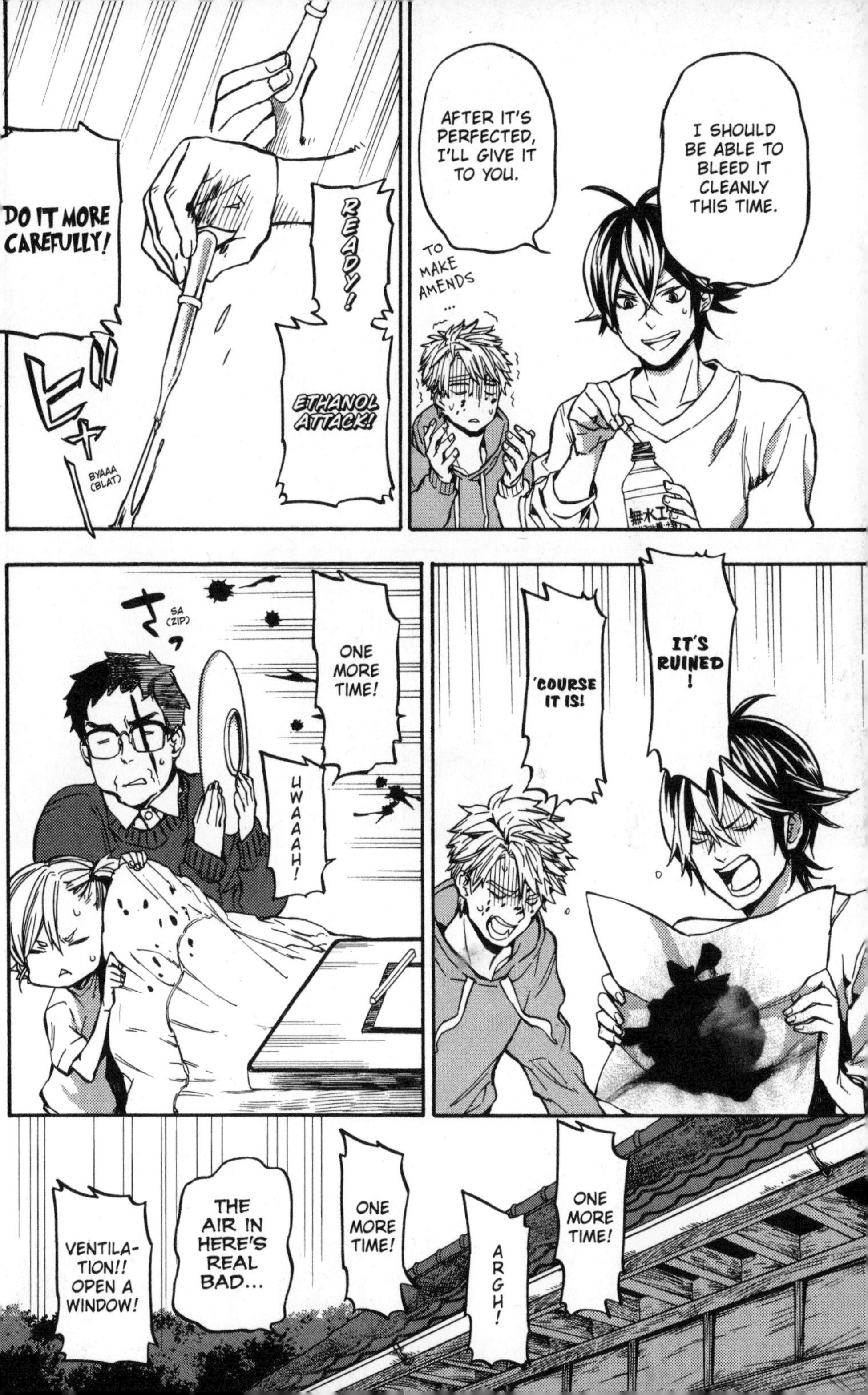
I SHOULD BE ABLE TO BLEED IT CLEANLY THIS TIME.
AFTER IT'S PERFECTED, I'LL GIVE IT TO YOU.
TO MAKE AMENDS ...
READY!
ETHANOL ATTACK!
DO IT MORE CAREFULLY!
BYAAA (BLAT)
IT'S RUINED!
'COURSE IT IS!
ONE MORE TIME!
UWAAAAH!
SA (ZIP)
ONE MORE TIME!
ARGH!
ONE MORE TIME!
THE AIR IN HERE'S REAL BAD...
VENTILA-TION!! OPEN A WINDOW!

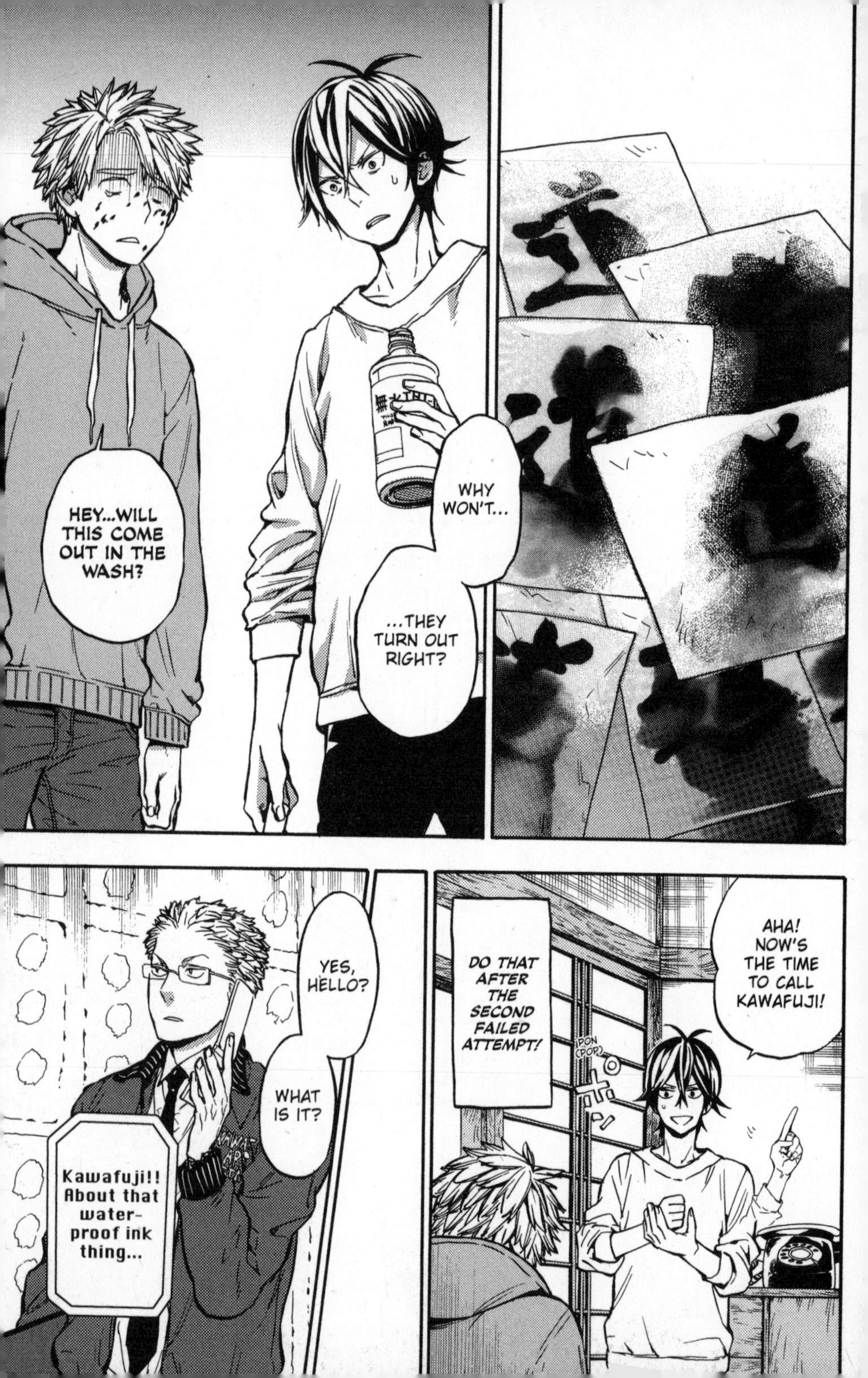
WHY WON'T...
...THEY TURN OUT RIGHT?
HEY...WILL THIS COME OUT IN THE WASH?
AHA! NOW'S THE TIME TO CALL KAWAFUJI!
DO THAT AFTER THE SECOND FAILED ATTEMPT!
PON (POP)
YES, HELLO?
WHAT IS IT?
Kawafuji!! About that water-proof ink thing...

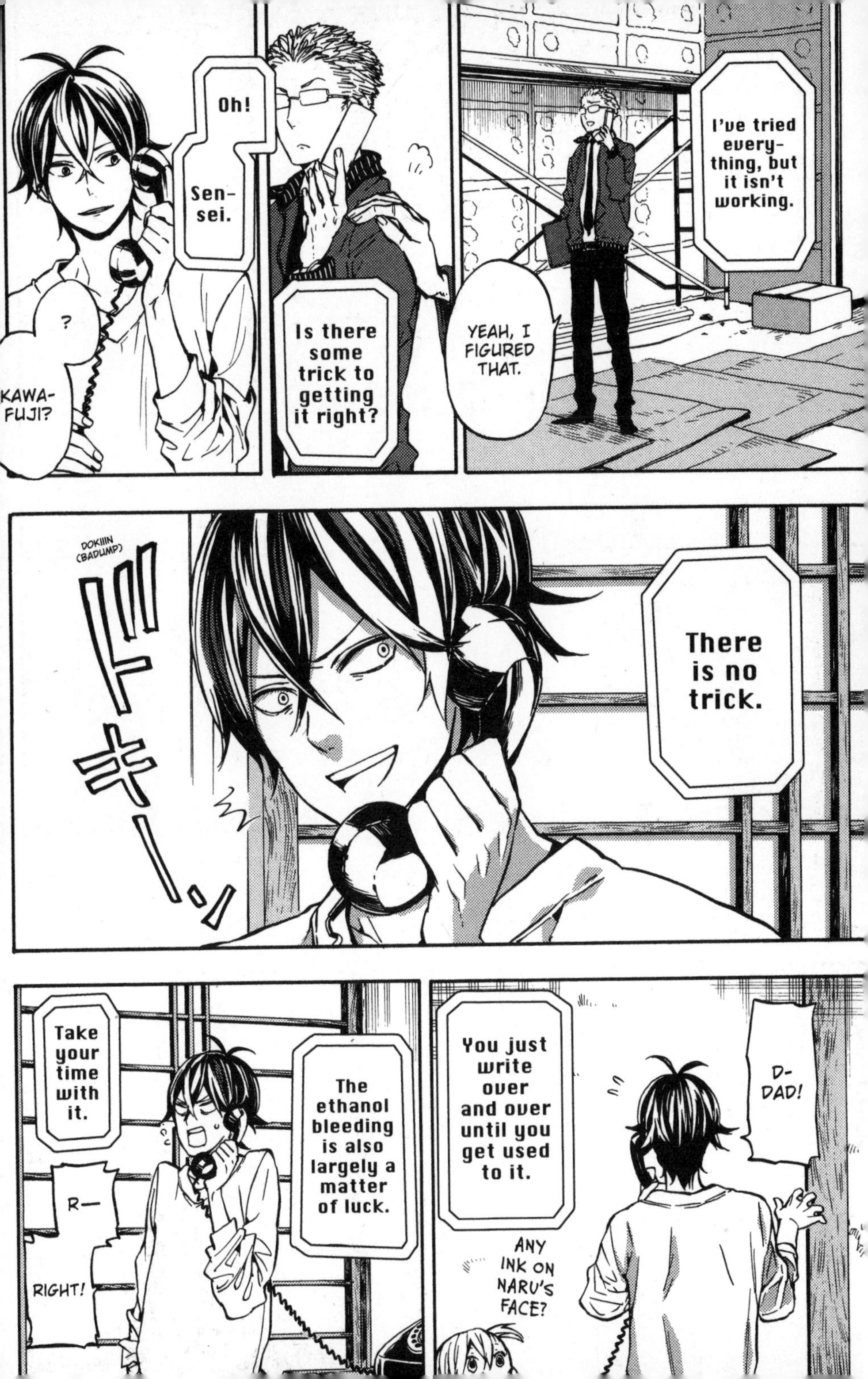
I've tried everything, but it isn't working.
YEAH, I FIGURED THAT.
Is there some trick to getting it right?
Oh!
Sen-sei.
?
KAWA-FUJI?
There is no trick.
DOKIIIN (BADUMP)
You just write over and over until you get used to it.
D-DAD!
ANY INK ON NARU'S FACE?
The ethanol bleeding is also largely a matter of luck.
Take your time with it.
R—
RIGHT!

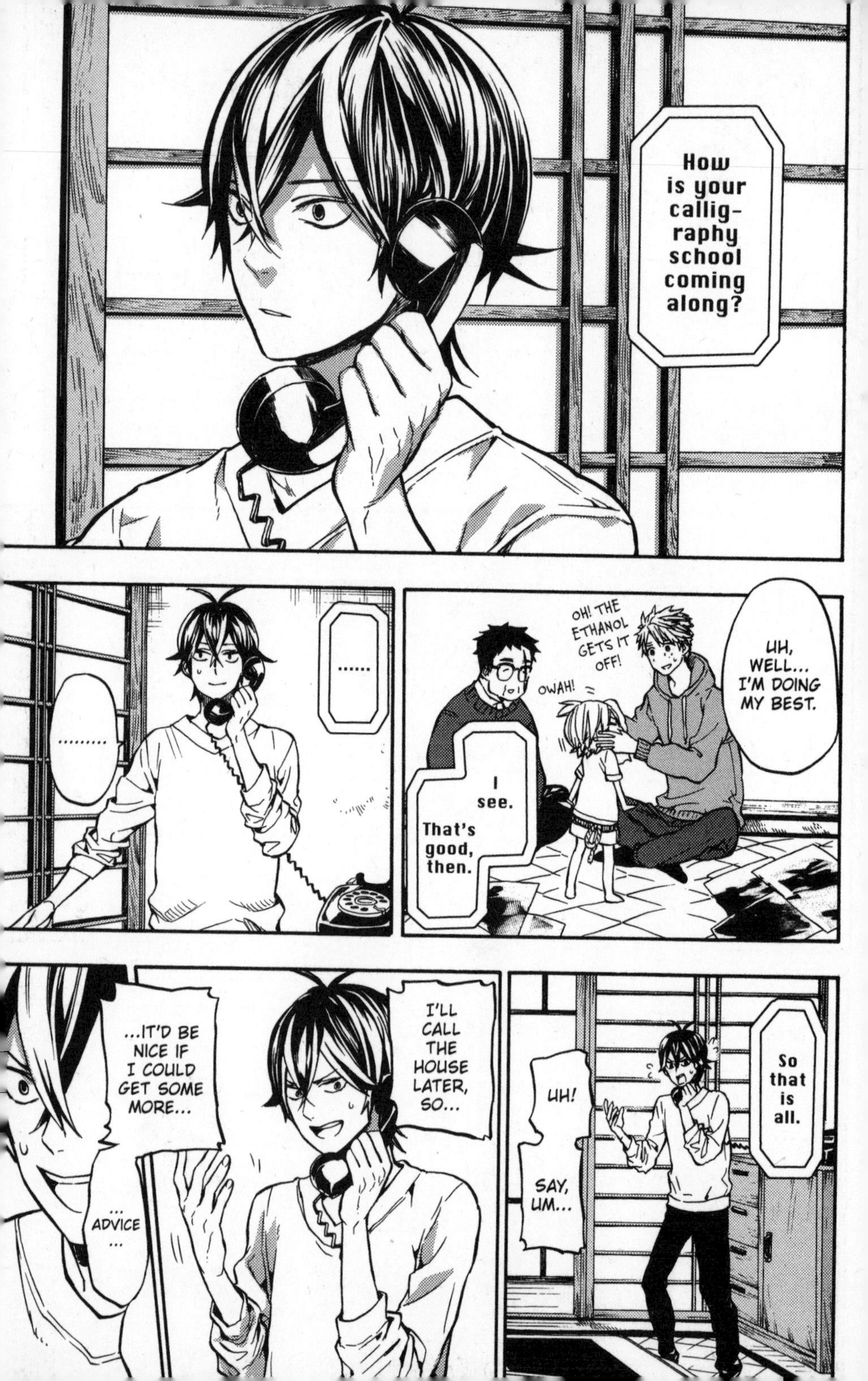
How is your callig-raphy school coming along?
UH, WELL... I'M DOING MY BEST.
OH! THE ETHANOL GETS IT OFF!
OWAH!
I see. That's good, then.
......
....
So that is all.
UH!
SAY, UM...
I'LL CALL THE HOUSE LATER, SO...
...IT'D BE NICE IF I COULD GET SOME MORE...
... ADVICE ...

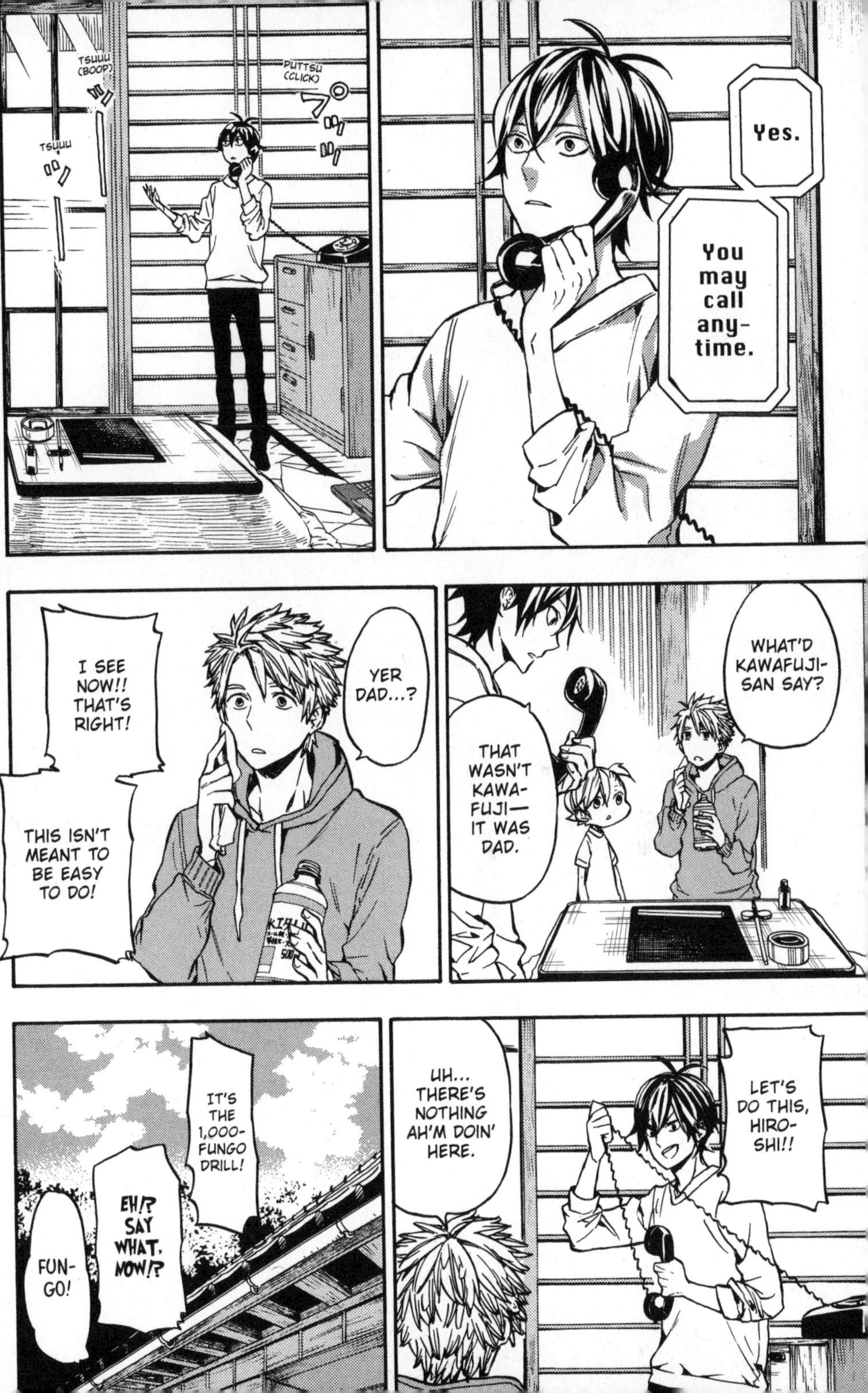
Yes.
You may call any-time.
PUTTSU (CLICK)
TSUUU (BOOP)
TSUUU
WHAT'D KAWAFUJI-SAN SAY?
THAT WASN'T KAWA-FUJI— IT WAS DAD.
YER DAD...?
I SEE NOW!! THAT'S RIGHT!
THIS ISN'T MEANT TO BE EASY TO DO!
LET'S DO THIS, HIRO-SHI!!
UH... THERE'S NOTHING AH'M DOIN' HERE.
IT'S THE 1,000-FUNGO DRILL!
EH!? SAY WHAT, NOW!?
FUN-GO!

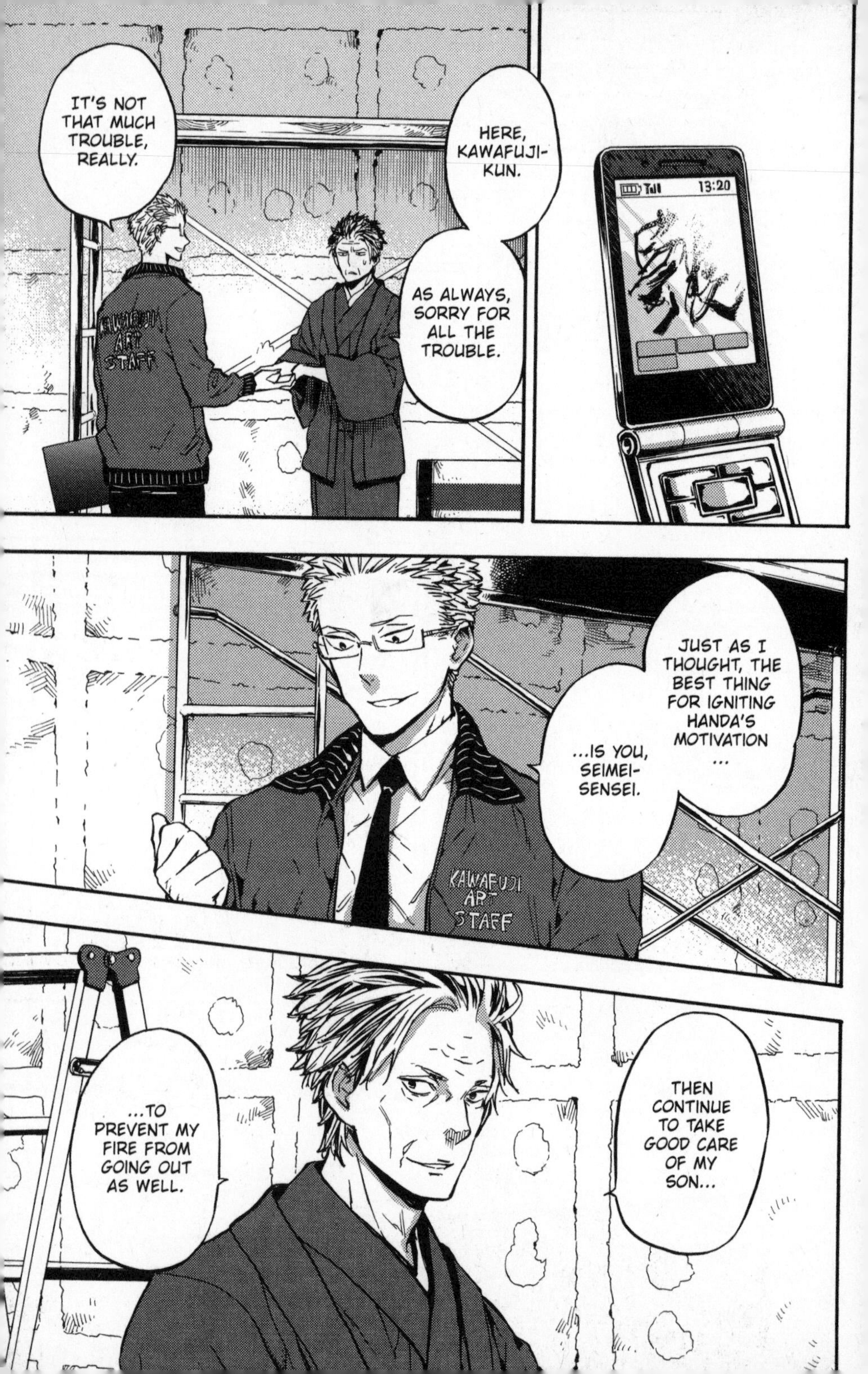
13:20
HERE, KAWAFUJI-KUN.
AS ALWAYS, SORRY FOR ALL THE TROUBLE.
IT'S NOT THAT MUCH TROUBLE, REALLY.
KAWAFUJI ART STAFF
JUST AS I THOUGHT, THE BEST THING FOR IGNITING HANDA'S MOTIVATION ...
...IS YOU, SEIMEI-SENSEI.
KAWAFUJI ART STAFF
THEN CONTINUE TO TAKE GOOD CARE OF MY SON...
...TO PREVENT MY FIRE FROM GOING OUT AS WELL.

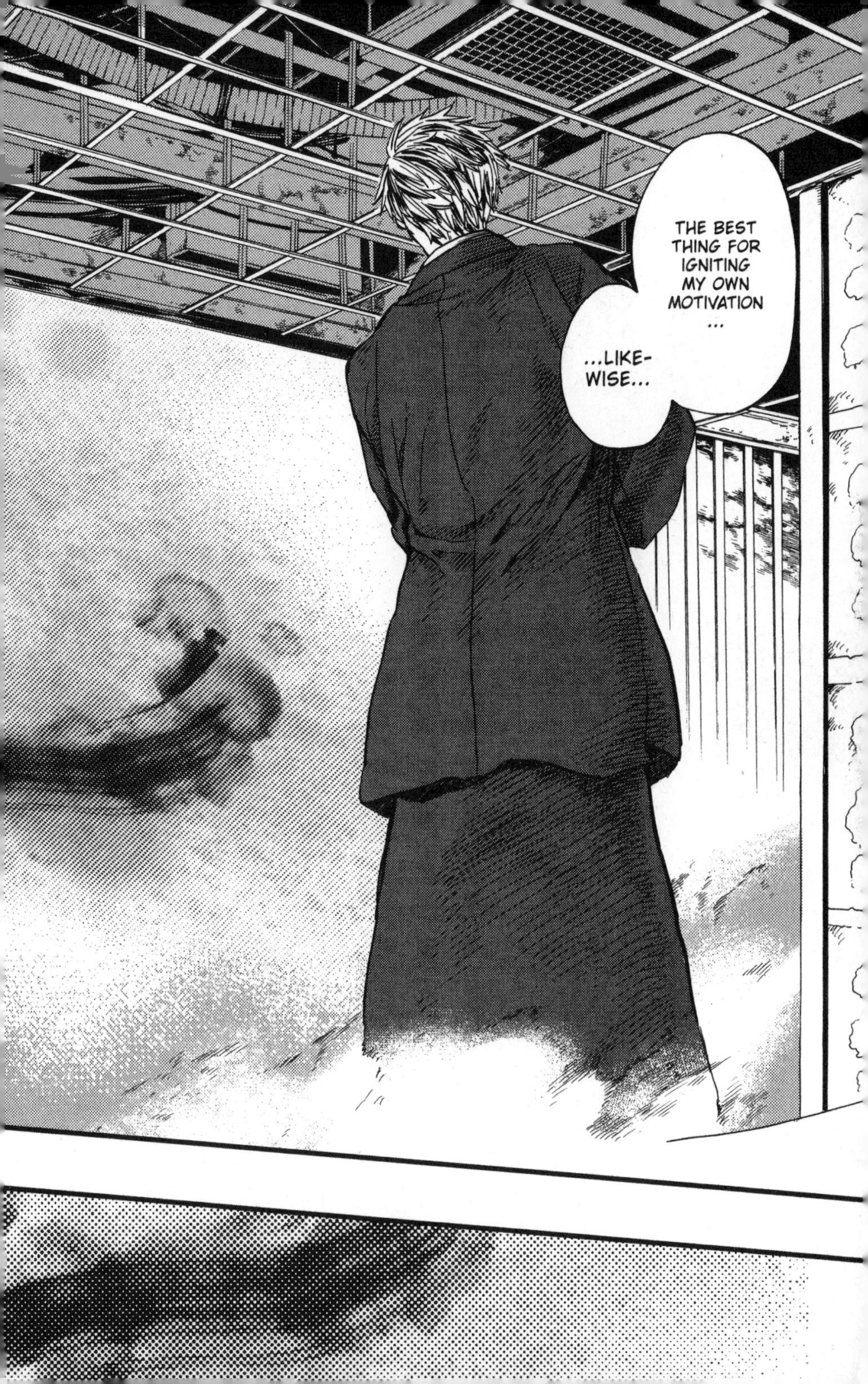
THE BEST THING FOR IGNITING MY OWN MOTIVATION ...
...LIKE-WISE...

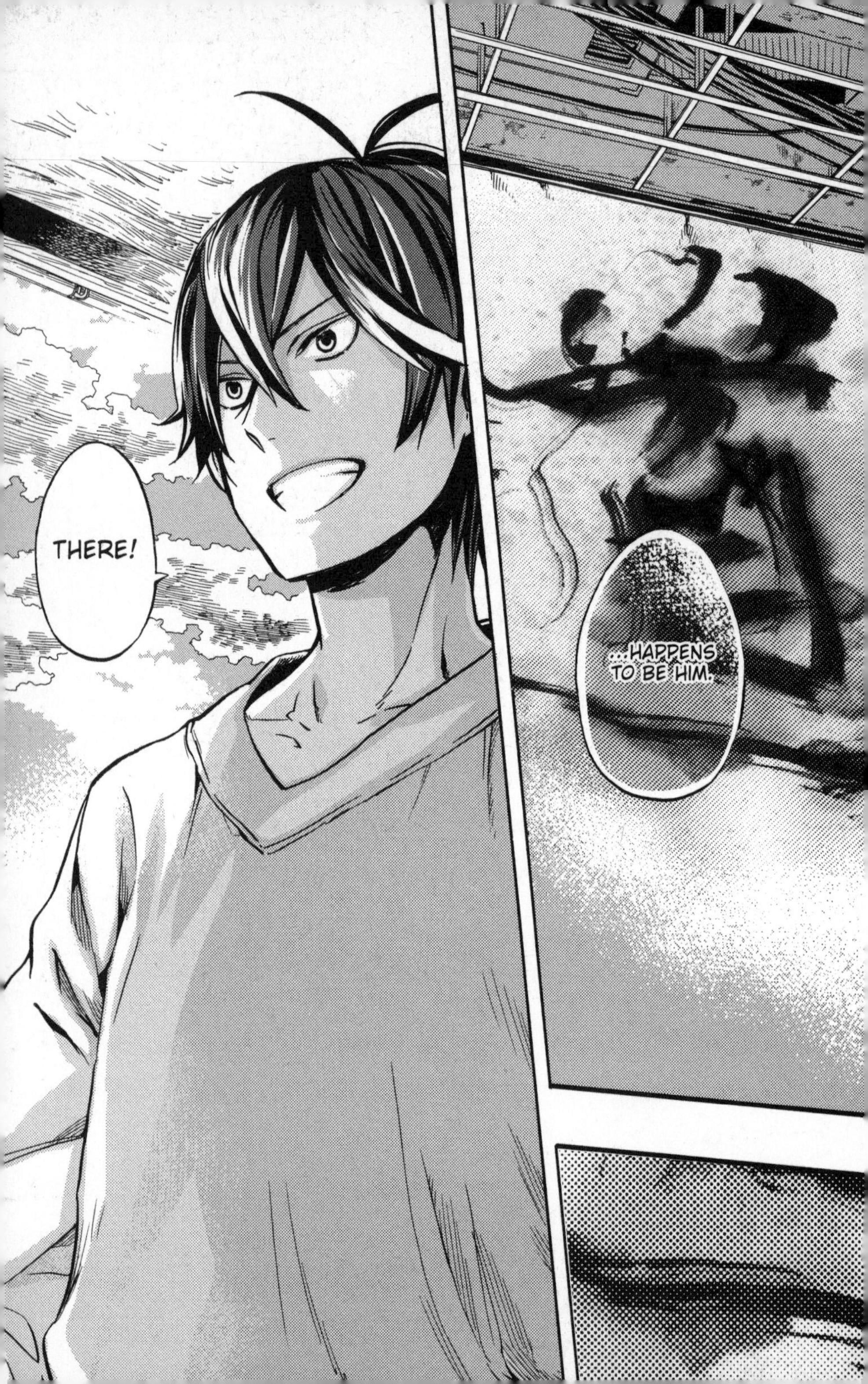
...HAPPENS TO BE HIM.
THERE!

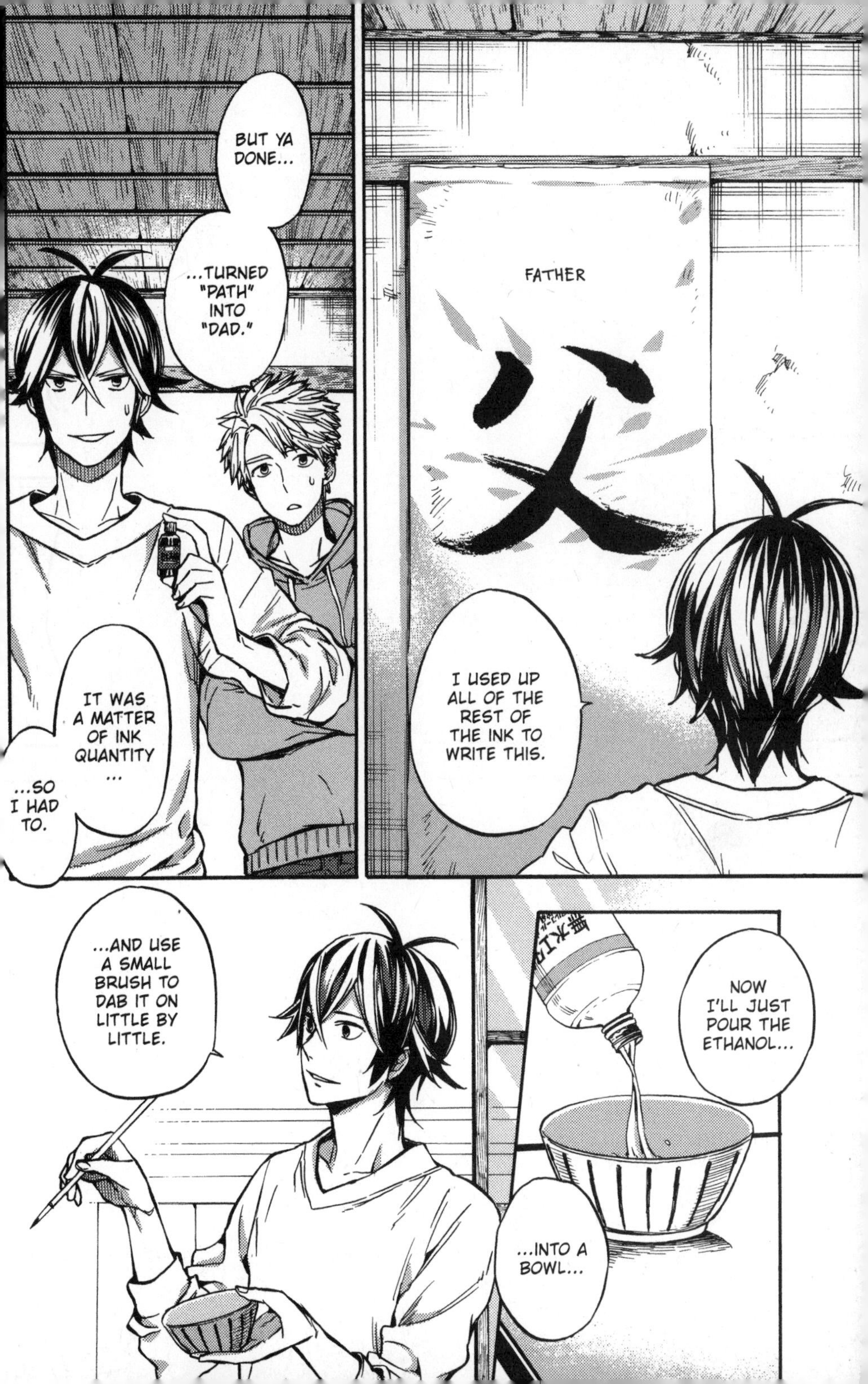
父
FATHER
I USED UP ALL OF THE REST OF THE INK TO WRITE THIS.
BUT YA DONE...
...TURNED "PATH" INTO "DAD."
IT WAS A MATTER OF INK QUANTITY...
...SO I HAD TO.
NOW I'LL JUST POUR THE ETHANOL...
...INTO A BOWL...
...AND USE A SMALL BRUSH TO DAB IT ON LITTLE BY LITTLE.

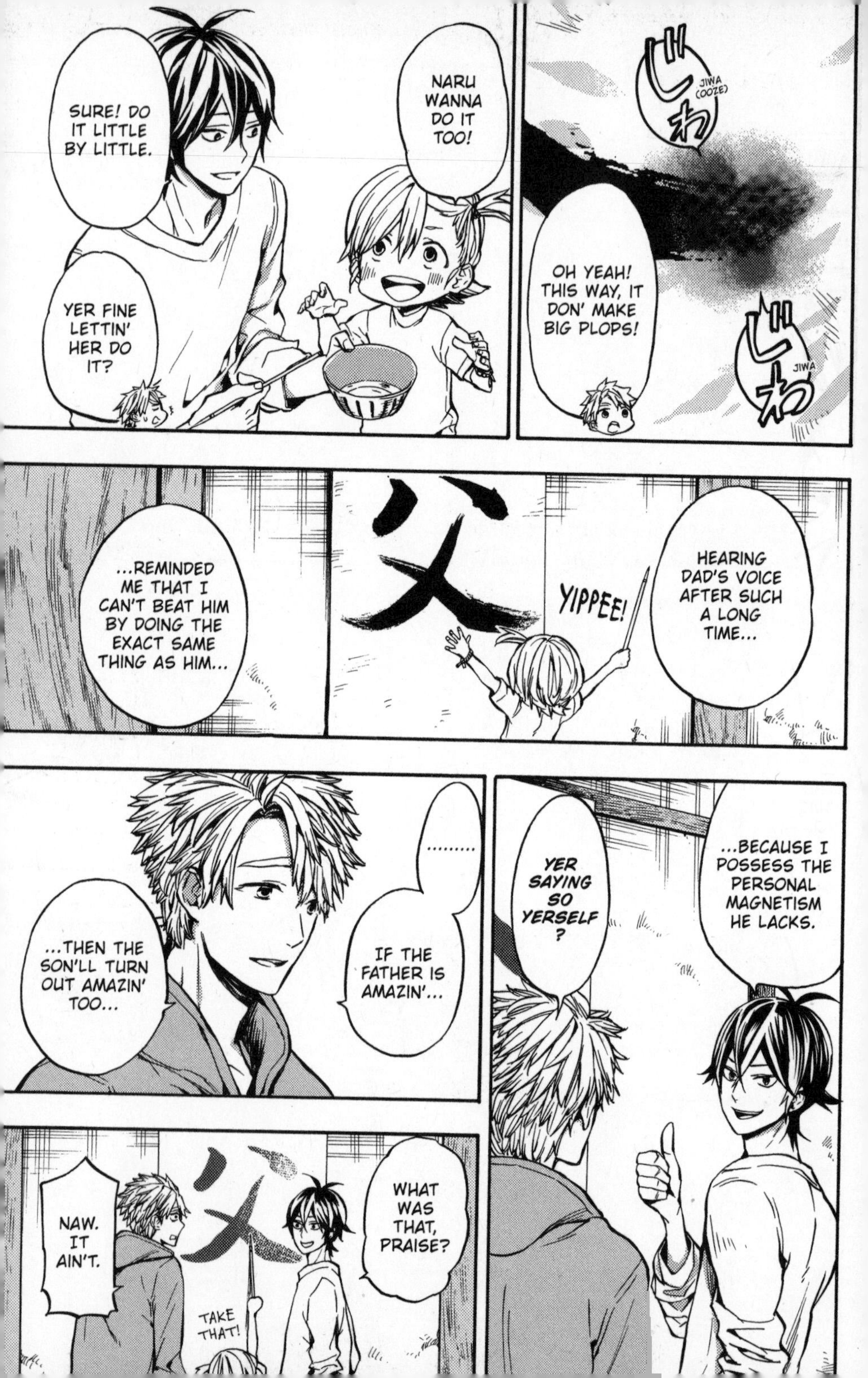
じわ
JIWA (OOZE)
OH YEAH! THIS WAY, IT DON' MAKE BIG PLOPS!
じわ
JIWA
NARU WANNA DO IT TOO!
SURE! DO IT LITTLE BY LITTLE.
YER FINE LETTIN' HER DO IT?
HEARING DAD'S VOICE AFTER SUCH A LONG TIME...
父
YIPPEE!
...REMINDED ME THAT I CAN'T BEAT HIM BY DOING THE EXACT SAME THING AS HIM...
...BECAUSE I POSSESS THE PERSONAL MAGNETISM HE LACKS.
YER SAYING SO YERSELF?
....
IF THE FATHER IS AMAZIN'...
...THEN THE SON'LL TURN OUT AMAZIN' TOO...
WHAT WAS THAT, PRAISE?
NAW. IT AIN'T.
TAKE THAT!

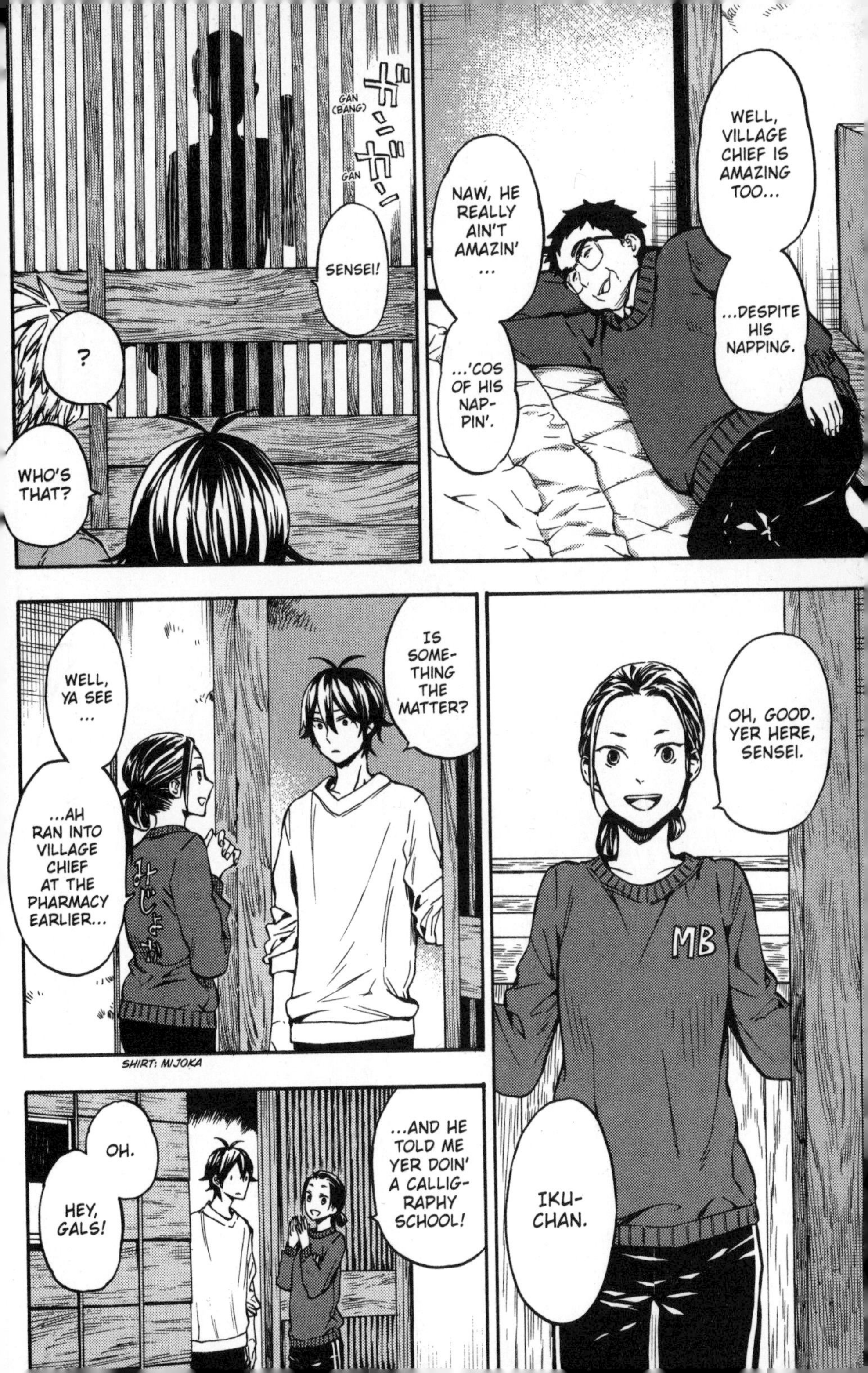
WELL, VILLAGE CHIEF IS AMAZING TOO…
…DESPITE HIS NAPPING.
NAW, HE REALLY AIN'T AMAZIN'…
…'COS OF HIS NAP-PIN'.
GAN (BANG)
GAN
SENSEI!
?
WHO'S THAT?
OH, GOOD. YER HERE, SENSEI.
IKU-CHAN.
IS SOME-THING THE MATTER?
WELL, YA SEE…
…AH RAN INTO VILLAGE CHIEF AT THE PHARMACY EARLIER…
SHIRT: MIJOKA
…AND HE TOLD ME YER DOIN' A CALLIG-RAPHY SCHOOL!
OH.
HEY, GALS!

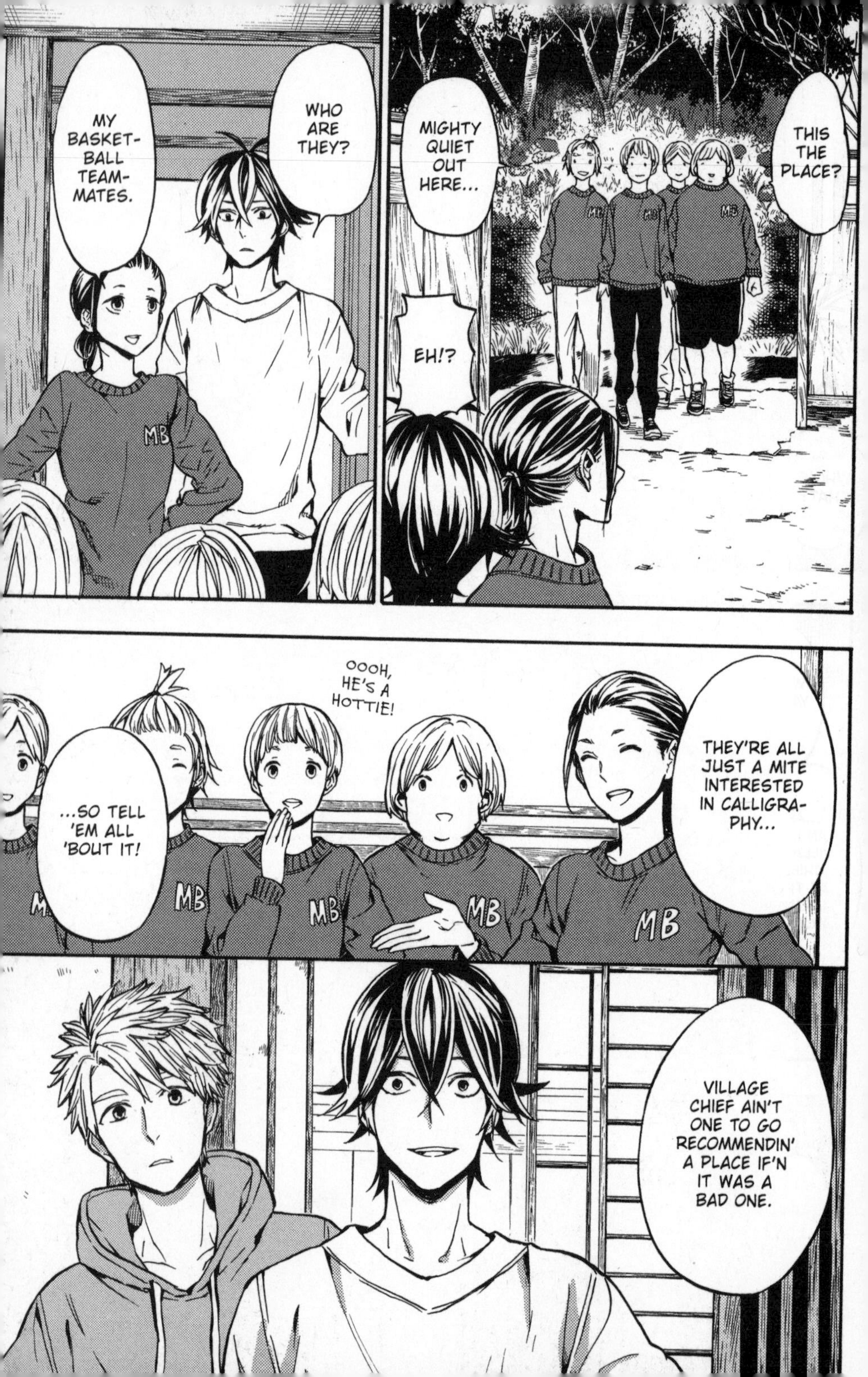
THIS THE PLACE?
MIGHTY QUIET OUT HERE...
EH!?
WHO ARE THEY?
MY BASKET-BALL TEAM-MATES.
THEY'RE ALL JUST A MITE INTERESTED IN CALLIGRA-PHY...
OOOH, HE'S A HOTTIE!
...SO TELL 'EM ALL 'BOUT IT!
MB
VILLAGE CHIEF AIN'T ONE TO GO RECOMMENDIN' A PLACE IF'N IT WAS A BAD ONE.

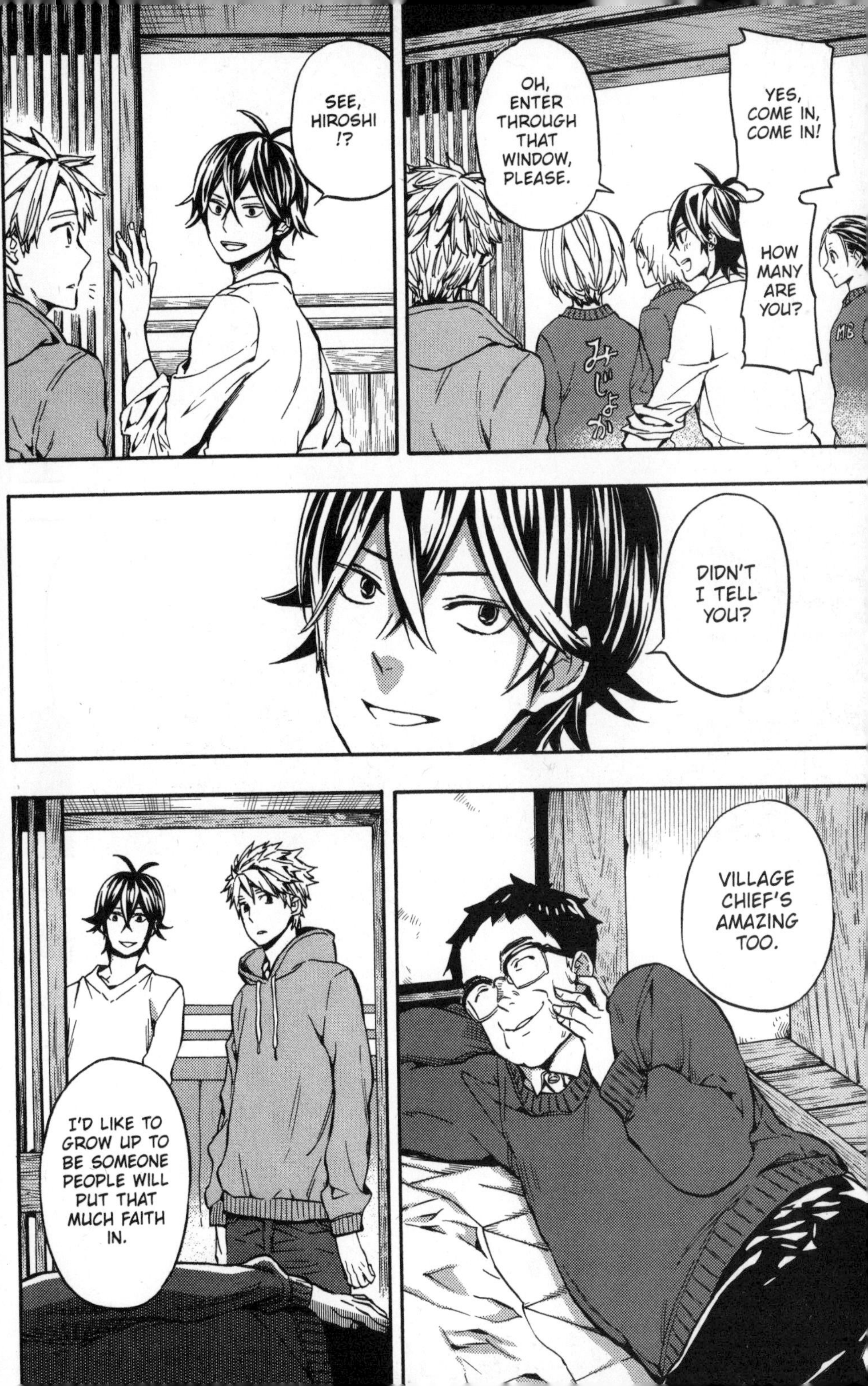
YES, COME IN, COME IN!
HOW MANY ARE YOU?
OH, ENTER THROUGH THAT WINDOW, PLEASE.
SEE, HIROSHI!?
DIDN'T I TELL YOU?
VILLAGE CHIEF'S AMAZING TOO.
I'D LIKE TO GROW UP TO BE SOMEONE PEOPLE WILL PUT THAT MUCH FAITH IN.

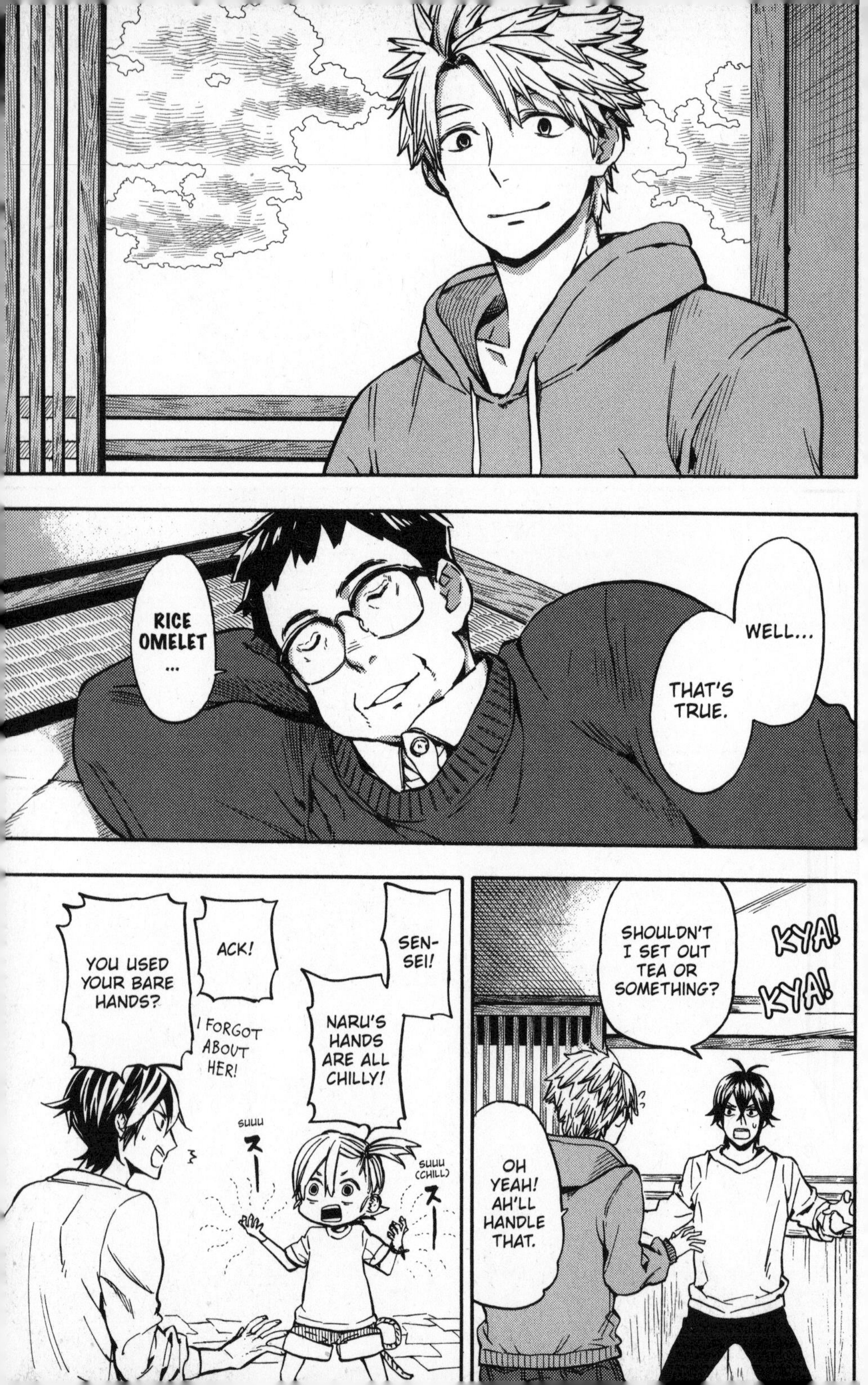
WELL... THAT'S TRUE.
RICE OMELET ...
SHOULDN'T I SET OUT TEA OR SOMETHING?
KYA! KYA!
OH YEAH! AH'LL HANDLE THAT.
SEN-SEI!
NARU'S HANDS ARE ALL CHILLY!
ACK!
I FORGOT ABOUT HER!
YOU USED YOUR BARE HANDS?
SUUU
SUUU (CHILL)

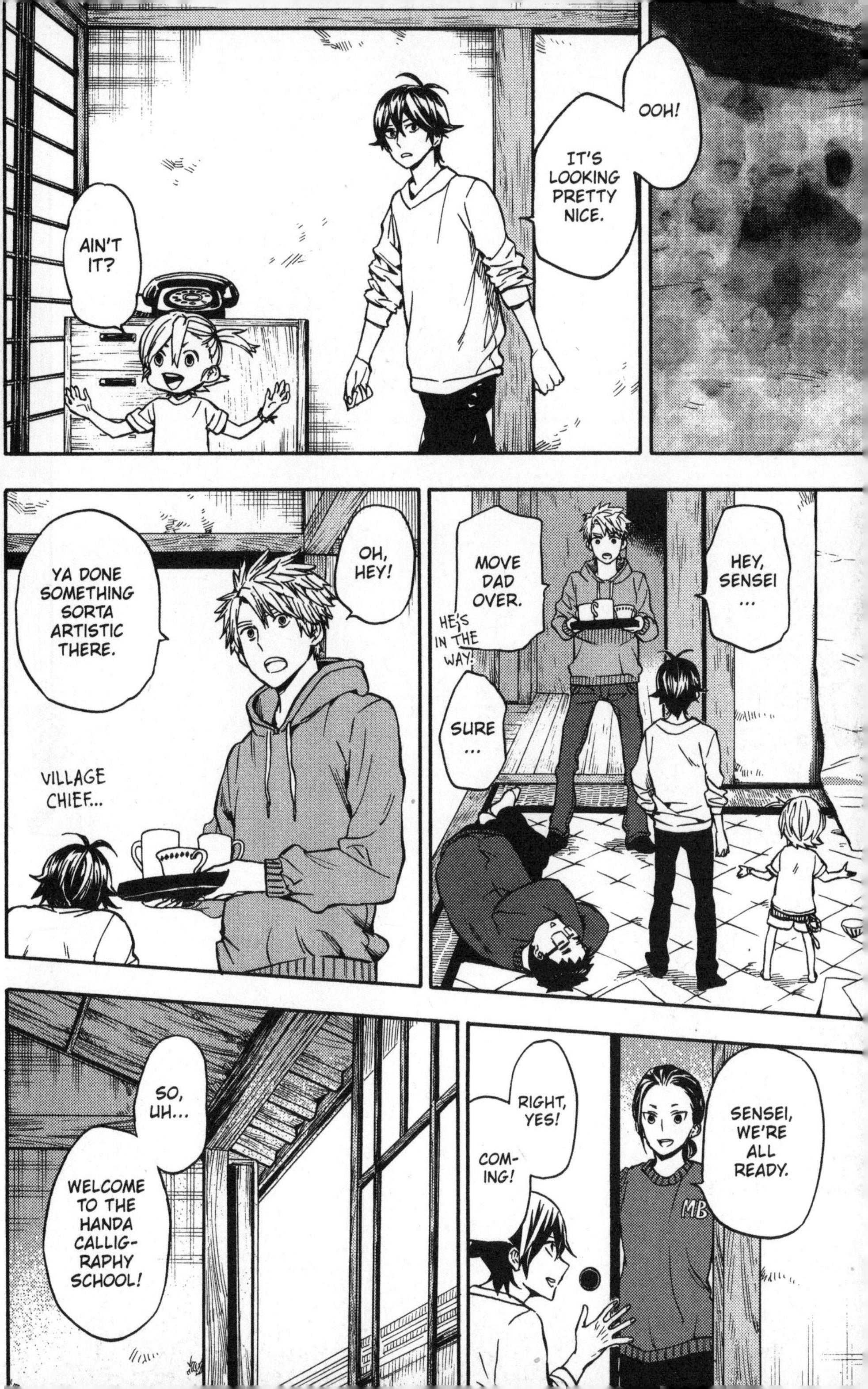
OOH!
IT'S LOOKING PRETTY NICE.
AIN'T IT?
HEY, SENSEI...
MOVE DAD OVER.
HE'S IN THE WAY.
SURE...
OH, HEY!
YA DONE SOMETHING SORTA ARTISTIC THERE.
VILLAGE CHIEF...
SENSEI, WE'RE ALL READY.
RIGHT, YES!
COMING!
SO, UH...
WELCOME TO THE HANDA CALLIGRAPHY SCHOOL!

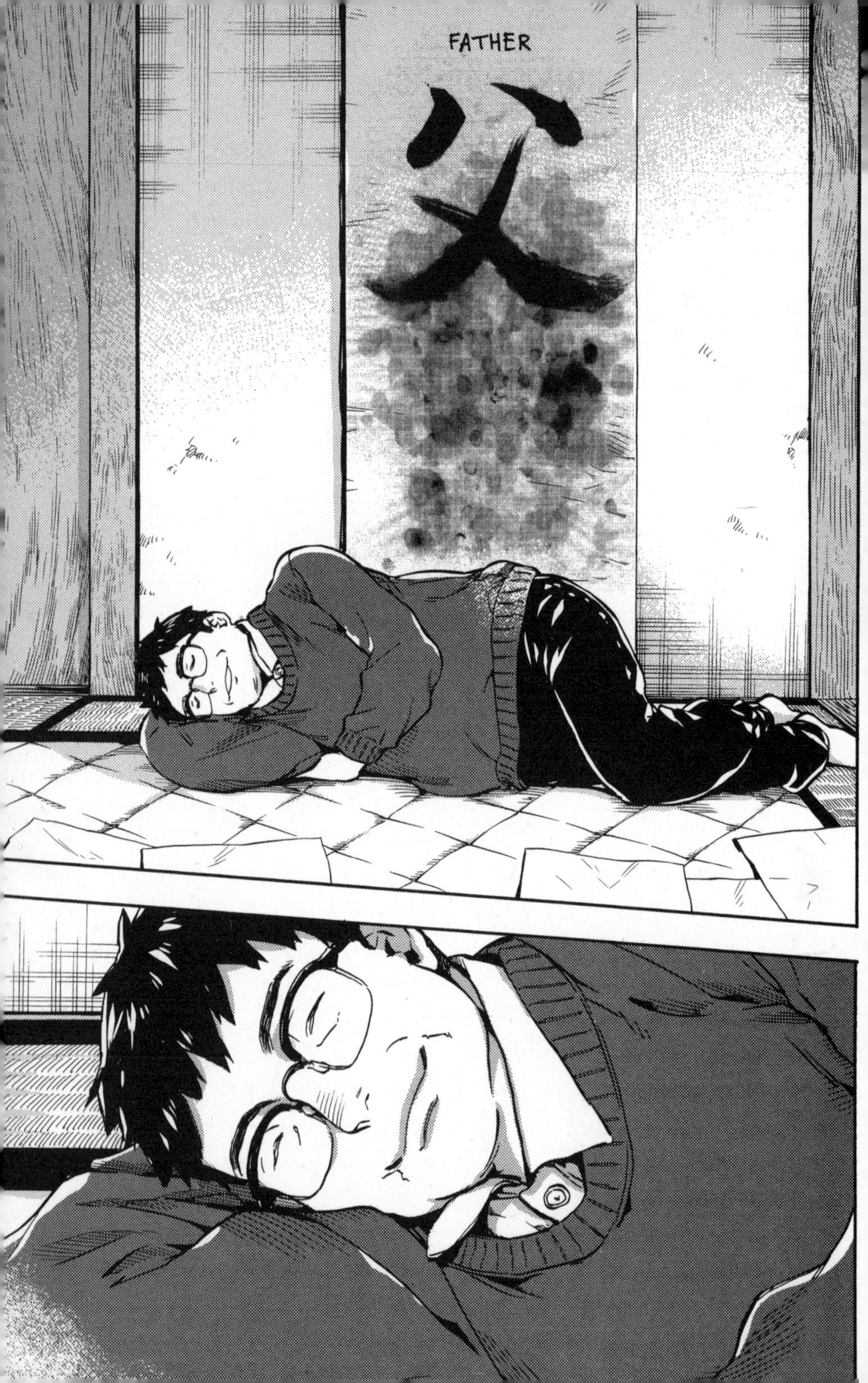

FATHER

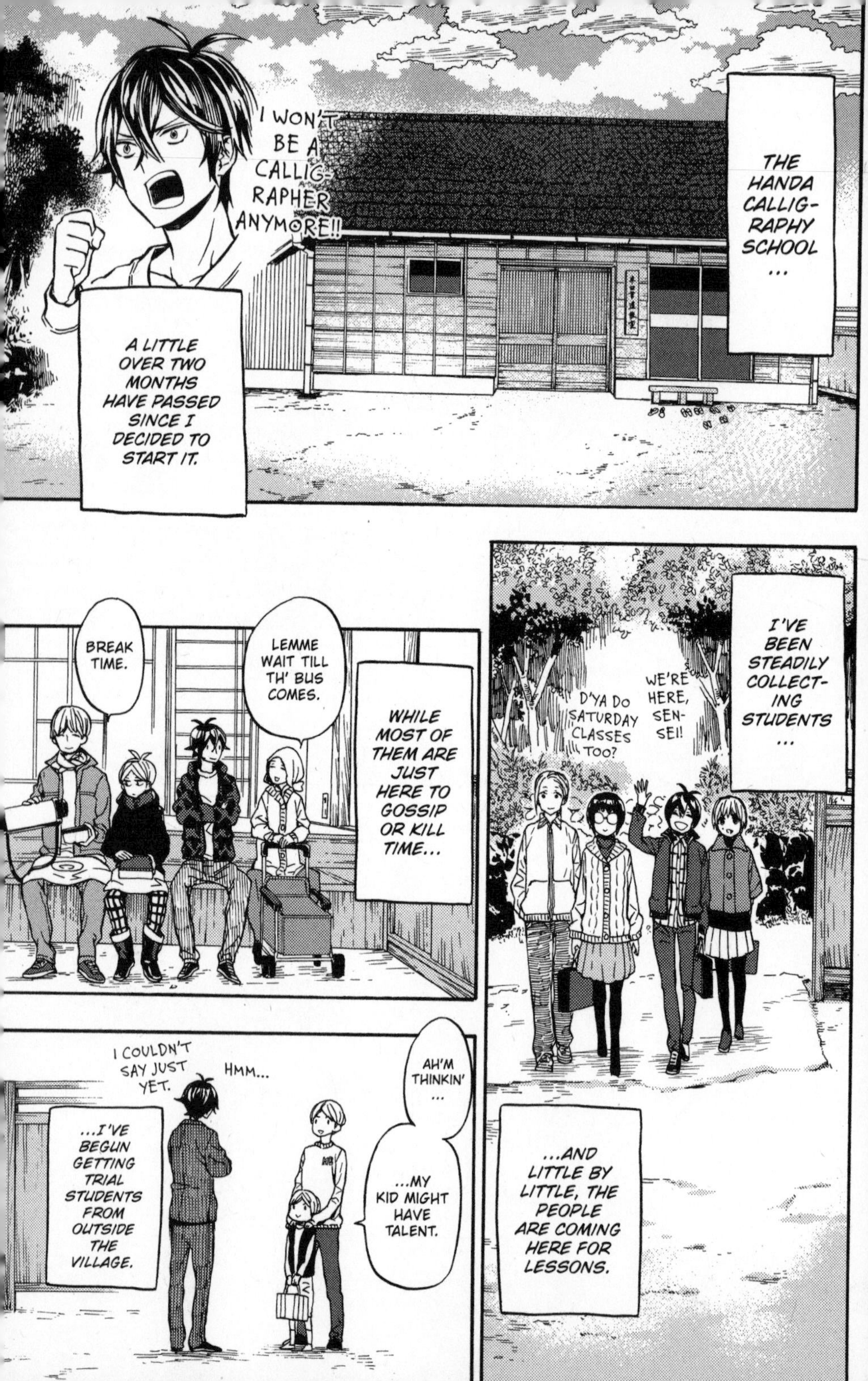
THE HANDA CALLIGRAPHY SCHOOL...
I WON'T BE A CALLIGRAPHER ANYMORE!!
A LITTLE OVER TWO MONTHS HAVE PASSED SINCE I DECIDED TO START IT.
I'VE BEEN STEADILY COLLECTING STUDENTS...
WE'RE HERE, SENSEI!
D'YA DO SATURDAY CLASSES TOO?
...AND LITTLE BY LITTLE, THE PEOPLE ARE COMING HERE FOR LESSONS.
WHILE MOST OF THEM ARE JUST HERE TO GOSSIP OR KILL TIME...
LEMME WAIT TILL TH' BUS COMES.
BREAK TIME.
AH'M THINKIN'...
...MY KID MIGHT HAVE TALENT.
HMM...
I COULDN'T SAY JUST YET.
...I'VE BEGUN GETTING TRIAL STUDENTS FROM OUTSIDE THE VILLAGE.

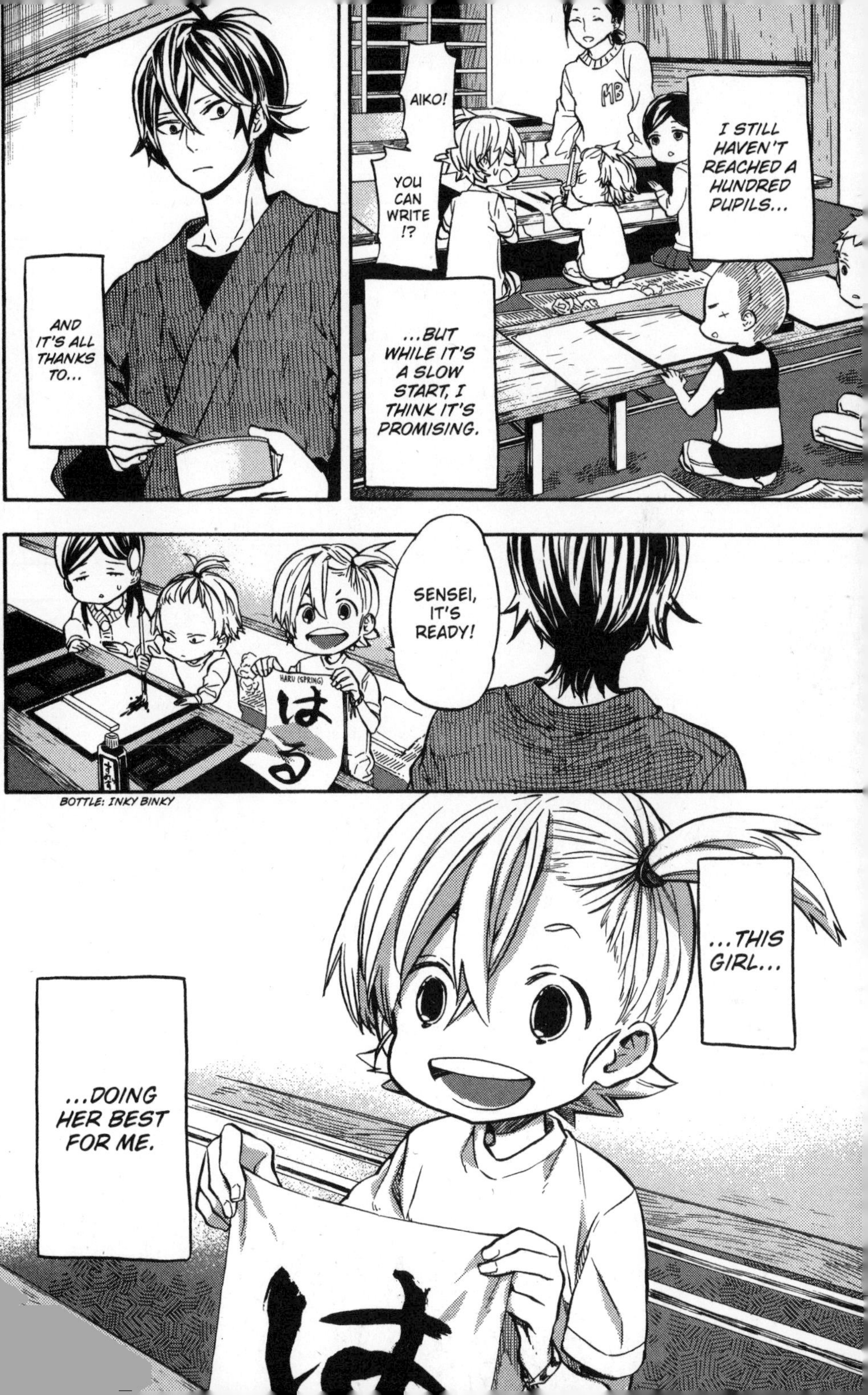
I STILL HAVEN'T REACHED A HUNDRED PUPILS...
AIKO!
YOU CAN WRITE !?
...BUT WHILE IT'S A SLOW START, I THINK IT'S PROMISING.
AND IT'S ALL THANKS TO...
SENSEI, IT'S READY!
HARU (SPRING)
BOTTLE: INKY BINKY
...THIS GIRL...
...DOING HER BEST FOR ME.

Act. 119
YATTATTOTTA
(Translation: Back-and-forth)

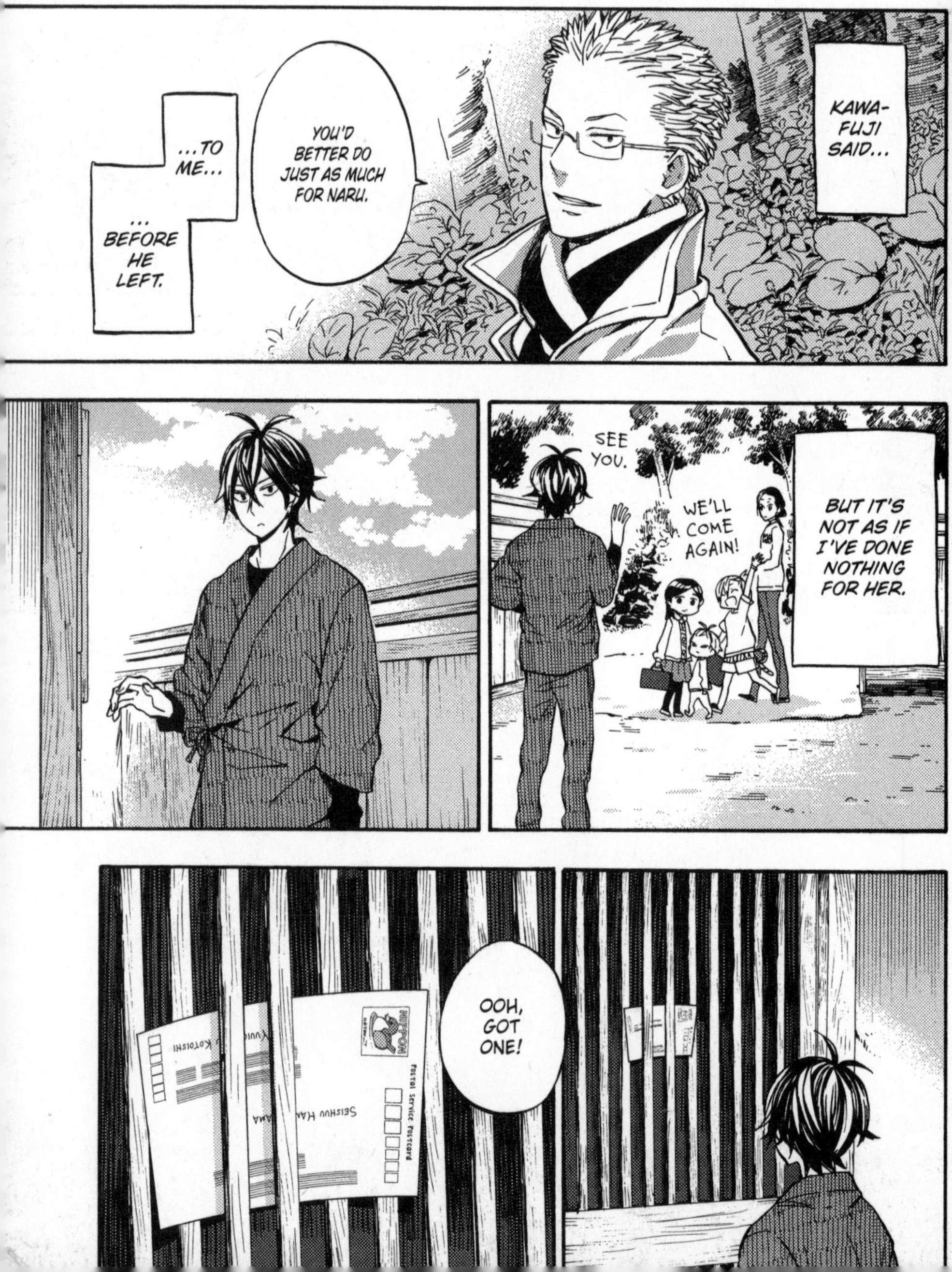
KAWAFUJI SAID...
YOU'D BETTER DO JUST AS MUCH FOR NARU.
...TO ME...
...BEFORE HE LEFT.
BUT IT'S NOT AS IF I'VE DONE NOTHING FOR HER.
SEE YOU.
WE'LL COME AGAIN!
OOH, GOT ONE!
NIPPON
Postal Service Postcard

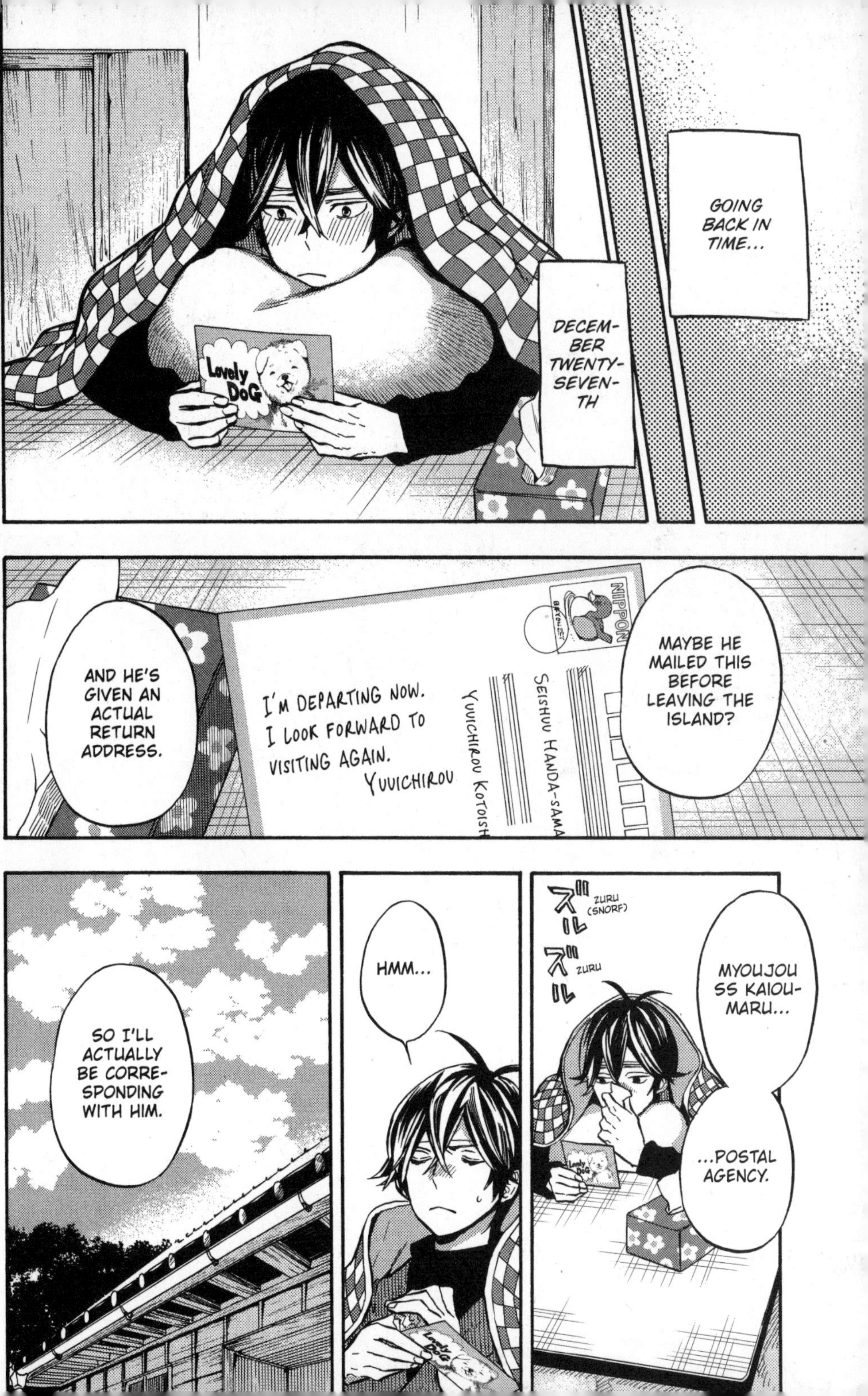
GOING BACK IN TIME...
DECEMBER TWENTY-SEVENTH
Lovely DoG
MAYBE HE MAILED THIS BEFORE LEAVING THE ISLAND?
NIPPON
Seishuu Handa-sama
Yuuichirou Kotoish
I'M DEPARTING NOW. I LOOK FORWARD TO VISITING AGAIN. Yuuichirou
AND HE'S GIVEN AN ACTUAL RETURN ADDRESS.
ZURU (SNORF)
ZURU
MYOUJOU SS KAIOU-MARU...
...POSTAL AGENCY.
Lovely DoG
HMM...
Lovely DoG
SO I'LL ACTUALLY BE CORRESPONDING WITH HIM.

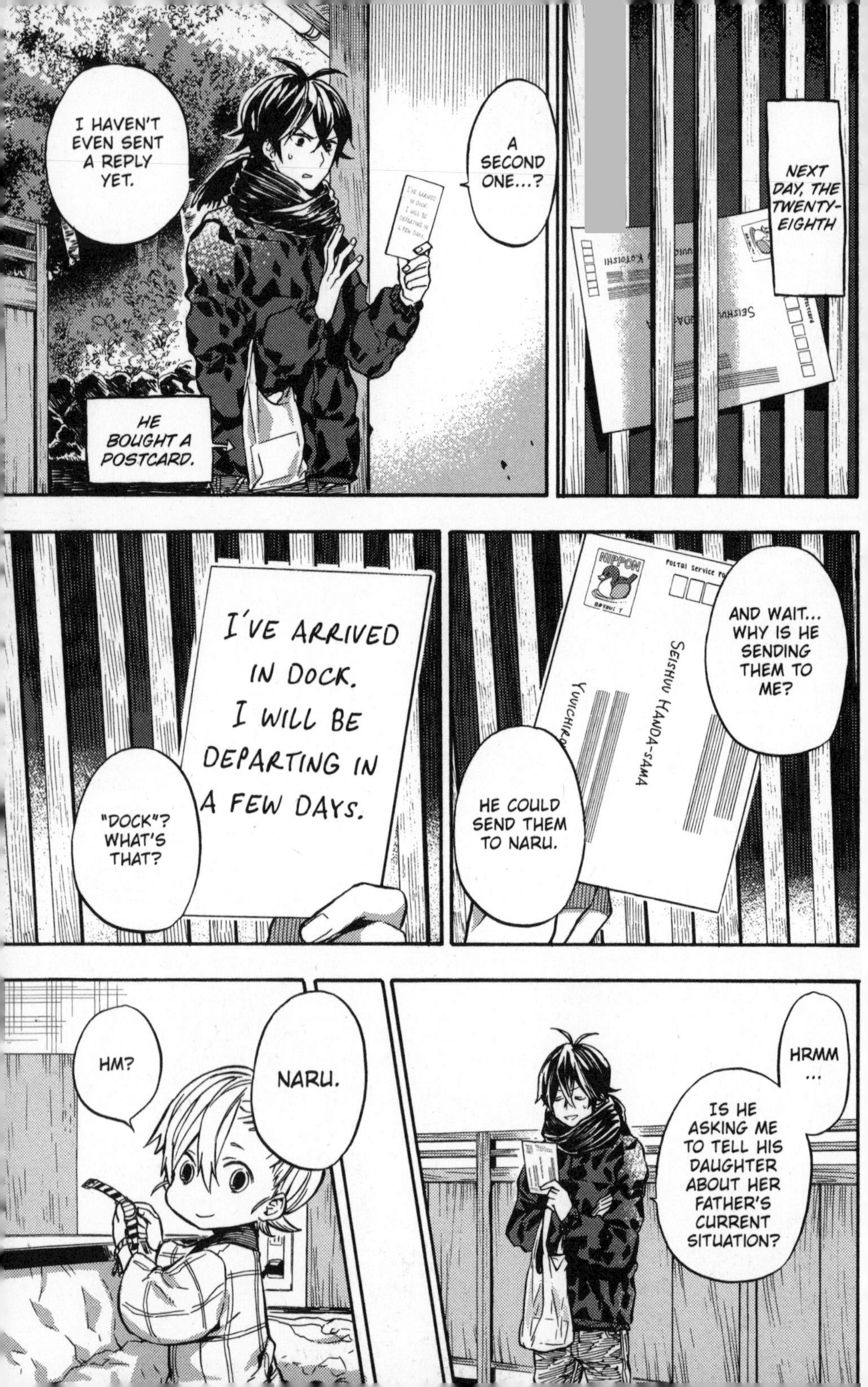
NEXT DAY, THE TWENTY-EIGHTH
A SECOND ONE...?
I HAVEN'T EVEN SENT A REPLY YET.
HE BOUGHT A POSTCARD.
AND WAIT... WHY IS HE SENDING THEM TO ME?
NIPPON
SEISHUU HANDA-SAMA
HE COULD SEND THEM TO NARU.
I'VE ARRIVED IN DOCK. I WILL BE DEPARTING IN A FEW DAYS.
"DOCK"? WHAT'S THAT?
HRMM ...
IS HE ASKING ME TO TELL HIS DAUGHTER ABOUT HER FATHER'S CURRENT SITUATION?
NARU.
HM?

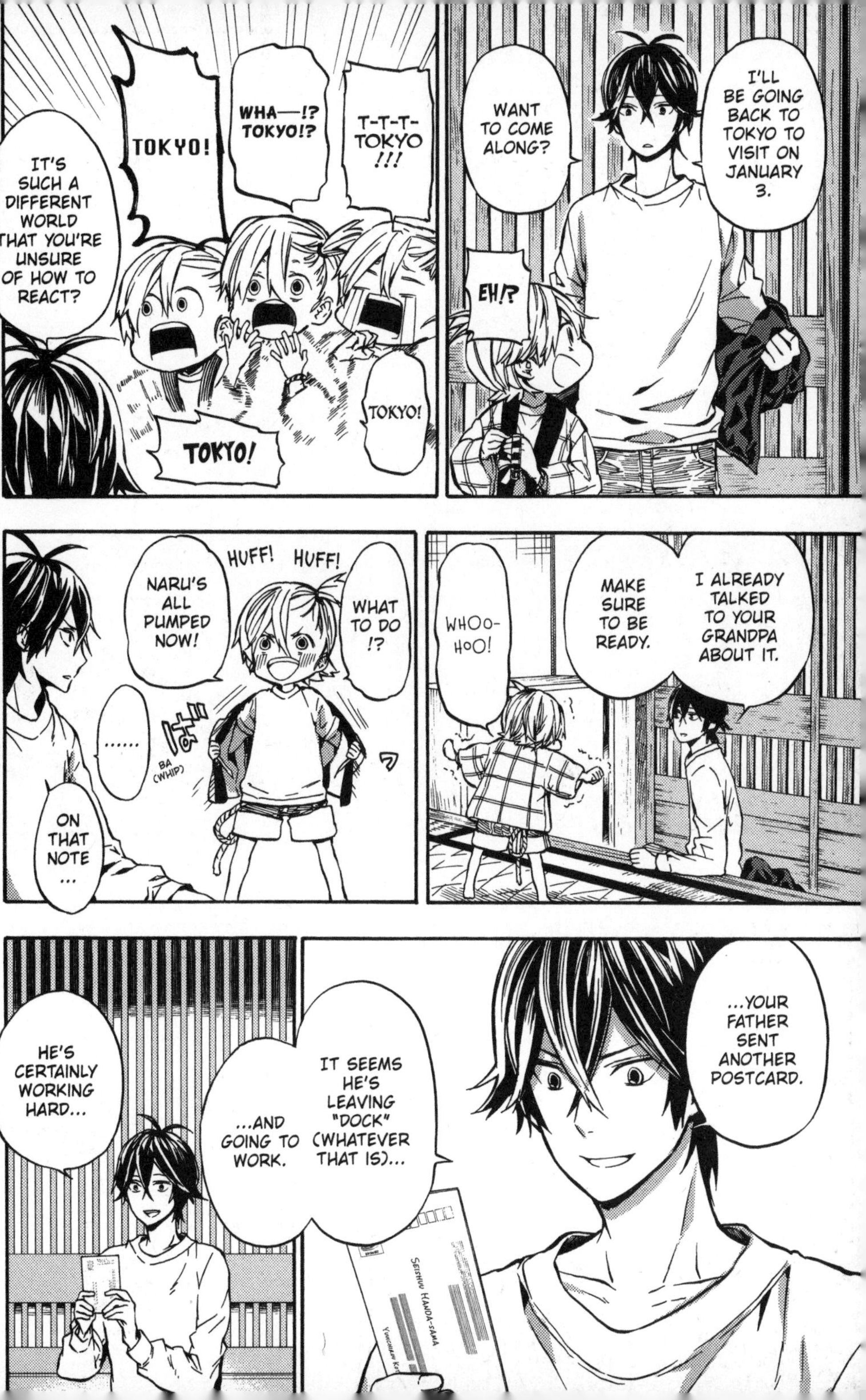
I'LL BE GOING BACK TO TOKYO TO VISIT ON JANUARY 3.
WANT TO COME ALONG?
EH!?
T-T-T-TOKYO!!!
WHA—!? TOKYO!?
TOKYO!
IT'S SUCH A DIFFERENT WORLD THAT YOU'RE UNSURE OF HOW TO REACT?
TOKYO!
TOKYO!
I ALREADY TALKED TO YOUR GRANDPA ABOUT IT.
MAKE SURE TO BE READY.
WHOO-HOO!
WHAT TO DO!?
HUFF! HUFF!
NARU'S ALL PUMPED NOW!
......
ばっ
BA (WHIP)
ON THAT NOTE...
...YOUR FATHER SENT ANOTHER POSTCARD.
IT SEEMS HE'S LEAVING "DOCK" (WHATEVER THAT IS)...
...AND GOING TO WORK.
HE'S CERTAINLY WORKING HARD...
SEISHUU HANDA-SAMA

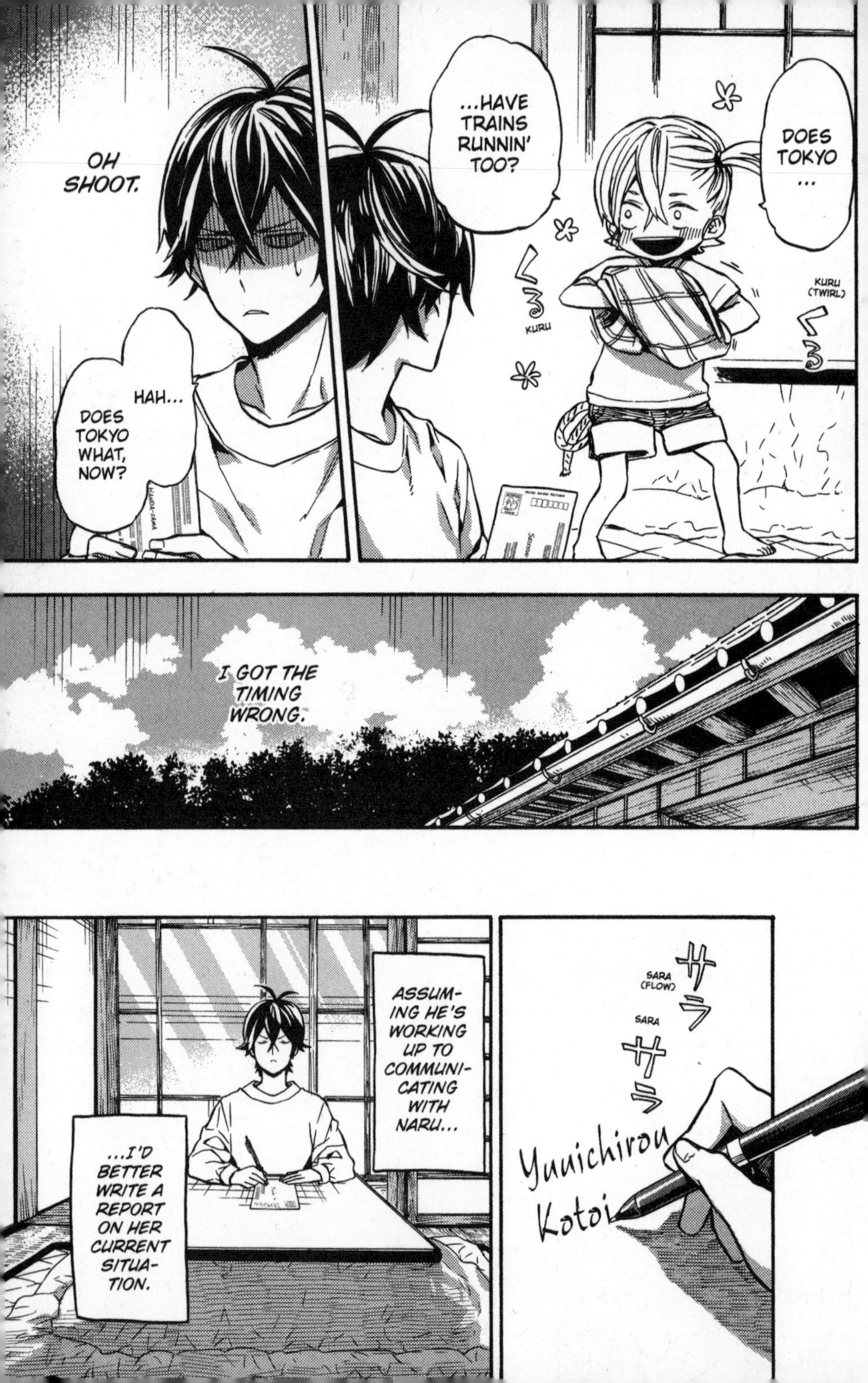
DOES TOKYO ...
KURU (TWIRL)
KURU
...HAVE TRAINS RUNNIN' TOO?
OH SHOOT.
HAH... DOES TOKYO WHAT, NOW?
I GOT THE TIMING WRONG.
SARA (FLOW)
SARA
Yuuichirou Kotoi
ASSUMING HE'S WORKING UP TO COMMUNICATING WITH NARU...
...I'D BETTER WRITE A REPORT ON HER CURRENT SITUATION.

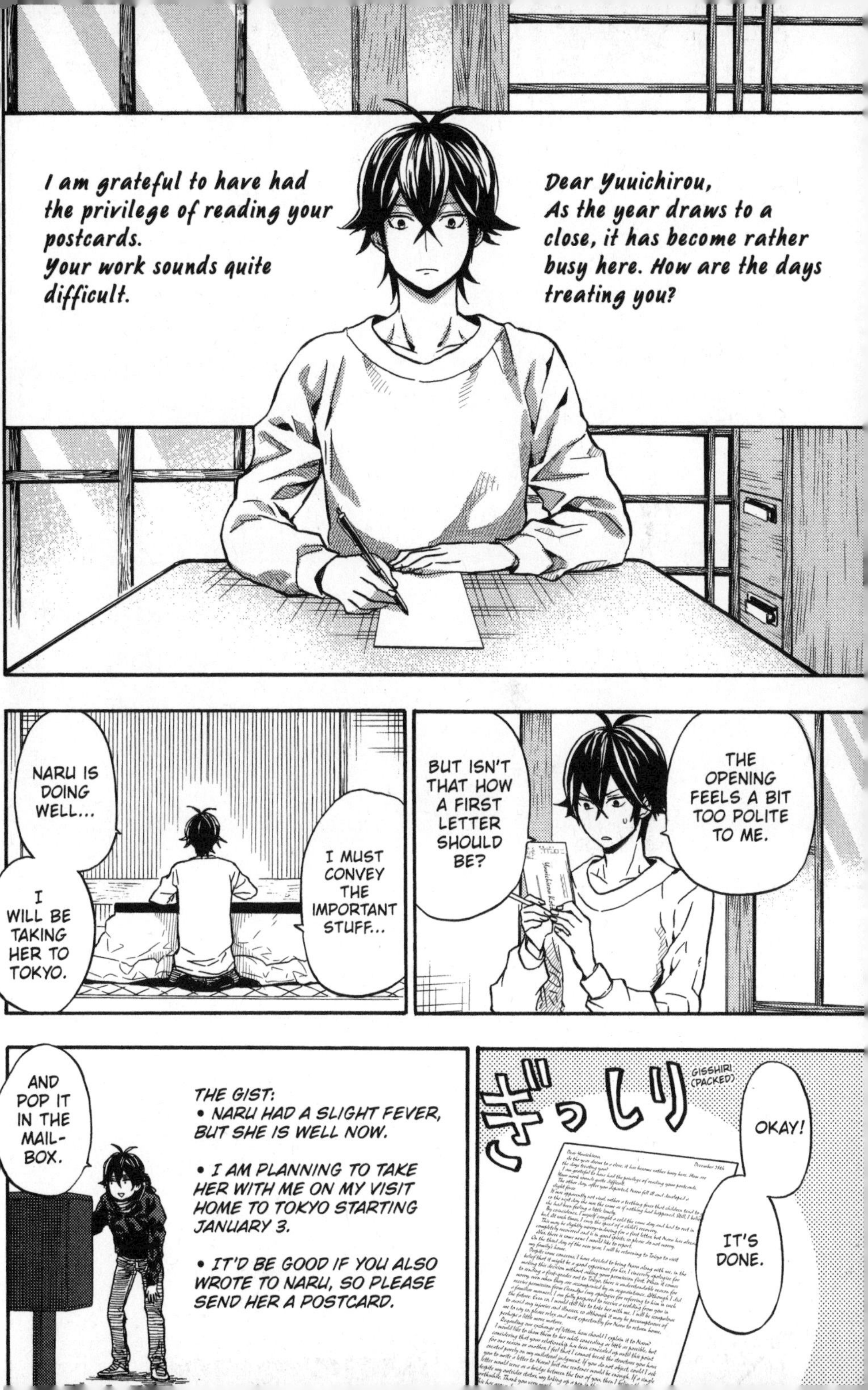

Dear Yuuichirou,
As the year draws to a close, it has become rather busy here. How are the days treating you?
I am grateful to have had the privilege of reading your postcards.
Your work sounds quite difficult.
THE OPENING FEELS A BIT TOO POLITE TO ME.
BUT ISN'T THAT HOW A FIRST LETTER SHOULD BE?
I MUST CONVEY THE IMPORTANT STUFF...
NARU IS DOING WELL...
I WILL BE TAKING HER TO TOKYO.
ぎっしり
GISSHIRI (PACKED)
OKAY!
IT'S DONE.
THE GIST:
• NARU HAD A SLIGHT FEVER, BUT SHE IS WELL NOW.
• I AM PLANNING TO TAKE HER WITH ME ON MY VISIT HOME TO TOKYO STARTING JANUARY 3.
• IT'D BE GOOD IF YOU ALSO WROTE TO NARU, SO PLEASE SEND HER A POSTCARD.
AND POP IT IN THE MAIL-BOX.

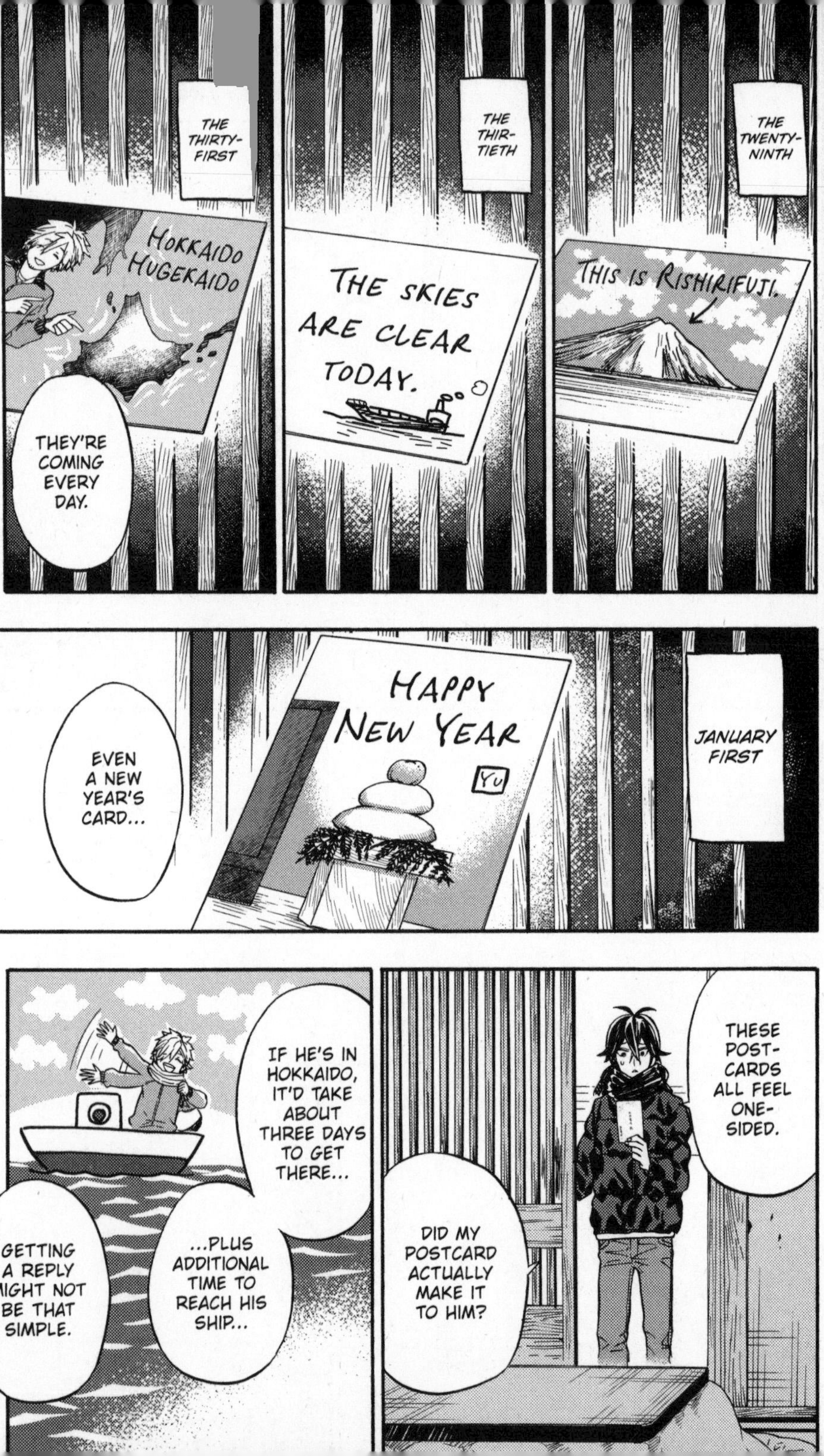
THE TWENTY-NINTH
THIS IS RISHIRIFUJI.
THE THIRTIETH
THE SKIES ARE CLEAR TODAY.
THE THIRTY-FIRST
HOKKAIDO HUGEKAIDO
THEY'RE COMING EVERY DAY.
JANUARY FIRST
HAPPY NEW YEAR
YU
EVEN A NEW YEAR'S CARD...
THESE POST-CARDS ALL FEEL ONE-SIDED.
DID MY POSTCARD ACTUALLY MAKE IT TO HIM?
IF HE'S IN HOKKAIDO, IT'D TAKE ABOUT THREE DAYS TO GET THERE...
...PLUS ADDITIONAL TIME TO REACH HIS SHIP...
GETTING A REPLY MIGHT NOT BE THAT SIMPLE.

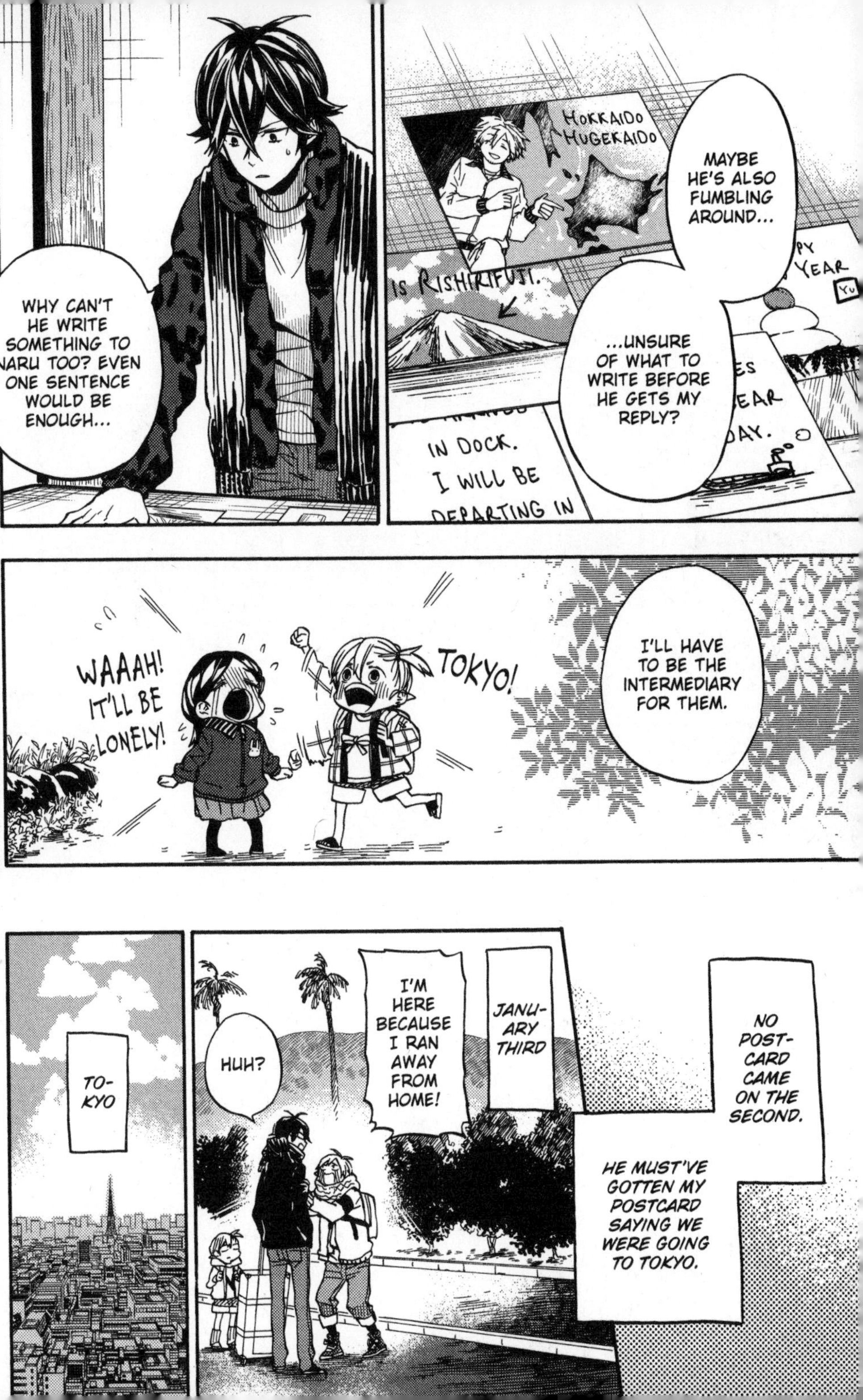
HOKKAIDO HUGEKAIDO
IS RISHIRIFUJI.
IN DOCK. I WILL BE DEPARTING IN
MAYBE HE'S ALSO FUMBLING AROUND...
...UNSURE OF WHAT TO WRITE BEFORE HE GETS MY REPLY?
WHY CAN'T HE WRITE SOMETHING TO NARU TOO? EVEN ONE SENTENCE WOULD BE ENOUGH...
I'LL HAVE TO BE THE INTERMEDIARY FOR THEM.
TOKYO!
WAAAH! IT'LL BE LONELY!
NO POST-CARD CAME ON THE SECOND.
HE MUST'VE GOTTEN MY POSTCARD SAYING WE WERE GOING TO TOKYO.
JANU-ARY THIRD
I'M HERE BECAUSE I RAN AWAY FROM HOME!
HUH?
TO-KYO

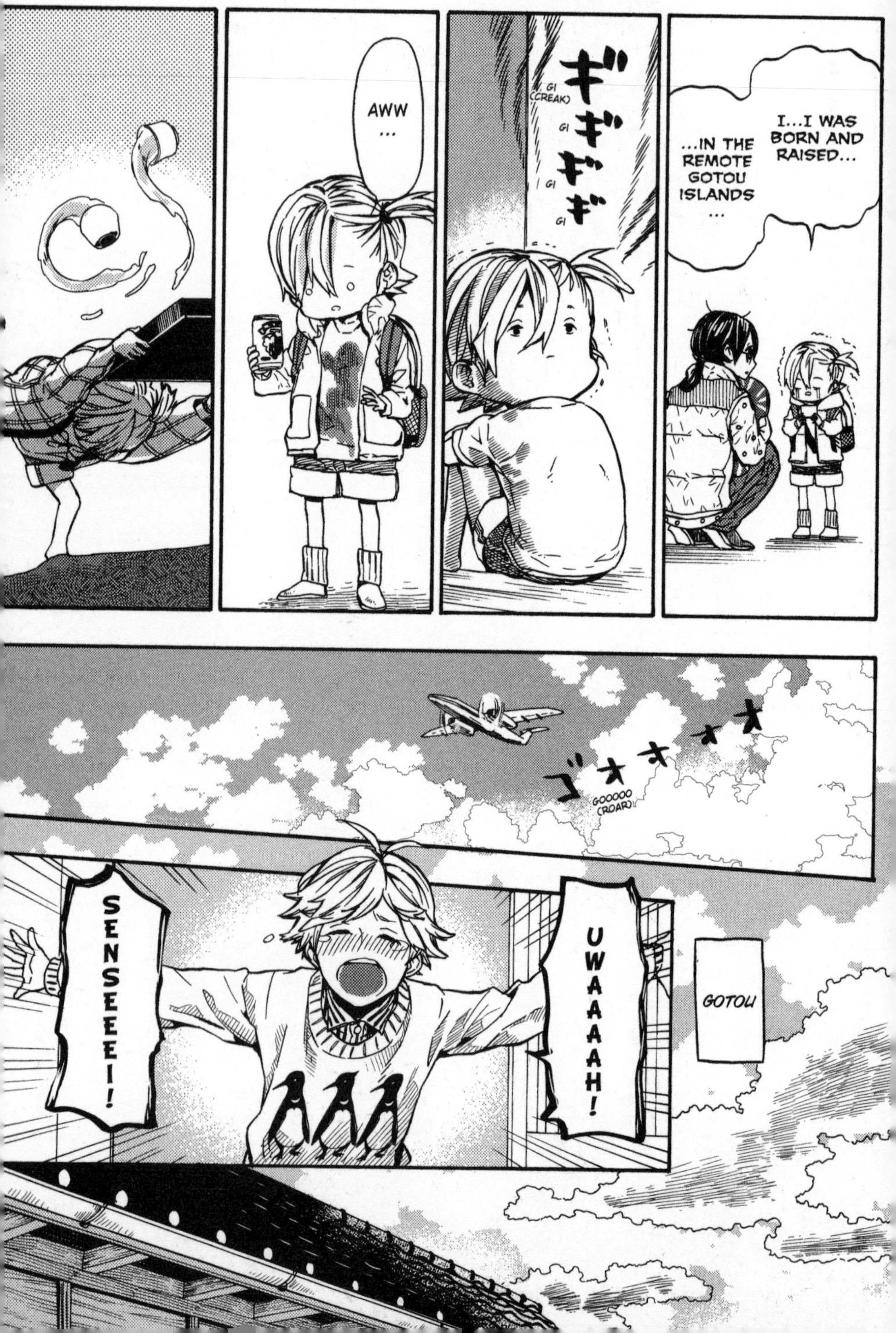
I...I WAS BORN AND RAISED...
...IN THE REMOTE GOTOU ISLANDS ...
ギギギギ
GI (CREAK) GI GI GI
AWW ...
ゴォォォォ
GOOOOO (ROAR)
GOTOU
UWAAAAAH!
SENSEEEI!

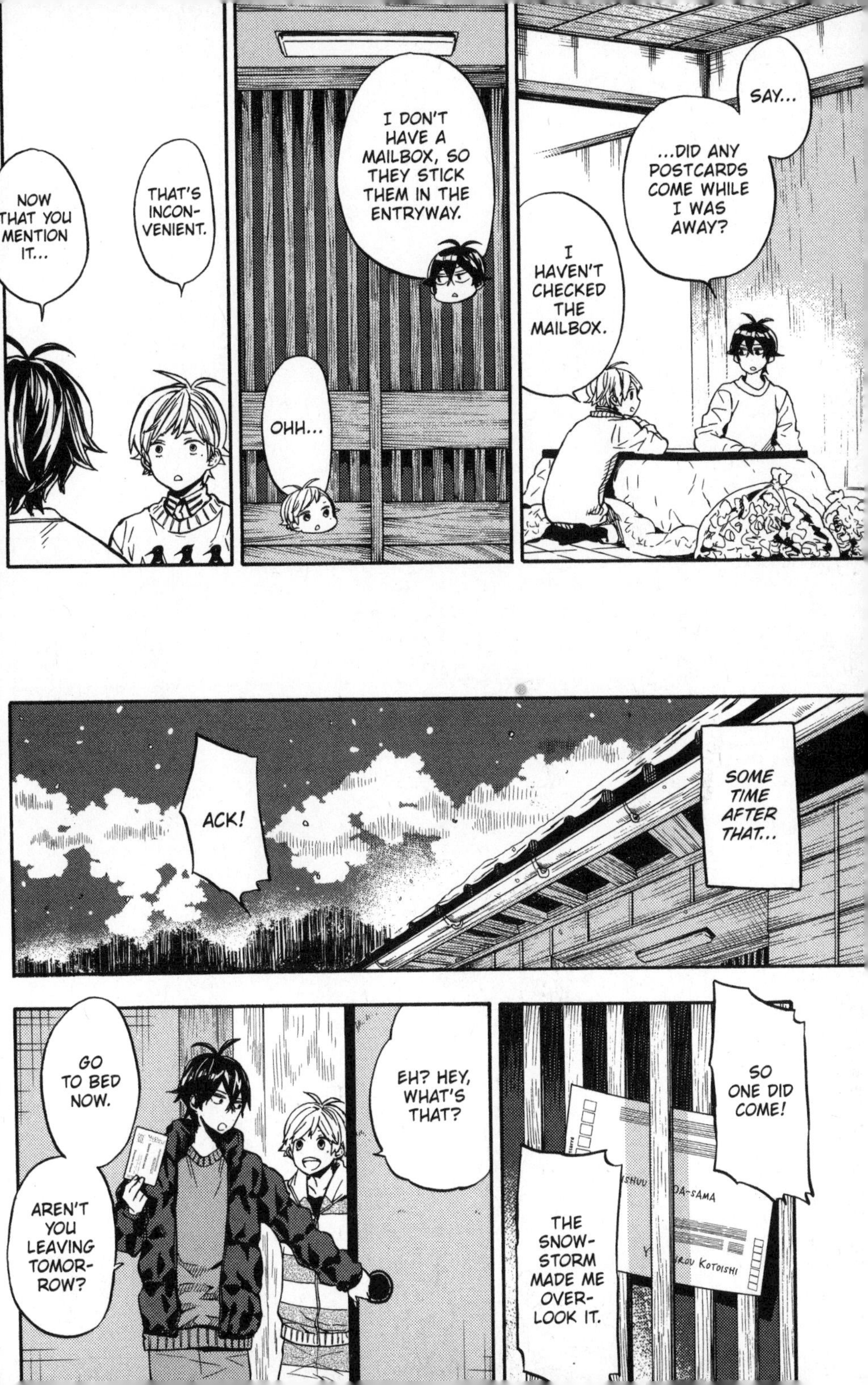
SAY...
...DID ANY POSTCARDS COME WHILE I WAS AWAY?
I HAVEN'T CHECKED THE MAILBOX.
I DON'T HAVE A MAILBOX, SO THEY STICK THEM IN THE ENTRYWAY.
OHH...
THAT'S INCON-VENIENT.
NOW THAT YOU MENTION IT...
SOME TIME AFTER THAT...
ACK!
SO ONE DID COME!
THE SNOW-STORM MADE ME OVER-LOOK IT.
EH? HEY, WHAT'S THAT?
GO TO BED NOW.
AREN'T YOU LEAVING TOMOR-ROW?

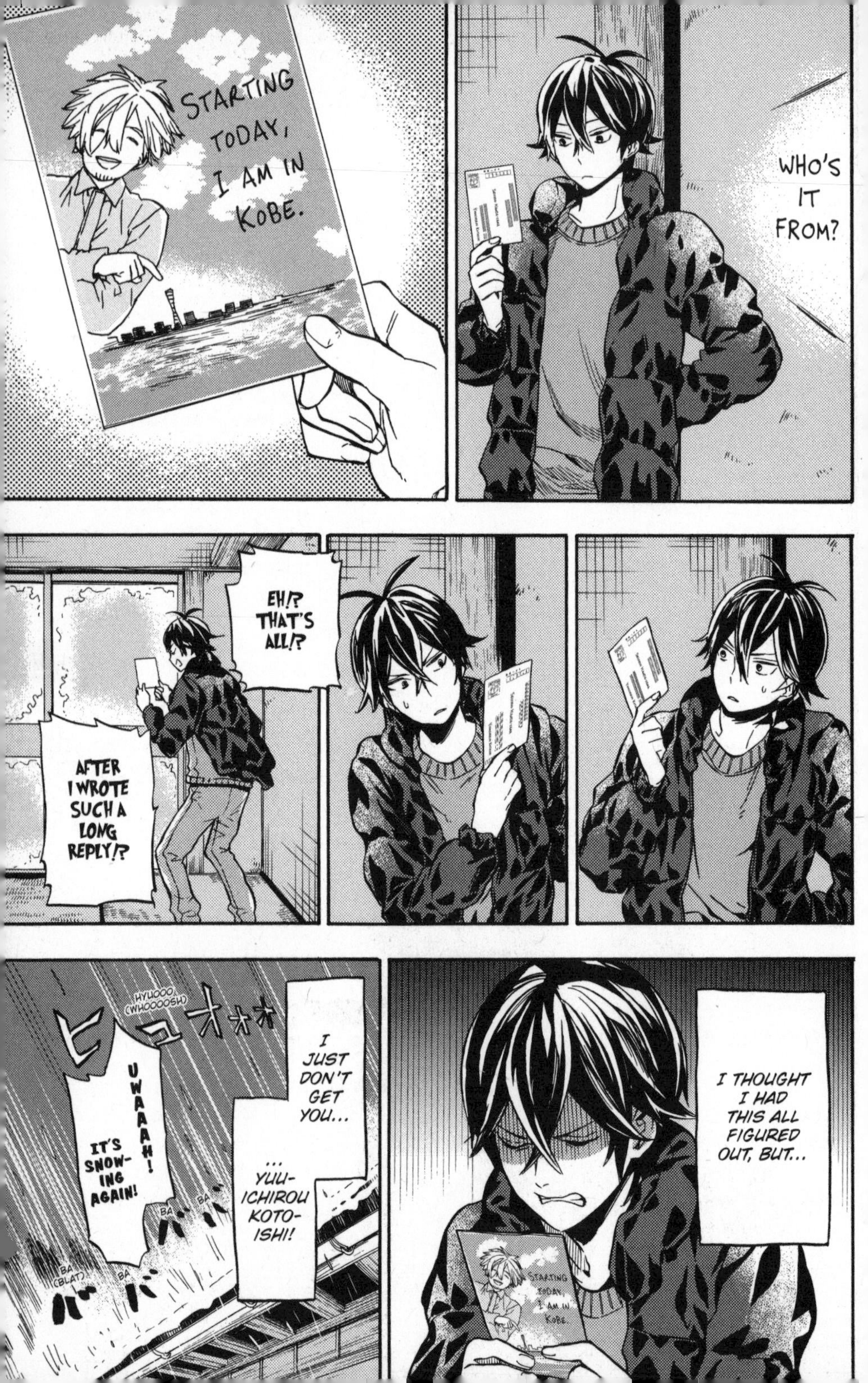
WHO'S IT FROM?
STARTING TODAY, I AM IN KOBE.
EH!? THAT'S ALL!?
AFTER I WROTE SUCH A LONG REPLY!?
I THOUGHT I HAD THIS ALL FIGURED OUT, BUT...
STARTING TODAY, I AM IN KOBE.
I JUST DON'T GET YOU...
...YUU-ICHIROU KOTO-ISHI!
ヒューオォォ
HYUOOO (WHOOOOSH)
UWAAAH! IT'S SNOWING AGAIN!
BA BA
BA (BLAT) BA

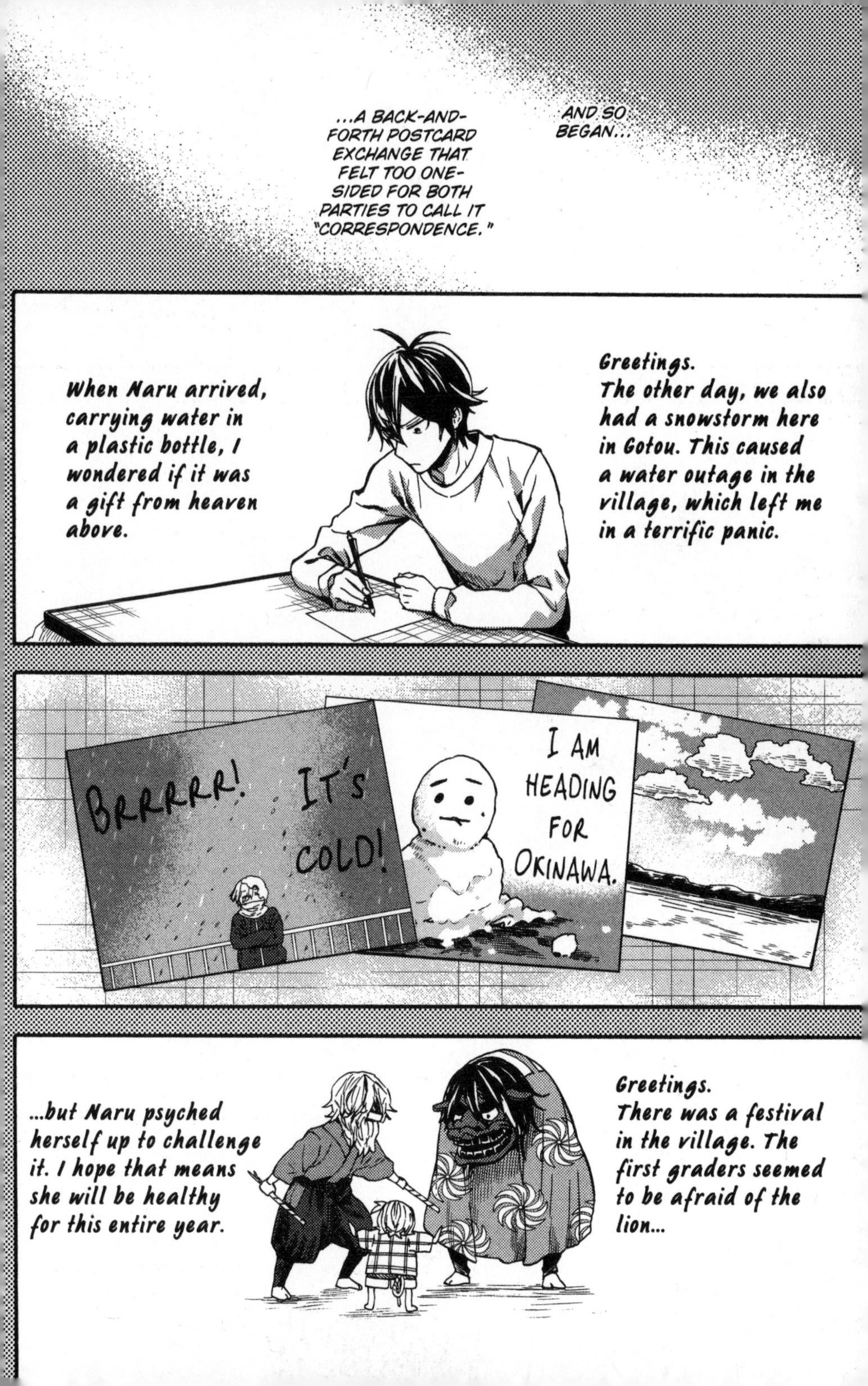
AND SO BEGAN...
...A BACK-AND-FORTH POSTCARD EXCHANGE THAT FELT TOO ONE-SIDED FOR BOTH PARTIES TO CALL IT "CORRESPONDENCE."
Greetings.
The other day, we also had a snowstorm here in Gotou. This caused a water outage in the village, which left me in a terrific panic.
When Naru arrived, carrying water in a plastic bottle, I wondered if it was a gift from heaven above.
I AM HEADING FOR OKINAWA.
BRRRRR! IT'S COLD!
Greetings.
There was a festival in the village. The first graders seemed to be afraid of the lion...
...but Naru psyched herself up to challenge it. I hope that means she will be healthy for this entire year.

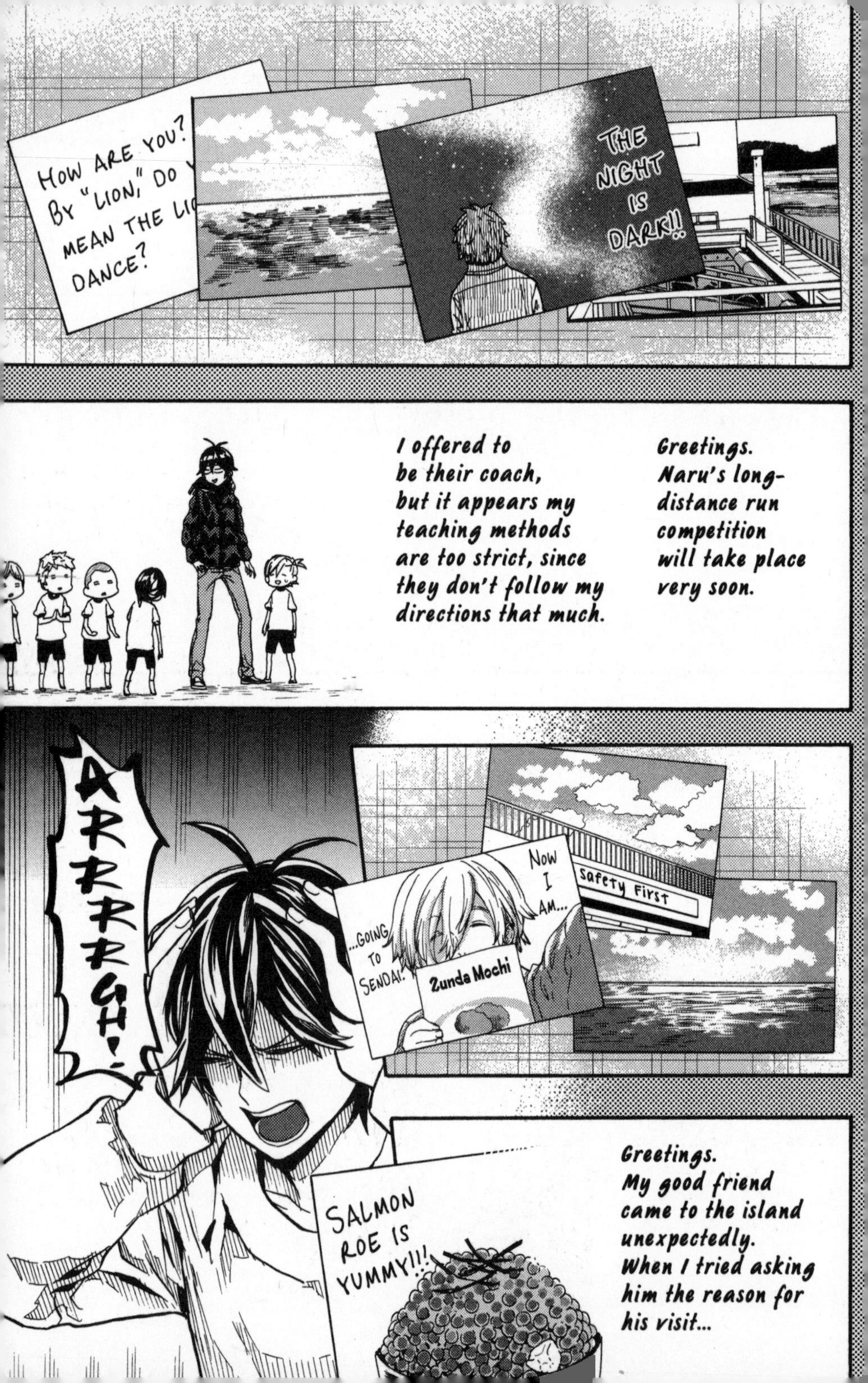
THE NIGHT IS DARK!!
HOW ARE YOU? BY "LION," DO Y
MEAN THE LI
DANCE?
Greetings. Naru's long-distance run competition will take place very soon.
I offered to be their coach, but it appears my teaching methods are too strict, since they don't follow my directions that much.
Safety First
NOW I AM...
...GOING TO SENDAI!
Zunda Mochi
ARRRRGH!
Greetings. My good friend came to the island unexpectedly. When I tried asking him the reason for his visit...
SALMON ROE IS YUMMY!!!

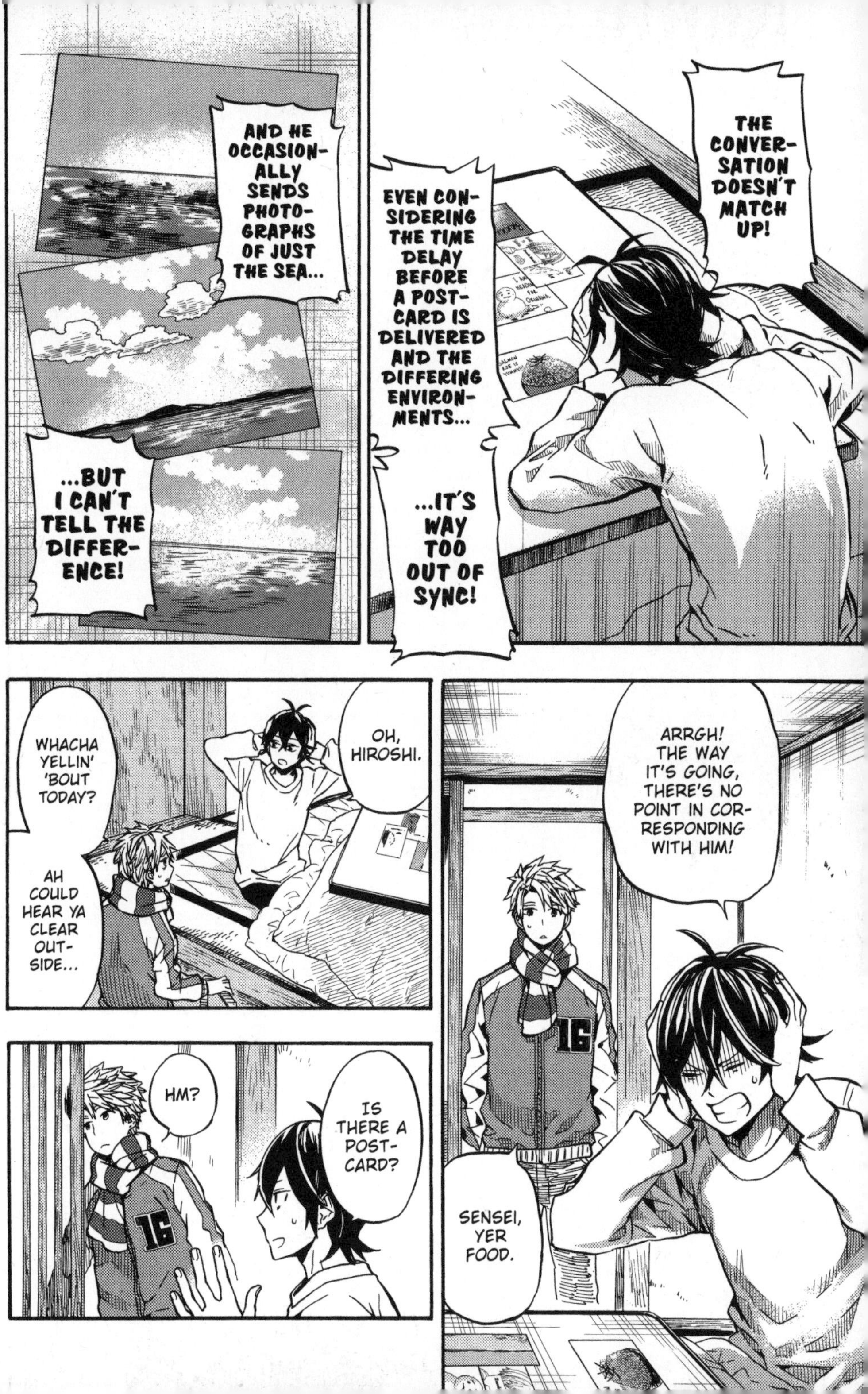
THE CONVERSATION DOESN'T MATCH UP!
EVEN CONSIDERING THE TIME DELAY BEFORE A POSTCARD IS DELIVERED AND THE DIFFERING ENVIRONMENTS...
...IT'S WAY TOO OUT OF SYNC!
AND HE OCCASIONALLY SENDS PHOTOGRAPHS OF JUST THE SEA...
...BUT I CAN'T TELL THE DIFFERENCE!
ARRGH! THE WAY IT'S GOING, THERE'S NO POINT IN CORRESPONDING WITH HIM!
SENSEI, YER FOOD.
OH, HIROSHI.
WHACHA YELLIN' 'BOUT TODAY?
AH COULD HEAR YA CLEAR OUTSIDE...
IS THERE A POSTCARD?
HM?

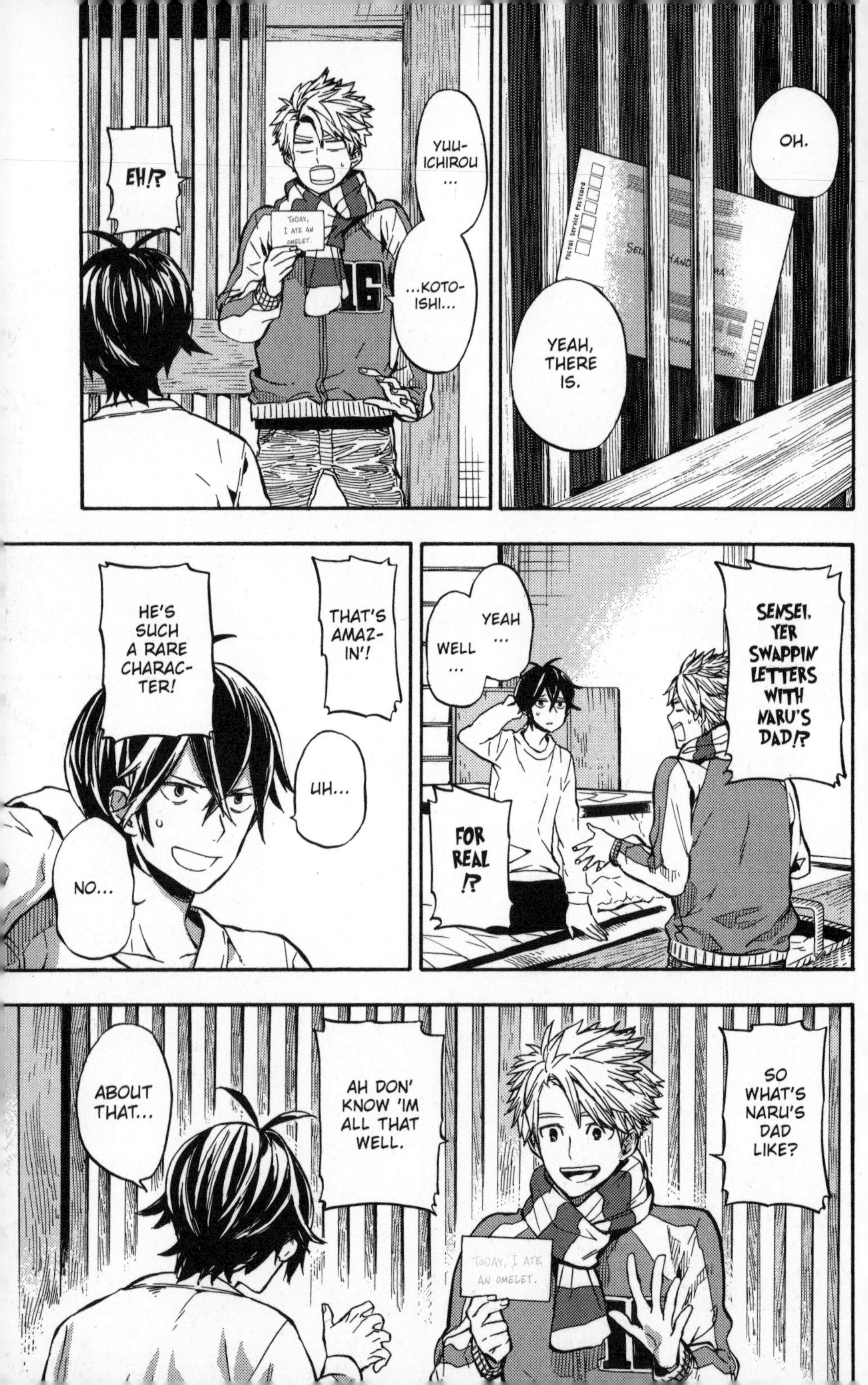
OH.
Postal Service Postcard
YEAH, THERE IS.
YUU-ICHIROU ...
...KOTO-ISHI...
TODAY, I ATE AN OMELET.
EH!?
SENSEI, YER SWAPPIN' LETTERS WITH NARU'S DAD!?
YEAH ... WELL ...
FOR REAL !?
THAT'S AMAZ-IN'!
HE'S SUCH A RARE CHARAC-TER!
UH...
NO...
SO WHAT'S NARU'S DAD LIKE?
TODAY, I ATE AN OMELET.
AH DON' KNOW 'IM ALL THAT WELL.
ABOUT THAT...

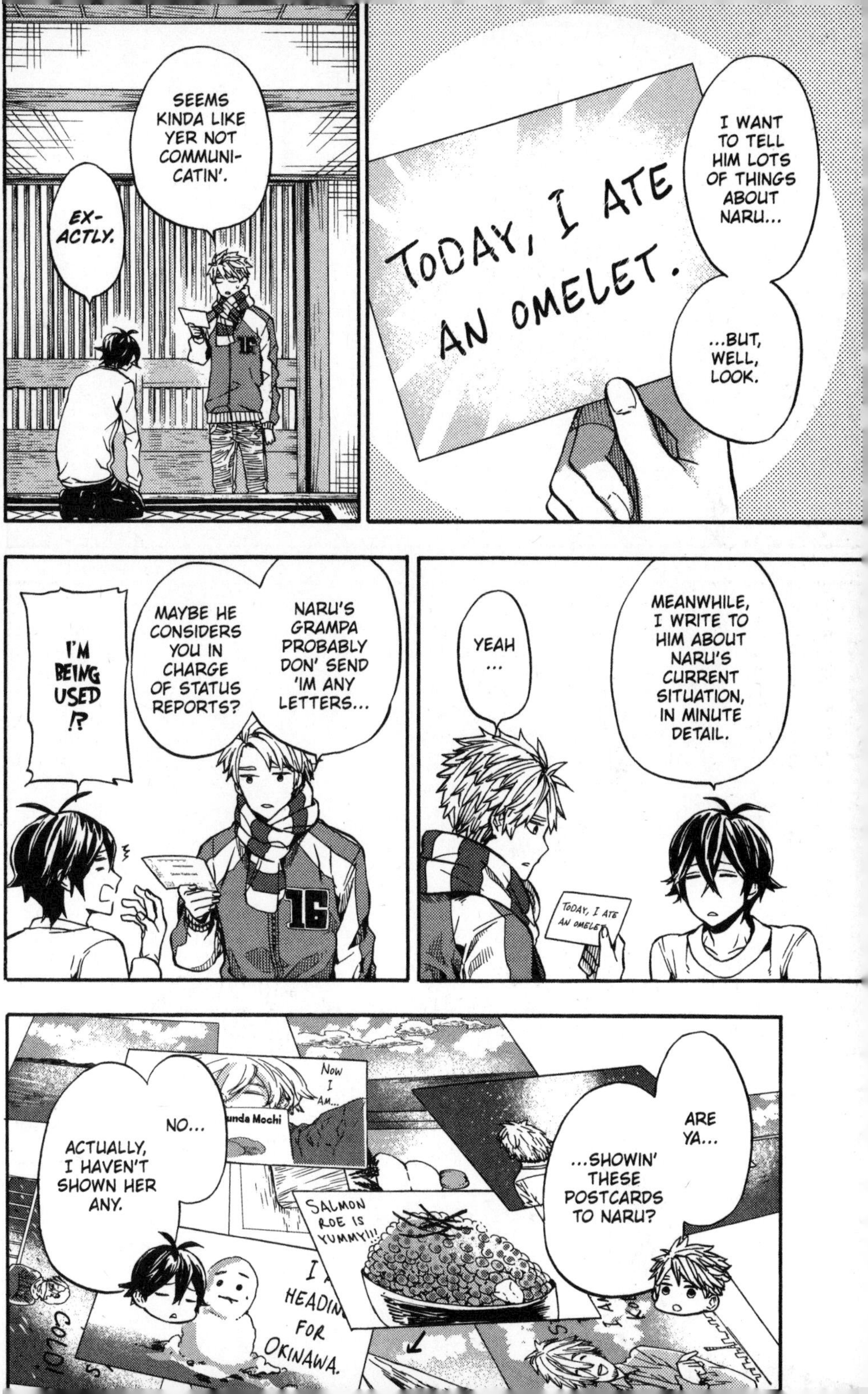
I WANT TO TELL HIM LOTS OF THINGS ABOUT NARU...
...BUT, WELL, LOOK.
TODAY, I ATE AN OMELET.
SEEMS KINDA LIKE YER NOT COMMUNICATIN'.
EXACTLY.
MEANWHILE, I WRITE TO HIM ABOUT NARU'S CURRENT SITUATION, IN MINUTE DETAIL.
YEAH...
TODAY, I ATE AN OMELET
NARU'S GRAMPA PROBABLY DON' SEND 'IM ANY LETTERS...
MAYBE HE CONSIDERS YOU IN CHARGE OF STATUS REPORTS?
I'M BEING USED!?
ARE YA...
...SHOWIN' THESE POSTCARDS TO NARU?
SALMON ROE IS YUMMY!!!
Now I AM...
NO...
ACTUALLY, I HAVEN'T SHOWN HER ANY.

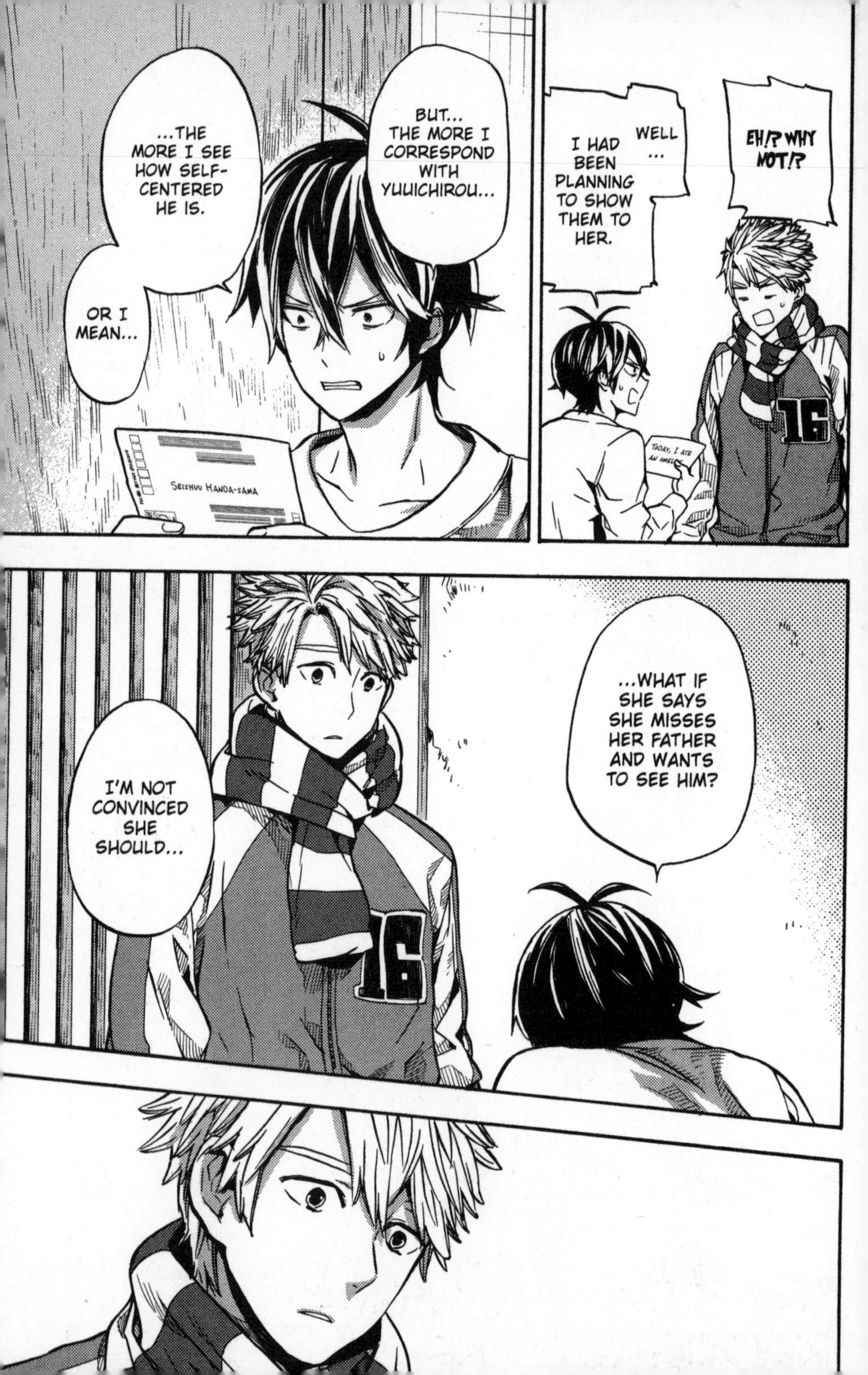
EH!? WHY NOT!?
WELL...
I HAD BEEN PLANNING TO SHOW THEM TO HER.
TODAY, I ATE
BUT... THE MORE I CORRESPOND WITH YUUICHIROU...
...THE MORE I SEE HOW SELF-CENTERED HE IS.
OR I MEAN...
SEISHUU HANDA-SAMA
...WHAT IF SHE SAYS SHE MISSES HER FATHER AND WANTS TO SEE HIM?
I'M NOT CONVINCED SHE SHOULD...

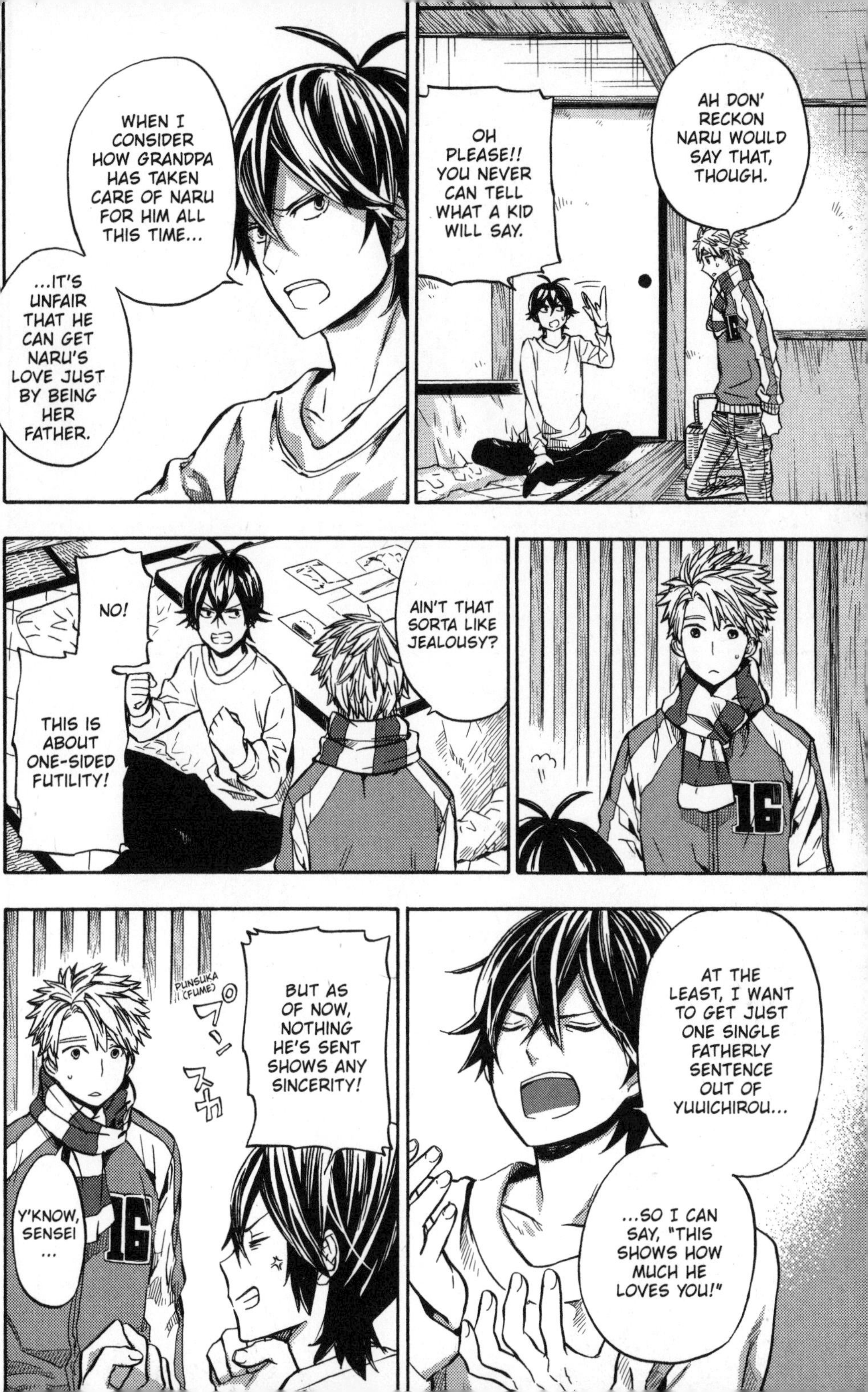
AH DON' RECKON NARU WOULD SAY THAT, THOUGH.
OH PLEASE!! YOU NEVER CAN TELL WHAT A KID WILL SAY.
WHEN I CONSIDER HOW GRANDPA HAS TAKEN CARE OF NARU FOR HIM ALL THIS TIME...
...IT'S UNFAIR THAT HE CAN GET NARU'S LOVE JUST BY BEING HER FATHER.
AIN'T THAT SORTA LIKE JEALOUSY?
NO!
THIS IS ABOUT ONE-SIDED FUTILITY!
AT THE LEAST, I WANT TO GET JUST ONE SINGLE FATHERLY SENTENCE OUT OF YUUICHIROU...
...SO I CAN SAY, "THIS SHOWS HOW MUCH HE LOVES YOU!"
BUT AS OF NOW, NOTHING HE'S SENT SHOWS ANY SINCERITY!
PUNSUKA (FUME)
Y'KNOW, SENSEI ...

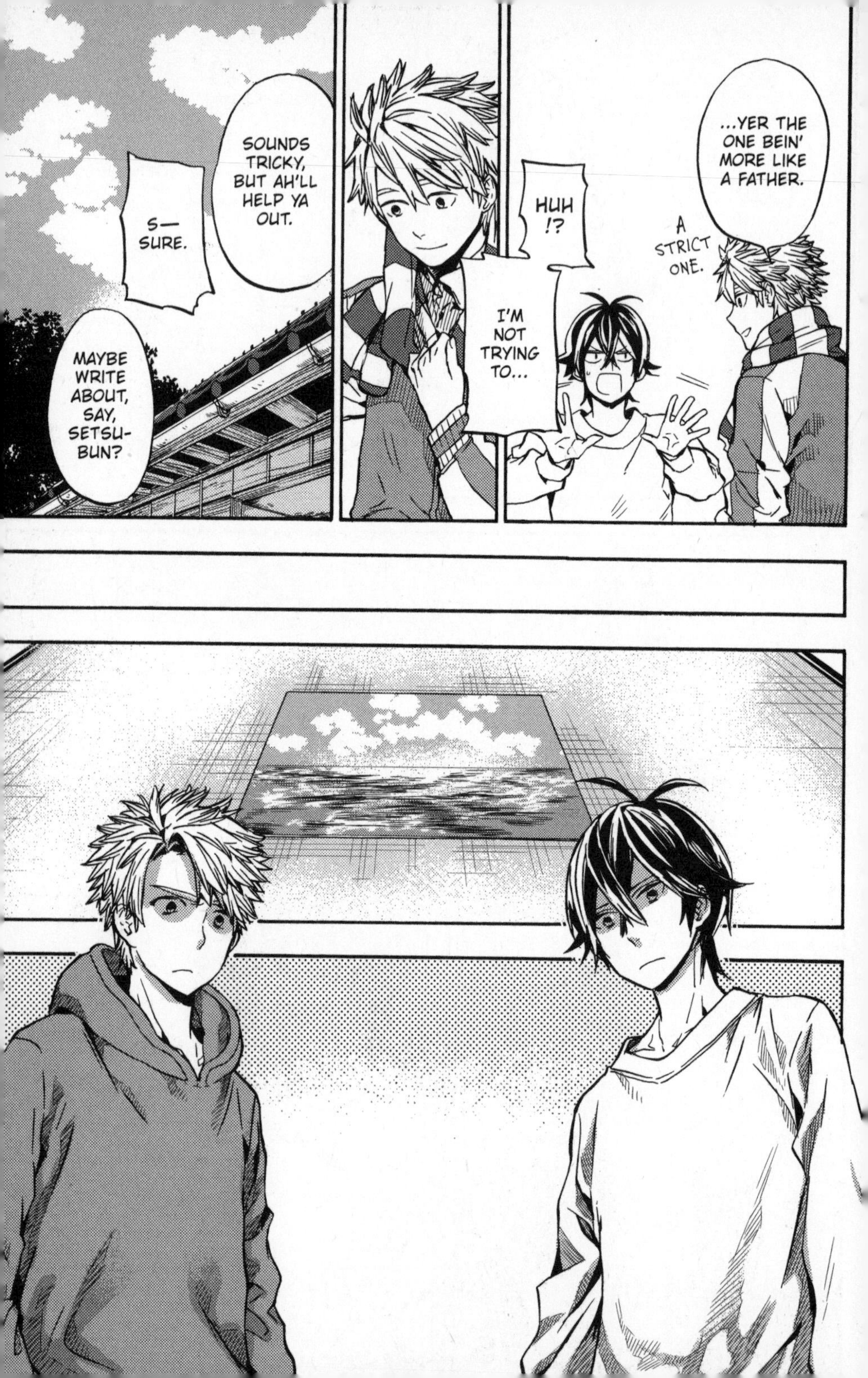
...YER THE ONE BEIN' MORE LIKE A FATHER.
A STRICT ONE.
HUH!?
I'M NOT TRYING TO...
SOUNDS TRICKY, BUT AH'LL HELP YA OUT.
S— SURE.
MAYBE WRITE ABOUT, SAY, SETSUBUN?

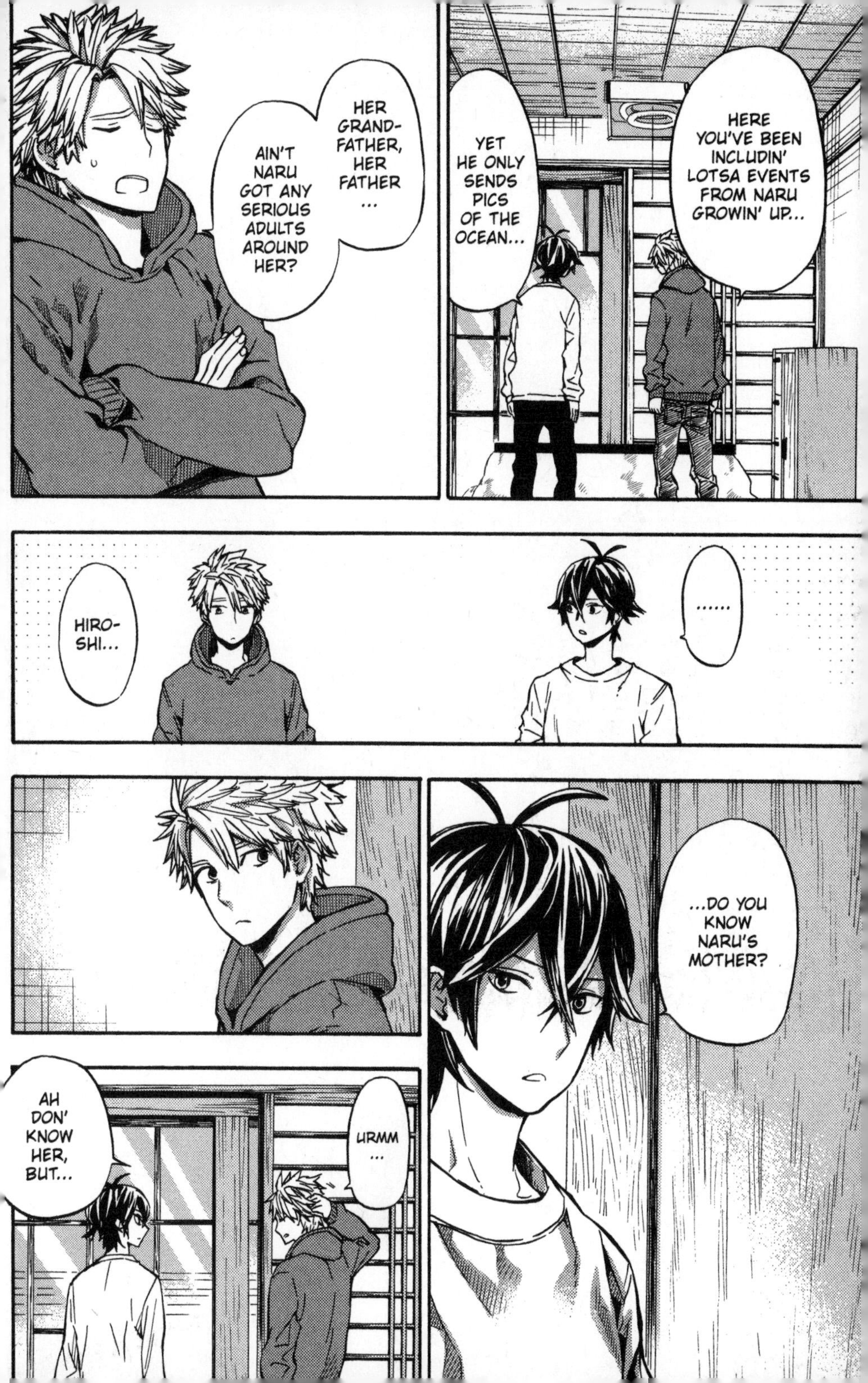
HERE YOU'VE BEEN INCLUDIN' LOTSA EVENTS FROM NARU GROWIN' UP...
YET HE ONLY SENDS PICS OF THE OCEAN...
HER GRAND-FATHER, HER FATHER...
AIN'T NARU GOT ANY SERIOUS ADULTS AROUND HER?
......
HIRO-SHI...
...DO YOU KNOW NARU'S MOTHER?
URMM...
AH DON' KNOW HER, BUT...

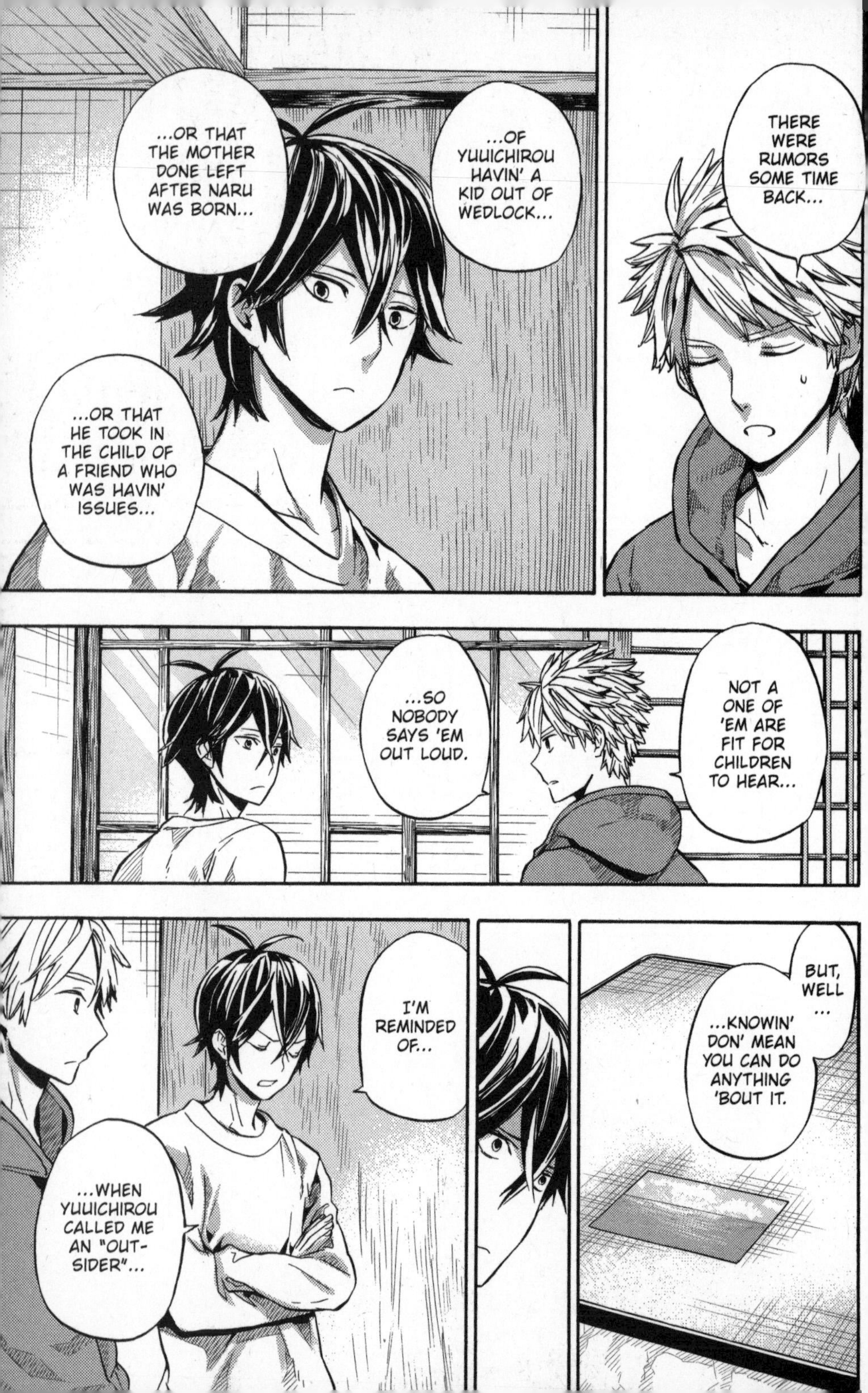
THERE WERE RUMORS SOME TIME BACK...
...OF YUUICHIROU HAVIN' A KID OUT OF WEDLOCK...
...OR THAT THE MOTHER DONE LEFT AFTER NARU WAS BORN...
...OR THAT HE TOOK IN THE CHILD OF A FRIEND WHO WAS HAVIN' ISSUES...
NOT A ONE OF 'EM ARE FIT FOR CHILDREN TO HEAR...
...SO NOBODY SAYS 'EM OUT LOUD.
BUT, WELL ...
...KNOWIN' DON' MEAN YOU CAN DO ANYTHING 'BOUT IT.
I'M REMINDED OF...
...WHEN YUUICHIROU CALLED ME AN "OUT-SIDER"...

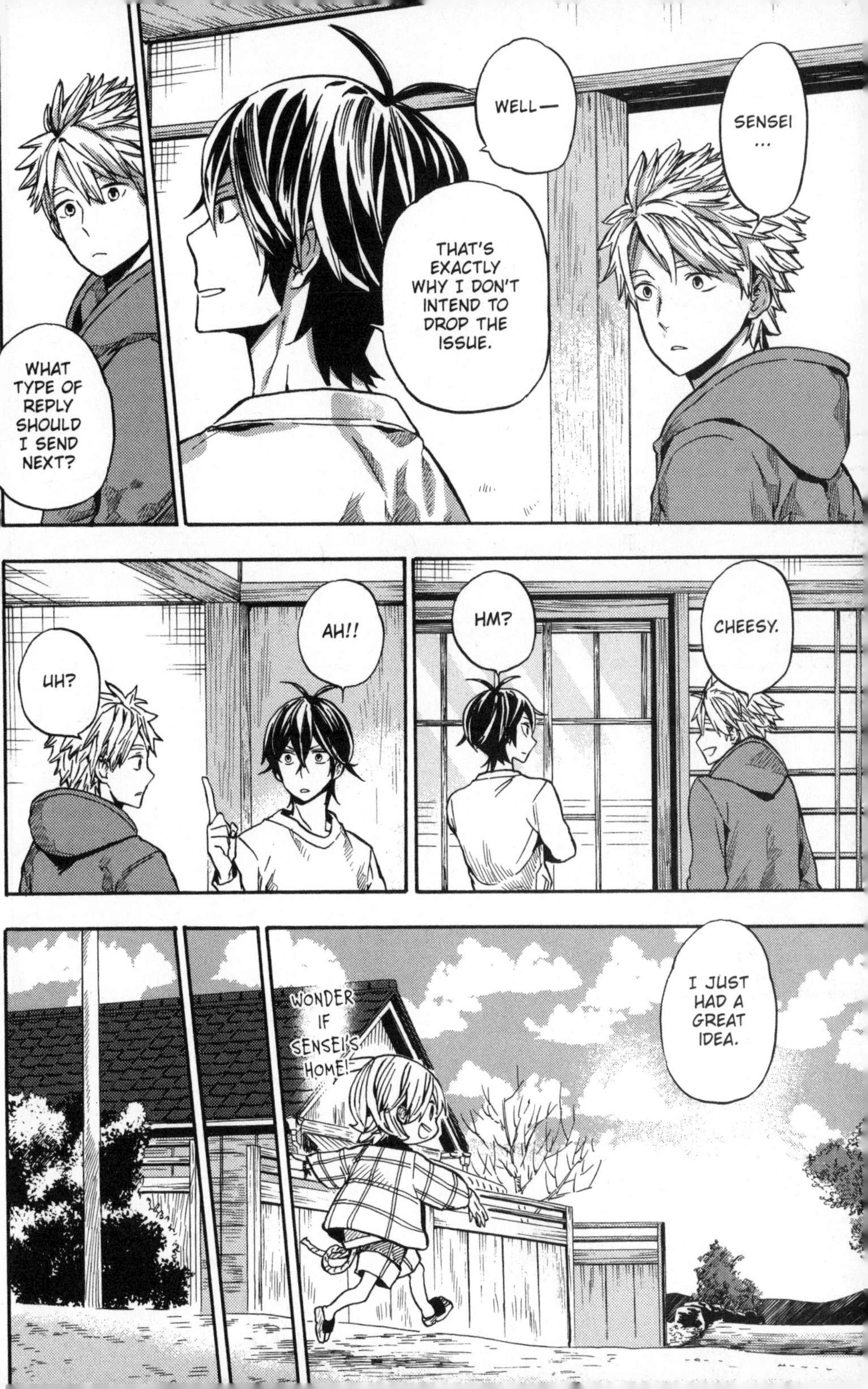
SENSEI...
WELL—
THAT'S EXACTLY WHY I DON'T INTEND TO DROP THE ISSUE.
WHAT TYPE OF REPLY SHOULD I SEND NEXT?
CHEESY.
HM?
AH!!
UH?
I JUST HAD A GREAT IDEA.
WONDER IF SENSEI'S HOME!

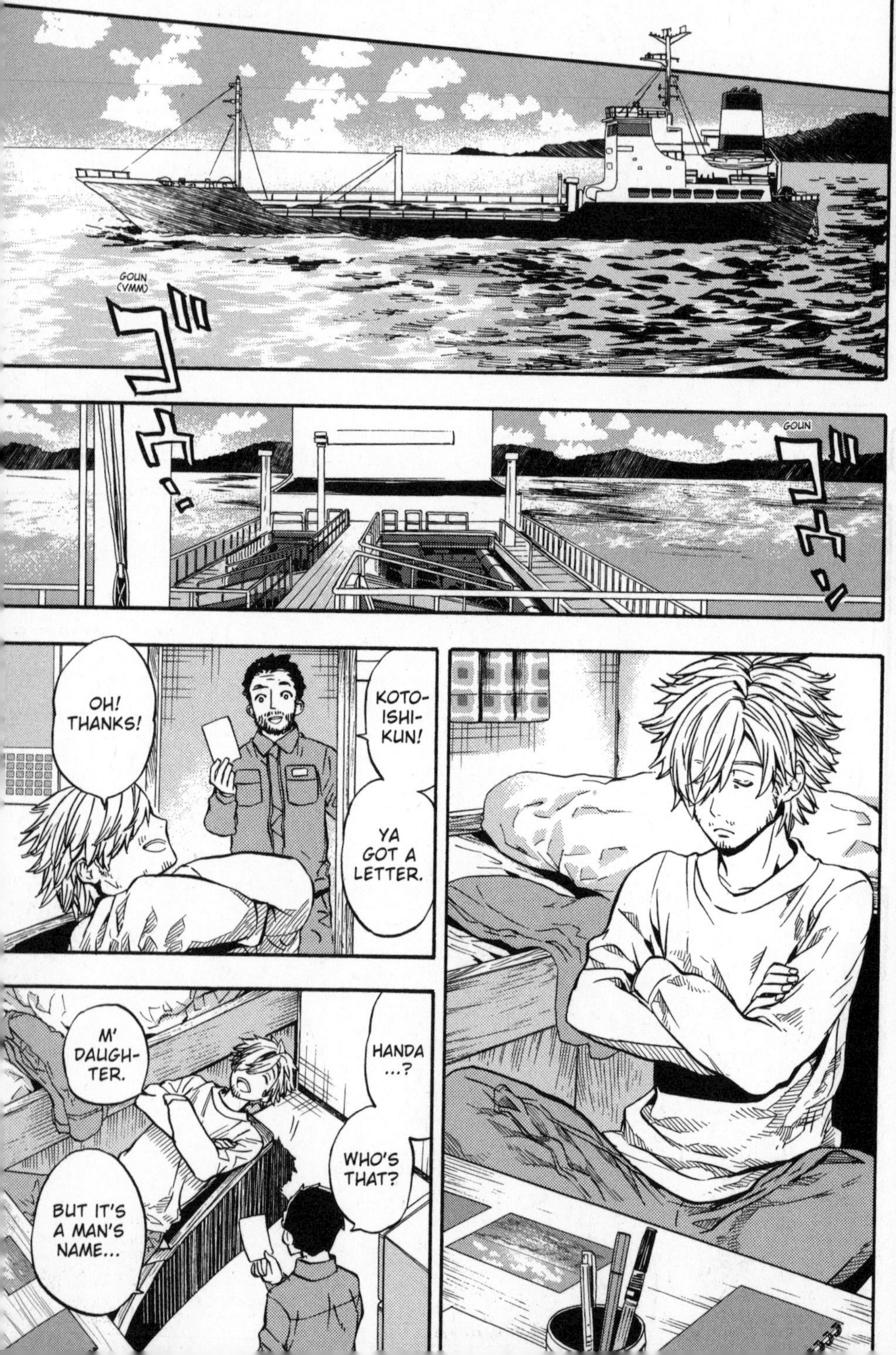
GOUN (VMM)
GOUN
KOTO-ISHI-KUN!
YA GOT A LETTER.
OH! THANKS!
HANDA ...?
WHO'S THAT?
M' DAUGHTER.
BUT IT'S A MAN'S NAME...

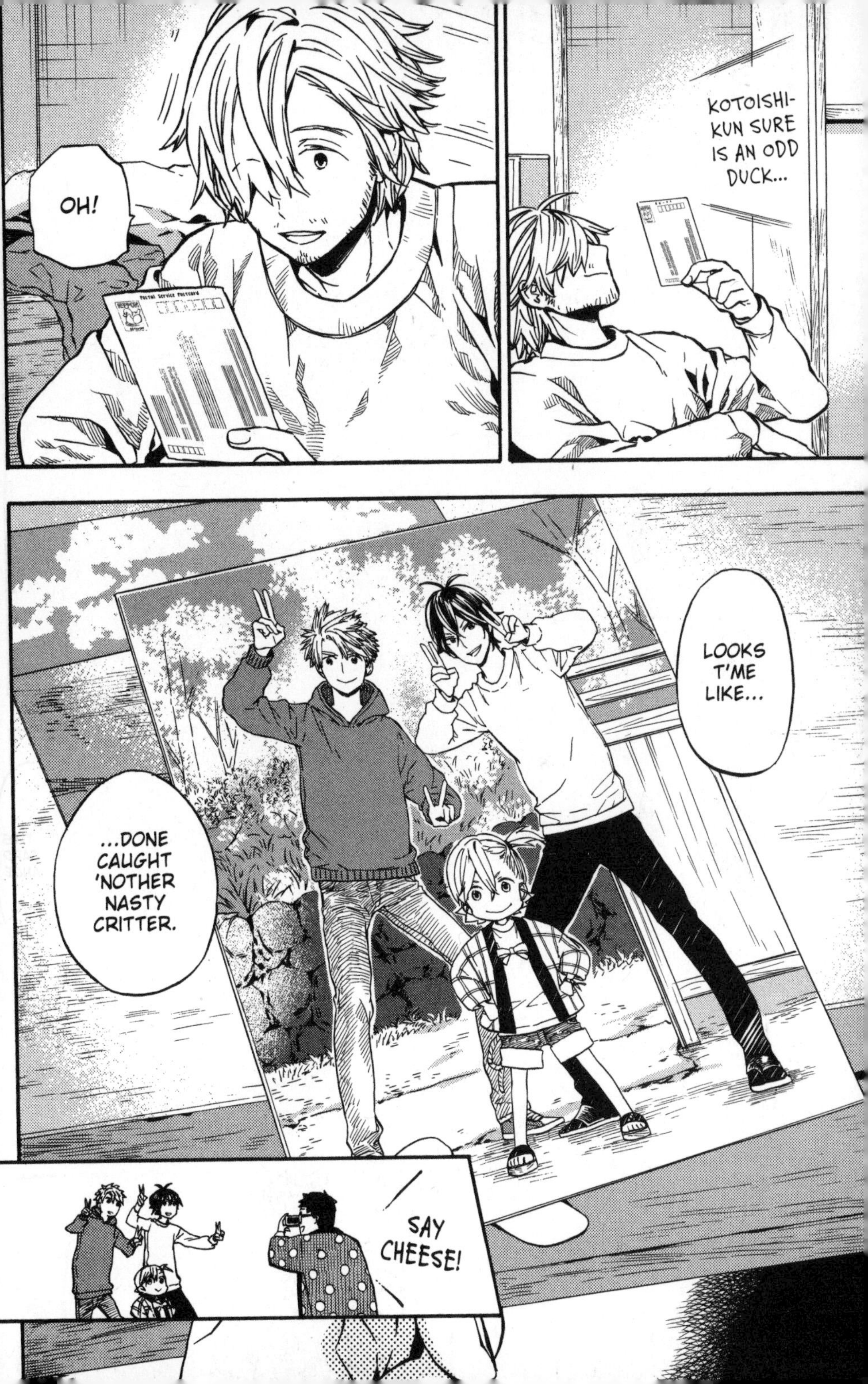
KOTOISHI-KUN SURE IS AN ODD DUCK...
OH!
LOOKS T'ME LIKE...
...DONE CAUGHT 'NOTHER NASTY CRITTER.
SAY CHEESE!

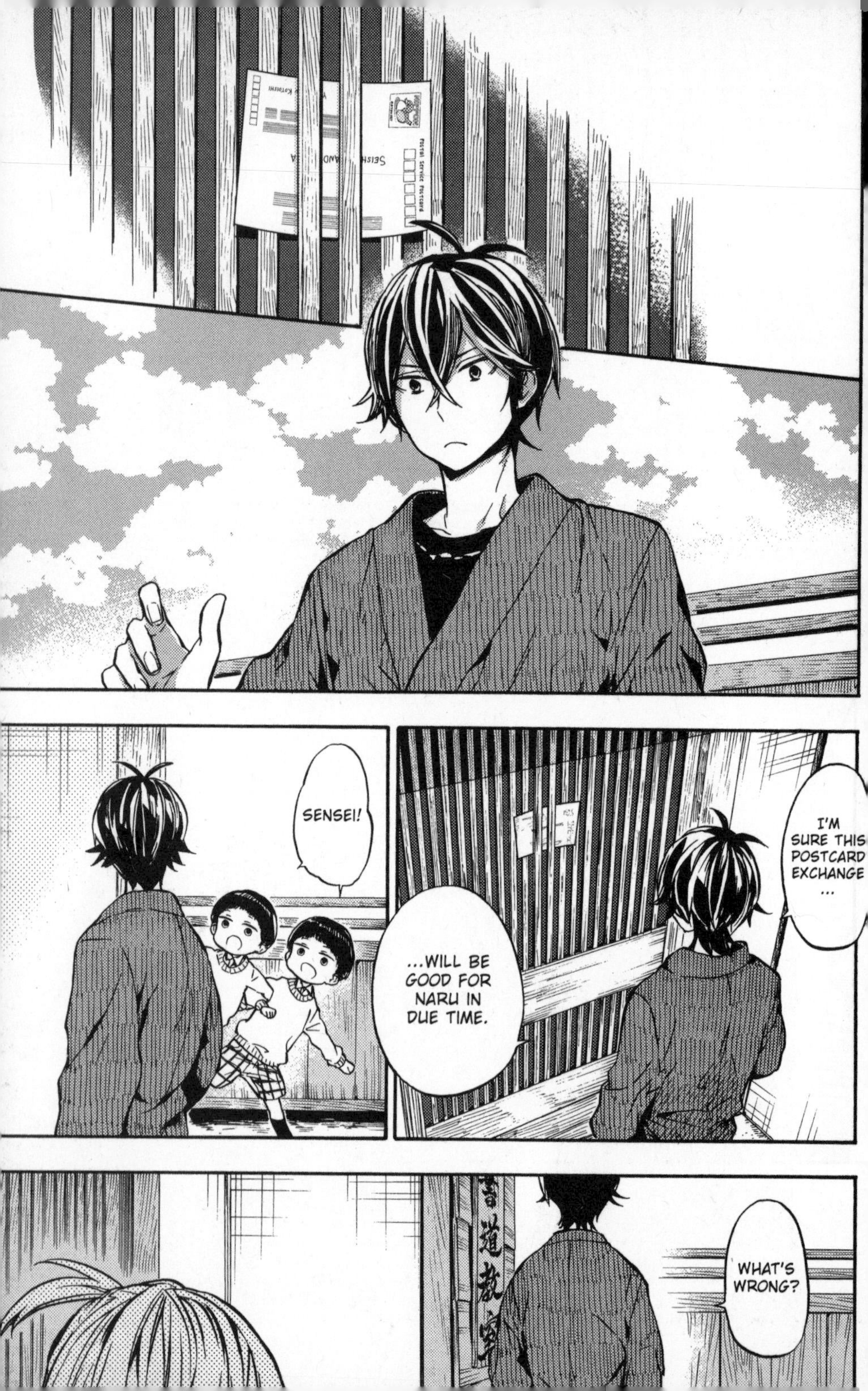
I'M SURE THIS POSTCARD EXCHANGE ...
...WILL BE GOOD FOR NARU IN DUE TIME.
SENSEI!
WHAT'S WRONG?

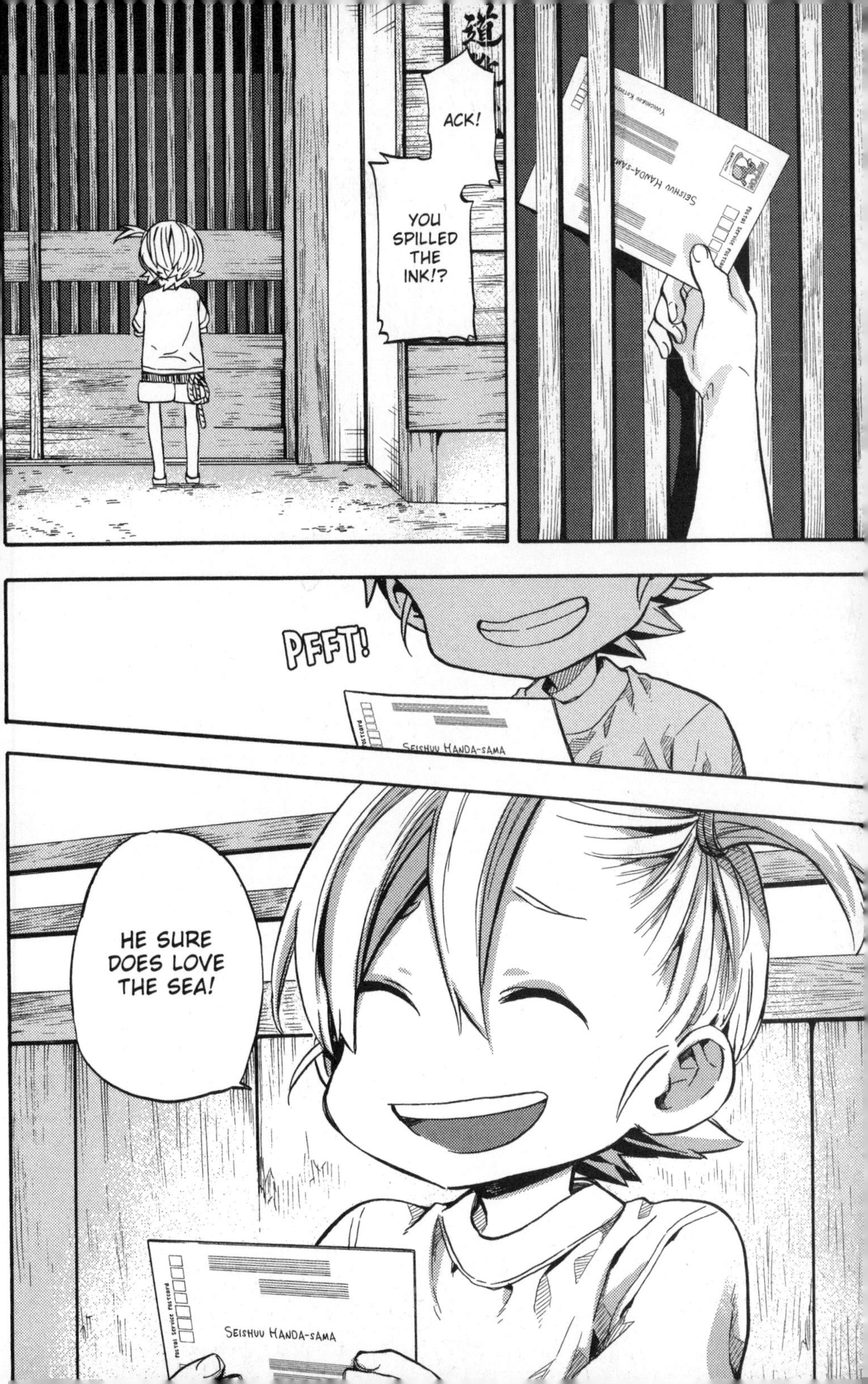
ACK!
YOU SPILLED THE INK!?
PFFT!
Seishuu Handa-sama
HE SURE DOES LOVE THE SEA!
Seishuu Handa-sama

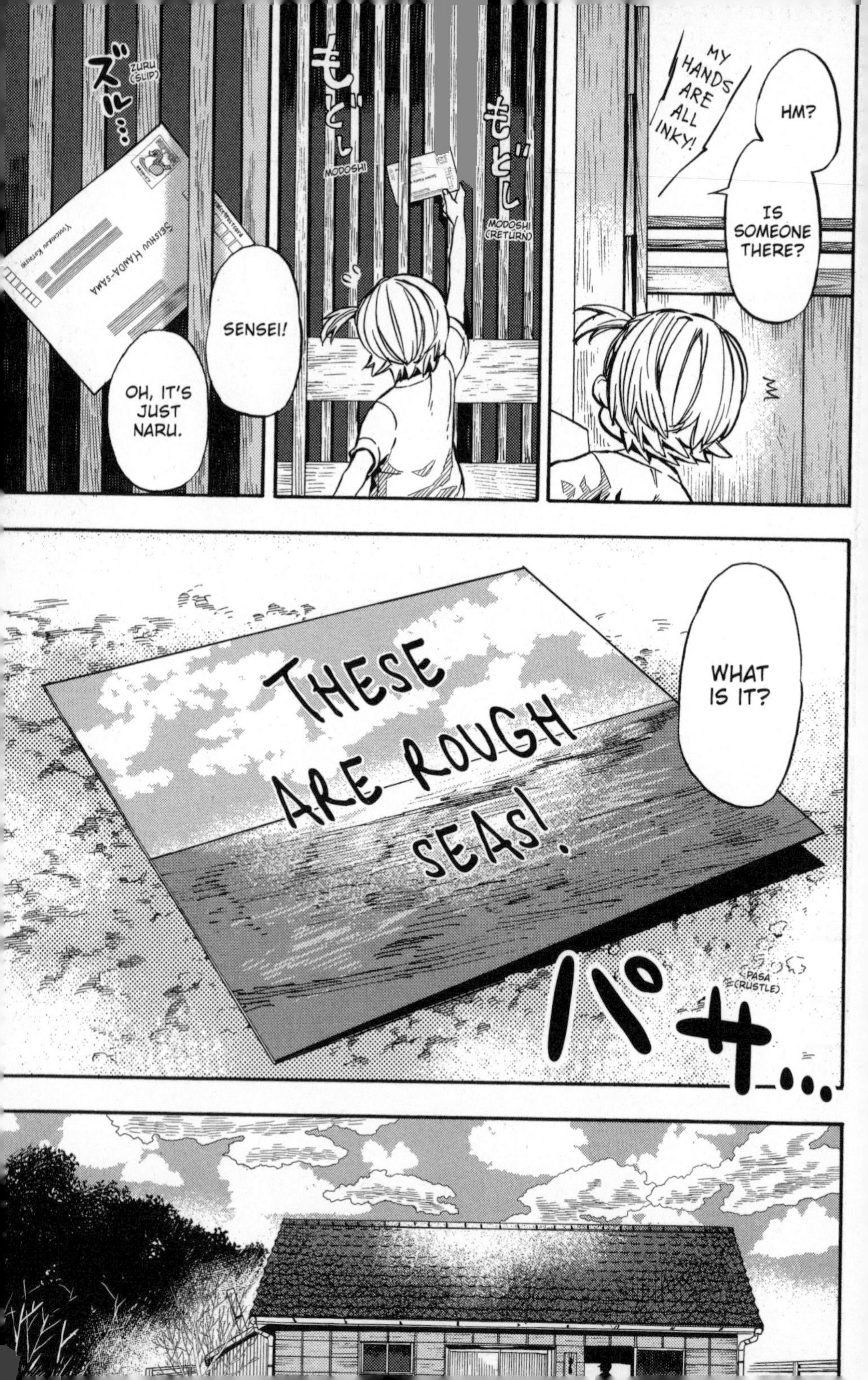
HM? IS SOMEONE THERE?
MY HANDS ARE ALL INKY!
もどし
MODOSHI (RETURN)
もどし
MODOSHI
SENSEI!
ズル…
ZURU (SLIP)
SEISHUU HANDA-SAMA
OH, IT'S JUST NARU.
WHAT IS IT?
THESE ARE ROUGH SEAS!
パサ…
PASA (RUSTLE)

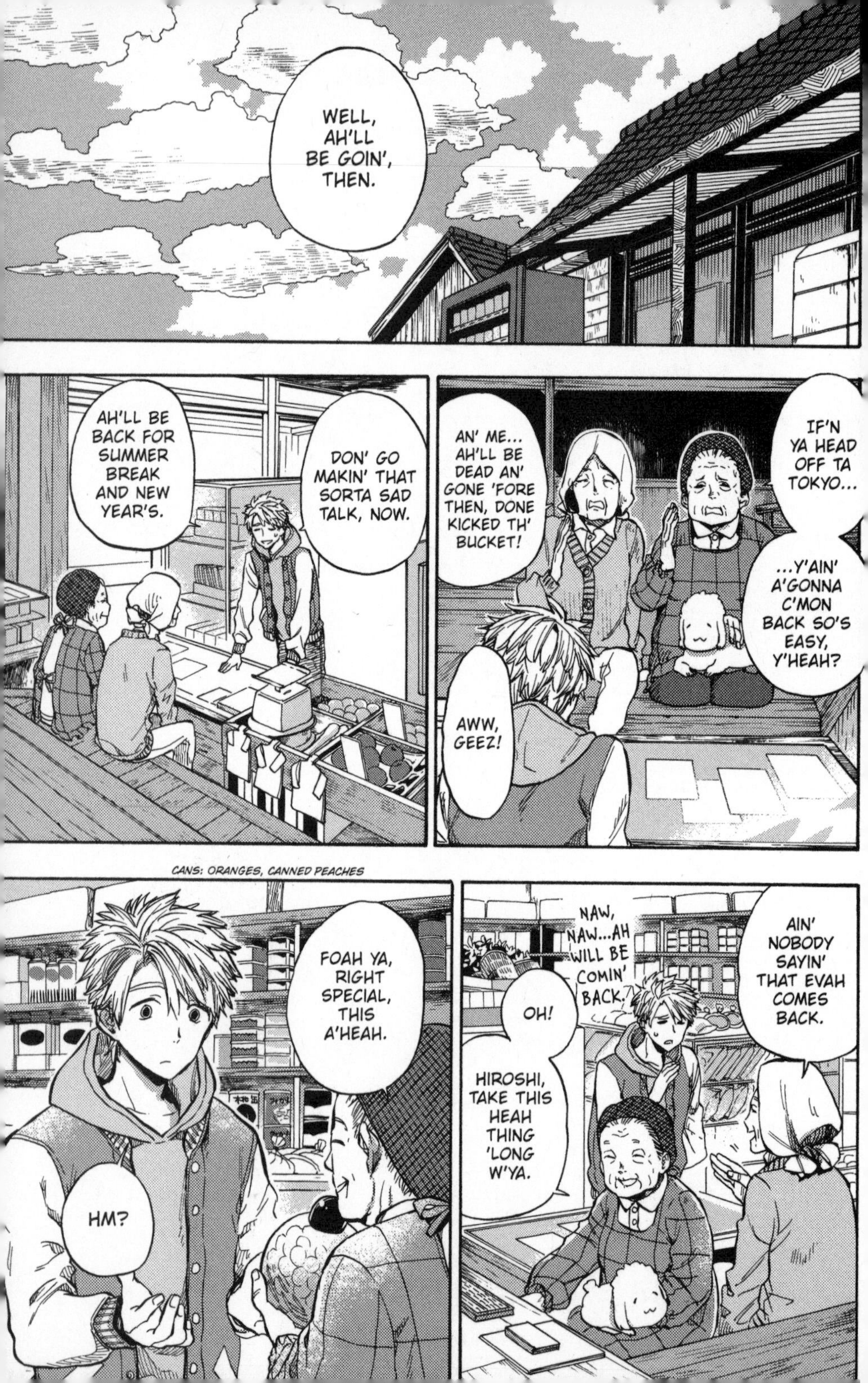
WELL, AH'LL BE GOIN', THEN.
IF'N YA HEAD OFF TA TOKYO...
...Y'AIN' A'GONNA C'MON BACK SO'S EASY, Y'HEAH?
AN' ME... AH'LL BE DEAD AN' GONE 'FORE THEN, DONE KICKED TH' BUCKET!
AWW, GEEZ!
DON' GO MAKIN' THAT SORTA SAD TALK, NOW.
AH'LL BE BACK FOR SUMMER BREAK AND NEW YEAR'S.
AIN' NOBODY SAYIN' THAT EVAH COMES BACK.
NAW, NAW...AH WILL BE COMIN' BACK.
OH!
HIROSHI, TAKE THIS HEAH THING 'LONG W'YA.
CANS: ORANGES, CANNED PEACHES
FOAH YA, RIGHT SPECIAL, THIS A'HEAH.
HM?

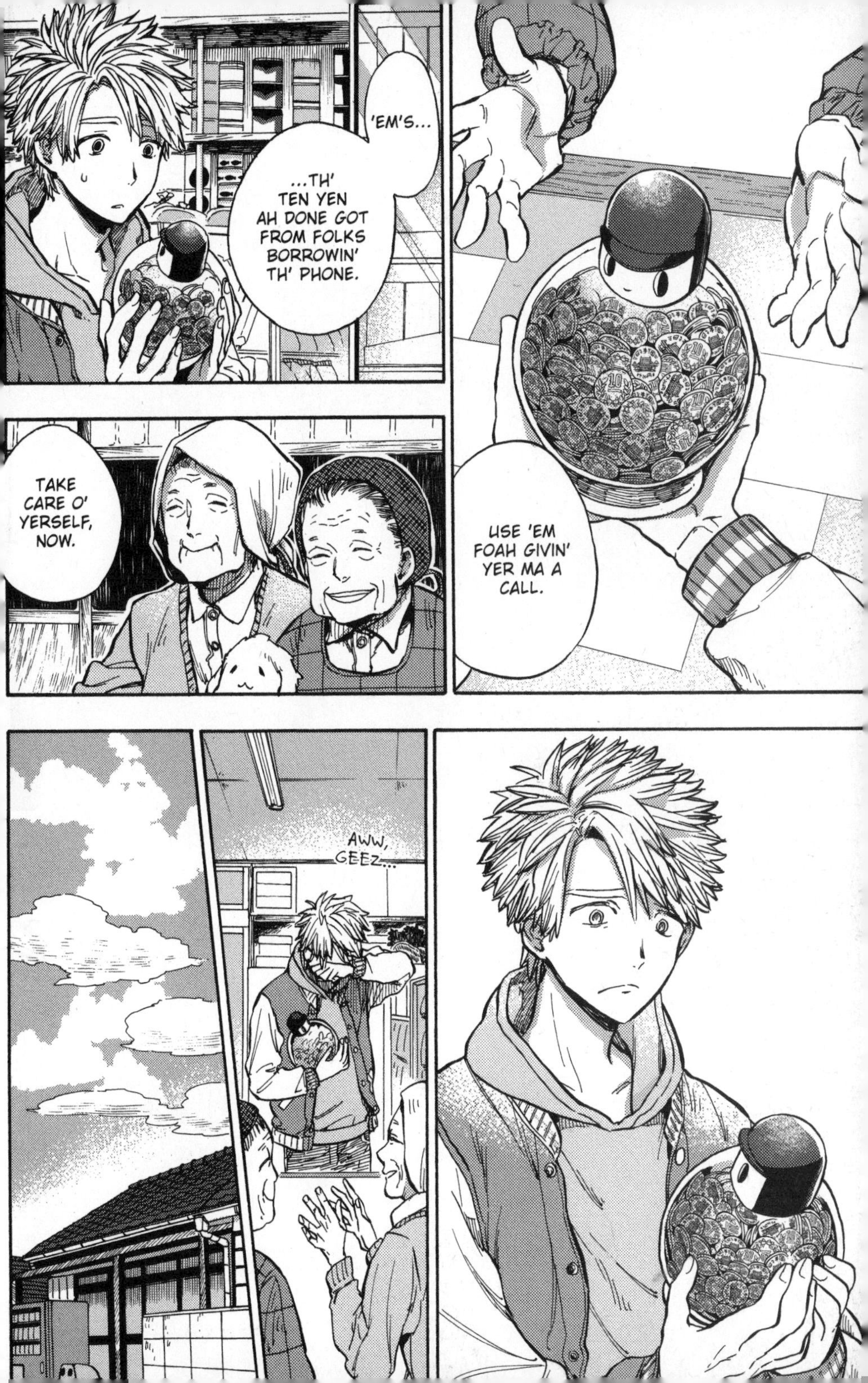
USE 'EM FOAH GIVIN' YER MA A CALL.
'EM'S...
...TH' TEN YEN AH DONE GOT FROM FOLKS BORROWIN' TH' PHONE.
TAKE CARE O' YERSELF, NOW.
AWW, GEEZ...

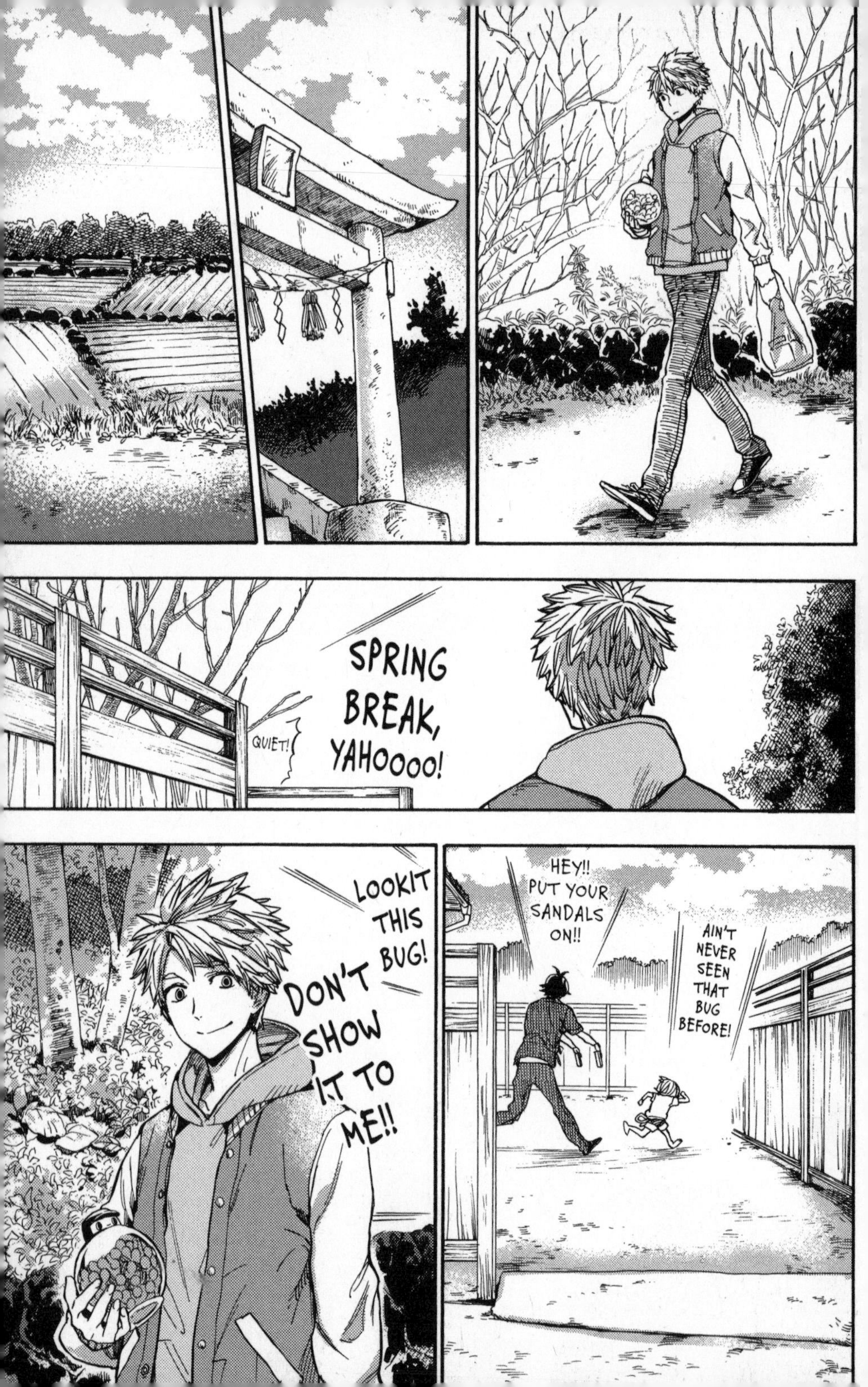
SPRING BREAK, YAHOOOO!
QUIET!
AIN'T NEVER SEEN THAT BUG BEFORE!
HEY!! PUT YOUR SANDALS ON!!
LOOKIT THIS BUG!
DON'T SHOW IT TO ME!!

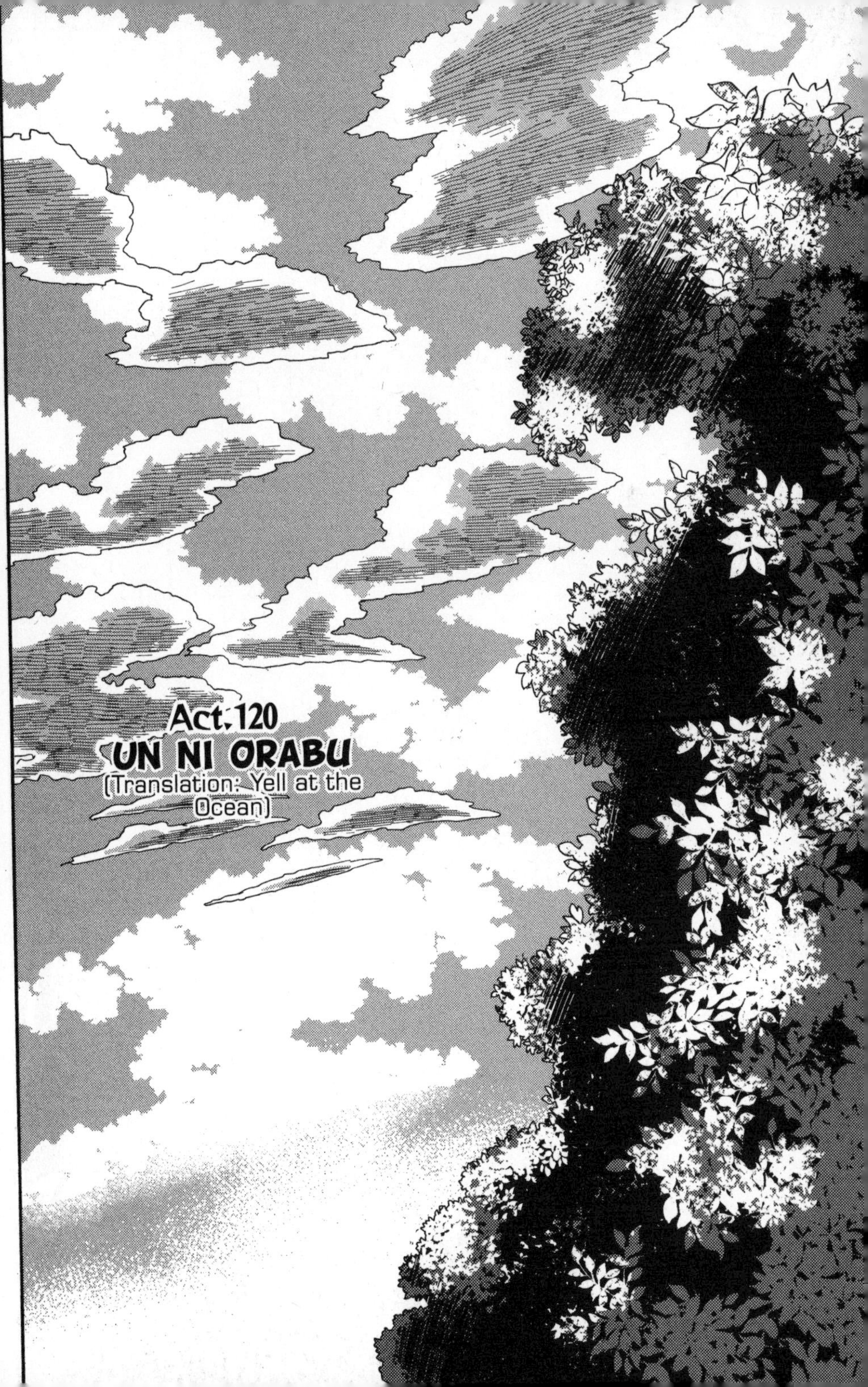
Act. 120
UN NI ORABU
(Translation: Yell at the Ocean)

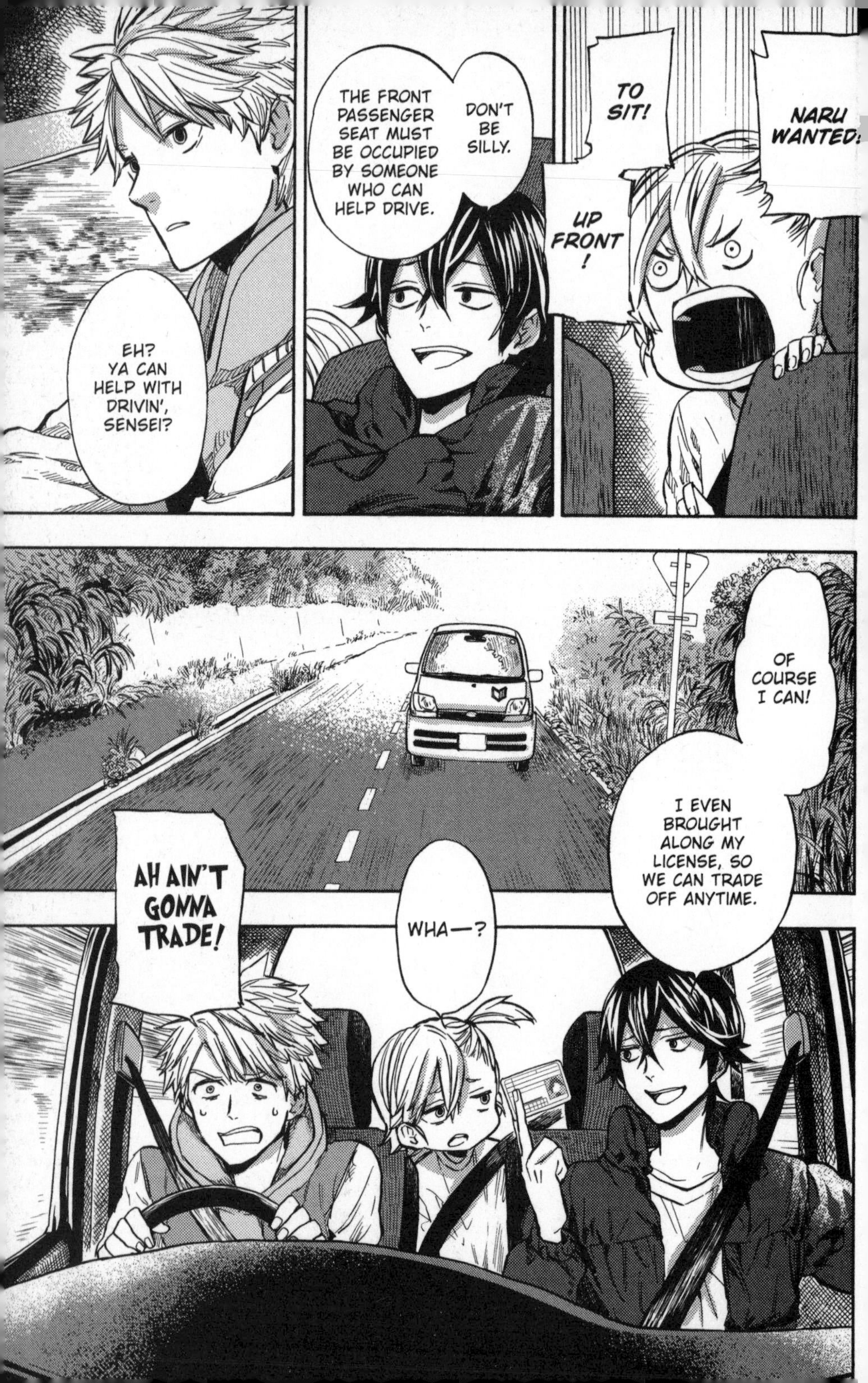
NARU WANTED!
TO SIT!
UP FRONT!
DON'T BE SILLY.
THE FRONT PASSENGER SEAT MUST BE OCCUPIED BY SOMEONE WHO CAN HELP DRIVE.
EH? YA CAN HELP WITH DRIVIN', SENSEI?
OF COURSE I CAN!
I EVEN BROUGHT ALONG MY LICENSE, SO WE CAN TRADE OFF ANYTIME.
WHA—?
AH AIN'T GONNA TRADE!

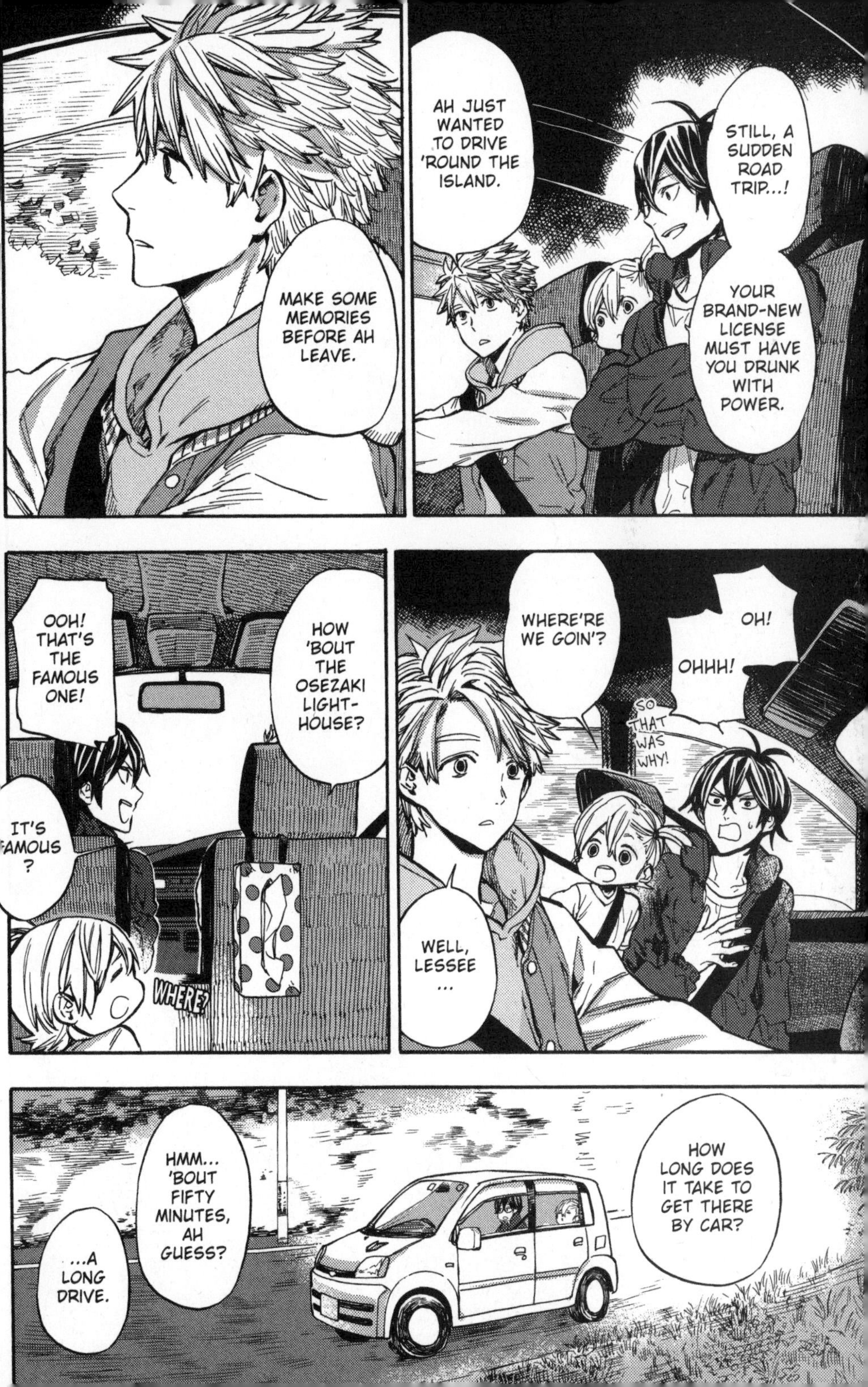
STILL, A SUDDEN ROAD TRIP...!
YOUR BRAND-NEW LICENSE MUST HAVE YOU DRUNK WITH POWER.
AH JUST WANTED TO DRIVE 'ROUND THE ISLAND.
MAKE SOME MEMORIES BEFORE AH LEAVE.
OH!
OHHH!
SO THAT WAS WHY!
WHERE'RE WE GOIN'?
WELL, LESSEE ...
HOW 'BOUT THE OSEZAKI LIGHT-HOUSE?
OOH! THAT'S THE FAMOUS ONE!
IT'S FAMOUS ?
WHERE?
HOW LONG DOES IT TAKE TO GET THERE BY CAR?
HMM... 'BOUT FIFTY MINUTES, AH GUESS?
...A LONG DRIVE.

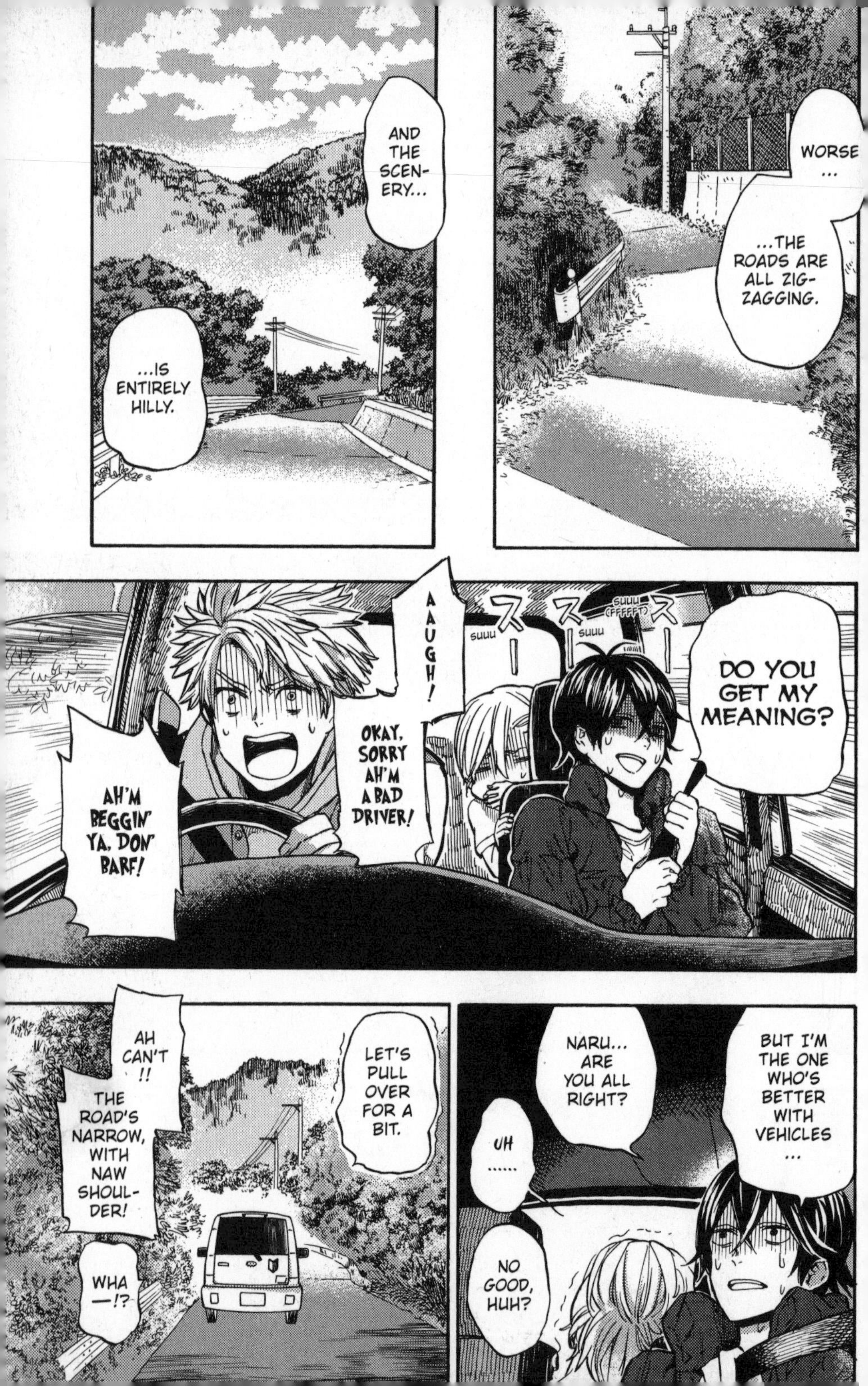
WORSE...
...THE ROADS ARE ALL ZIG-ZAGGING.
AND THE SCEN-ERY...
...IS ENTIRELY HILLY.
DO YOU GET MY MEANING?
スー
SUUU (PFFFFFT)
スー
SUUU
スー
SUUU
AAUGH!
OKAY, SORRY AH'M A BAD DRIVER!
AH'M BEGGIN' YA, DON' BARF!
BUT I'M THE ONE WHO'S BETTER WITH VEHICLES...
NARU... ARE YOU ALL RIGHT?
UH......
NO GOOD, HUH?
LET'S PULL OVER FOR A BIT.
AH CAN'T!!
THE ROAD'S NARROW, WITH NAW SHOULDER!
WHA—!?

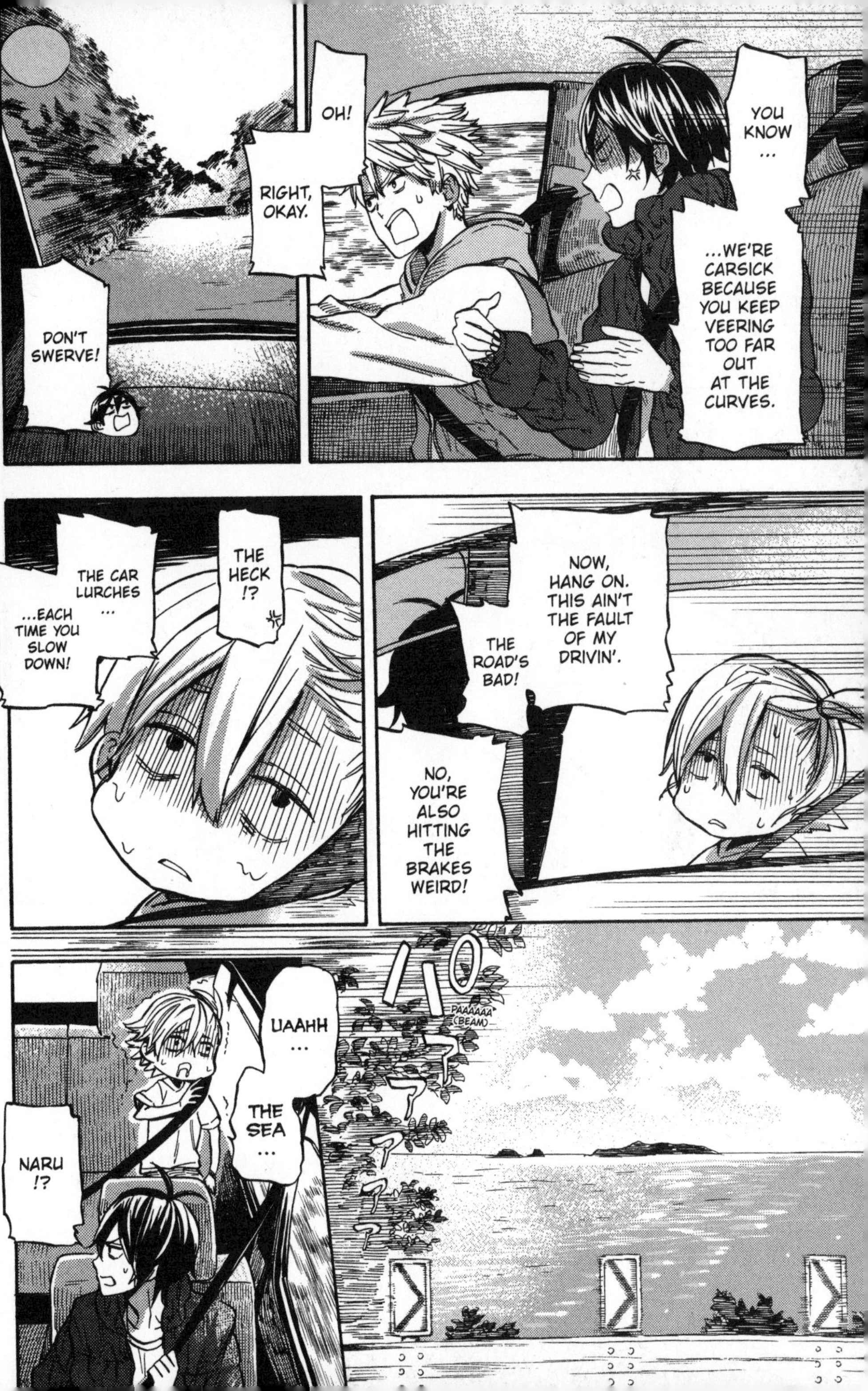
YOU KNOW ...
...WE'RE CARSICK BECAUSE YOU KEEP VEERING TOO FAR OUT AT THE CURVES.
OH!
RIGHT, OKAY.
DON'T SWERVE!
NOW, HANG ON. THIS AIN'T THE FAULT OF MY DRIVIN'.
THE ROAD'S BAD!
NO, YOU'RE ALSO HITTING THE BRAKES WEIRD!
THE HECK !?
THE CAR LURCHES ...
...EACH TIME YOU SLOW DOWN!
PAAAAAA (BEAM)
UAAHH ...
THE SEA ...
NARU !?

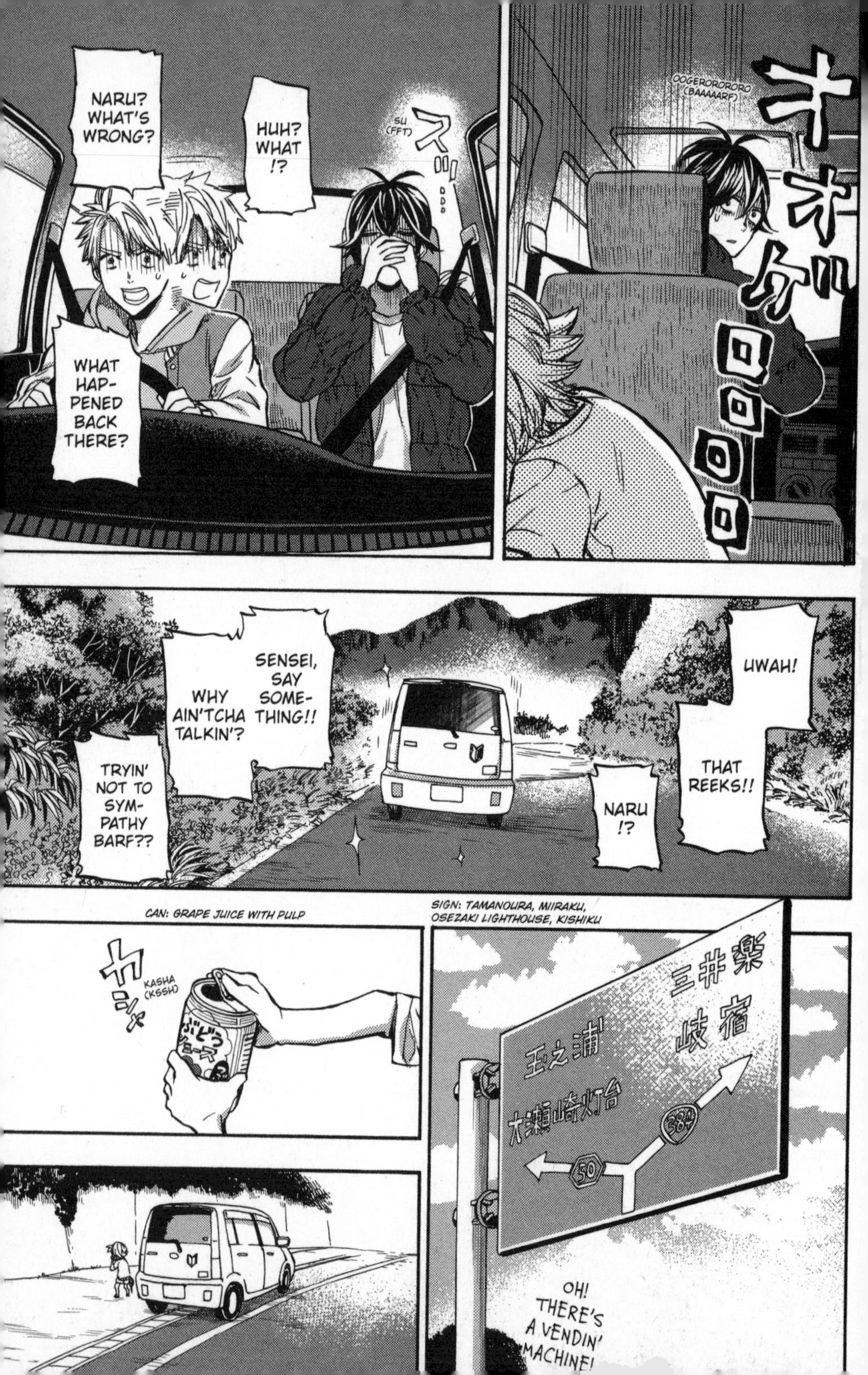
OOGEROROROR (BAAAAARF)
オボゲロロロロ
SU (FFT)
スッ
HUH? WHAT!?
NARU? WHAT'S WRONG?
WHAT HAP-PENED BACK THERE?
UWAH! THAT REEKS!!
NARU!?
SENSEI, SAY SOME-THING!!
WHY AIN'TCHA TALKIN'?
TRYIN' NOT TO SYM-PATHY BARF??
SIGN: TAMANOURA, MIIRAKU, OSEZAKI LIGHTHOUSE, KISHIKU
三井楽
岐宿
玉之浦
大瀬崎灯台
384
50
OH! THERE'S A VENDIN' MACHINE!
CAN: GRAPE JUICE WITH PULP
KASHA (KSSH)
カシャ

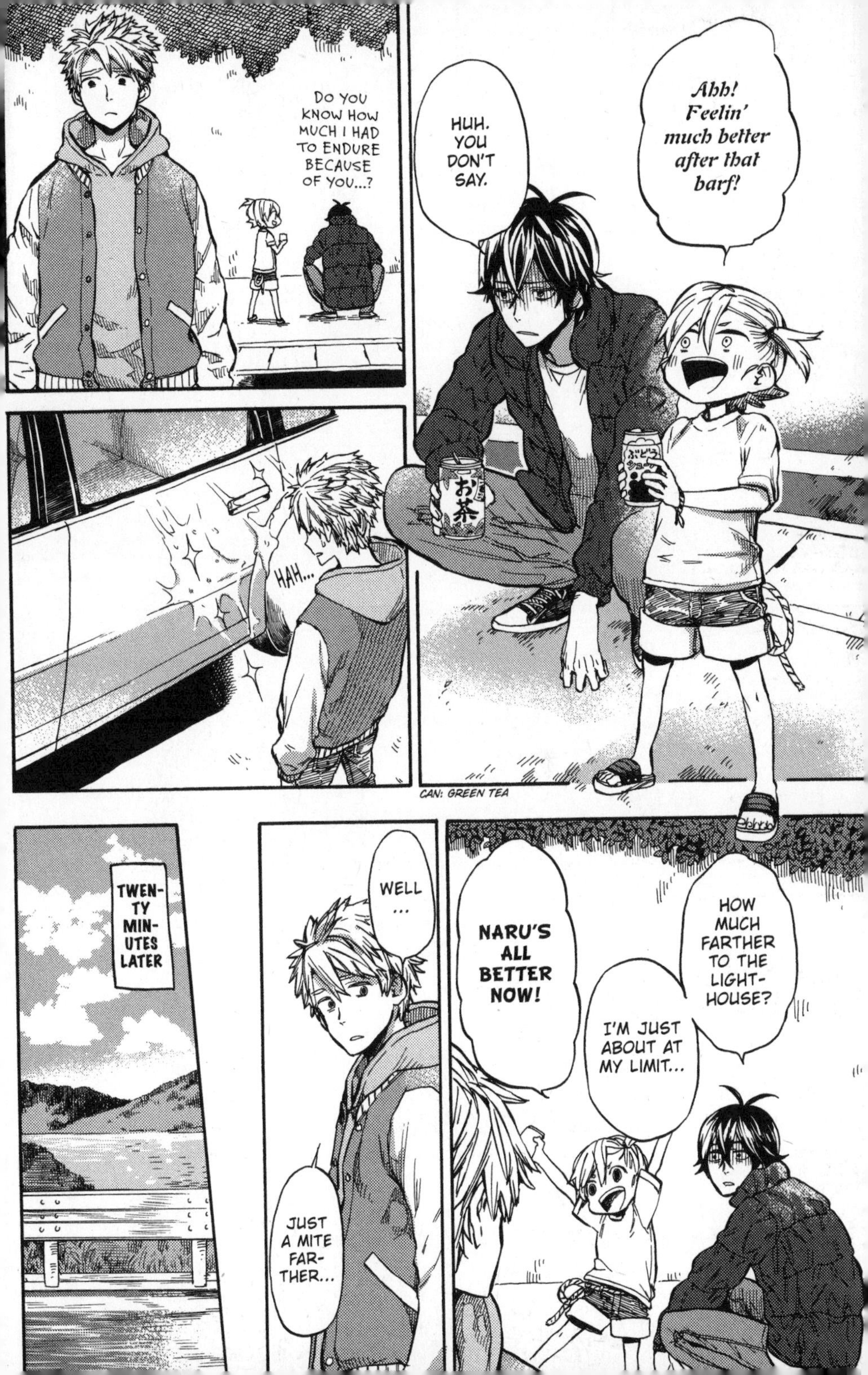
Ahh! Feelin' much better after that barf!
HUH. YOU DON'T SAY.
お茶
CAN: GREEN TEA
DO YOU KNOW HOW MUCH I HAD TO ENDURE BECAUSE OF YOU...?
HAH...
HOW MUCH FARTHER TO THE LIGHT-HOUSE?
I'M JUST ABOUT AT MY LIMIT...
NARU'S ALL BETTER NOW!
WELL...
JUST A MITE FAR-THER...
TWEN-TY MIN-UTES LATER

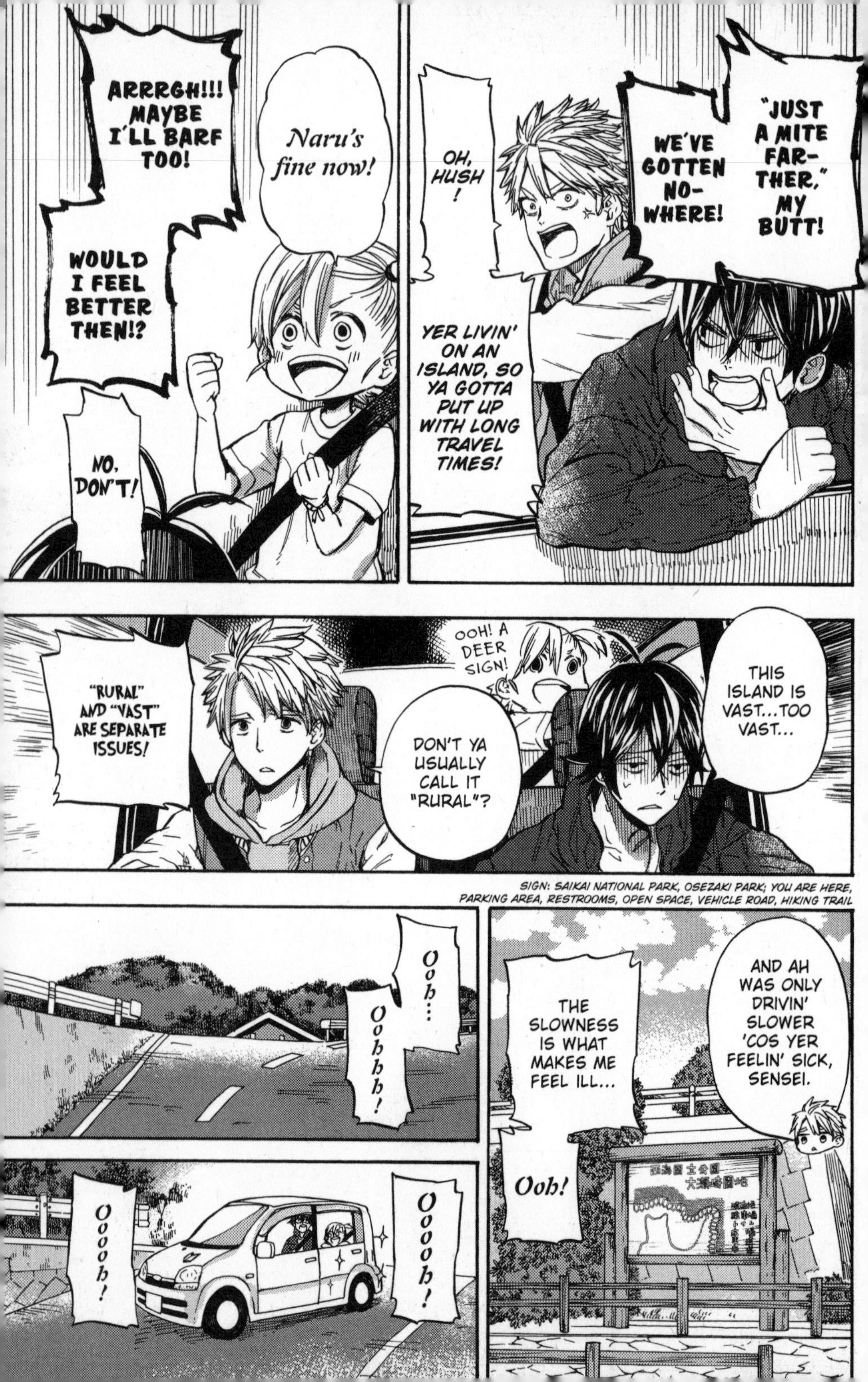
"JUST A MITE FARTHER," MY BUTT!
WE'VE GOTTEN NOWHERE!
OH, HUSH!
YER LIVIN' ON AN ISLAND, SO YA GOTTA PUT UP WITH LONG TRAVEL TIMES!
Naru's fine now!
ARRRGH!!! MAYBE I'LL BARF TOO!
WOULD I FEEL BETTER THEN!?
NO, DON'T!
THIS ISLAND IS VAST...TOO VAST...
OOH! A DEER SIGN!
DON'T YA USUALLY CALL IT "RURAL"?
"RURAL" AND "VAST" ARE SEPARATE ISSUES!
SIGN: SAIKAI NATIONAL PARK, OSEZAKI PARK; YOU ARE HERE, PARKING AREA, RESTROOMS, OPEN SPACE, VEHICLE ROAD, HIKING TRAIL
AND AH WAS ONLY DRIVIN' SLOWER 'COS YER FEELIN' SICK, SENSEI.
THE SLOWNESS IS WHAT MAKES ME FEEL ILL...
Ooh!
Ooh...
Oohhhh!
Ooooh!
Ooooh!

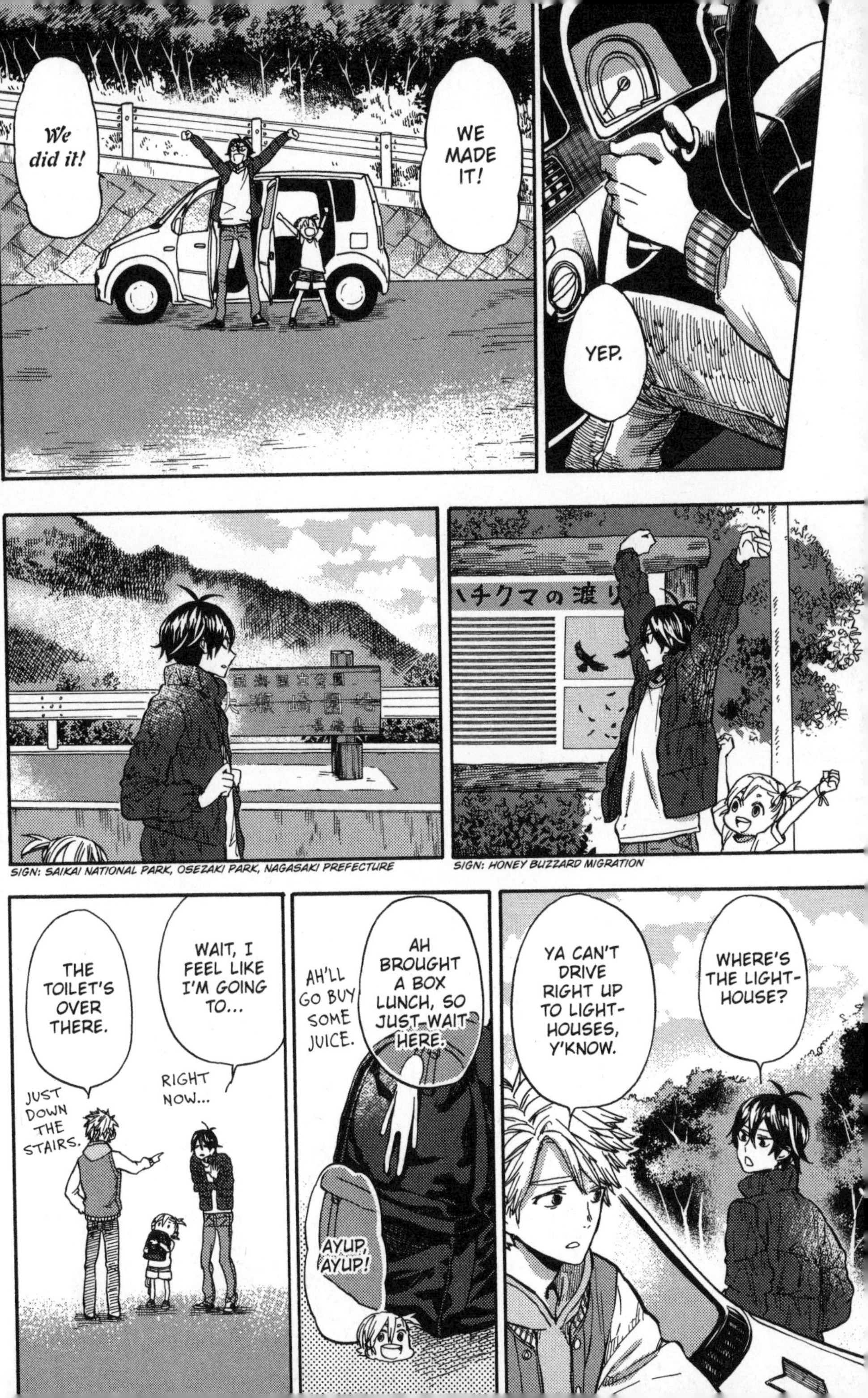
YEP.
WE MADE IT!
We did it!
ハチクマの渡り
SIGN: HONEY BUZZARD MIGRATION
SIGN: SAIKAI NATIONAL PARK, OSEZAKI PARK, NAGASAKI PREFECTURE
WHERE'S THE LIGHT-HOUSE?
YA CAN'T DRIVE RIGHT UP TO LIGHT-HOUSES, Y'KNOW.
AH BROUGHT A BOX LUNCH, SO JUST WAIT HERE.
AH'LL GO BUY SOME JUICE.
AYUP, AYUP!
WAIT, I FEEL LIKE I'M GOING TO...
RIGHT NOW...
THE TOILET'S OVER THERE.
JUST DOWN THE STAIRS.

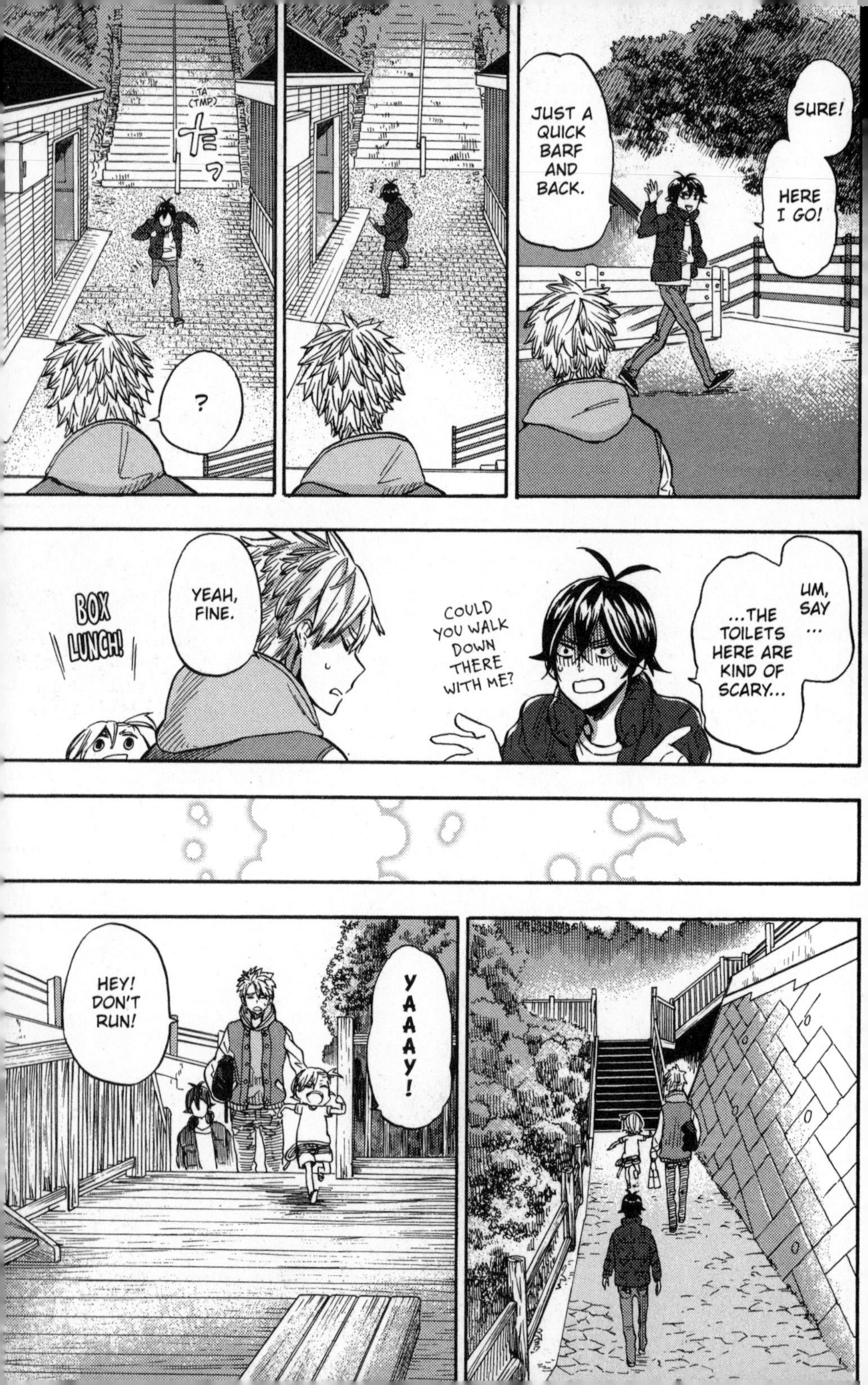
SURE!
HERE I GO!
JUST A QUICK BARF AND BACK.
TA (TMP)
?
UM, SAY ...
...THE TOILETS HERE ARE KIND OF SCARY...
COULD YOU WALK DOWN THERE WITH ME?
YEAH, FINE.
BOX LUNCH!
YAAAAY!
HEY! DON'T RUN!

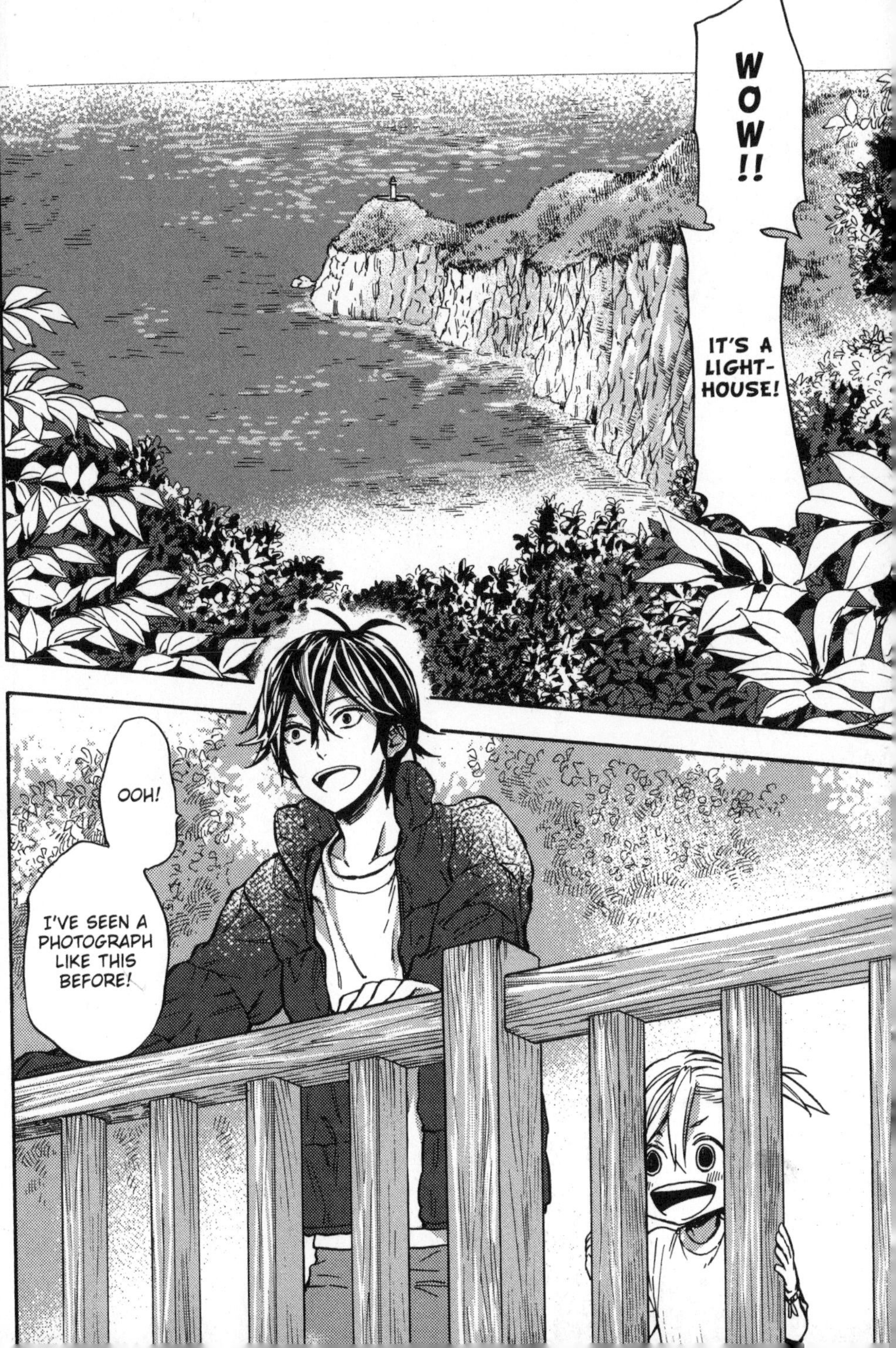
WOW!!
IT'S A LIGHT-HOUSE!
OOH!
I'VE SEEN A PHOTOGRAPH LIKE THIS BEFORE!

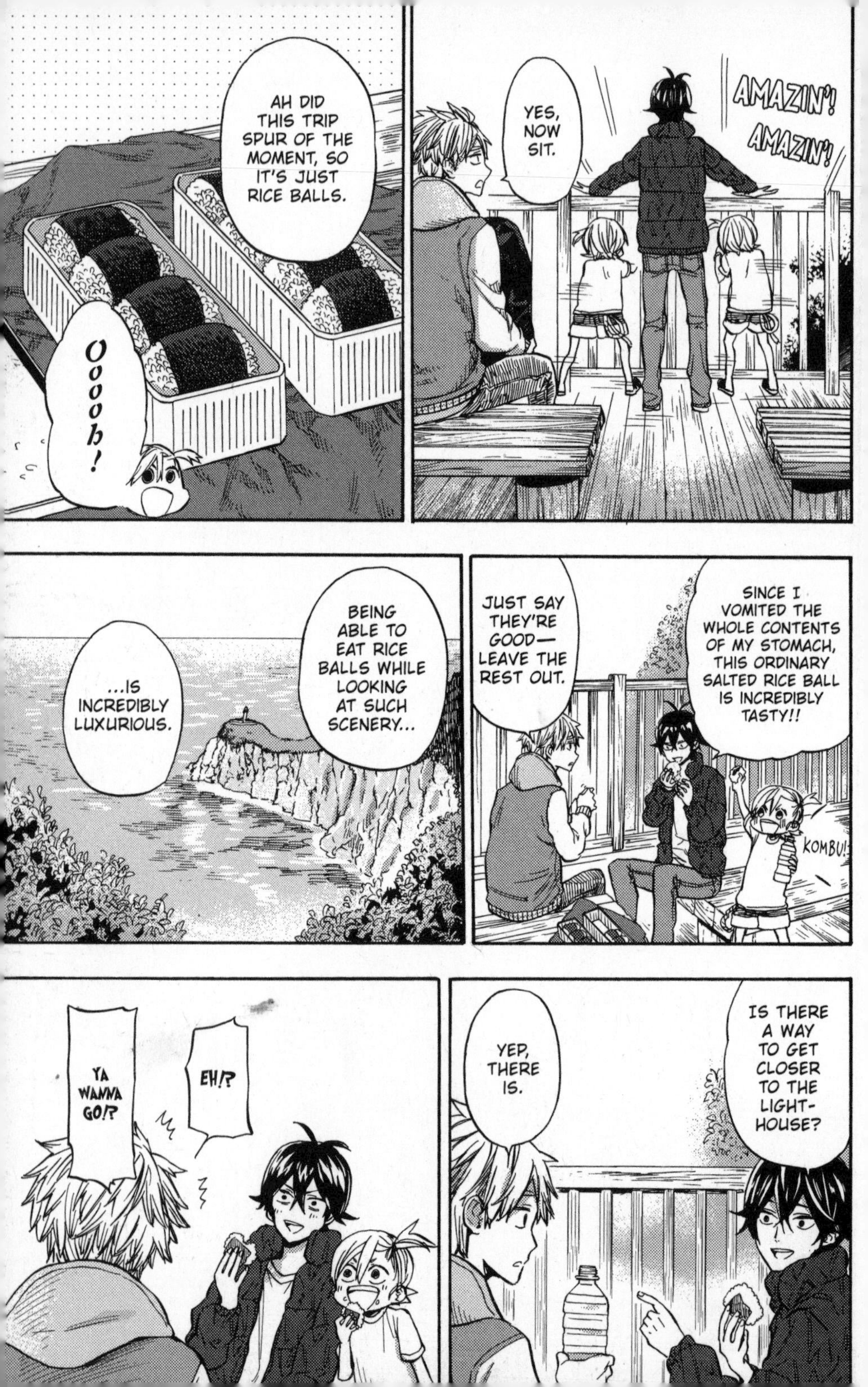
AMAZIN'!
AMAZIN'!
YES, NOW SIT.
AH DID THIS TRIP SPUR OF THE MOMENT, SO IT'S JUST RICE BALLS.
Ooooh!
SINCE I VOMITED THE WHOLE CONTENTS OF MY STOMACH, THIS ORDINARY SALTED RICE BALL IS INCREDIBLY TASTY!!
KOMBU!
JUST SAY THEY'RE GOOD— LEAVE THE REST OUT.
BEING ABLE TO EAT RICE BALLS WHILE LOOKING AT SUCH SCENERY...
...IS INCREDIBLY LUXURIOUS.
IS THERE A WAY TO GET CLOSER TO THE LIGHT-HOUSE?
YEP, THERE IS.
EH!?
YA WANNA GO!?

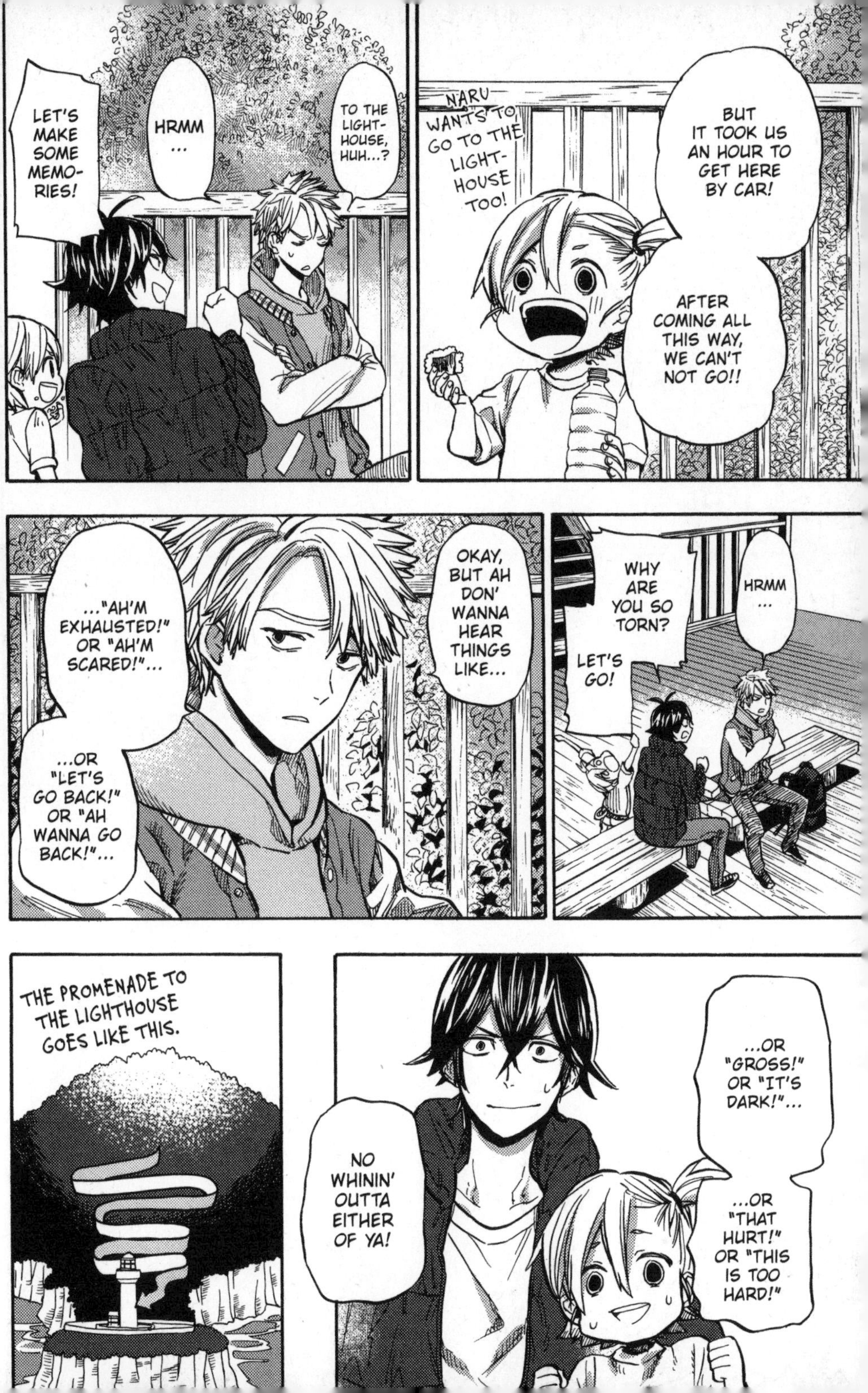
BUT IT TOOK US AN HOUR TO GET HERE BY CAR!
NARU WANTS TO GO TO THE LIGHTHOUSE TOO!
AFTER COMING ALL THIS WAY, WE CAN'T NOT GO!!
TO THE LIGHTHOUSE, HUH...?
HRMM...
LET'S MAKE SOME MEMORIES!
HRMM...
WHY ARE YOU SO TORN?
LET'S GO!
OKAY, BUT AH DON' WANNA HEAR THINGS LIKE...
..."AH'M EXHAUSTED!" OR "AH'M SCARED!"...
...OR "LET'S GO BACK!" OR "AH WANNA GO BACK!"...
...OR "GROSS!" OR "IT'S DARK!"...
...OR "THAT HURT!" OR "THIS IS TOO HARD!"
NO WHININ' OUTTA EITHER OF YA!
THE PROMENADE TO THE LIGHTHOUSE GOES LIKE THIS.

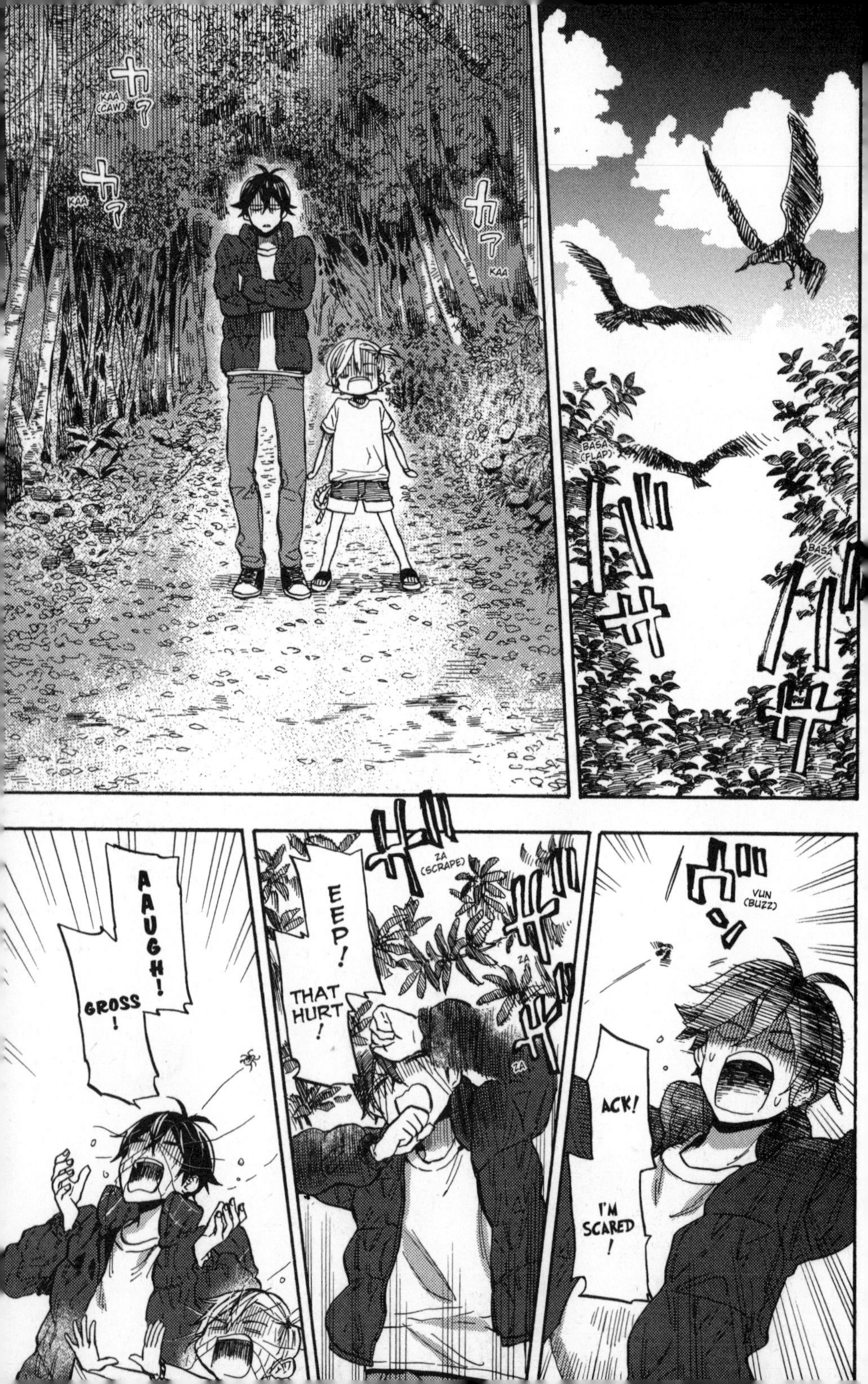
BASA (FLAP)
BASA
カァ
KAA (CAW)
カァ
KAA
カァ
KAA
VUN (BUZZ)
ACK!
I'M SCARED!
ZA (SCRAPE)
ZA
ZA
EEP!
THAT HURT!
AAUGH!
GROSS!

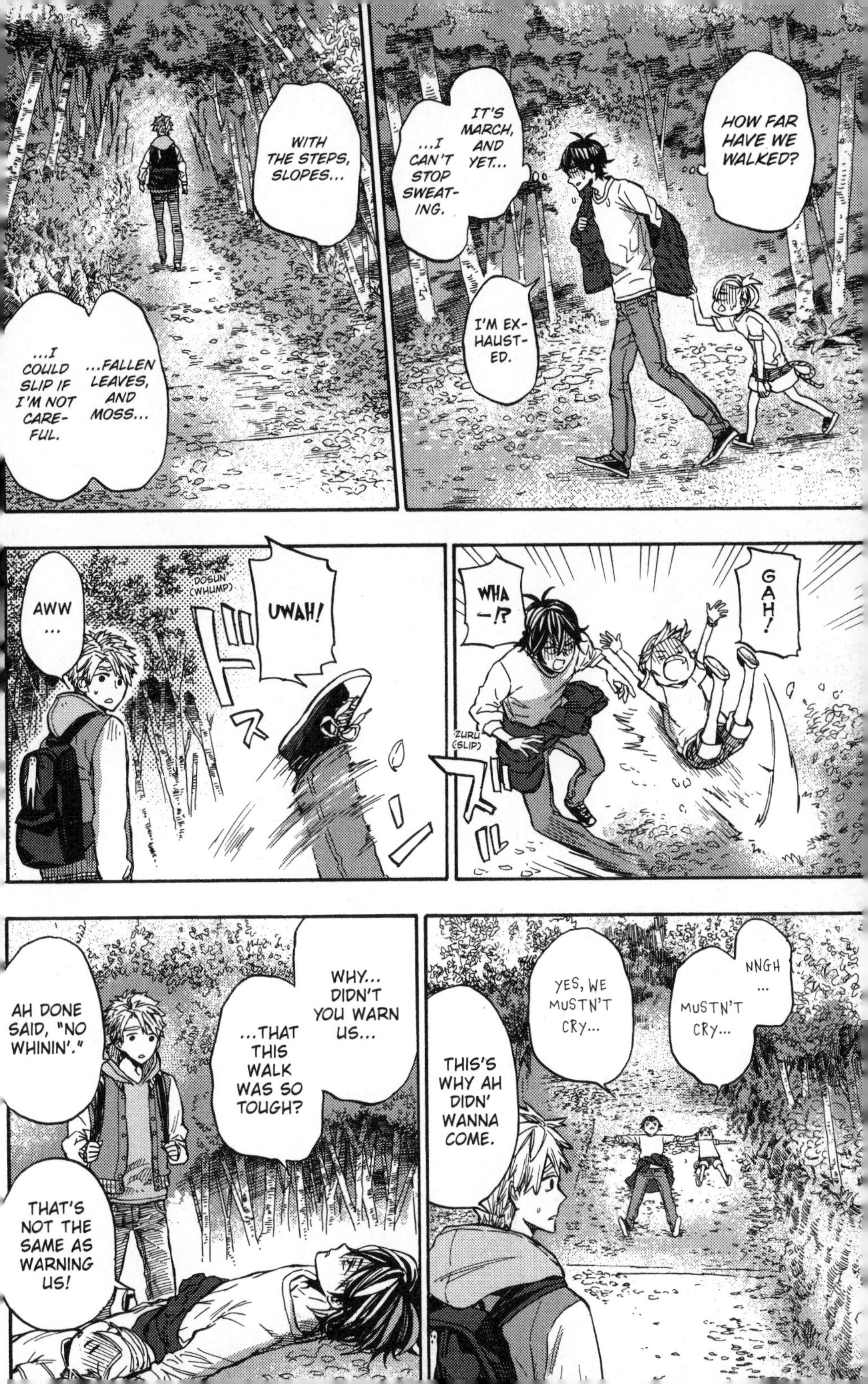
HOW FAR HAVE WE WALKED?
IT'S MARCH, AND YET...
...I CAN'T STOP SWEATING.
I'M EXHAUSTED.
WITH THE STEPS, SLOPES...
...FALLEN LEAVES, AND MOSS...
...I COULD SLIP IF I'M NOT CAREFUL.
GAH!
WHA—!?
ZURU (SLIP)
UWAH!
DOSUN (WHUMP)
AWW...
NNGH...
MUSTN'T CRY...
YES, WE MUSTN'T CRY...
THIS'S WHY AH DIDN' WANNA COME.
WHY... DIDN'T YOU WARN US...
...THAT THIS WALK WAS SO TOUGH?
AH DONE SAID, "NO WHININ'."
THAT'S NOT THE SAME AS WARNING US!

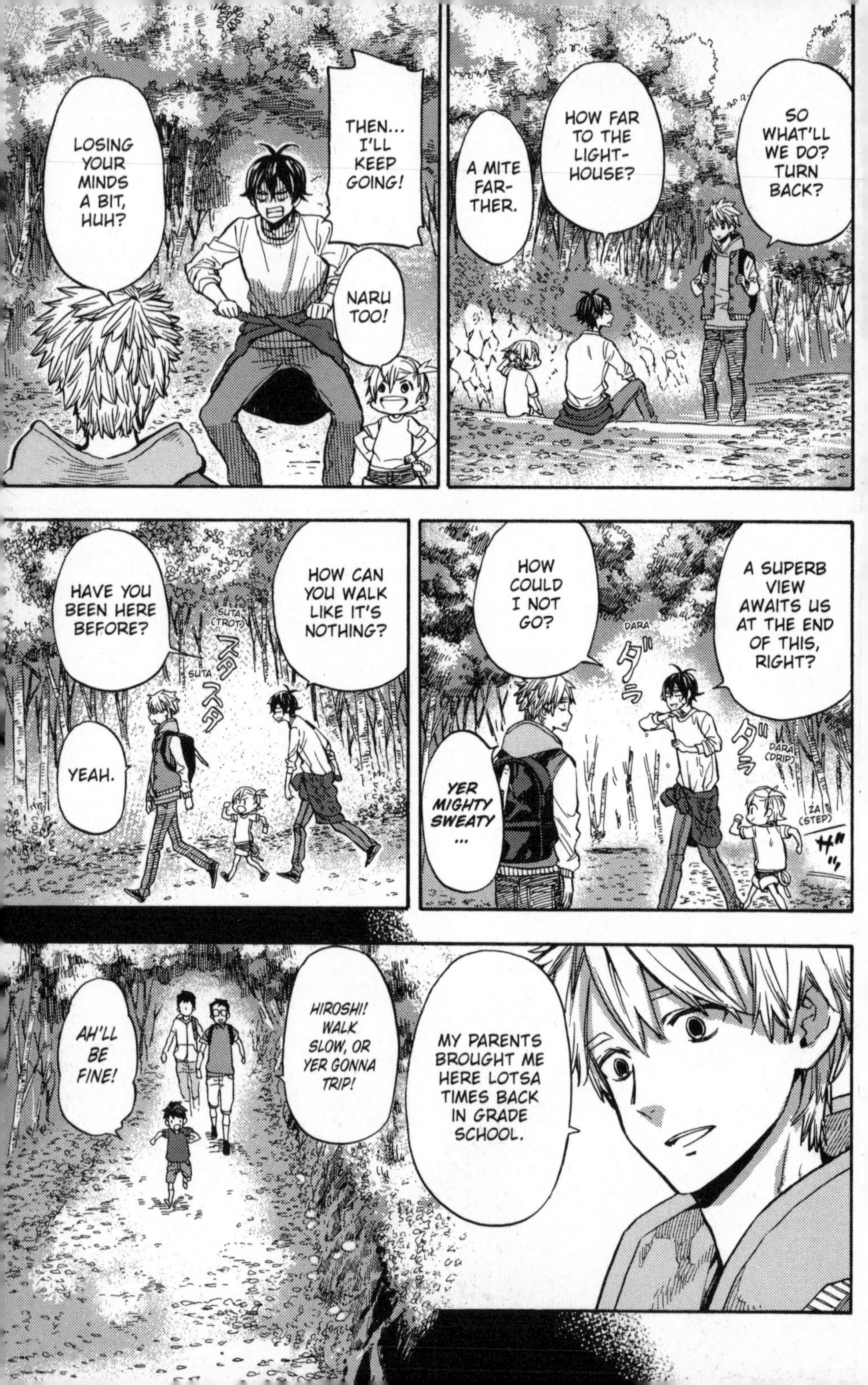
SO WHAT'LL WE DO? TURN BACK?
HOW FAR TO THE LIGHT-HOUSE?
A MITE FAR-THER.
THEN... I'LL KEEP GOING!
NARU TOO!
LOSING YOUR MINDS A BIT, HUH?
A SUPERB VIEW AWAITS US AT THE END OF THIS, RIGHT?
HOW COULD I NOT GO?
DARA
ダラ
DARA (DRIP)
ダラ
ZA (STEP)
ザッ
YER MIGHTY SWEATY ...
HOW CAN YOU WALK LIKE IT'S NOTHING?
HAVE YOU BEEN HERE BEFORE?
SUTA (TROT)
スタ
SUTA
スタ
YEAH.
MY PARENTS BROUGHT ME HERE LOTSA TIMES BACK IN GRADE SCHOOL.
HIROSHI! WALK SLOW, OR YER GONNA TRIP!
AH'LL BE FINE!

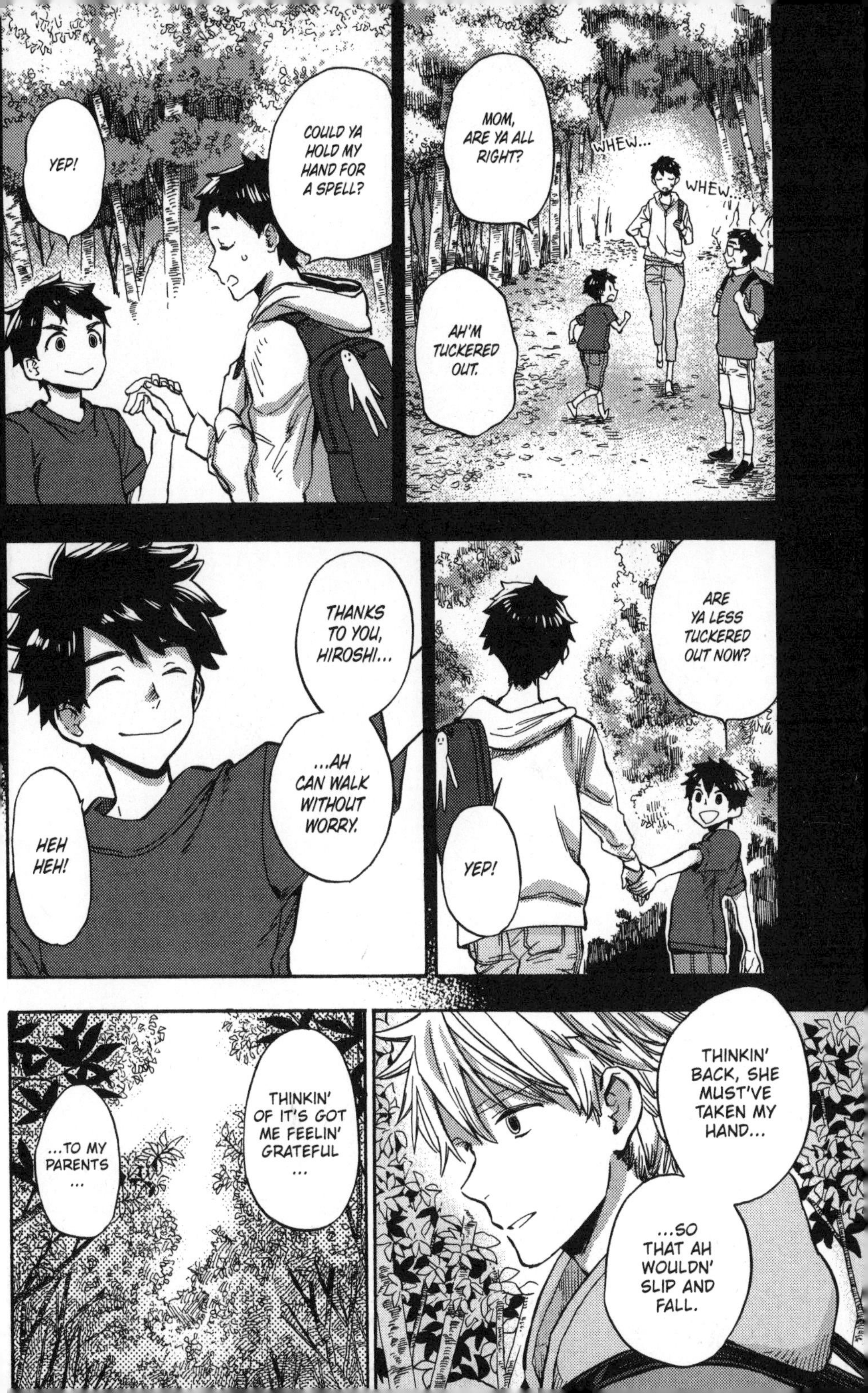
MOM, ARE YA ALL RIGHT?
WHEW...
WHEW...
AH'M TUCKERED OUT.
COULD YA HOLD MY HAND FOR A SPELL?
YEP!
ARE YA LESS TUCKERED OUT NOW?
YEP!
THANKS TO YOU, HIROSHI...
...AH CAN WALK WITHOUT WORRY.
HEH HEH!
THINKIN' BACK, SHE MUST'VE TAKEN MY HAND...
...SO THAT AH WOULDN' SLIP AND FALL.
THINKIN' OF IT'S GOT ME FEELIN' GRATEFUL ...
...TO MY PARENTS ...

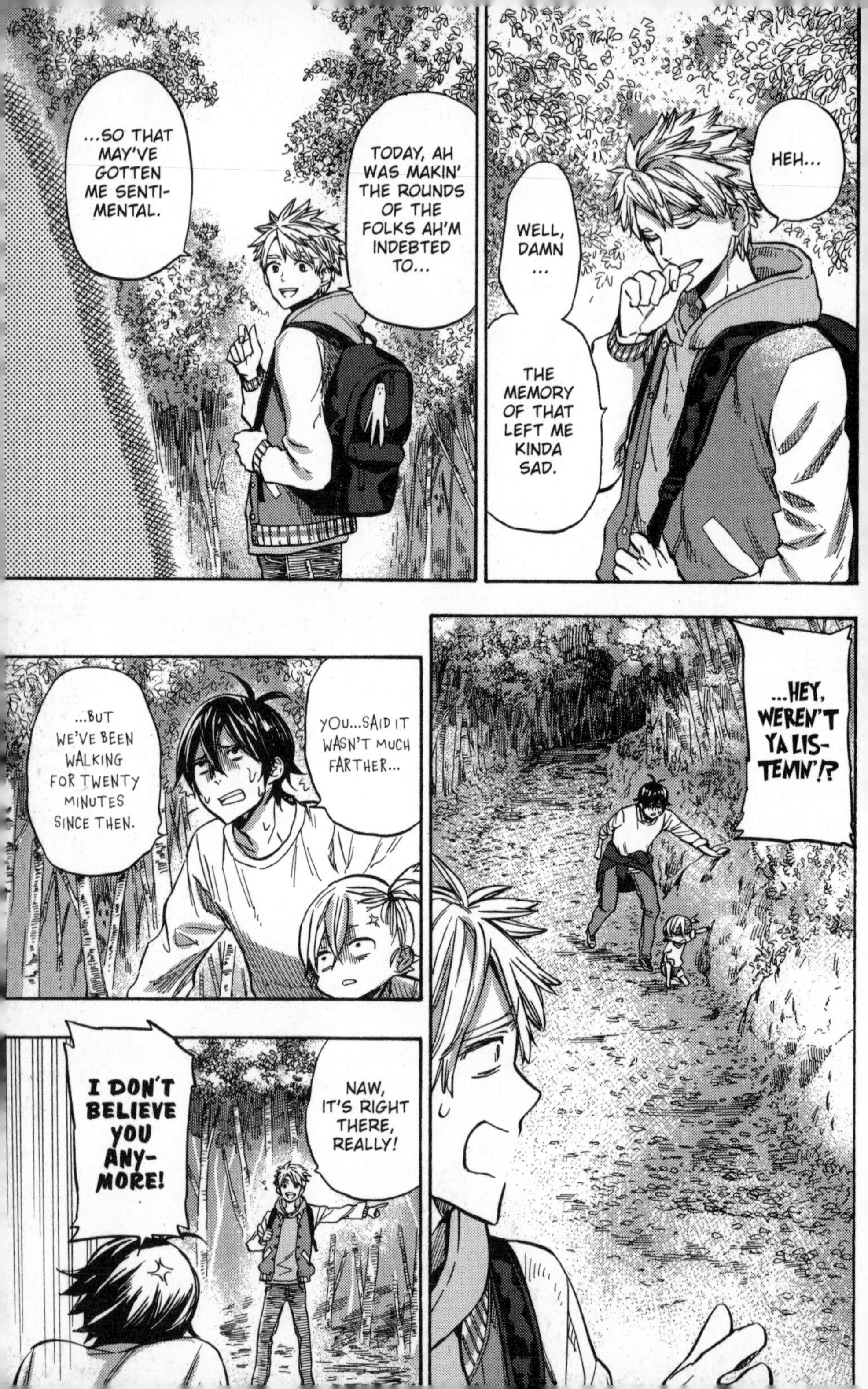
HEH...
WELL, DAMN...
THE MEMORY OF THAT LEFT ME KINDA SAD.
TODAY, AH WAS MAKIN' THE ROUNDS OF THE FOLKS AH'M INDEBTED TO...
...SO THAT MAY'VE GOTTEN ME SENTI-MENTAL.
...HEY, WEREN'T YA LIS-TEMN'!?
YOU...SAID IT WASN'T MUCH FARTHER...
...BUT WE'VE BEEN WALKING FOR TWENTY MINUTES SINCE THEN.
NAW, IT'S RIGHT THERE, REALLY!
I DON'T BELIEVE YOU ANY-MORE!

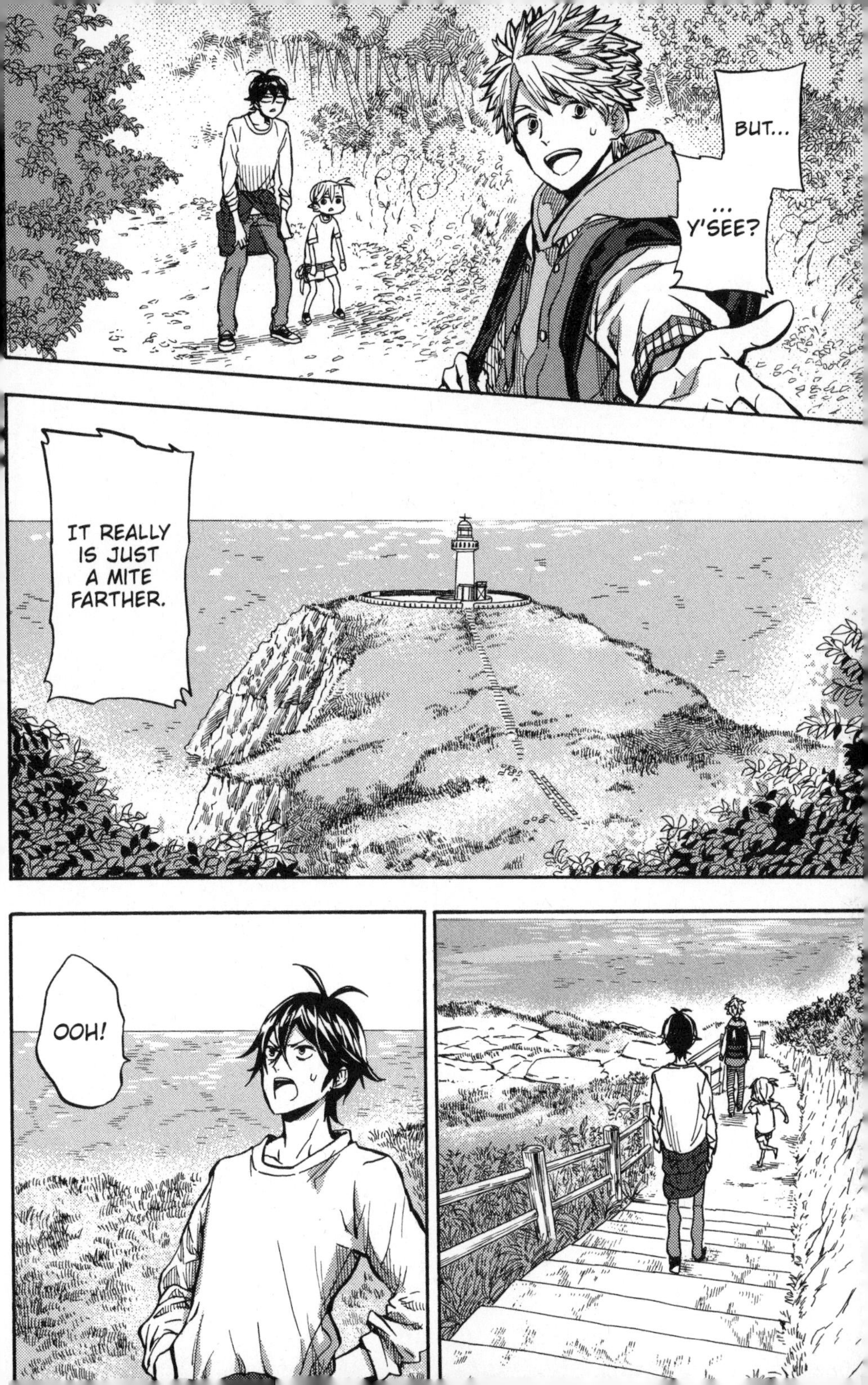
BUT...
... Y'SEE?
IT REALLY IS JUST A MITE FARTHER.
OOH!

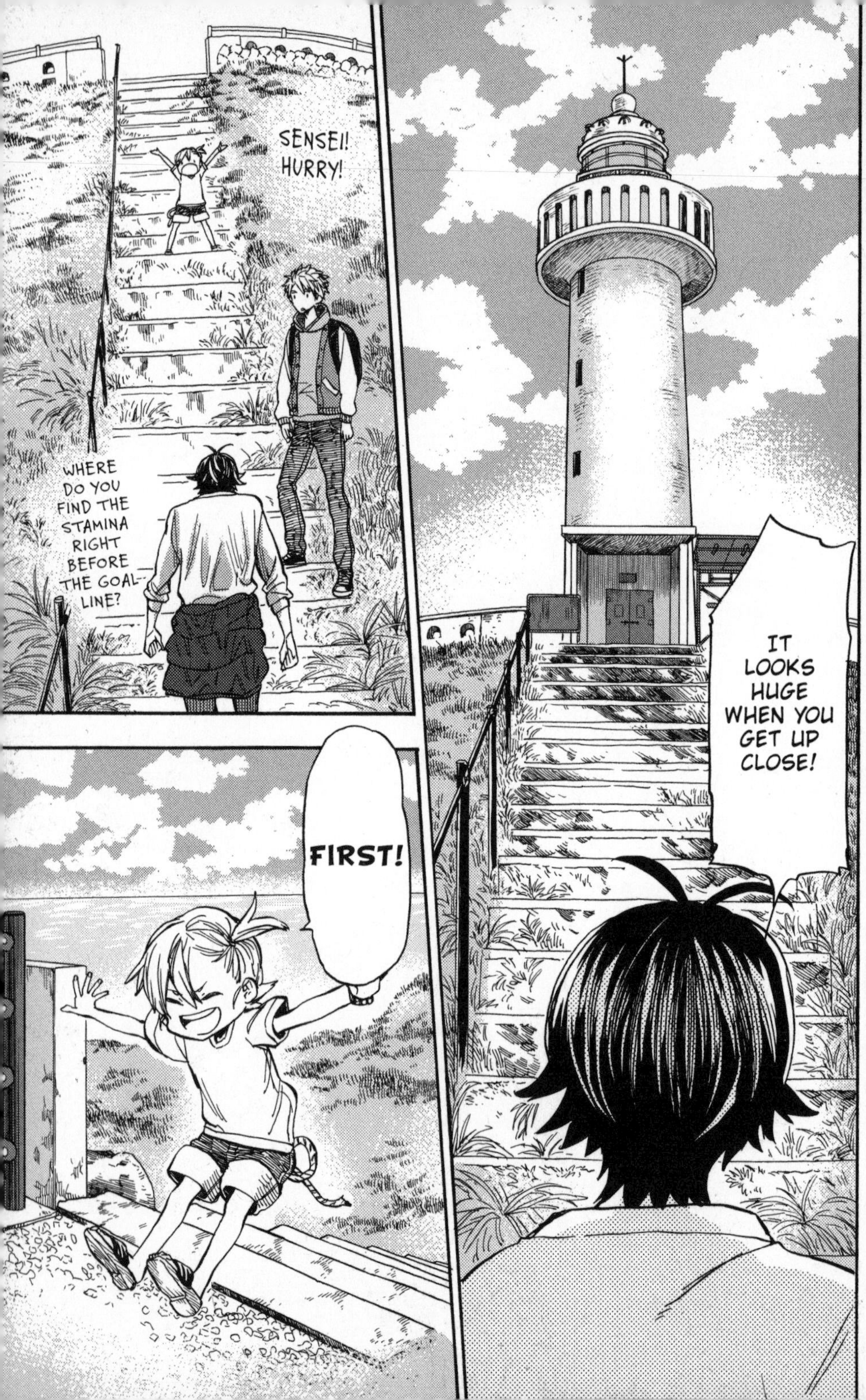
IT LOOKS HUGE WHEN YOU GET UP CLOSE!
SENSEI! HURRY!
WHERE DO YOU FIND THE STAMINA RIGHT BEFORE THE GOAL LINE?
FIRST!

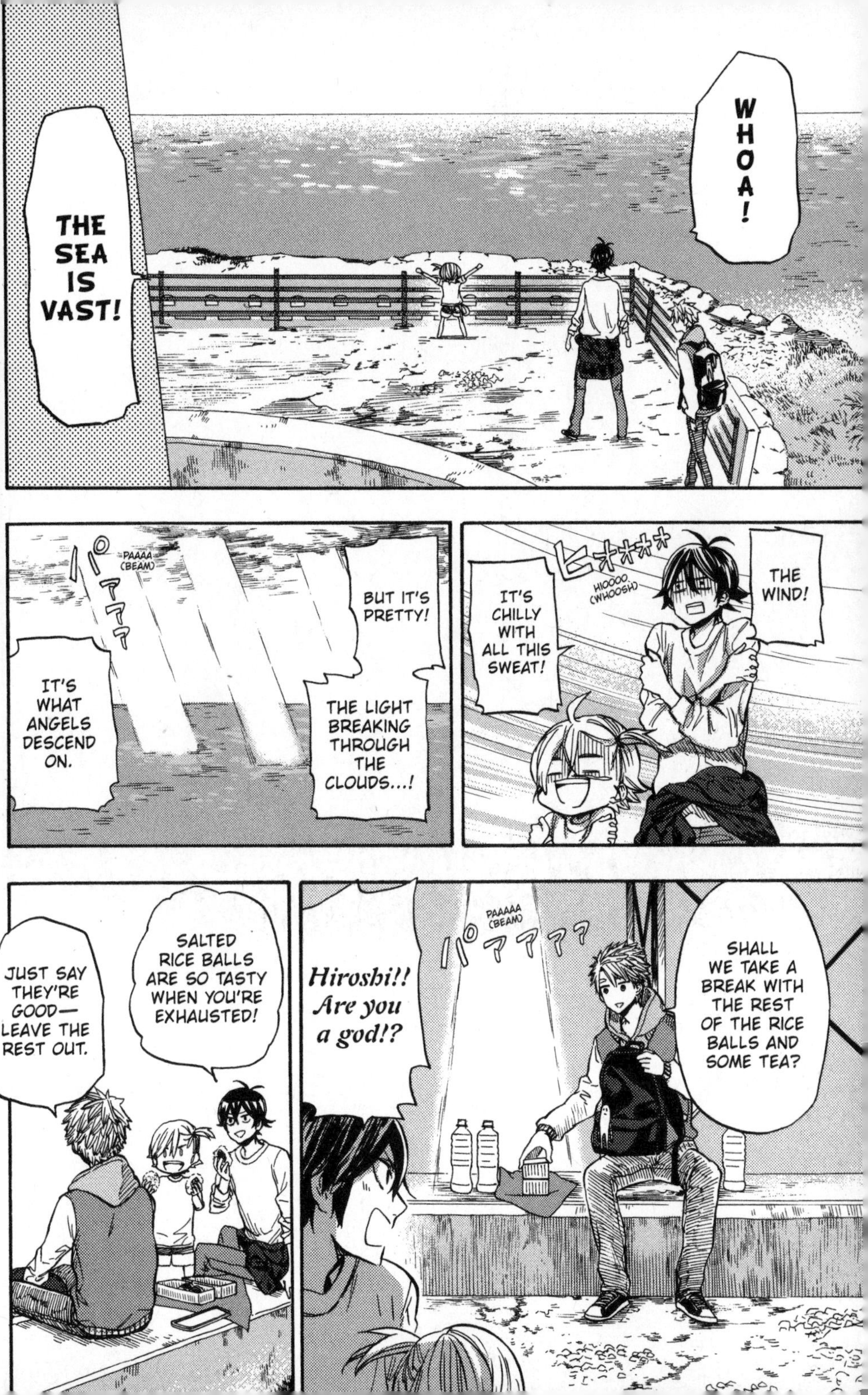
WHOA!
THE SEA IS VAST!
THE WIND!
ヒオォォォ
HIOOOO (WHOOSH)
IT'S CHILLY WITH ALL THIS SWEAT!
BUT IT'S PRETTY!
THE LIGHT BREAKING THROUGH THE CLOUDS...!
パアアア
PAAAA (BEAM)
IT'S WHAT ANGELS DESCEND ON.
SHALL WE TAKE A BREAK WITH THE REST OF THE RICE BALLS AND SOME TEA?
パアアアア
PAAAAA (BEAM)
Hiroshi!! Are you a god!?
SALTED RICE BALLS ARE SO TASTY WHEN YOU'RE EXHAUSTED!
JUST SAY THEY'RE GOOD—LEAVE THE REST OUT.

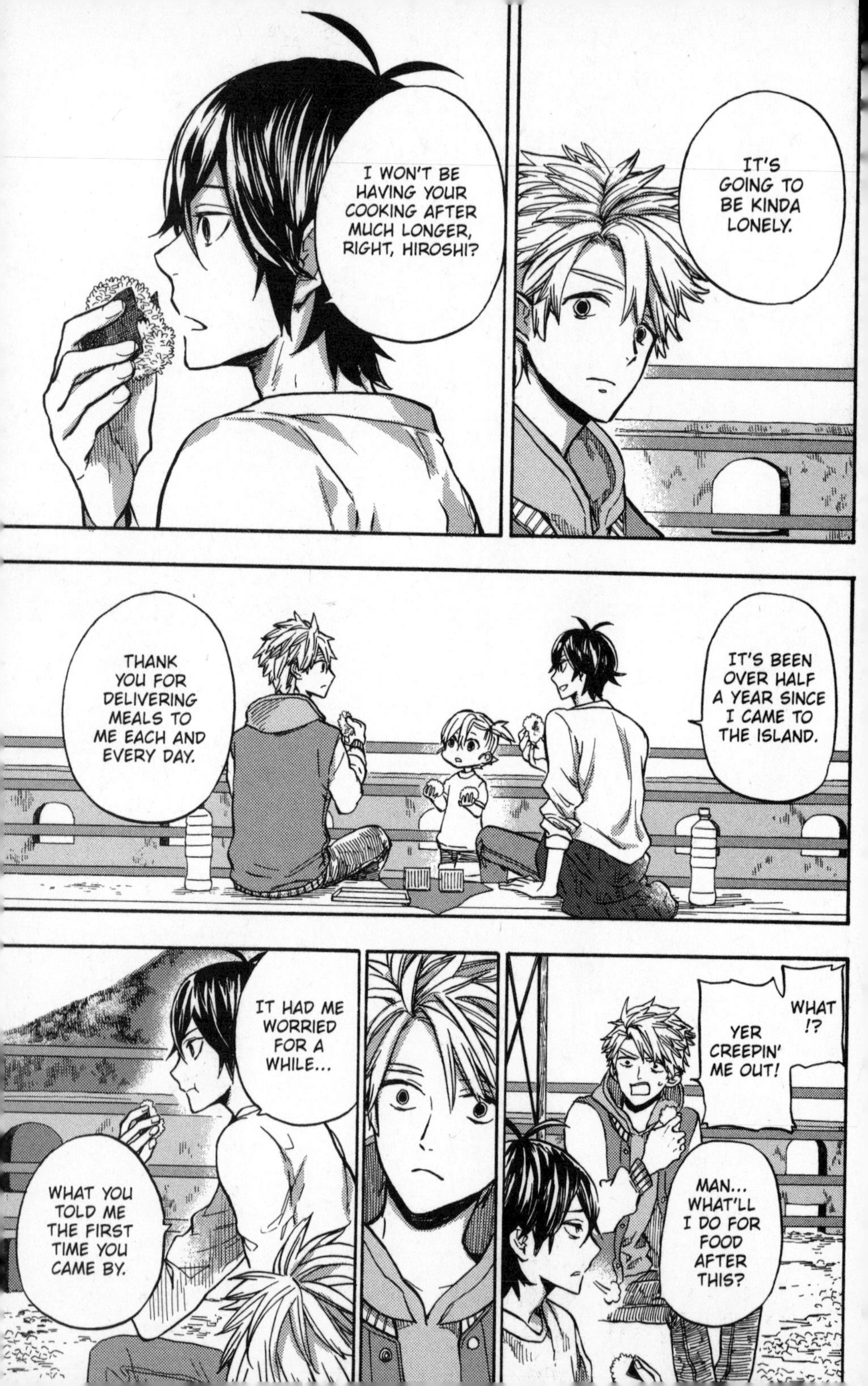
IT'S GOING TO BE KINDA LONELY.
I WON'T BE HAVING YOUR COOKING AFTER MUCH LONGER, RIGHT, HIROSHI?
IT'S BEEN OVER HALF A YEAR SINCE I CAME TO THE ISLAND.
THANK YOU FOR DELIVERING MEALS TO ME EACH AND EVERY DAY.
WHAT!?
YER CREEPIN' ME OUT!
MAN... WHAT'LL I DO FOR FOOD AFTER THIS?
IT HAD ME WORRIED FOR A WHILE...
WHAT YOU TOLD ME THE FIRST TIME YOU CAME BY.

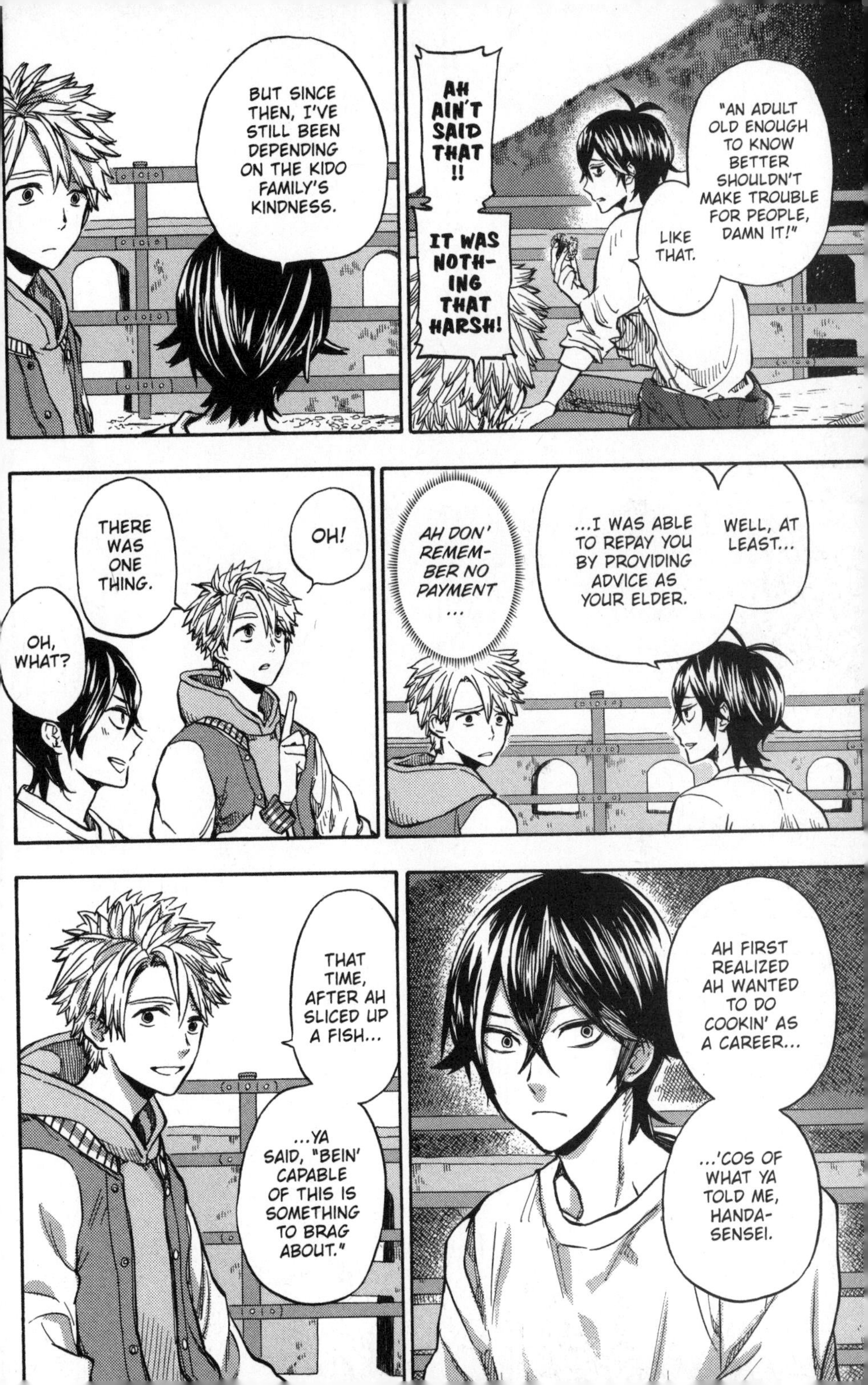
"AN ADULT OLD ENOUGH TO KNOW BETTER SHOULDN'T MAKE TROUBLE FOR PEOPLE, DAMN IT!"
LIKE THAT.
AH AIN'T SAID THAT!!
IT WAS NOTHING THAT HARSH!
BUT SINCE THEN, I'VE STILL BEEN DEPENDING ON THE KIDO FAMILY'S KINDNESS.
WELL, AT LEAST...
...I WAS ABLE TO REPAY YOU BY PROVIDING ADVICE AS YOUR ELDER.
AH DON' REMEMBER NO PAYMENT...
OH!
THERE WAS ONE THING.
OH, WHAT?
AH FIRST REALIZED AH WANTED TO DO COOKIN' AS A CAREER...
...'COS OF WHAT YA TOLD ME, HANDA-SENSEI.
THAT TIME, AFTER AH SLICED UP A FISH...
...YA SAID, "BEIN' CAPABLE OF THIS IS SOMETHING TO BRAG ABOUT."

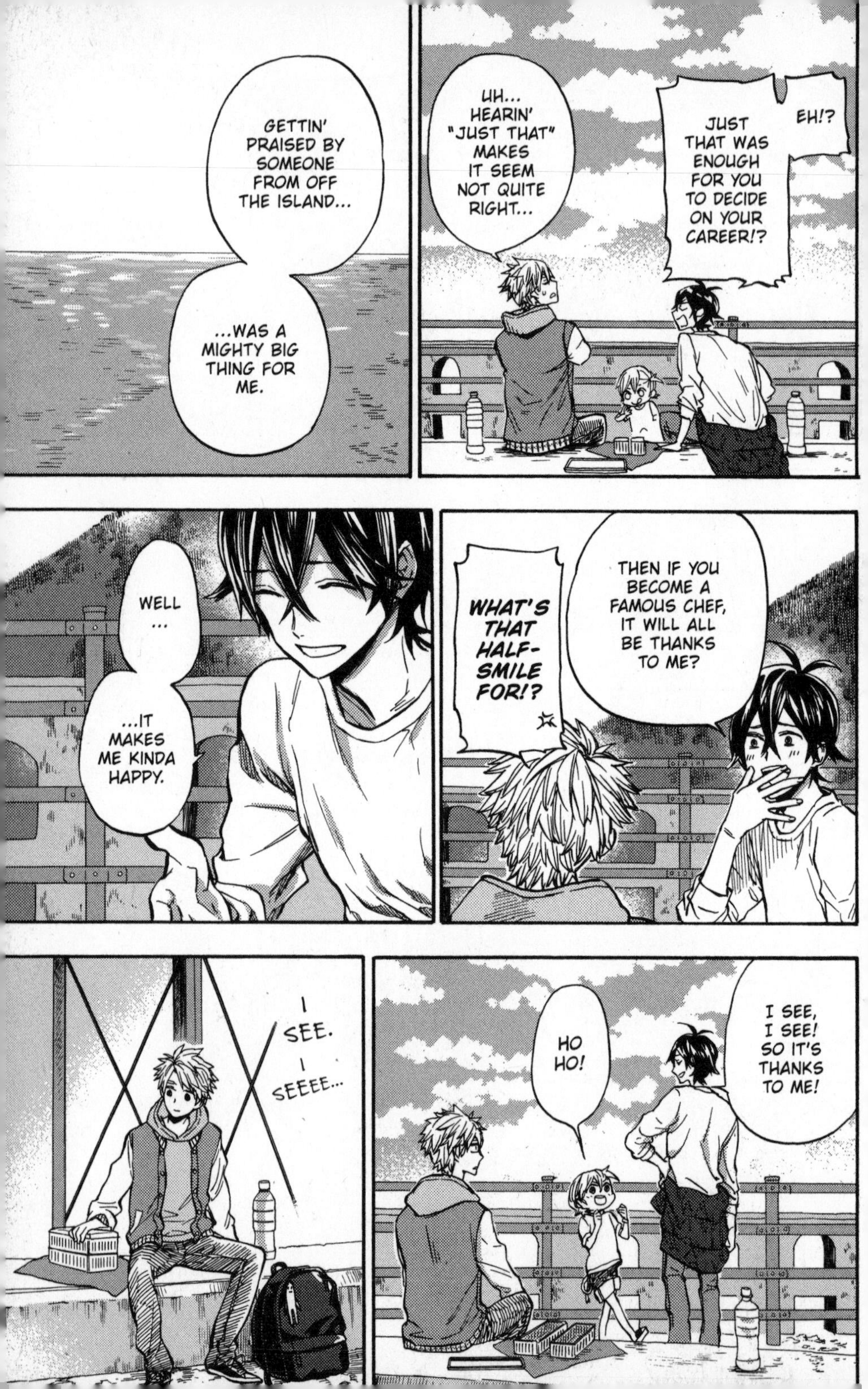
EH!?
JUST THAT WAS ENOUGH FOR YOU TO DECIDE ON YOUR CAREER!?
UH... HEARIN' "JUST THAT" MAKES IT SEEM NOT QUITE RIGHT...
GETTIN' PRAISED BY SOMEONE FROM OFF THE ISLAND...
...WAS A MIGHTY BIG THING FOR ME.
THEN IF YOU BECOME A FAMOUS CHEF, IT WILL ALL BE THANKS TO ME?
WHAT'S THAT HALF-SMILE FOR!?
WELL ...
...IT MAKES ME KINDA HAPPY.
I SEE, I SEE! SO IT'S THANKS TO ME!
HO HO!
I SEE. I SEEEE...

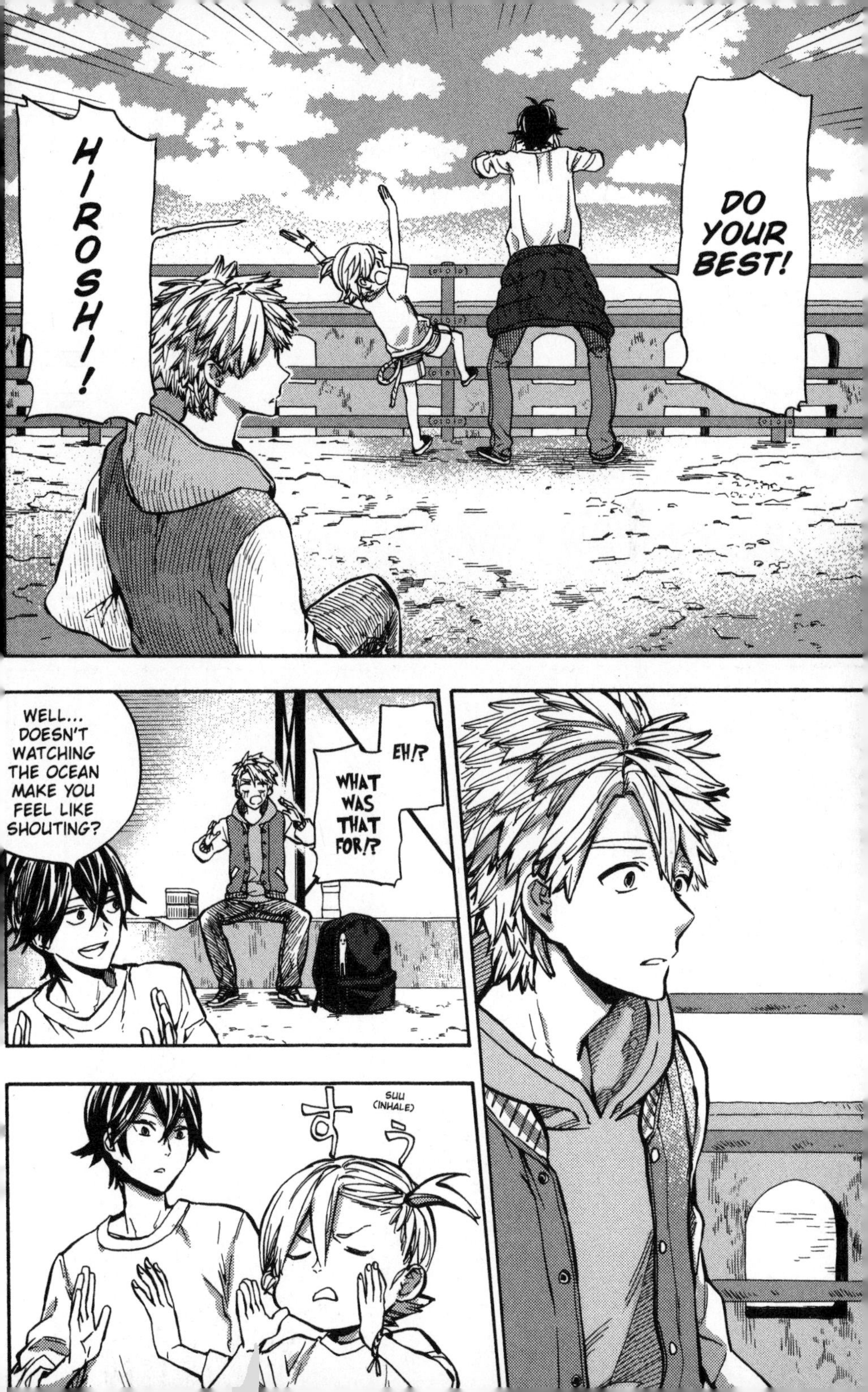
DO YOUR BEST!
HIROSHI!!
EH!? WHAT WAS THAT FOR!?
WELL... DOESN'T WATCHING THE OCEAN MAKE YOU FEEL LIKE SHOUTING?
すう
SUU (INHALE)

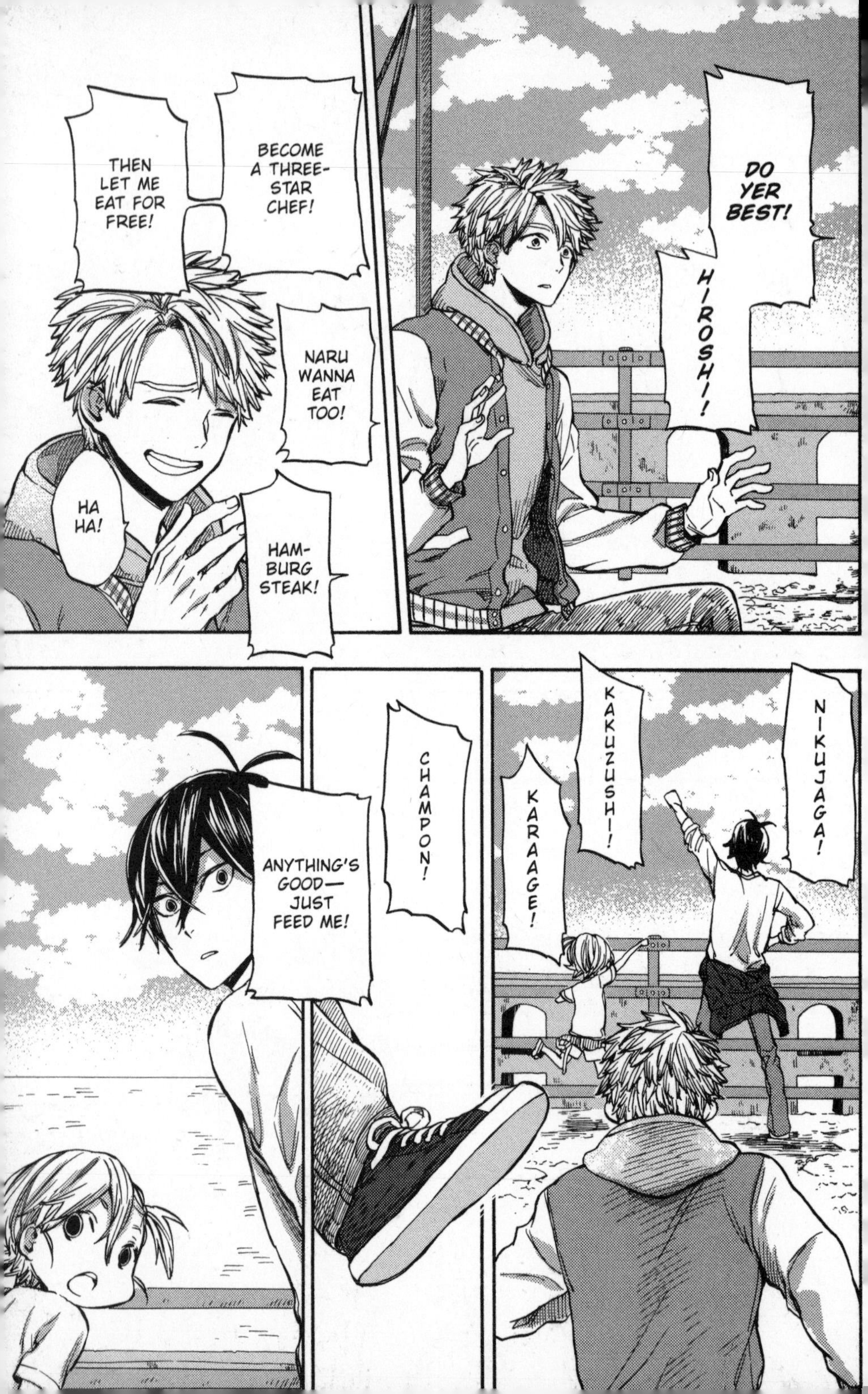
DO YER BEST!
HIROSHI!
BECOME A THREE-STAR CHEF!
THEN LET ME EAT FOR FREE!
NARU WANNA EAT TOO!
HAM-BURG STEAK!
HA HA!
NIKUJAGA!
KAKUZUSHI!
KARAAGE!
CHAMPON!
ANYTHING'S GOOD—JUST FEED ME!

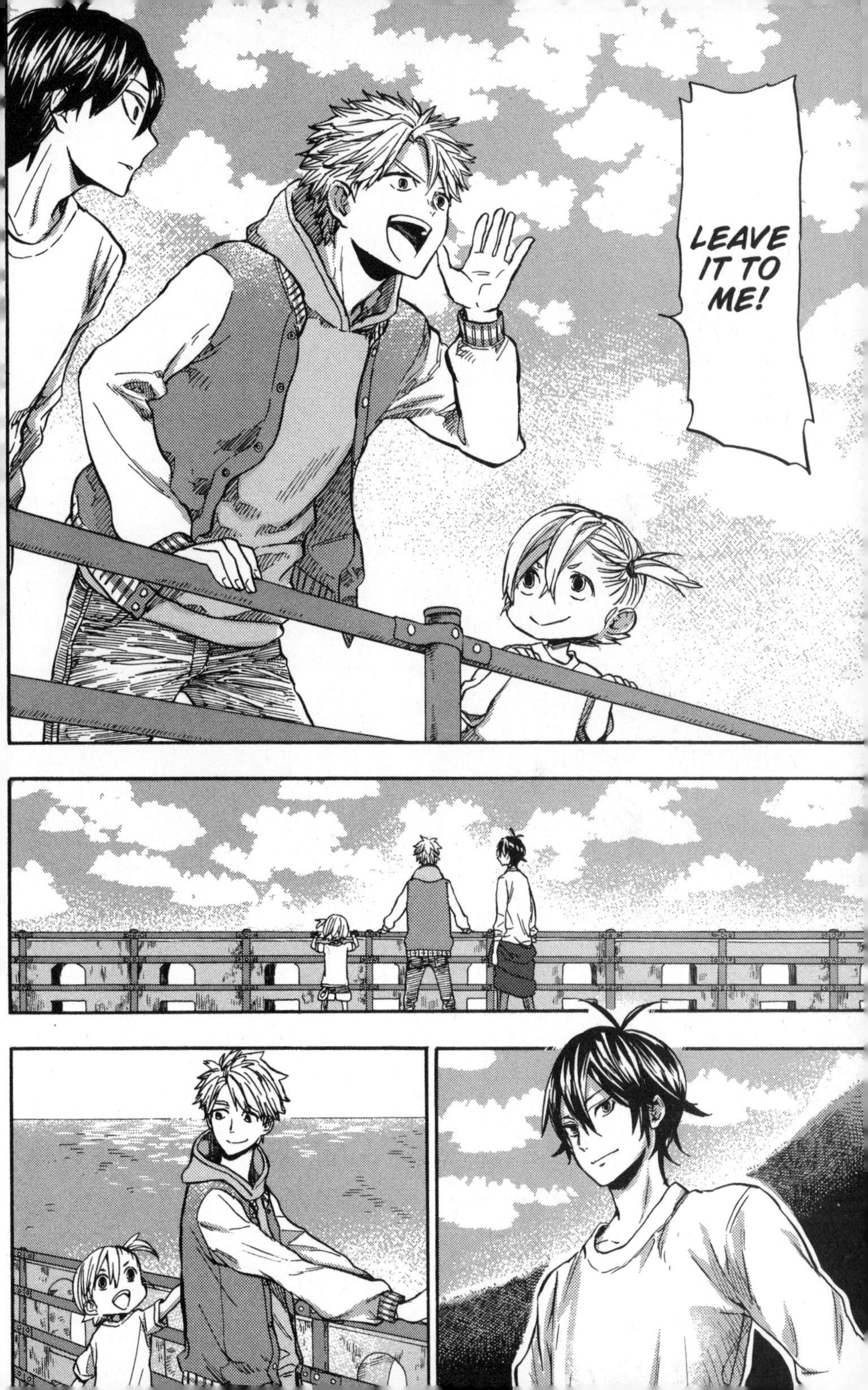
LEAVE IT TO ME!

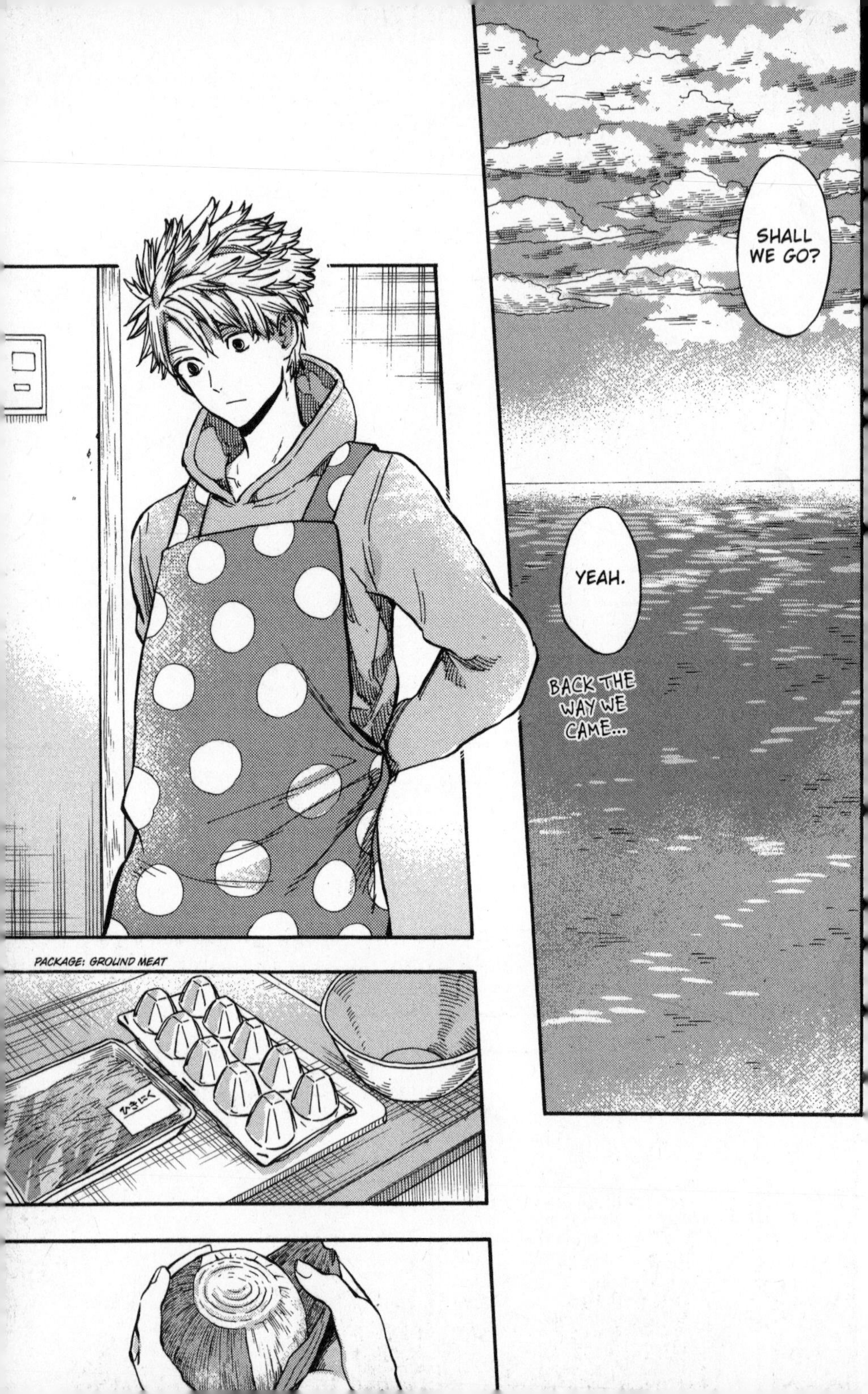
SHALL WE GO?
YEAH.
BACK THE WAY WE CAME...
PACKAGE: GROUND MEAT
ひきにく

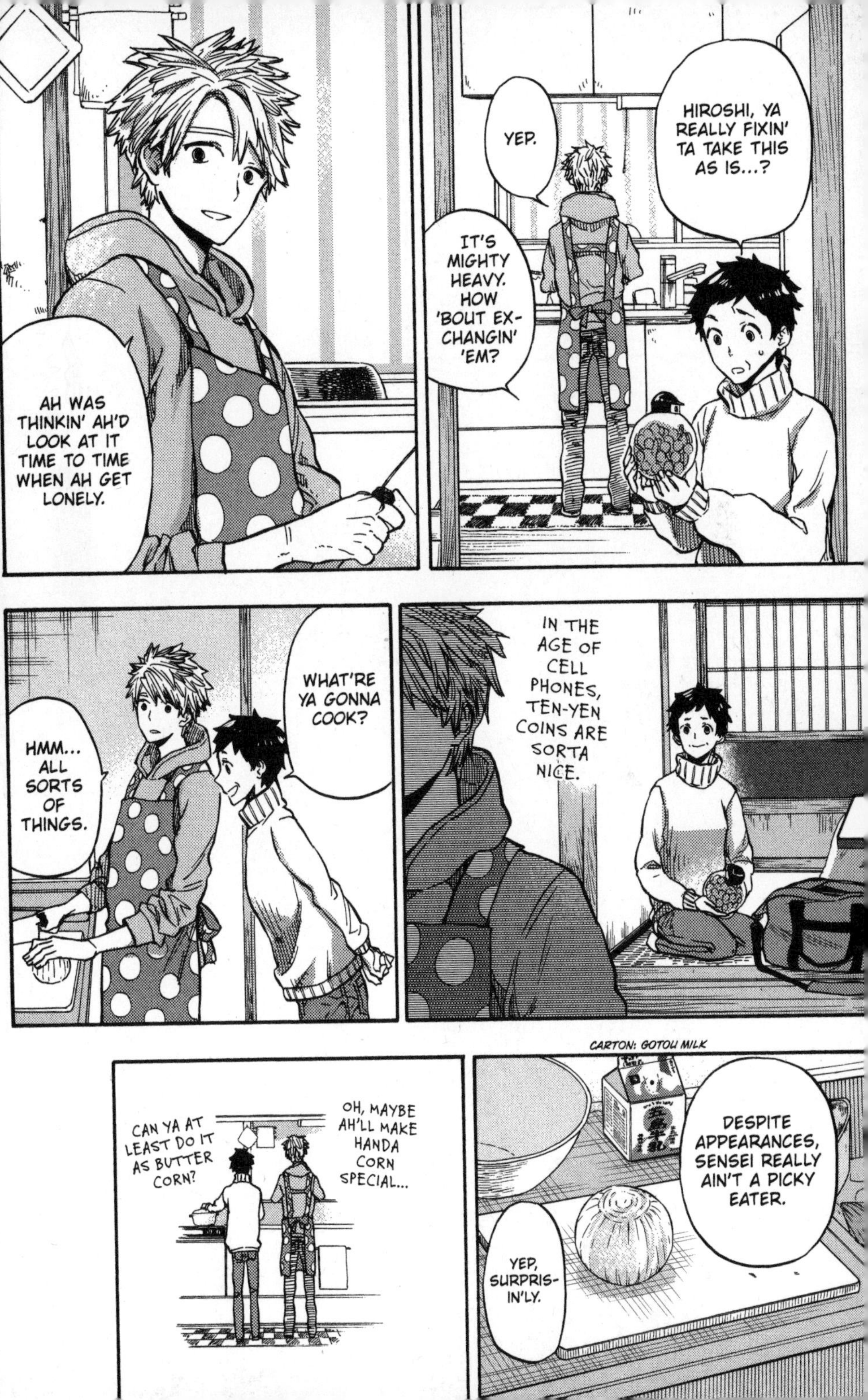
HIROSHI, YA REALLY FIXIN' TA TAKE THIS AS IS...?
YEP.
IT'S MIGHTY HEAVY. HOW 'BOUT EX-CHANGIN' 'EM?
AH WAS THINKIN' AH'D LOOK AT IT TIME TO TIME WHEN AH GET LONELY.
IN THE AGE OF CELL PHONES, TEN-YEN COINS ARE SORTA NICE.
WHAT'RE YA GONNA COOK?
HMM... ALL SORTS OF THINGS.
CARTON: GOTOU MILK
DESPITE APPEARANCES, SENSEI REALLY AIN'T A PICKY EATER.
YEP, SURPRIS-IN'LY.
OH, MAYBE AH'LL MAKE HANDA CORN SPECIAL...
CAN YA AT LEAST DO IT AS BUTTER CORN?

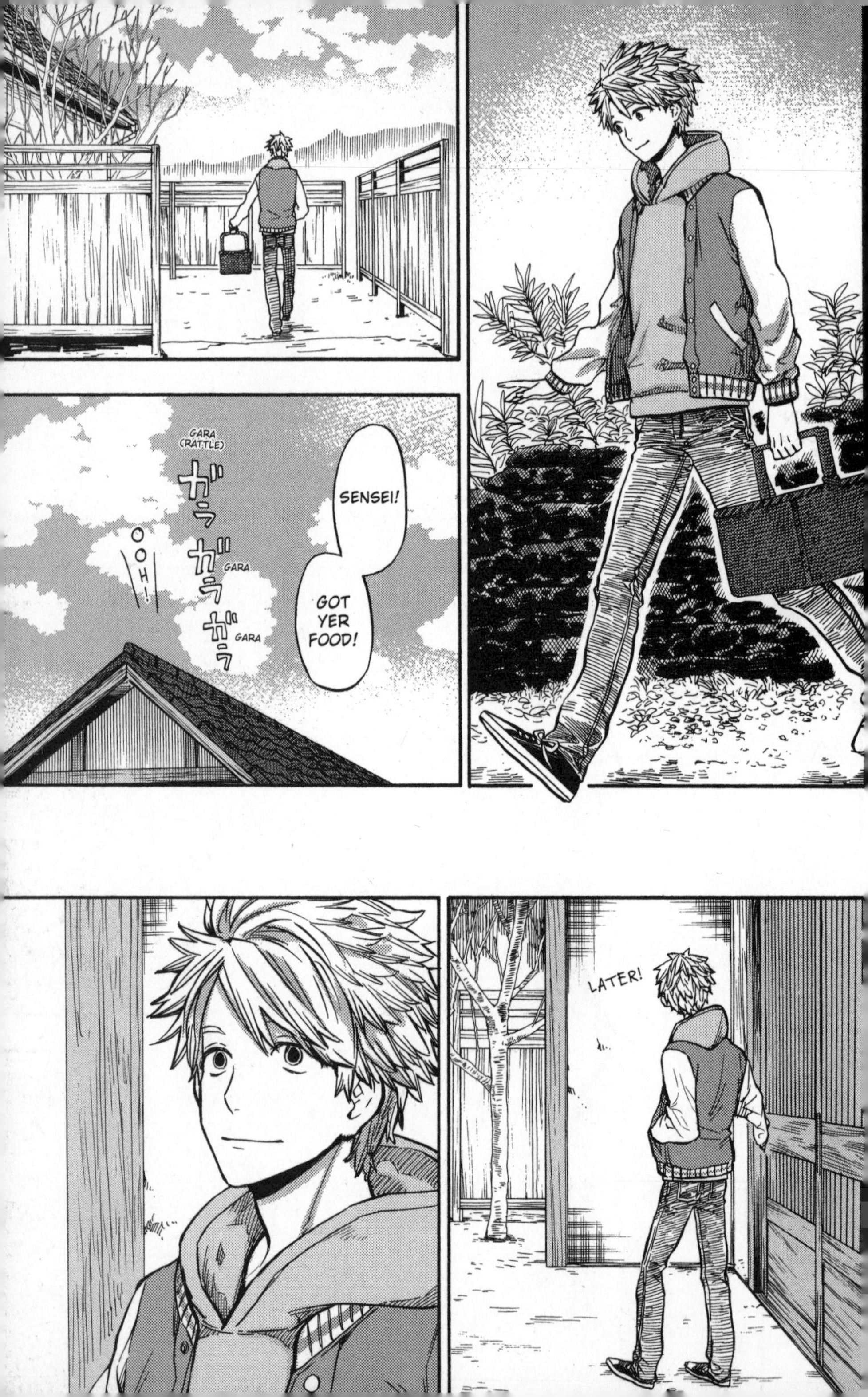
SENSEI!
GOT YER FOOD!
ガラガラガラ
GARA (RATTLE)
GARA
GARA
OOH!
LATER!

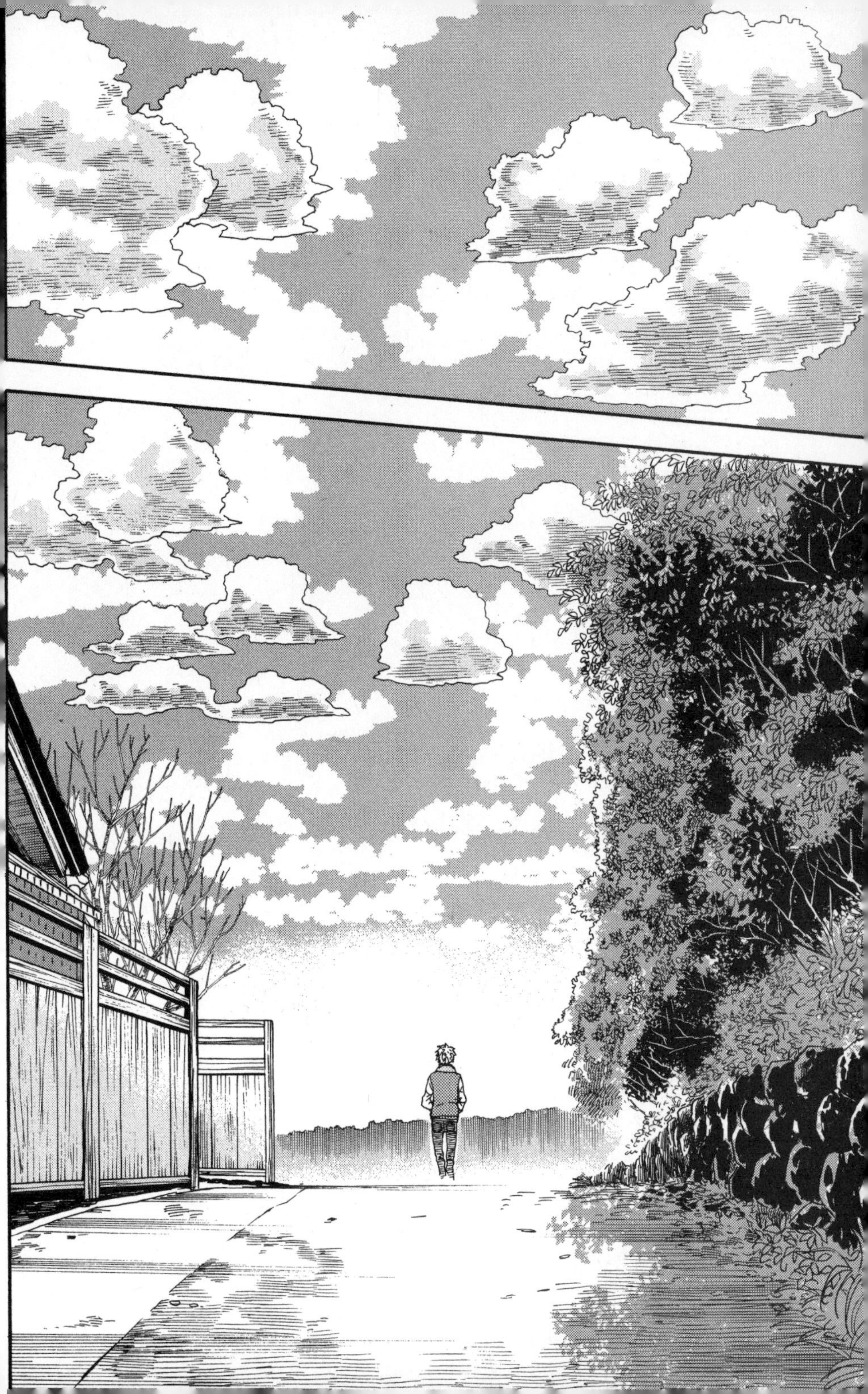

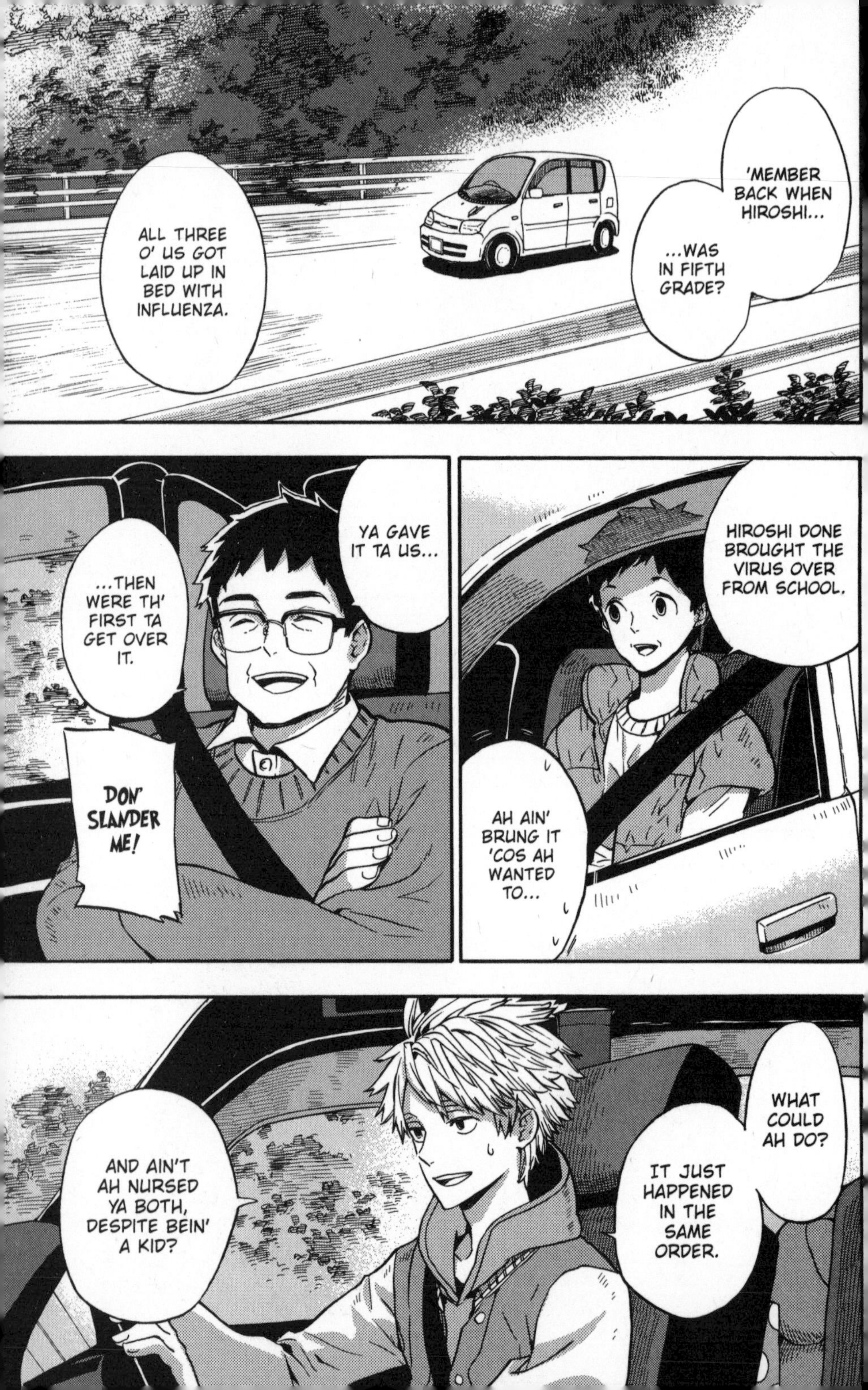
'MEMBER BACK WHEN HIROSHI...
...WAS IN FIFTH GRADE?
ALL THREE O' US GOT LAID UP IN BED WITH INFLUENZA.
HIROSHI DONE BROUGHT THE VIRUS OVER FROM SCHOOL.
AH AIN' BRUNG IT 'COS AH WANTED TO...
YA GAVE IT TA US...
...THEN WERE TH' FIRST TA GET OVER IT.
DON' SLANDER ME!
WHAT COULD AH DO?
IT JUST HAPPENED IN THE SAME ORDER.
AND AIN'T AH NURSED YA BOTH, DESPITE BEIN' A KID?

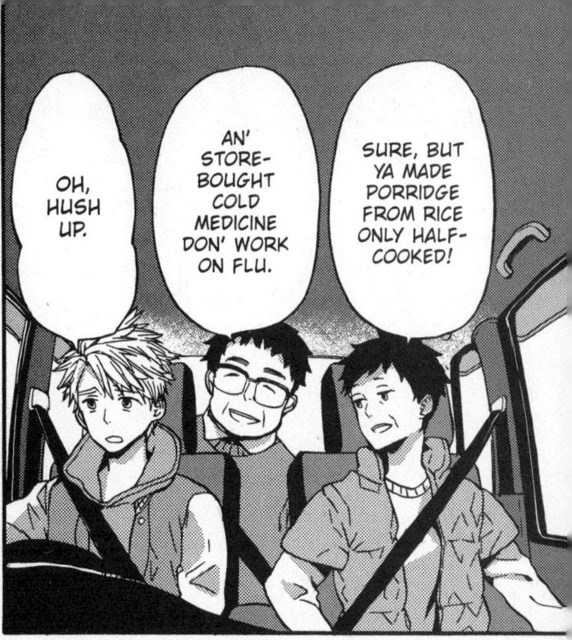
SURE, BUT YA MADE PORRIDGE FROM RICE ONLY HALF-COOKED!
AN' STORE-BOUGHT COLD MEDICINE DON' WORK ON FLU.
OH, HUSH UP.

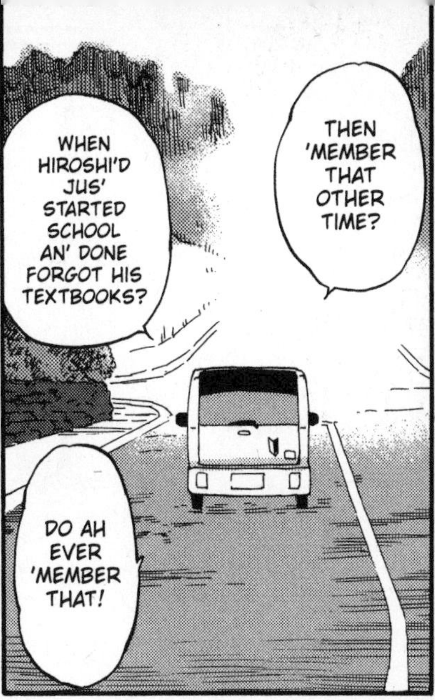
THEN 'MEMBER THAT OTHER TIME?
WHEN HIROSHI'D JUS' STARTED SCHOOL AN' DONE FORGOT HIS TEXTBOOKS?
DO AH EVER 'MEMBER THAT!

Act. 121
ITEKOI HIROSHI
(Translation: Bon Voyage, Hiroshi)

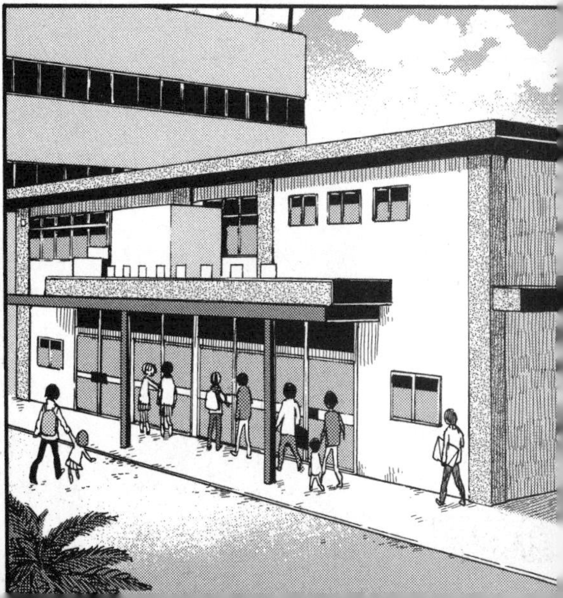

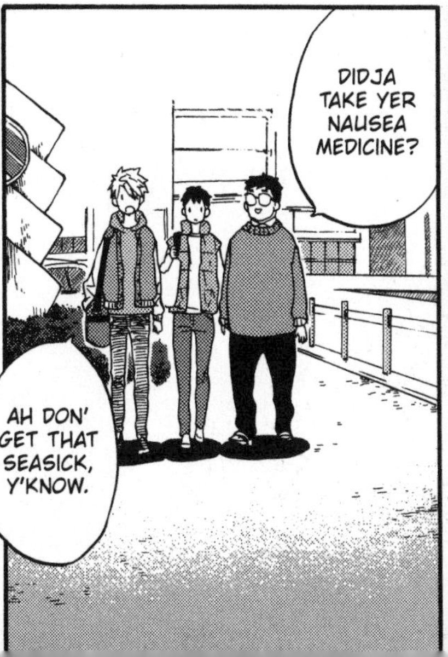
DIDJA TAKE YER NAUSEA MEDICINE?
AH DON' GET THAT SEASICK, Y'KNOW.

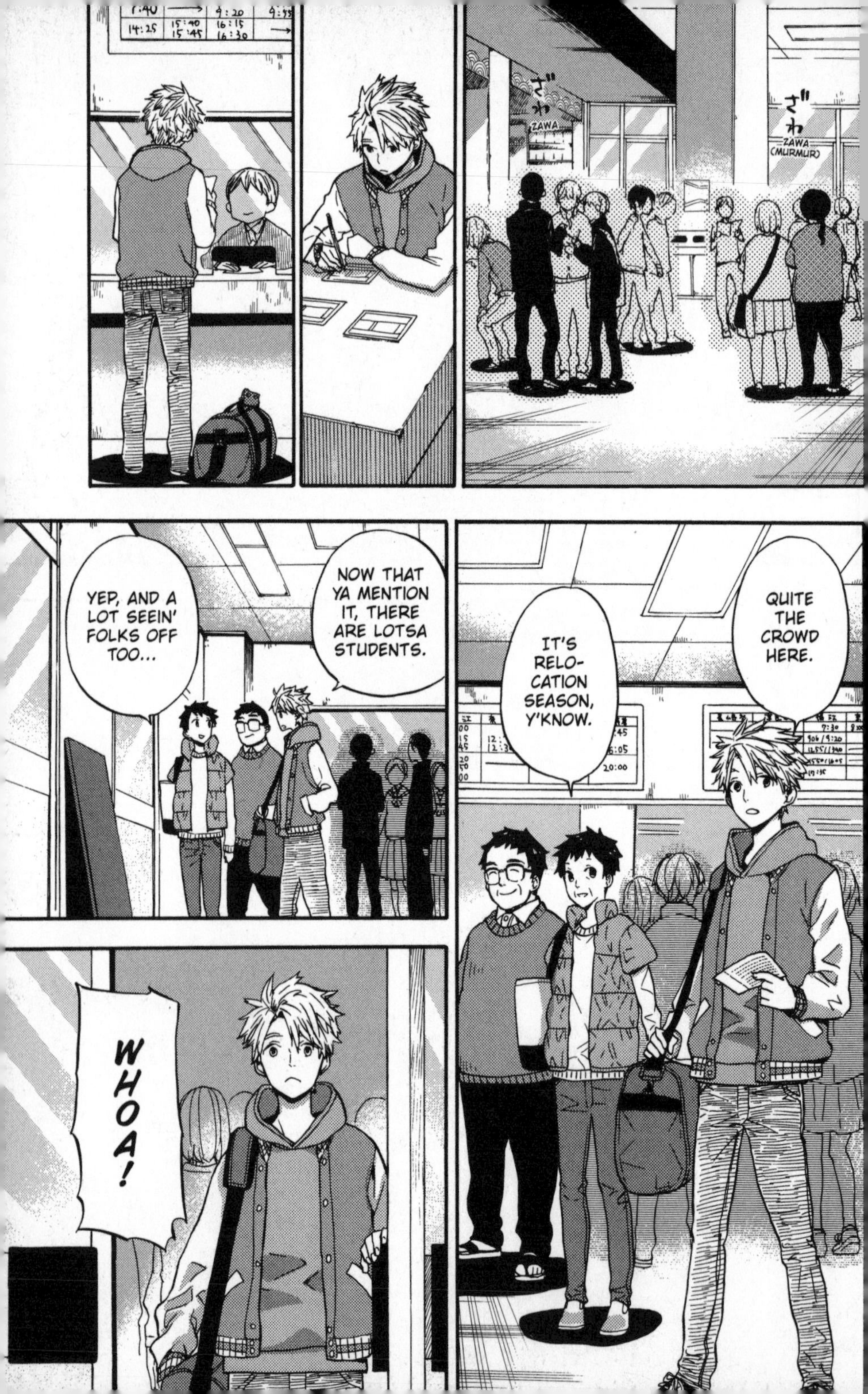
ざわ
ZAWA (MURMUR)
ざわ
ZAWA
QUITE THE CROWD HERE.
IT'S RELO-CATION SEASON, Y'KNOW.
NOW THAT YA MENTION IT, THERE ARE LOTSA STUDENTS.
YEP, AND A LOT SEEIN' FOLKS OFF TOO...
WHOA!

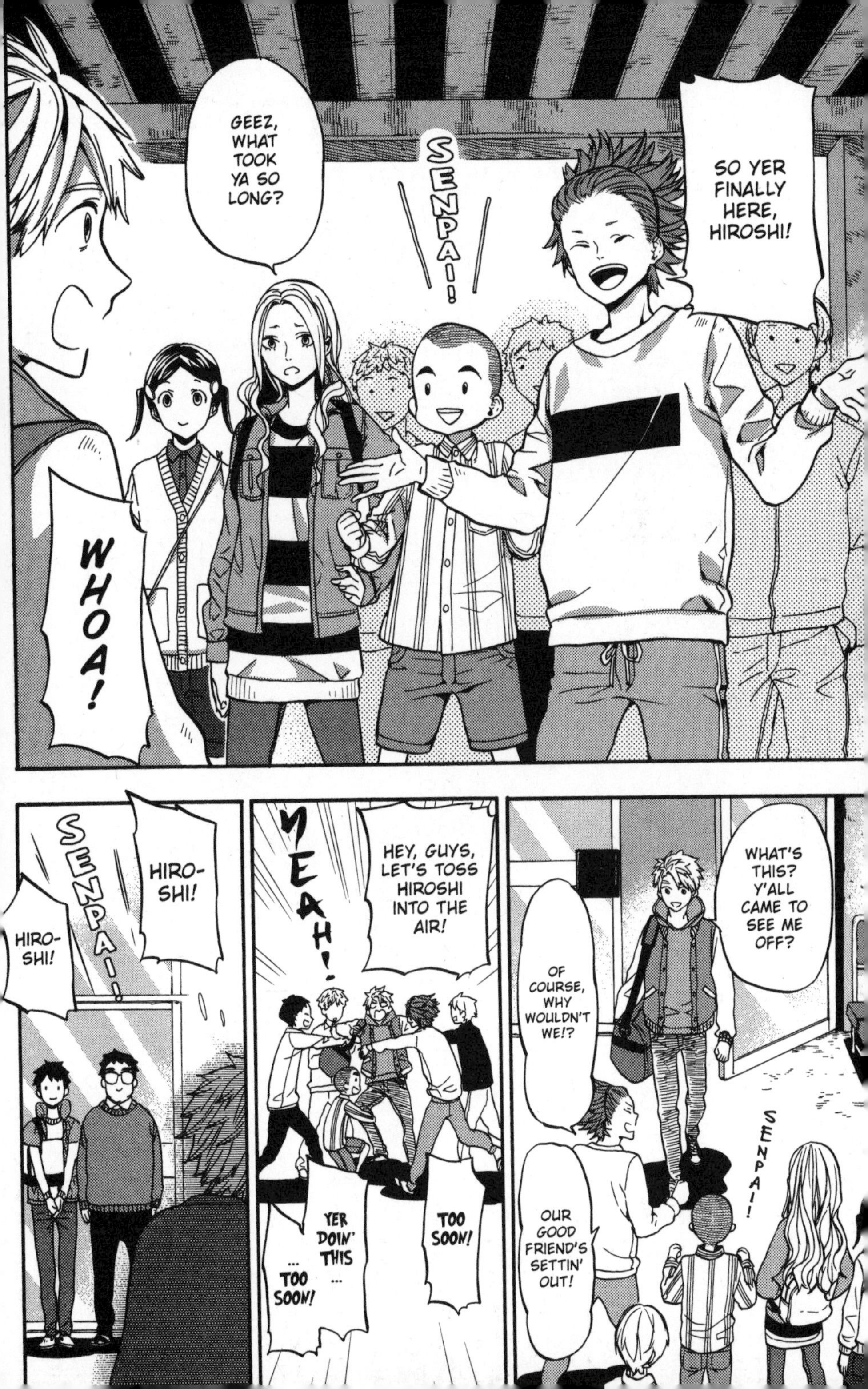
SO YER FINALLY HERE, HIROSHI!
SENPAI!
GEEZ, WHAT TOOK YA SO LONG?
WHOA!
WHAT'S THIS? Y'ALL CAME TO SEE ME OFF?
OF COURSE, WHY WOULDN'T WE!?
SENPAI!
OUR GOOD FRIEND'S SETTIN' OUT!
HEY, GUYS, LET'S TOSS HIROSHI INTO THE AIR!
YEAH!
TOO SOON!
YER DOIN' THIS ... ... TOO SOON!
HIRO-SHI!
SENPAI!
HIRO-SHI!

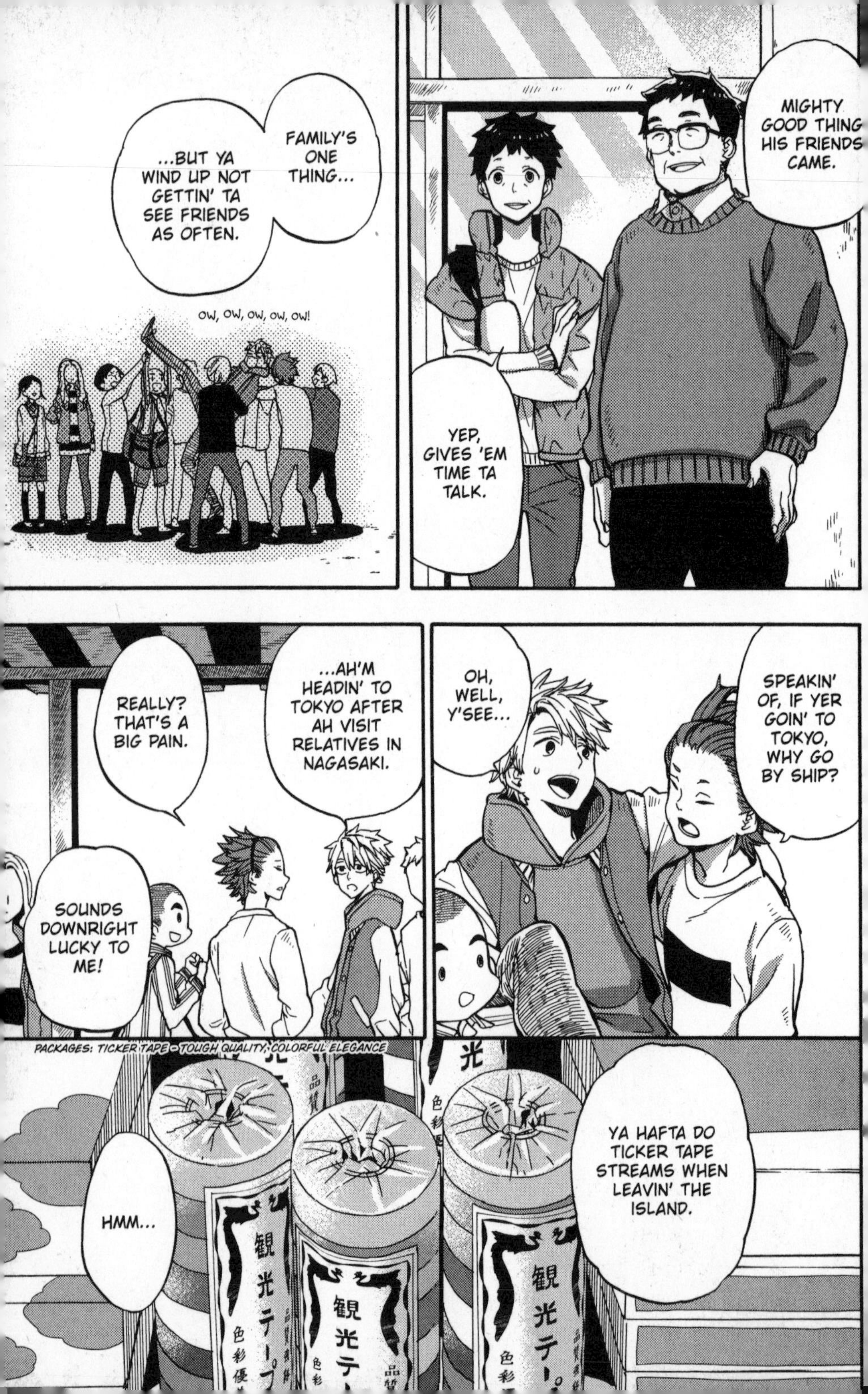
MIGHTY GOOD THING HIS FRIENDS CAME.
YEP, GIVES 'EM TIME TA TALK.
FAMILY'S ONE THING...
...BUT YA WIND UP NOT GETTIN' TA SEE FRIENDS AS OFTEN.
OW, OW, OW, OW, OW!
SPEAKIN' OF, IF YER GOIN' TO TOKYO, WHY GO BY SHIP?
OH, WELL, Y'SEE...
...AH'M HEADIN' TO TOKYO AFTER AH VISIT RELATIVES IN NAGASAKI.
REALLY? THAT'S A BIG PAIN.
SOUNDS DOWNRIGHT LUCKY TO ME!
PACKAGES: TICKER TAPE - TOUGH QUALITY, COLORFUL ELEGANCE
YA HAFTA DO TICKER TAPE STREAMS WHEN LEAVIN' THE ISLAND.
HMM...

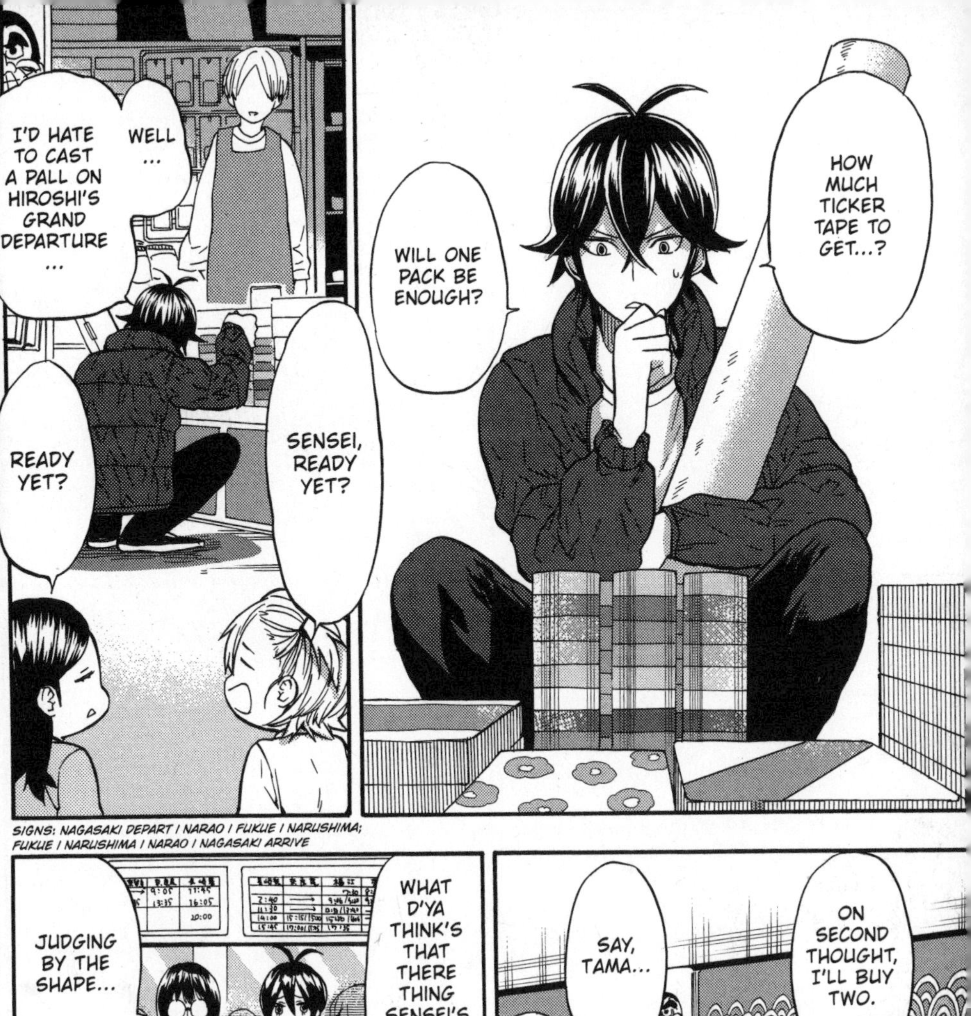
HOW MUCH TICKER TAPE TO GET...?
WILL ONE PACK BE ENOUGH?
WELL...
I'D HATE TO CAST A PALL ON HIROSHI'S GRAND DEPARTURE...
SENSEI, READY YET?
READY YET?

SIGNS: NAGASAKI DEPART / NARAO / FUKUE / NARUSHIMA; FUKUE / NARUSHIMA / NARAO / NAGASAKI ARRIVE

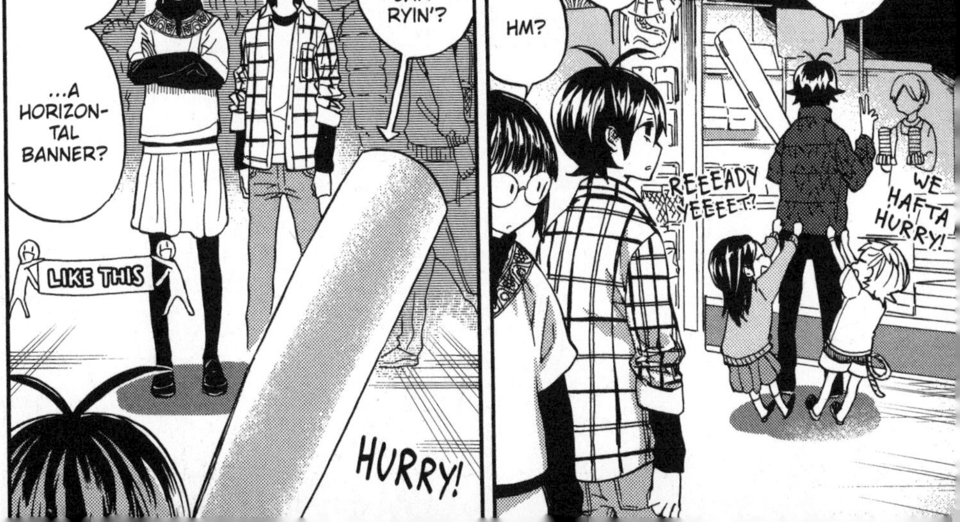
ON SECOND THOUGHT, I'LL BUY TWO.
SAY, TAMA...
HM?
WE HAFTA HURRY!
REEEADY YEEEET?
WHAT D'YA THINK'S THAT THERE THING SENSEI'S CAR-RYIN'?
JUDGING BY THE SHAPE...
...A HORIZON-TAL BANNER?
LIKE THIS
HURRY!

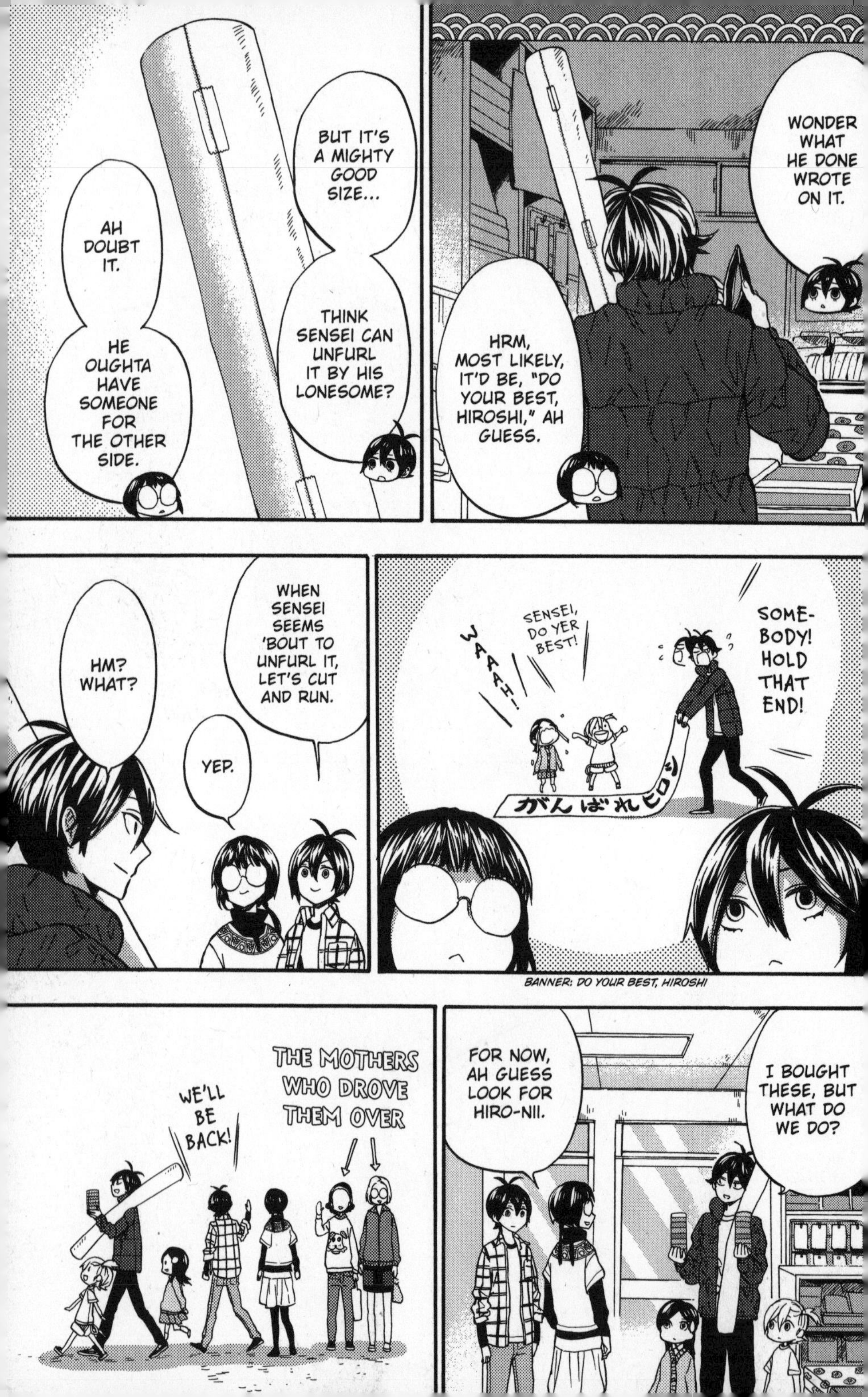
WONDER WHAT HE DONE WROTE ON IT.
HRM, MOST LIKELY, IT'D BE, "DO YOUR BEST, HIROSHI," AH GUESS.
BUT IT'S A MIGHTY GOOD SIZE...
THINK SENSEI CAN UNFURL IT BY HIS LONESOME?
AH DOUBT IT.
HE OUGHTA HAVE SOMEONE FOR THE OTHER SIDE.
SOME-BODY! HOLD THAT END!
SENSEI, DO YER BEST!
WAAAH!
がんばれヒロシ
WHEN SENSEI SEEMS 'BOUT TO UNFURL IT, LET'S CUT AND RUN.
HM? WHAT?
YEP.
I BOUGHT THESE, BUT WHAT DO WE DO?
FOR NOW, AH GUESS LOOK FOR HIRO-NII.
THE MOTHERS WHO DROVE THEM OVER
WE'LL BE BACK!

BANNER: DO YOUR BEST, HIROSHI

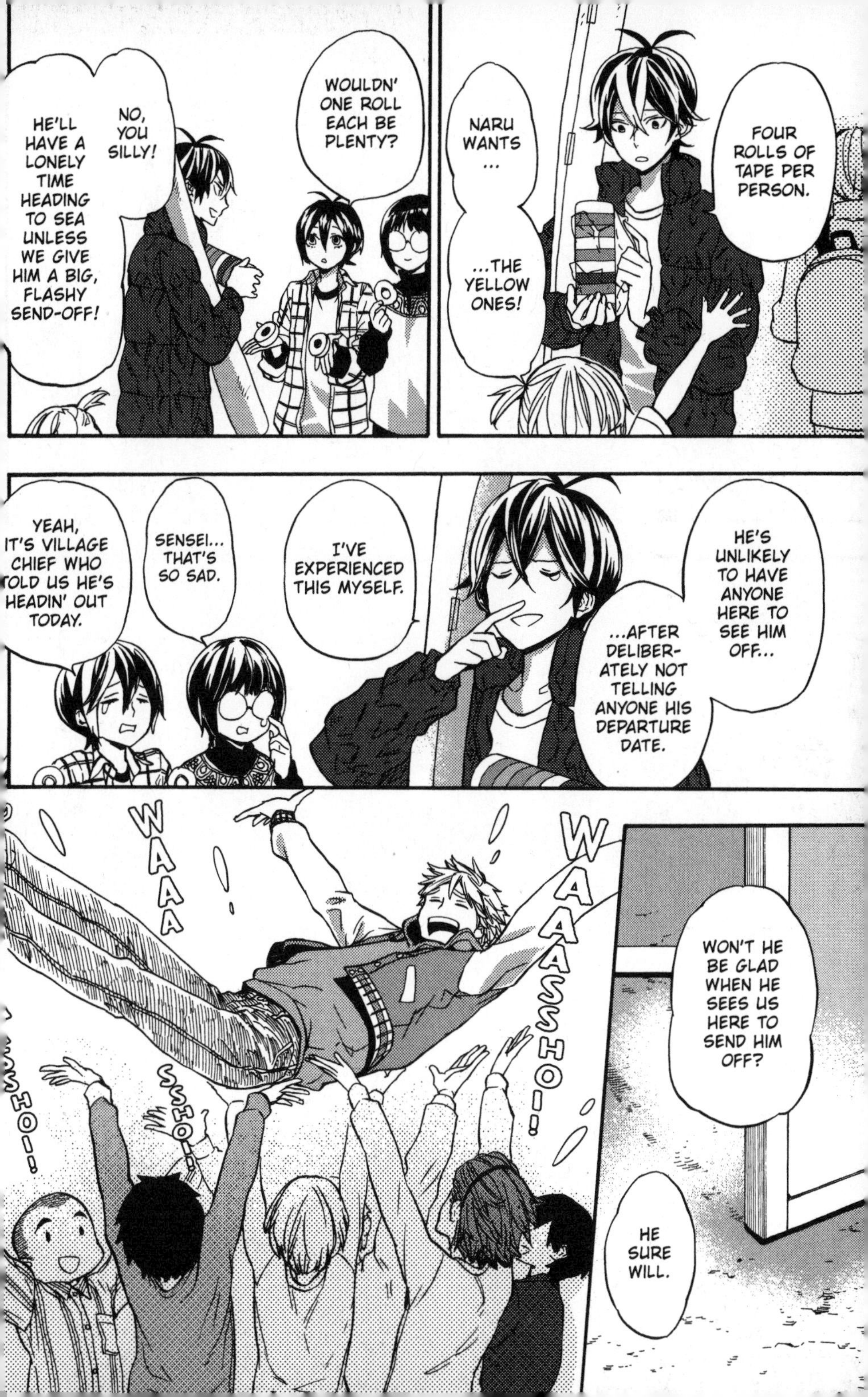
FOUR ROLLS OF TAPE PER PERSON.
NARU WANTS ...
...THE YELLOW ONES!
WOULDN' ONE ROLL EACH BE PLENTY?
NO, YOU SILLY!
HE'LL HAVE A LONELY TIME HEADING TO SEA UNLESS WE GIVE HIM A BIG, FLASHY SEND-OFF!
HE'S UNLIKELY TO HAVE ANYONE HERE TO SEE HIM OFF...
...AFTER DELIBER-ATELY NOT TELLING ANYONE HIS DEPARTURE DATE.
I'VE EXPERIENCED THIS MYSELF.
SENSEI... THAT'S SO SAD.
YEAH, IT'S VILLAGE CHIEF WHO TOLD US HE'S HEADIN' OUT TODAY.
WON'T HE BE GLAD WHEN HE SEES US HERE TO SEND HIM OFF?
HE SURE WILL.
WAAAASSHOI!
WAAAA
SSHOI!
SSHOI!

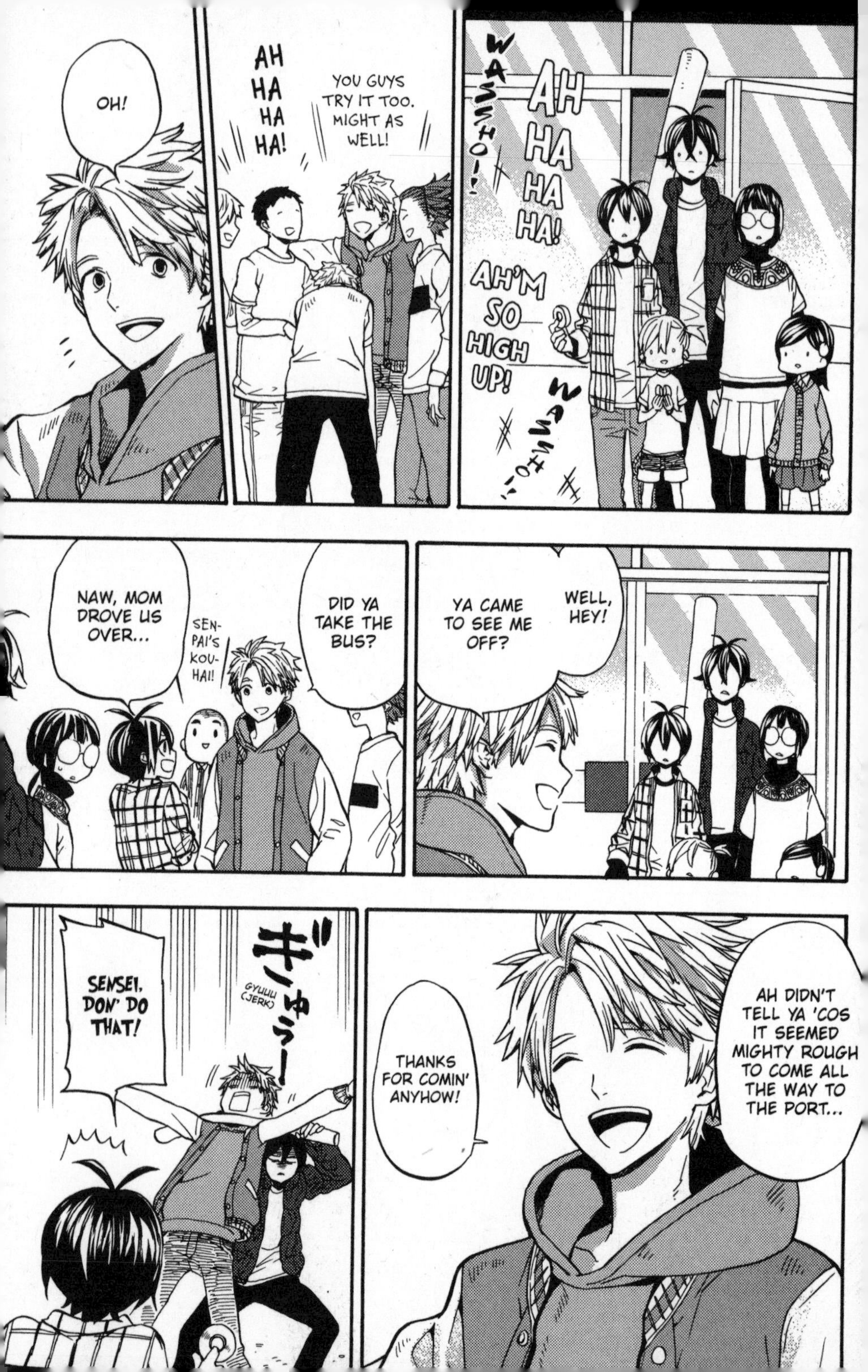
WASSHO!!
AH HA HA HA!
AH'M SO HIGH UP!
WASSHO!!
AH HA HA HA!
YOU GUYS TRY IT TOO. MIGHT AS WELL!
OH!
WELL, HEY!
YA CAME TO SEE ME OFF?
DID YA TAKE THE BUS?
NAW, MOM DROVE US OVER...
SEN-PAI'S KOU-HAI!
AH DIDN'T TELL YA 'COS IT SEEMED MIGHTY ROUGH TO COME ALL THE WAY TO THE PORT...
THANKS FOR COMIN' ANYHOW!
ぎゅうー
GYUUU (JERK)
SENSEI, DON' DO THAT!

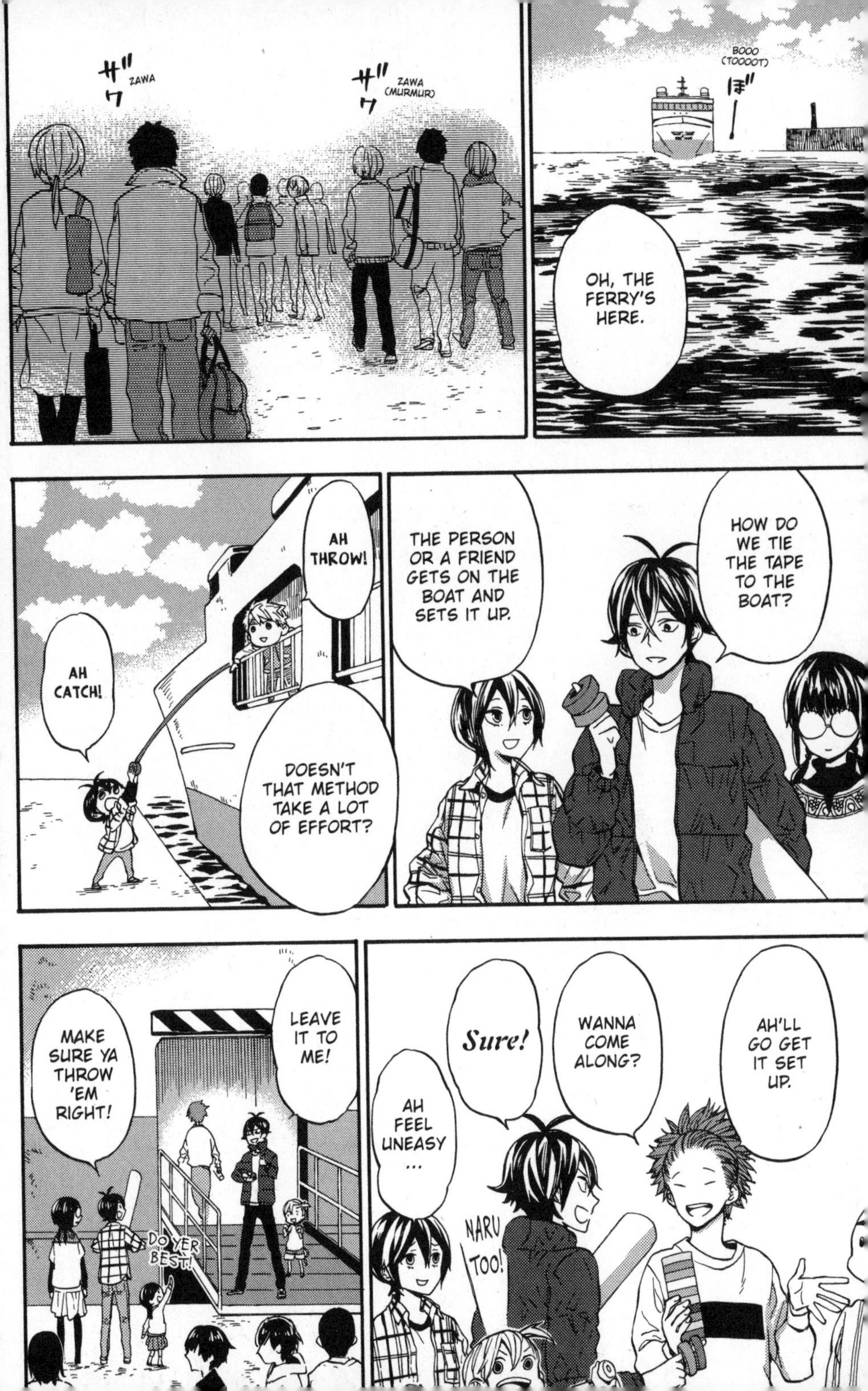
BOOO (TOOOOT)
ぼー
OH, THE FERRY'S HERE.
ザワ ZAWA (MURMUR)
ザワ ZAWA
HOW DO WE TIE THE TAPE TO THE BOAT?
THE PERSON OR A FRIEND GETS ON THE BOAT AND SETS IT UP.
AH THROW!
AH CATCH!
DOESN'T THAT METHOD TAKE A LOT OF EFFORT?
AH'LL GO GET IT SET UP.
WANNA COME ALONG?
Sure!
AH FEEL UNEASY ...
NARU TOO!
LEAVE IT TO ME!
MAKE SURE YA THROW 'EM RIGHT!
DO YER BEST!

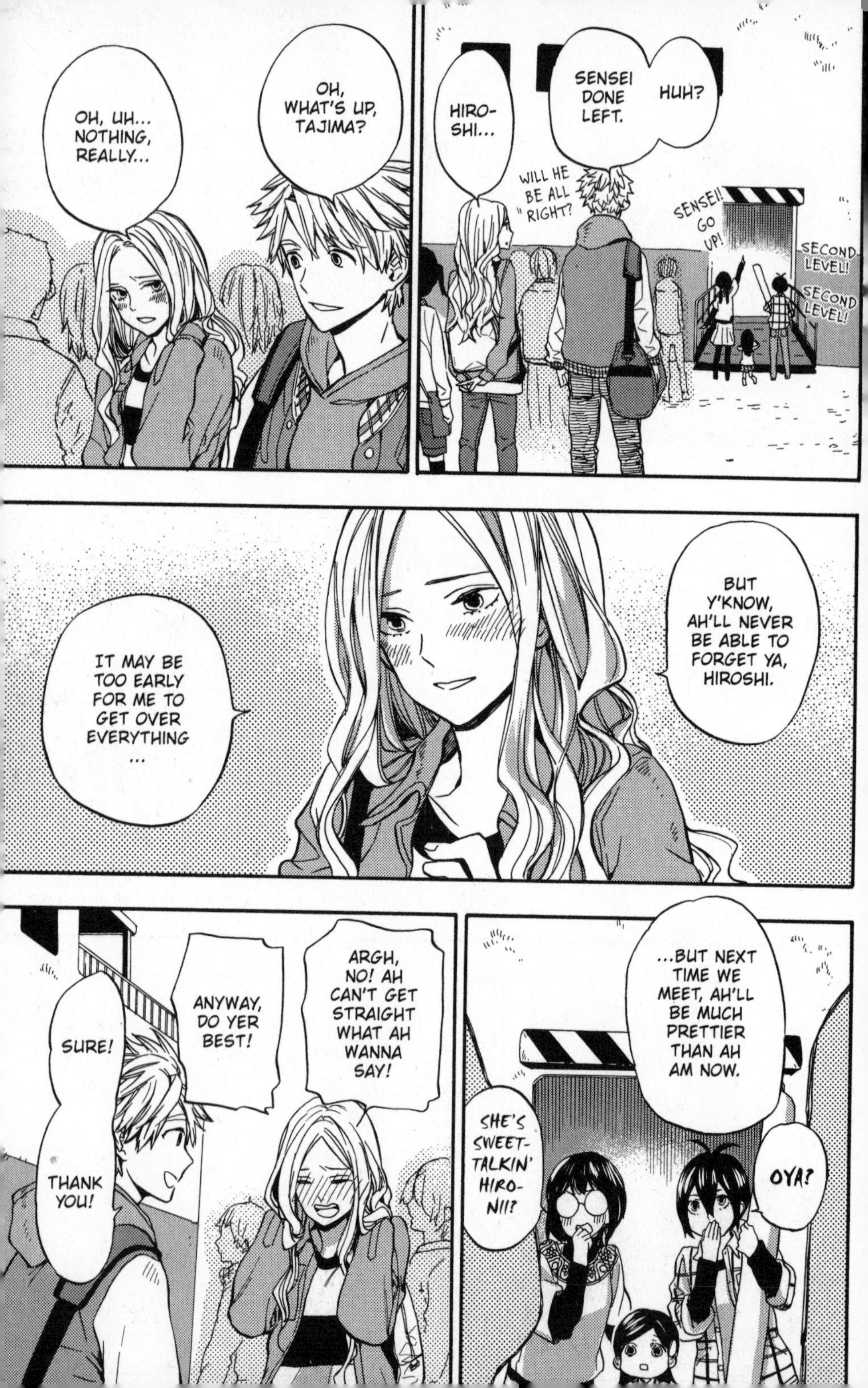
HUH?
SENSEI DONE LEFT.
HIRO-SHI...
WILL HE BE ALL RIGHT?
SENSEI! GO UP!
SECOND LEVEL!
SECOND LEVEL!
OH, WHAT'S UP, TAJIMA?
OH, UH... NOTHING, REALLY...
BUT Y'KNOW, AH'LL NEVER BE ABLE TO FORGET YA, HIROSHI.
IT MAY BE TOO EARLY FOR ME TO GET OVER EVERYTHING...
...BUT NEXT TIME WE MEET, AH'LL BE MUCH PRETTIER THAN AH AM NOW.
OYA?
SHE'S SWEET-TALKIN' HIRO-NII?
ARGH, NO! AH CAN'T GET STRAIGHT WHAT AH WANNA SAY!
ANYWAY, DO YER BEST!
SURE!
THANK YOU!

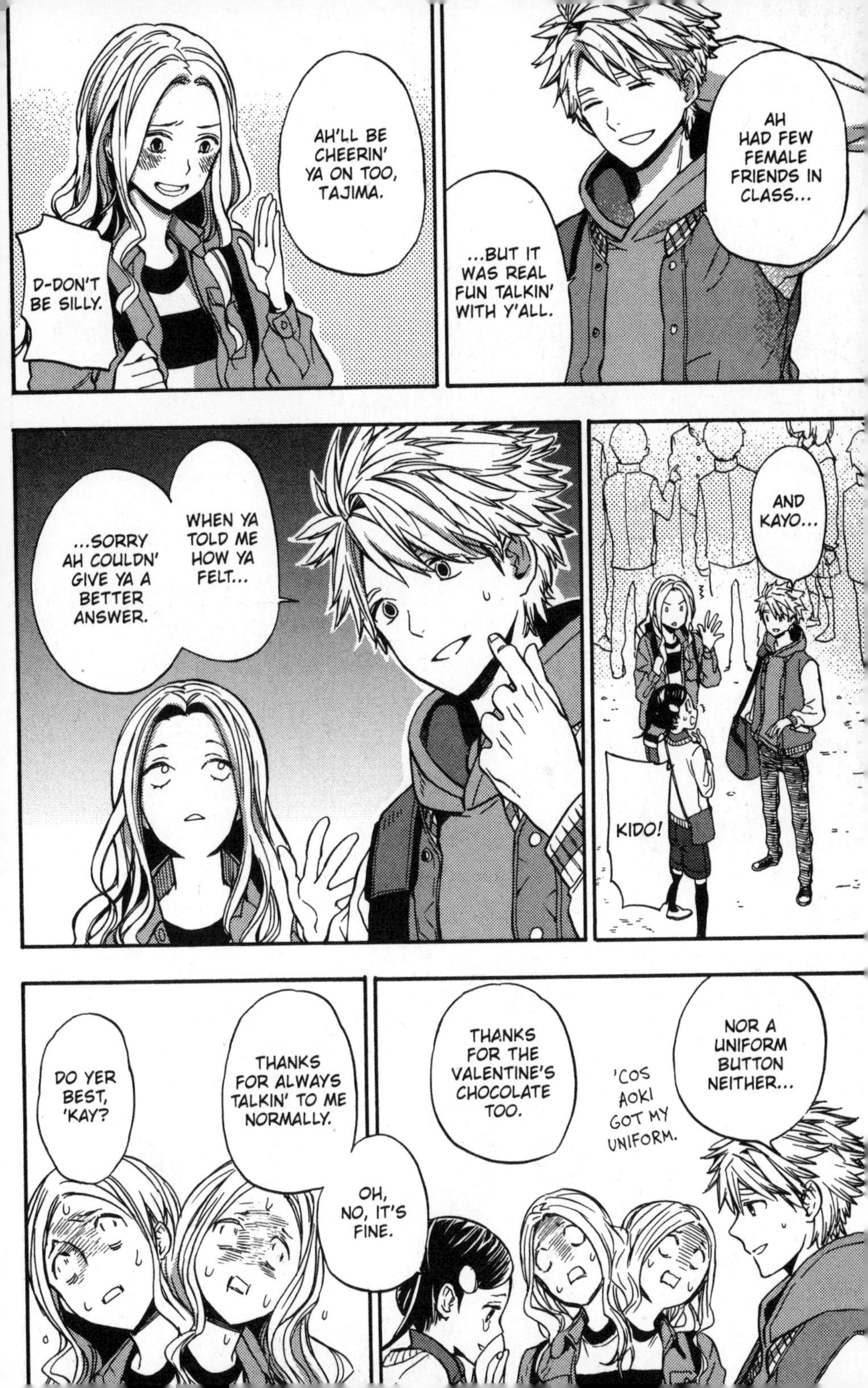
AH HAD FEW FEMALE FRIENDS IN CLASS...
...BUT IT WAS REAL FUN TALKIN' WITH Y'ALL.
AH'LL BE CHEERIN' YA ON TOO, TAJIMA.
D-DON'T BE SILLY.
AND KAYO...
KIDO!
WHEN YA TOLD ME HOW YA FELT...
...SORRY AH COULDN' GIVE YA A BETTER ANSWER.
NOR A UNIFORM BUTTON NEITHER...
'COS AOKI GOT MY UNIFORM.
THANKS FOR THE VALENTINE'S CHOCOLATE TOO.
THANKS FOR ALWAYS TALKIN' TO ME NORMALLY.
OH, NO, IT'S FINE.
DO YER BEST, 'KAY?

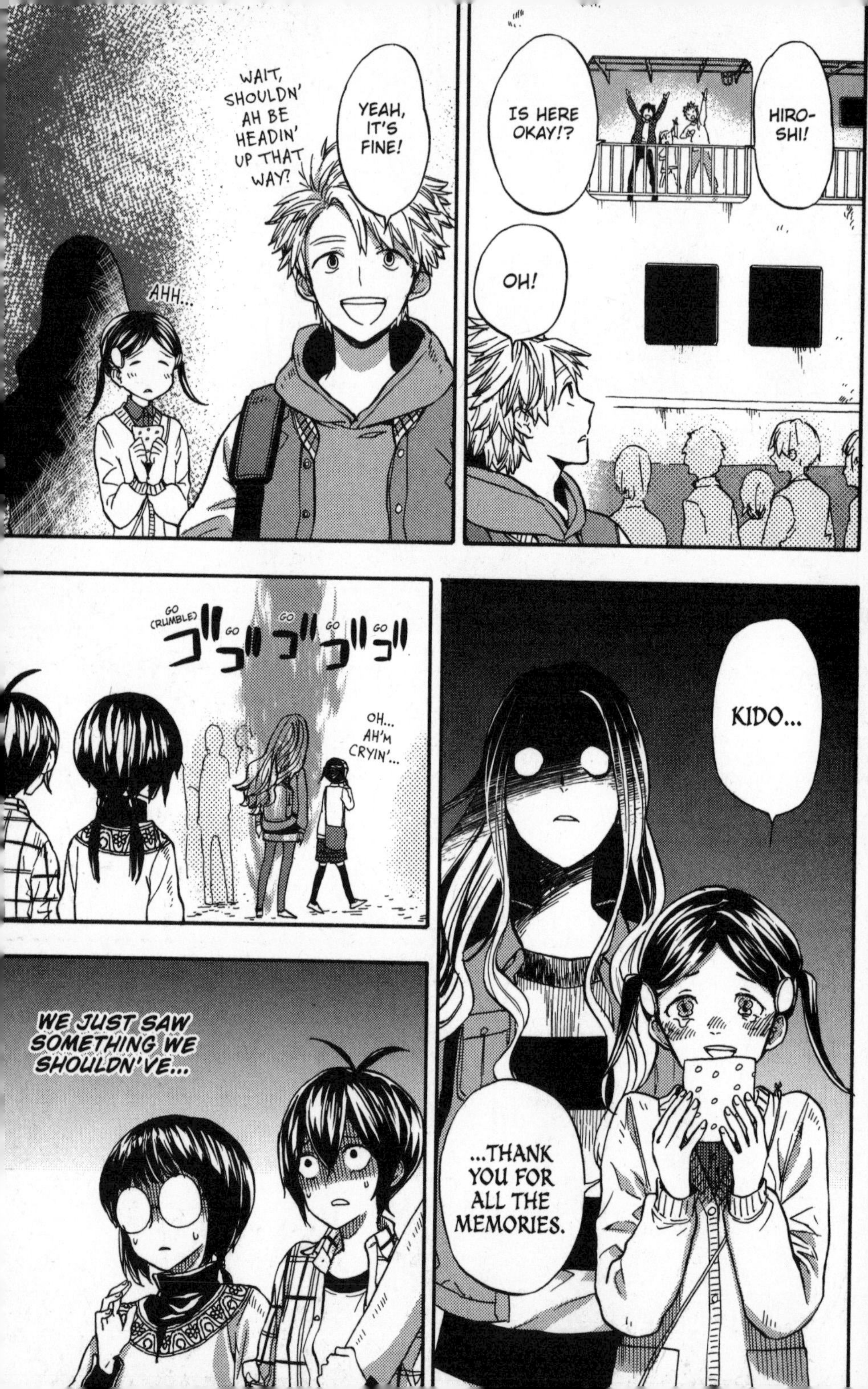
HIRO-SHI!
IS HERE OKAY!?
OH!
YEAH, IT'S FINE!
WAIT, SHOULDN' AH BE HEADIN' UP THAT WAY?
AHH...
KIDO...
...THANK YOU FOR ALL THE MEMORIES.
GO (RUMBLE) GO GO GO GO
ゴゴゴゴゴ
OH... AH'M CRYIN'...
WE JUST SAW SOMETHING WE SHOULDN'VE...

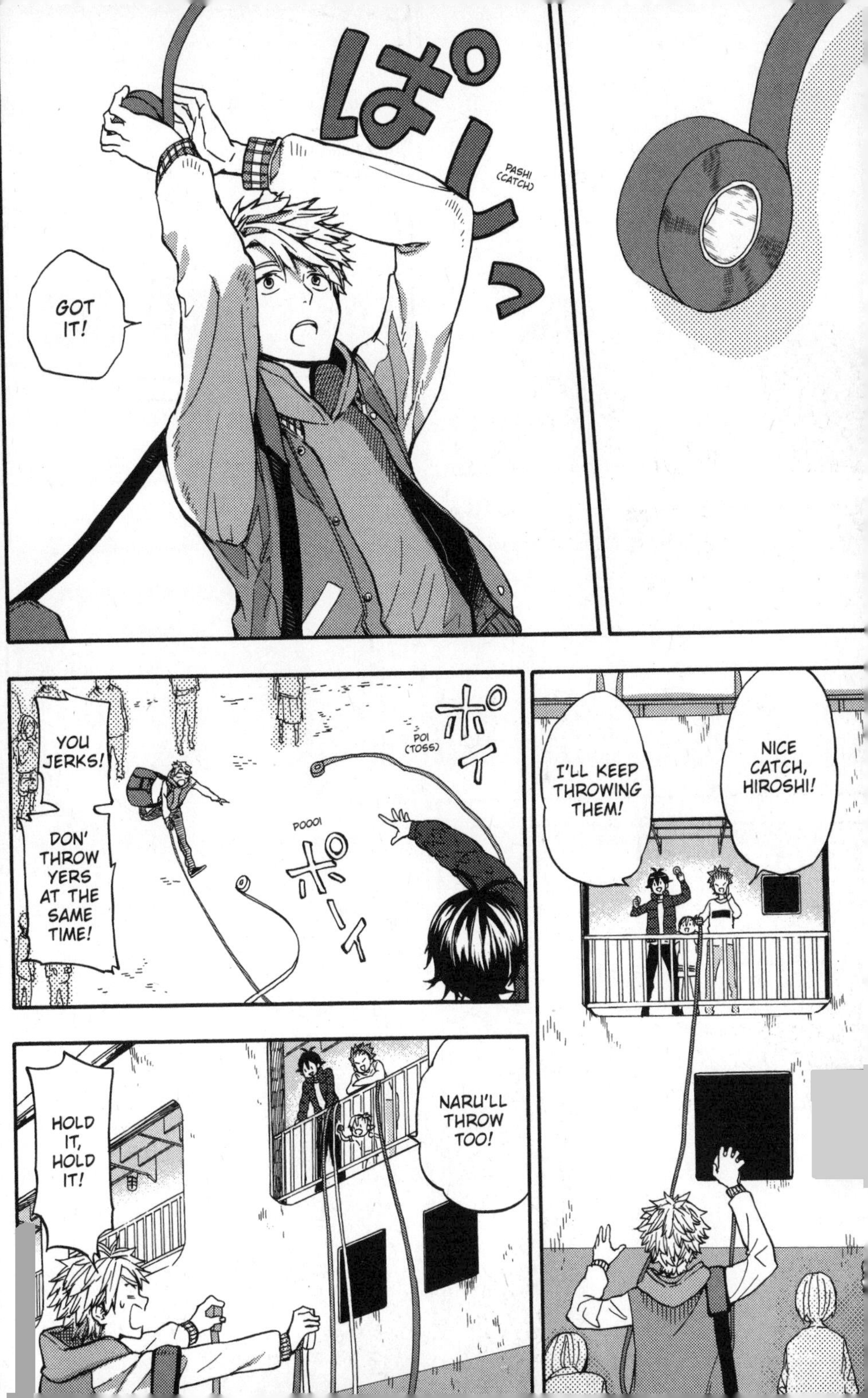

ぱしっ
PASHI (CATCH)
GOT IT!
NICE CATCH, HIROSHI!
I'LL KEEP THROWING THEM!
ポイ
POI (TOSS)
ポーイ
POOOI
YOU JERKS!
DON' THROW YERS AT THE SAME TIME!
NARU'LL THROW TOO!
HOLD IT, HOLD IT!

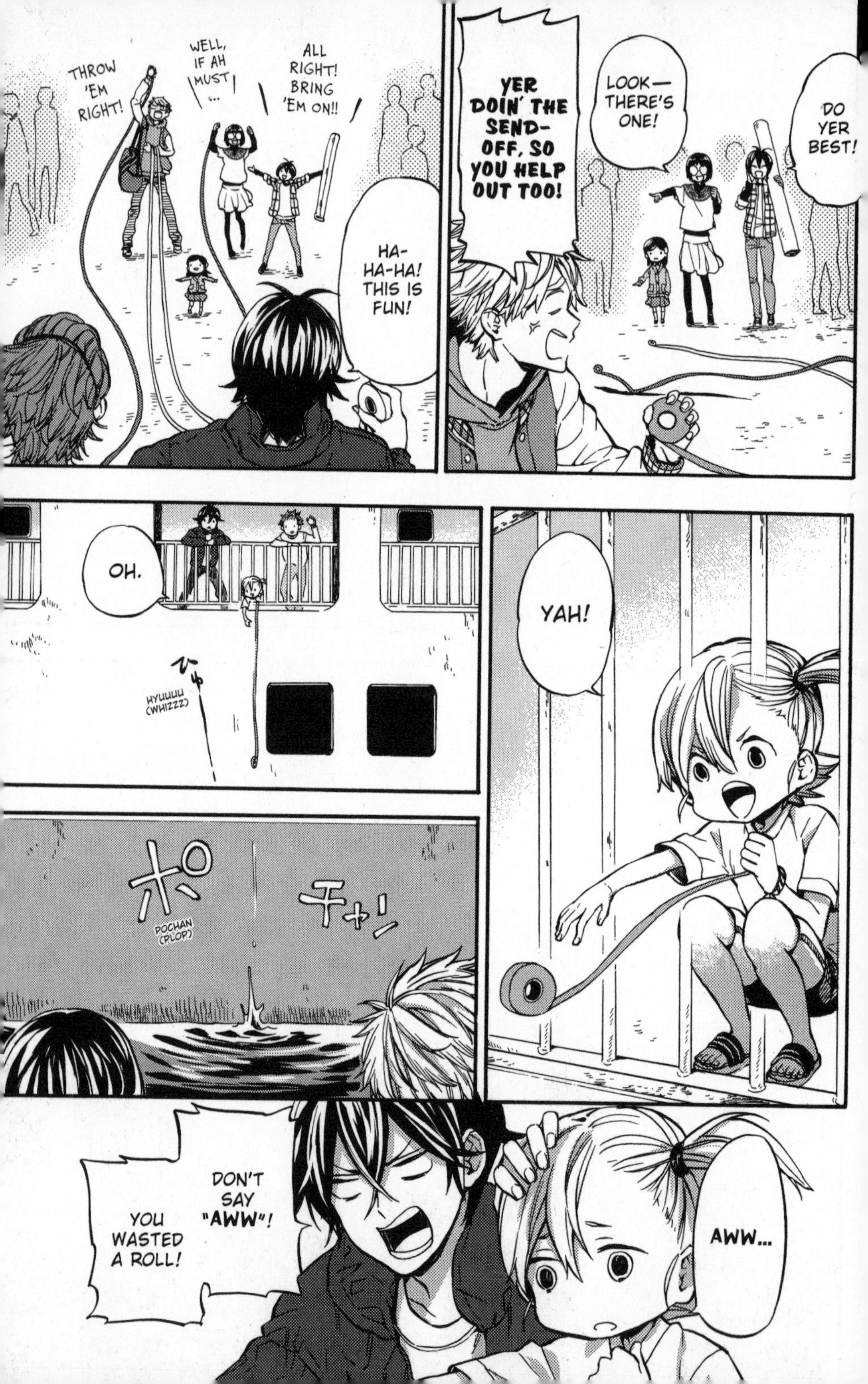
DO YER BEST!
LOOK—THERE'S ONE!
YER DOIN' THE SEND-OFF, SO YOU HELP OUT TOO!
ALL RIGHT! BRING 'EM ON!!
WELL, IF AH MUST...
THROW 'EM RIGHT!
HA-HA-HA! THIS IS FUN!
YAH!
OH.
ひゅ
HYUUUU (WHIZZZ)
ポチャン
POCHAN (PLOP)
AWW...
DON'T SAY "AWW"!
YOU WASTED A ROLL!

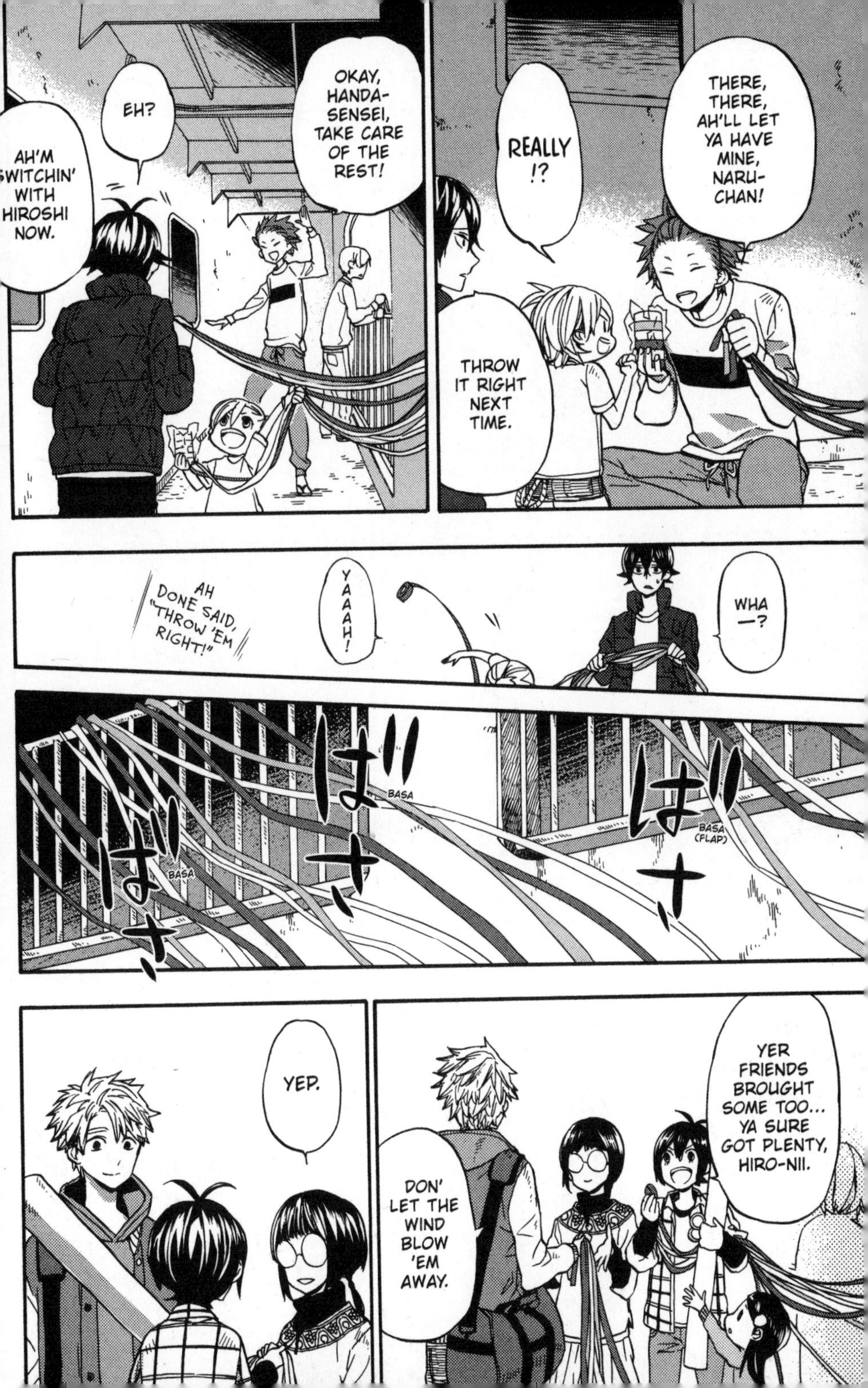
THERE, THERE, AH'LL LET YA HAVE MINE, NARU-CHAN!
REALLY !?
THROW IT RIGHT NEXT TIME.
OKAY, HANDA-SENSEI, TAKE CARE OF THE REST!
EH?
AH'M SWITCHIN' WITH HIROSHI NOW.
WHA—?
YAAAAH!
AH DONE SAID, "THROW 'EM RIGHT!"
BASA (FLAP)
BASA
BASA
YER FRIENDS BROUGHT SOME TOO… YA SURE GOT PLENTY, HIRO-NII.
DON' LET THE WIND BLOW 'EM AWAY.
YEP.

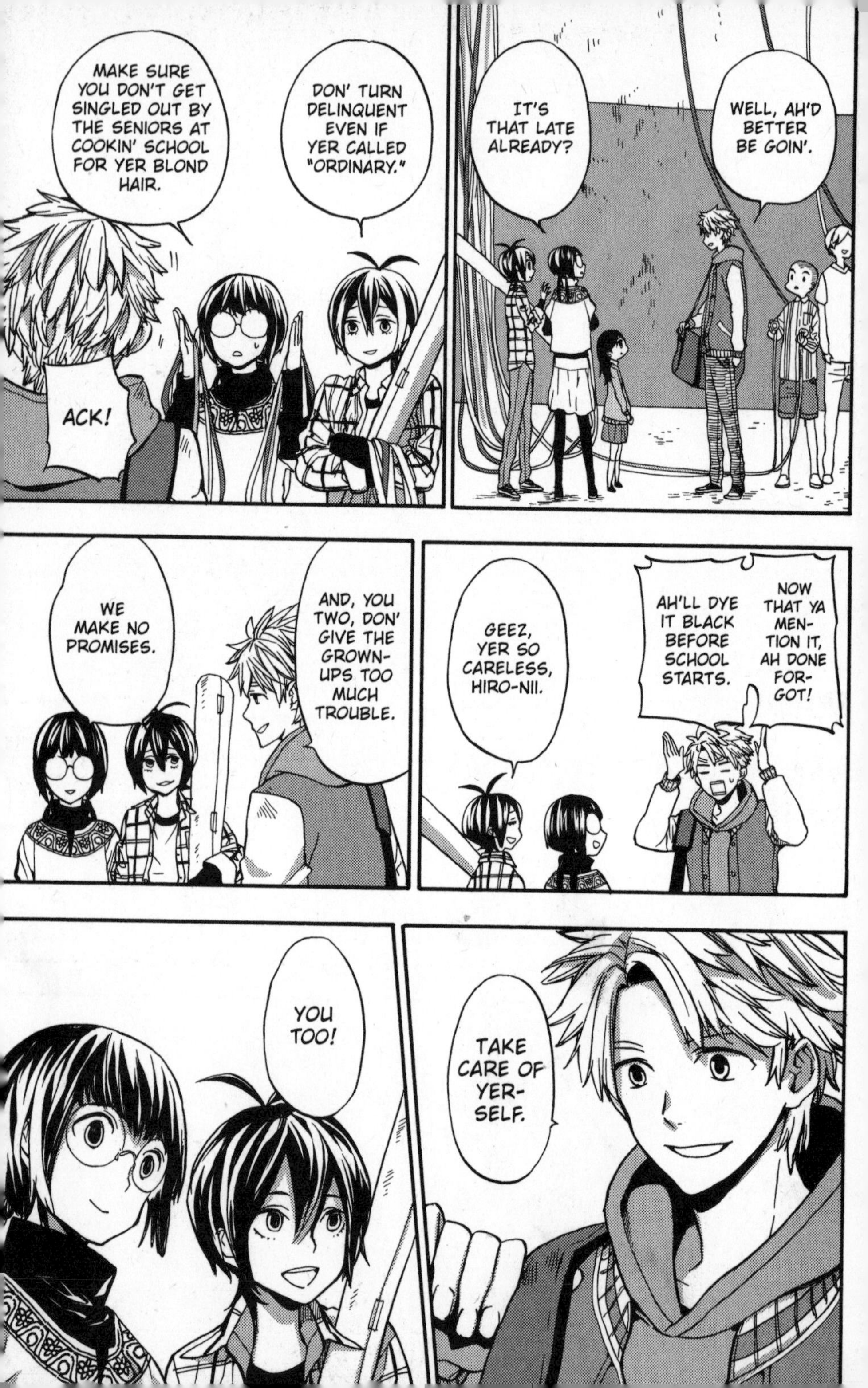
WELL, AH'D BETTER BE GOIN'.
IT'S THAT LATE ALREADY?
DON' TURN DELINQUENT EVEN IF YER CALLED "ORDINARY."
MAKE SURE YOU DON'T GET SINGLED OUT BY THE SENIORS AT COOKIN' SCHOOL FOR YER BLOND HAIR.
ACK!
NOW THAT YA MENTION IT, AH DONE FORGOT!
AH'LL DYE IT BLACK BEFORE SCHOOL STARTS.
GEEZ, YER SO CARELESS, HIRO-NII.
AND, YOU TWO, DON' GIVE THE GROWN-UPS TOO MUCH TROUBLE.
WE MAKE NO PROMISES.
TAKE CARE OF YERSELF.
YOU TOO!

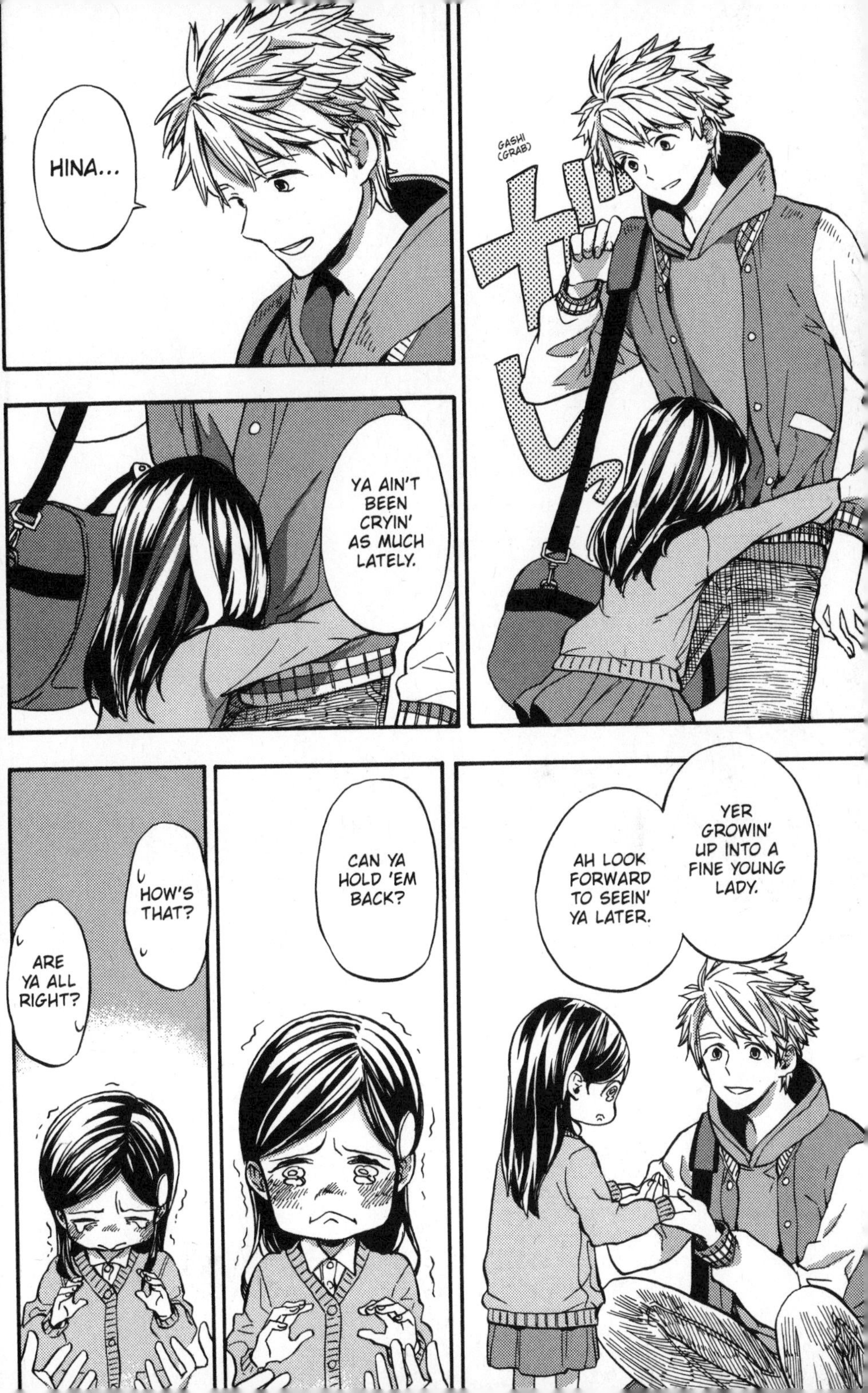
GASHI (GRAB)
HINA...
YA AIN'T BEEN CRYIN' AS MUCH LATELY.
YER GROWIN' UP INTO A FINE YOUNG LADY.
AH LOOK FORWARD TO SEEIN' YA LATER.
CAN YA HOLD 'EM BACK?
HOW'S THAT?
ARE YA ALL RIGHT?

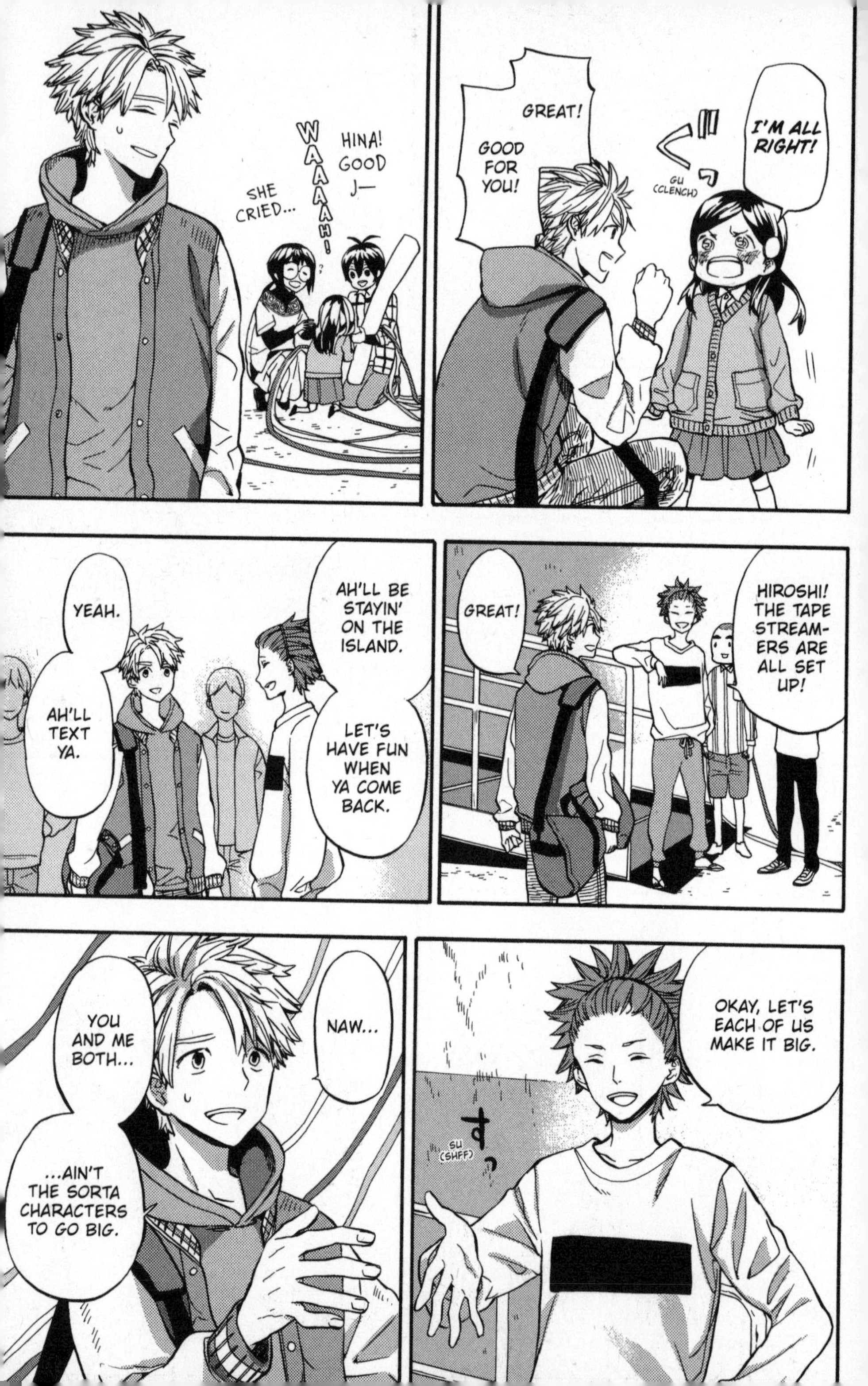
I'M ALL RIGHT!
GU (CLENCH)
GREAT!
GOOD FOR YOU!
HINA! GOOD J—
WAAAAAH!
SHE CRIED...
HIROSHI! THE TAPE STREAMERS ARE ALL SET UP!
GREAT!
AH'LL BE STAYIN' ON THE ISLAND.
LET'S HAVE FUN WHEN YA COME BACK.
YEAH.
AH'LL TEXT YA.
OKAY, LET'S EACH OF US MAKE IT BIG.
SU (SHFF)
NAW...
YOU AND ME BOTH...
...AIN'T THE SORTA CHARACTERS TO GO BIG.

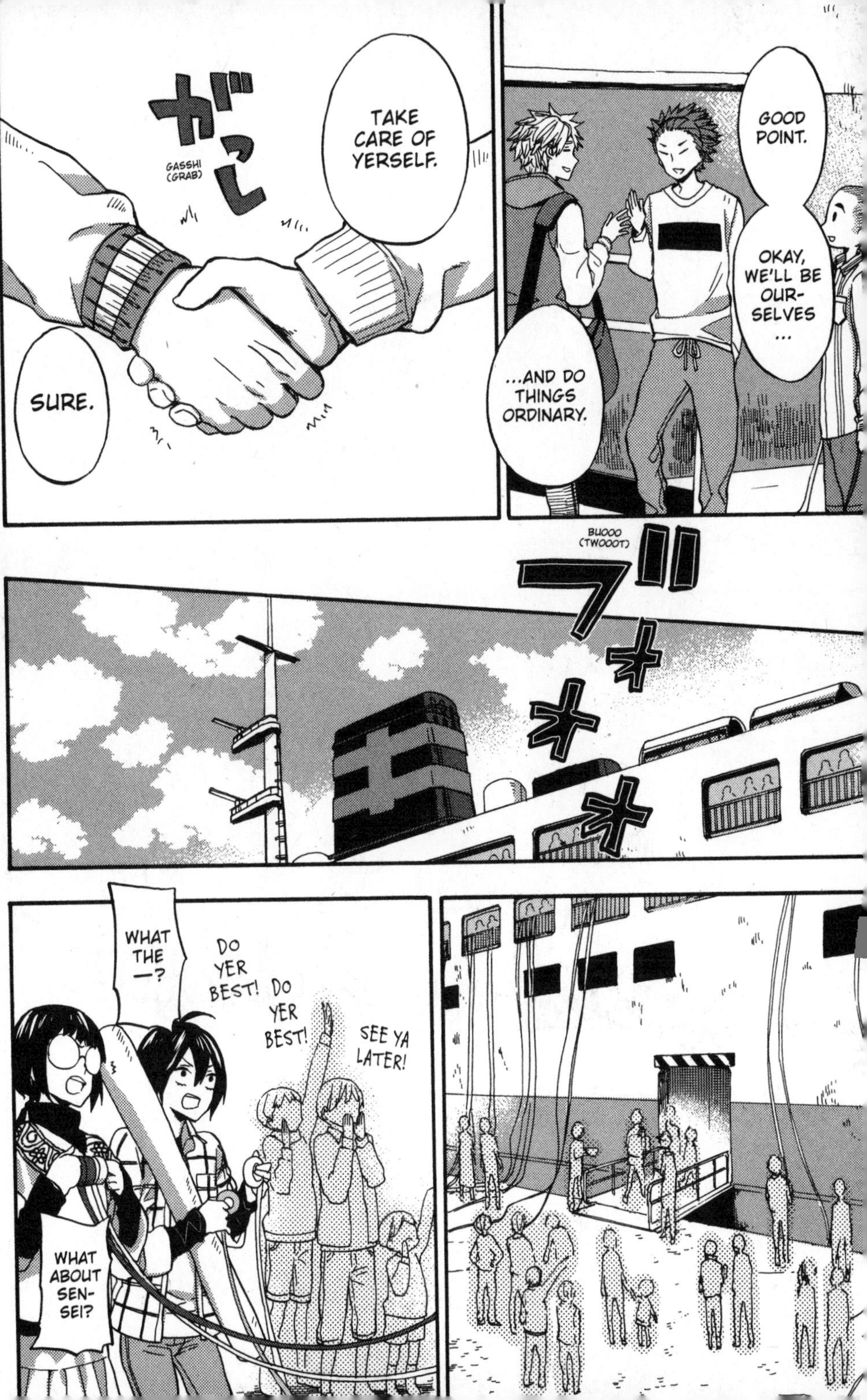
GOOD POINT.
OKAY, WE'LL BE OURSELVES...
...AND DO THINGS ORDINARY.
TAKE CARE OF YERSELF.
がっし
GASSHI (GRAB)
SURE.
BUOOO (TWOOOT)
ブォォォ
SEE YA LATER!
DO YER BEST!
DO YER BEST!
WHAT THE—?
WHAT ABOUT SEN-SEI?

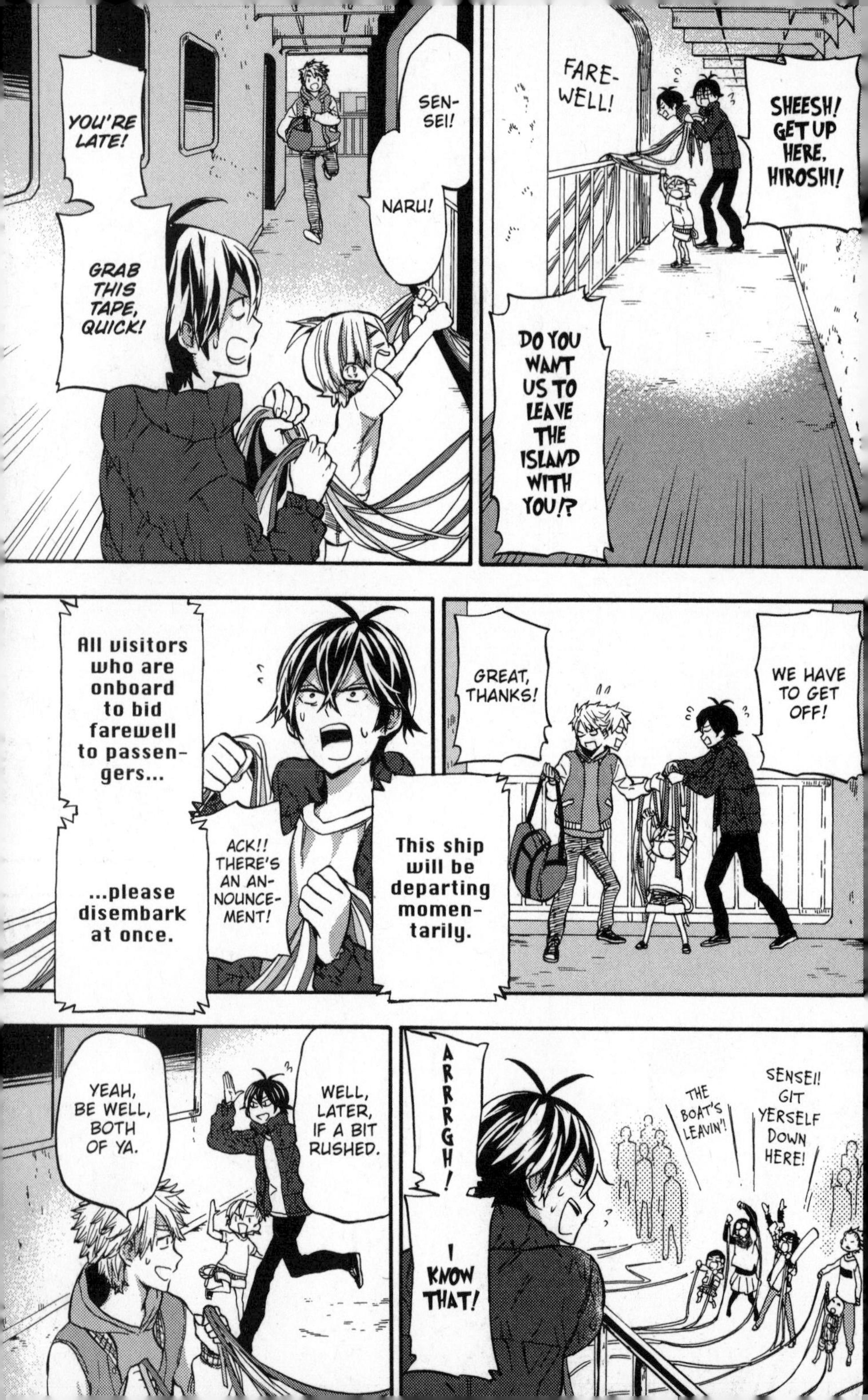
SHEESH! GET UP HERE, HIROSHI!
FARE-WELL!
DO YOU WANT US TO LEAVE THE ISLAND WITH YOU!?
SEN-SEI!
NARU!
YOU'RE LATE!
GRAB THIS TAPE, QUICK!
WE HAVE TO GET OFF!
GREAT, THANKS!
All visitors who are onboard to bid farewell to passen-gers...
...please disembark at once.
This ship will be departing momen-tarily.
ACK!! THERE'S AN AN-NOUNCE-MENT!
SENSEI! GIT YERSELF DOWN HERE!
THE BOAT'S LEAVIN'!
ARRRGH!
I KNOW THAT!
WELL, LATER, IF A BIT RUSHED.
YEAH, BE WELL, BOTH OF YA.

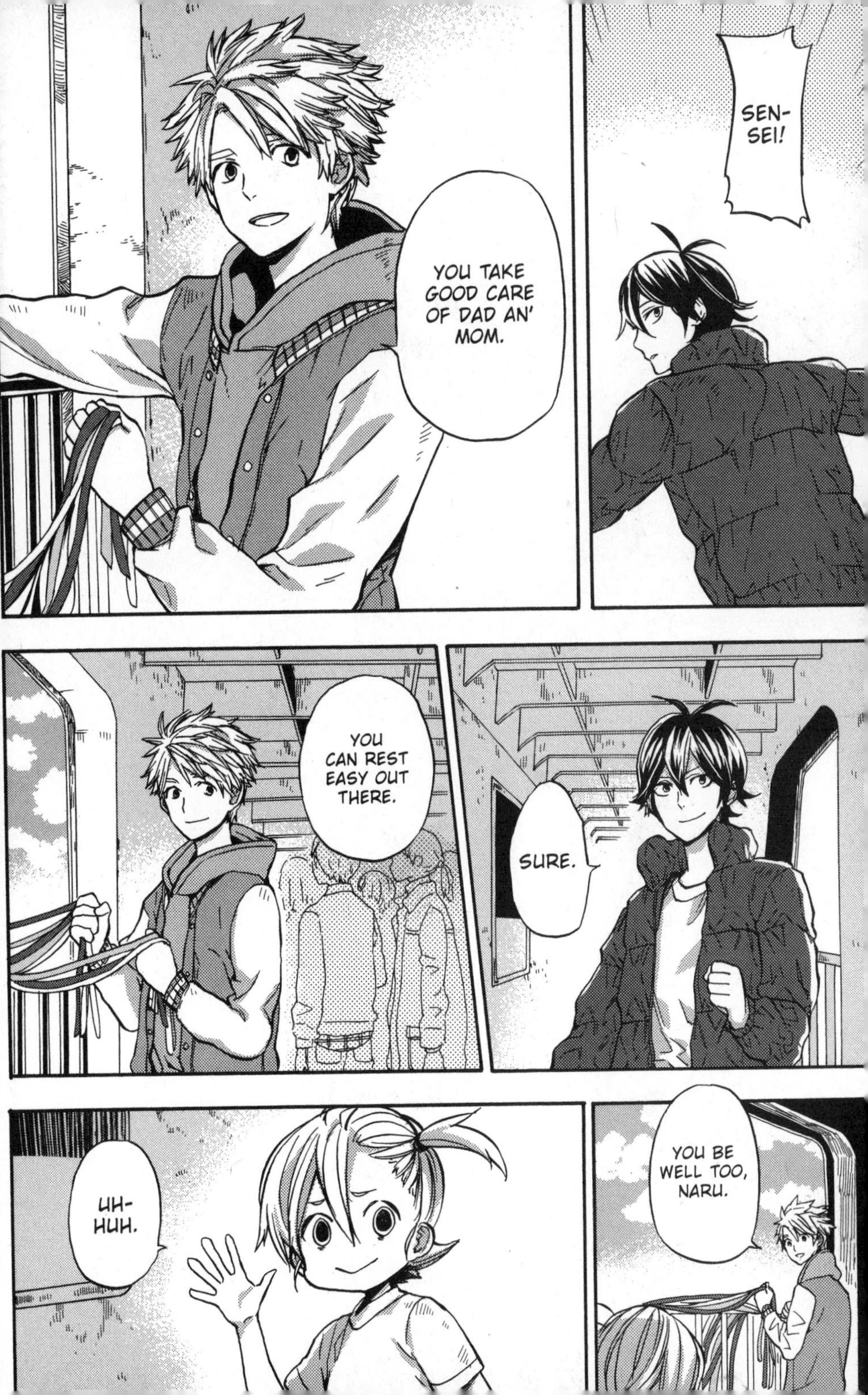
SEN-SEI!
YOU TAKE GOOD CARE OF DAD AN' MOM.
SURE.
YOU CAN REST EASY OUT THERE.
YOU BE WELL TOO, NARU.
UH-HUH.

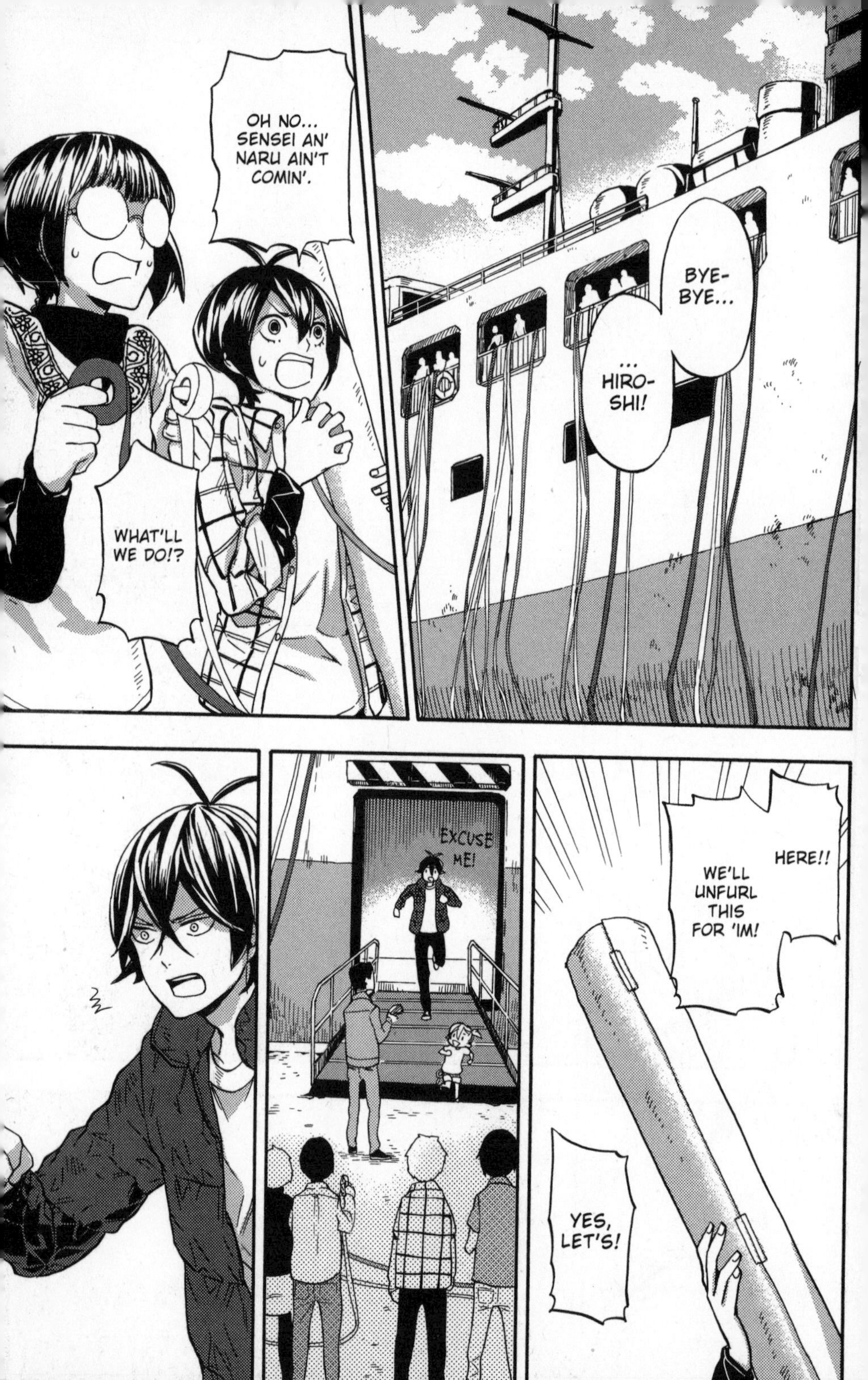
BYE-BYE...
...HIRO-SHI!
OH NO... SENSEI AN' NARU AIN'T COMIN'.
WHAT'LL WE DO!?
HERE!! WE'LL UNFURL THIS FOR 'IM!
YES, LET'S!
EXCUSE ME!

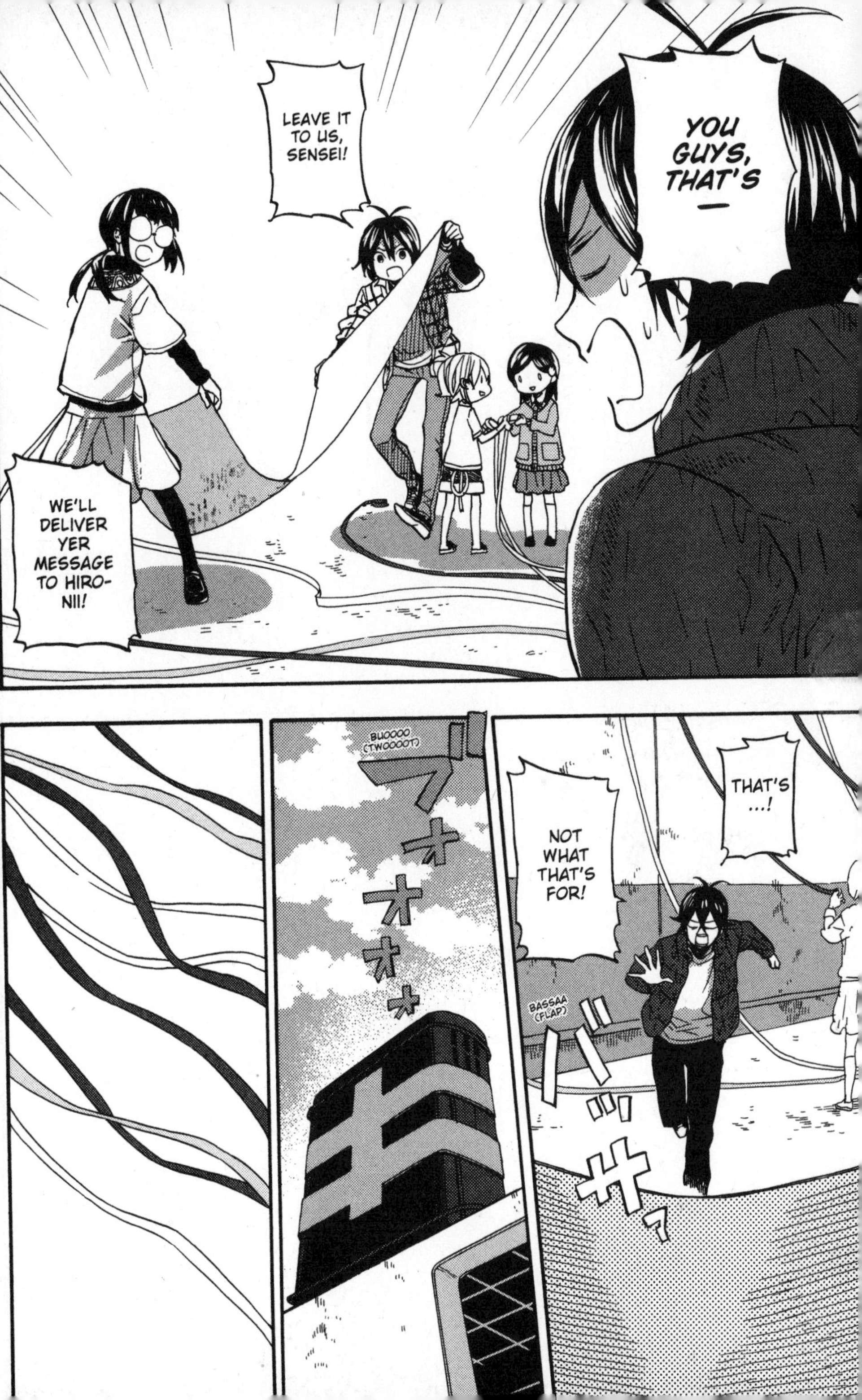
YOU GUYS, THAT'S —
LEAVE IT TO US, SENSEI!
WE'LL DELIVER YER MESSAGE TO HIRO-NII!
THAT'S ...!
NOT WHAT THAT'S FOR!
BASSAA (FLAP)
BUOOOO (TWOOOOT)

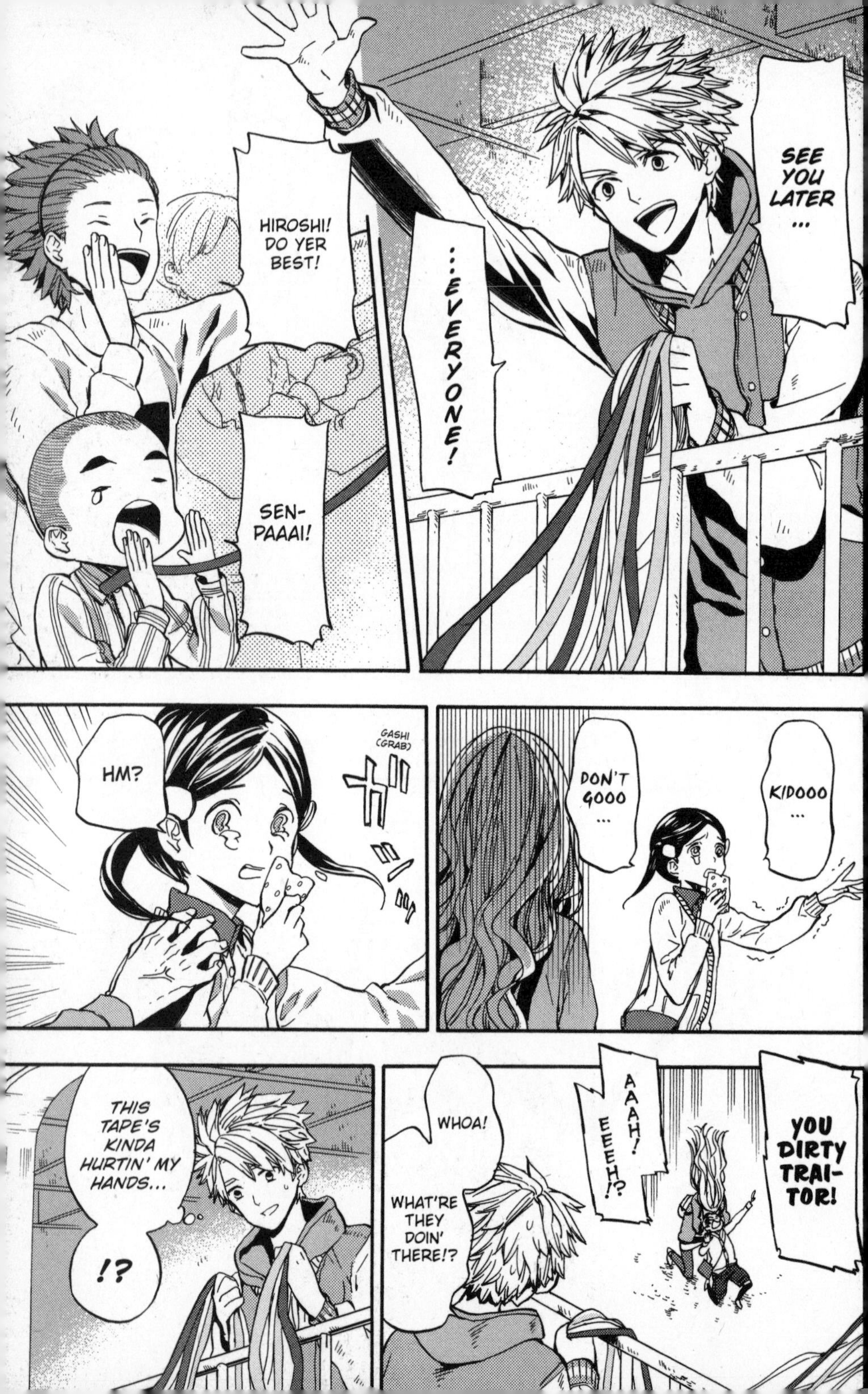
SEE YOU LATER...
...EVERYONE!
HIROSHI! DO YER BEST!
SEN-PAAAI!
KIDOOO...
DON'T GOOO...
GASHI (GRAB)
HM?
YOU DIRTY TRAI-TOR!
AAAH! EEEH!?
WHOA!
WHAT'RE THEY DOIN' THERE!?
THIS TAPE'S KINDA HURTIN' MY HANDS...
!?

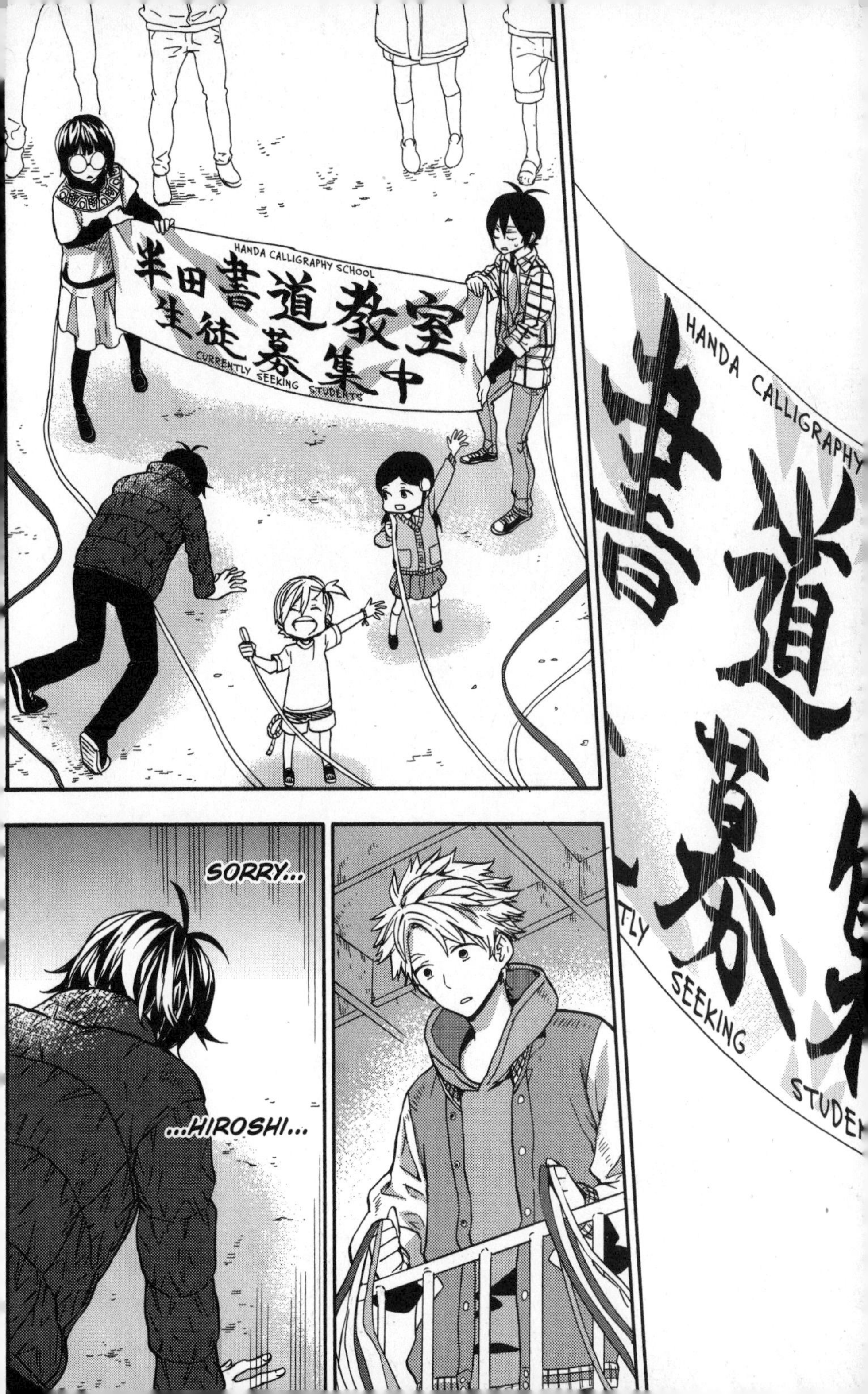

HANDA CALLIGRAPHY
書道
募
SEEKING
半田書道教室
HANDA CALLIGRAPHY SCHOOL
生徒募集中
CURRENTLY SEEKING STUDENTS
SORRY...
...HIROSHI...

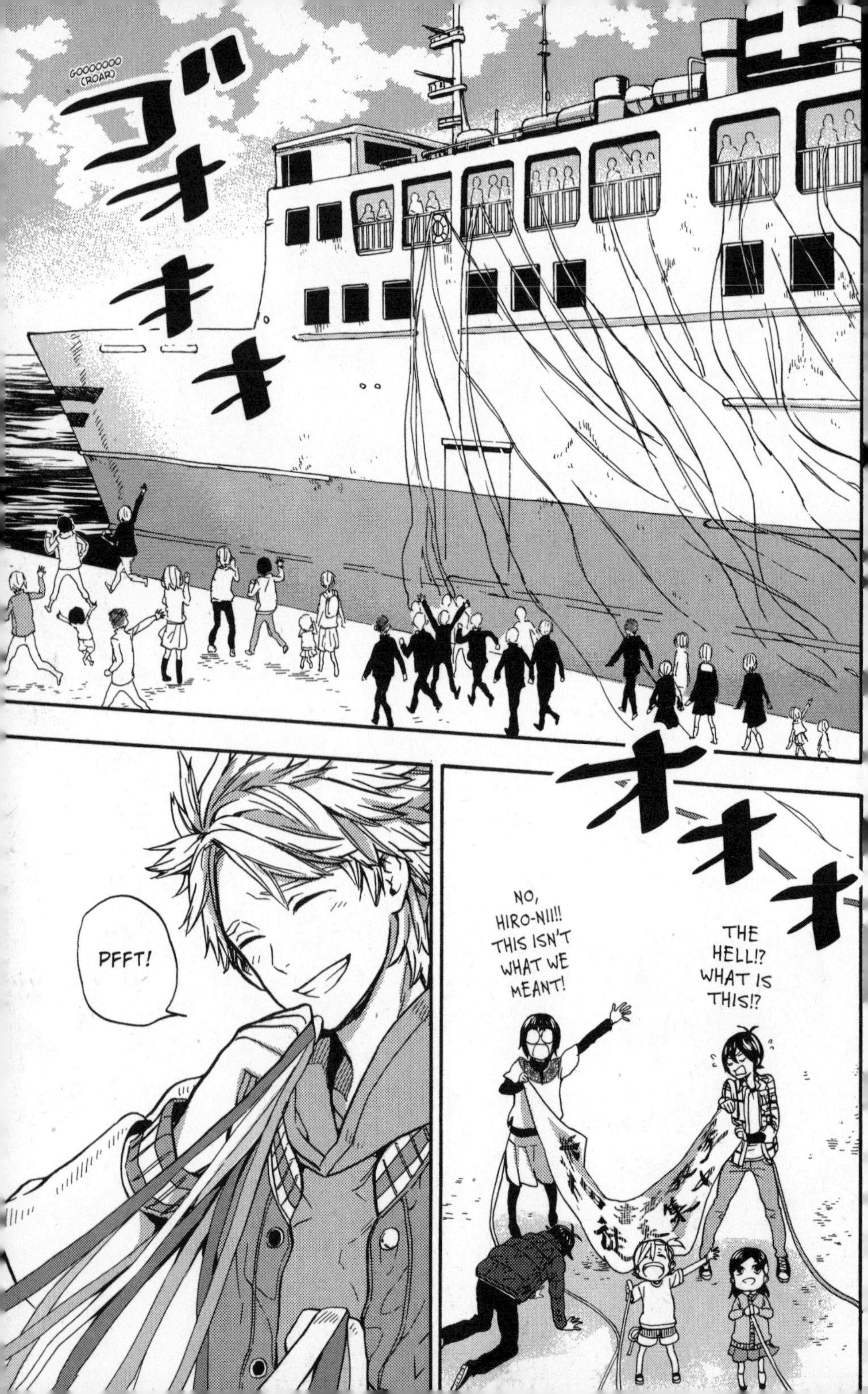
GOOOOOOO
(ROAR)
THE HELL!? WHAT IS THIS!?
NO, HIRO-NII!! THIS ISN'T WHAT WE MEANT!
PFFT!

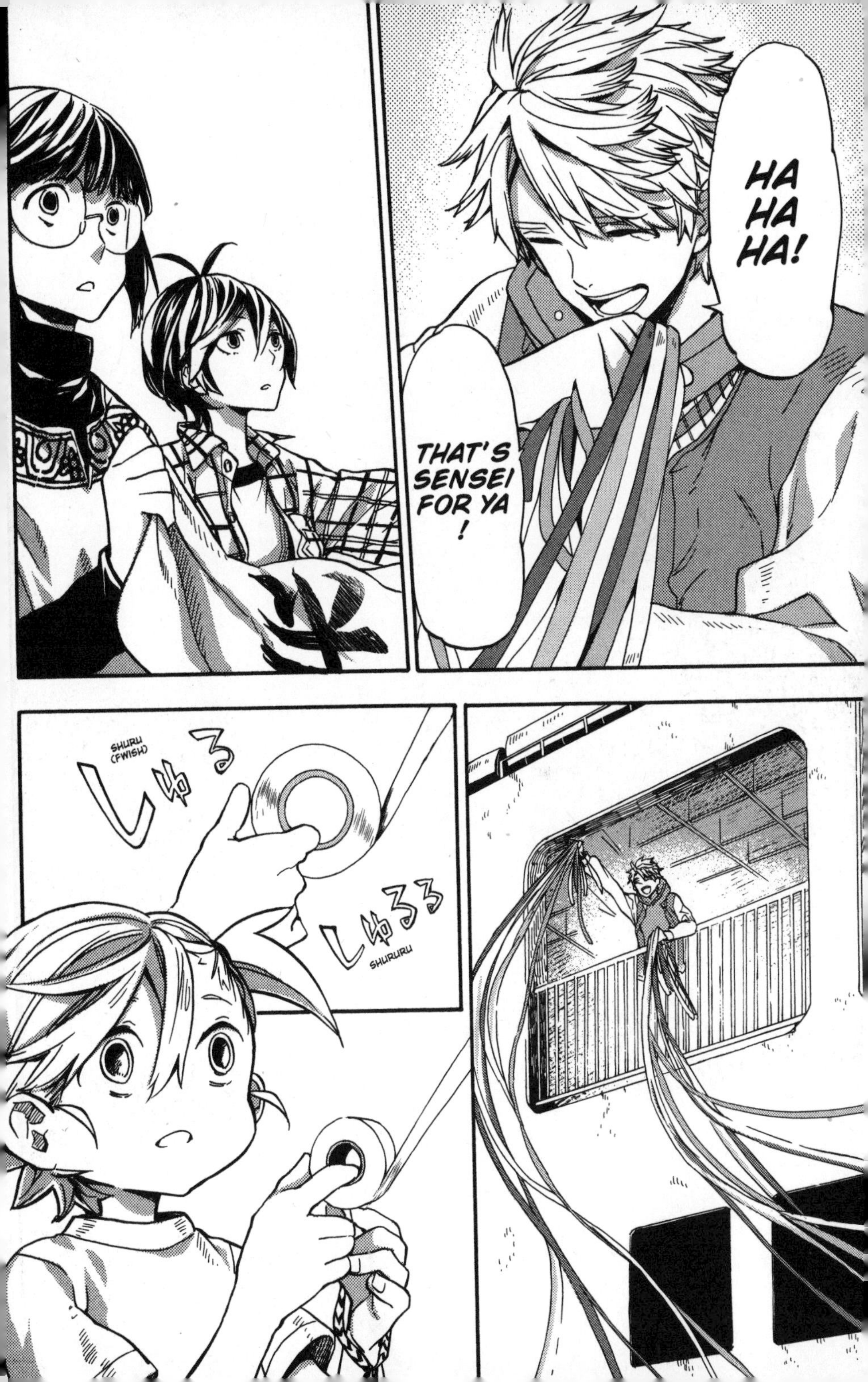
HA HA HA!
THAT'S SENSEI FOR YA!
しゅる
SHURU (FWISH)
しゅるる
SHURURU

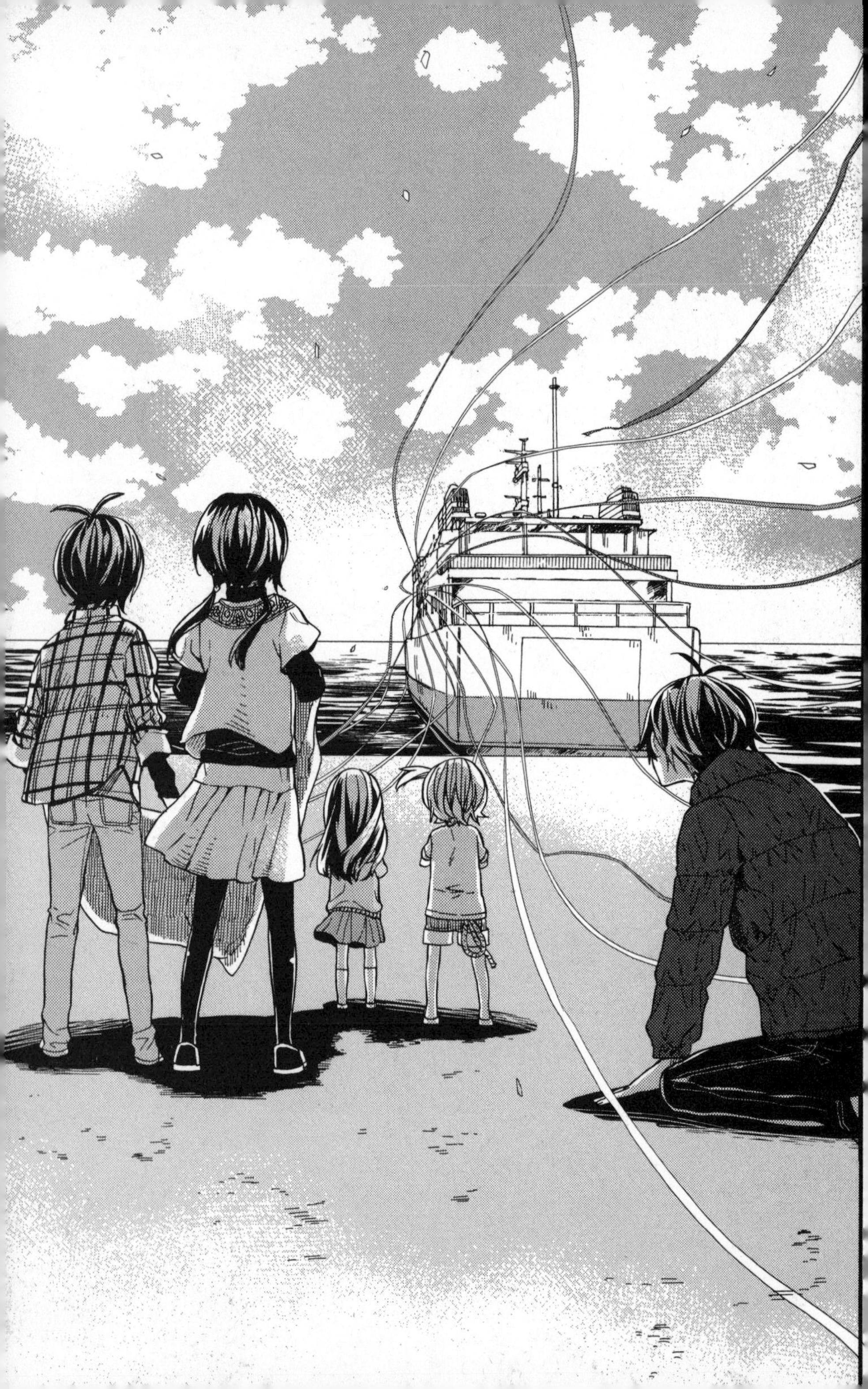

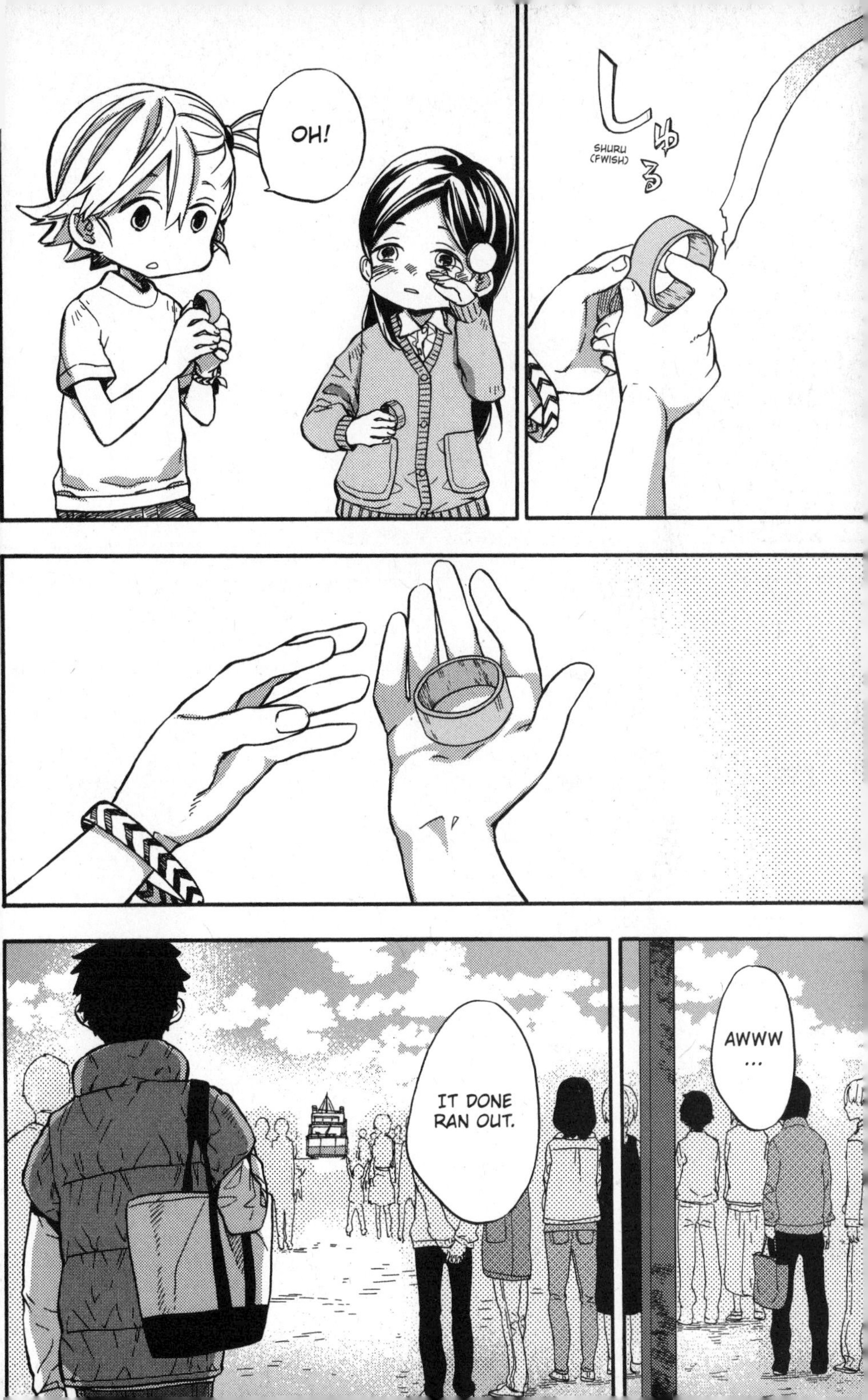
しゅる
SHURU
(FWISH)
OH!
AWWW
...
IT DONE
RAN OUT.

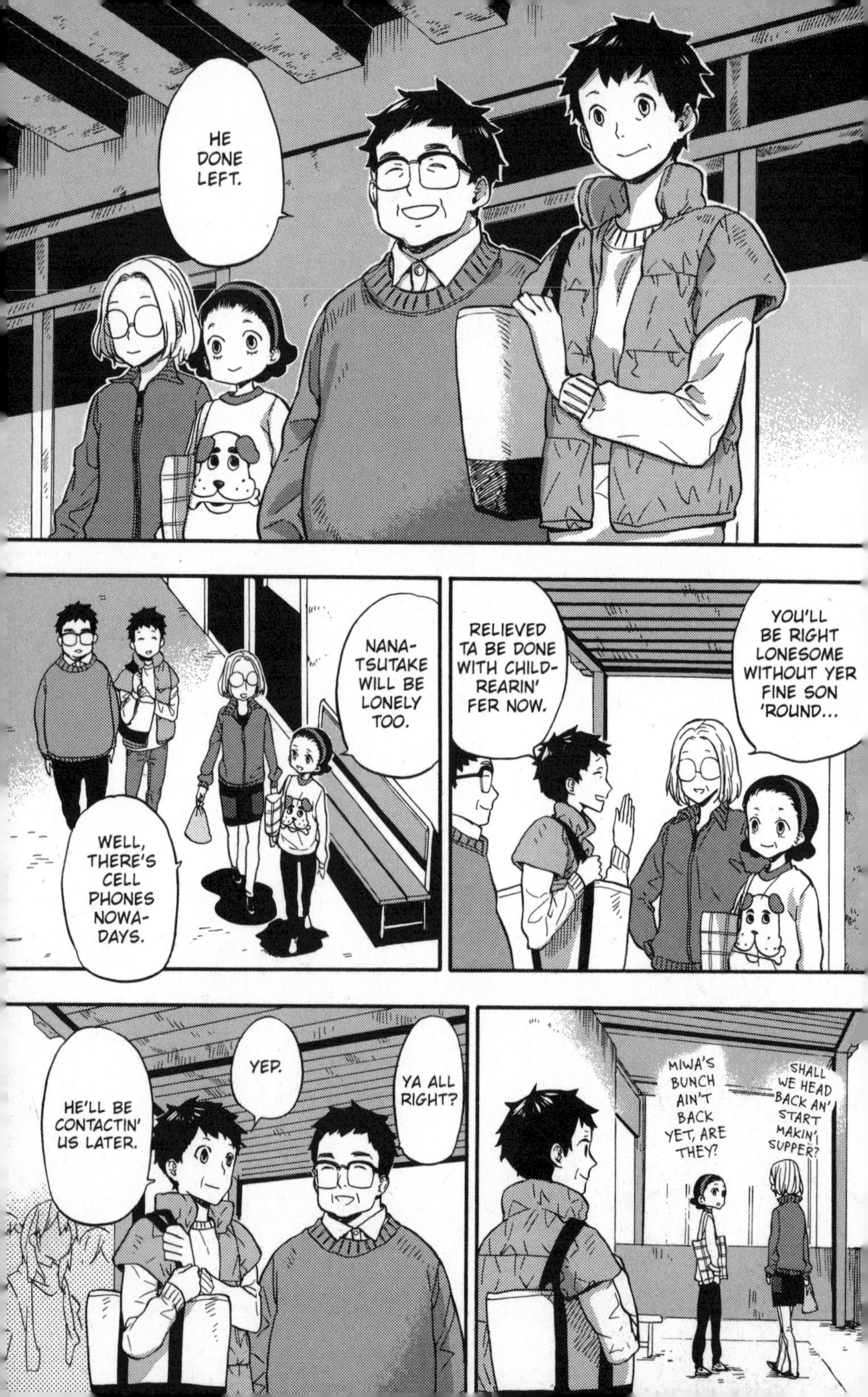
HE DONE LEFT.
YOU'LL BE RIGHT LONESOME WITHOUT YER FINE SON 'ROUND...
RELIEVED TA BE DONE WITH CHILD-REARIN' FER NOW.
NANA-TSUTAKE WILL BE LONELY TOO.
WELL, THERE'S CELL PHONES NOWA-DAYS.
SHALL WE HEAD BACK AN' START MAKIN' SUPPER?
MIWA'S BUNCH AIN'T BACK YET, ARE THEY?
YA ALL RIGHT?
YEP.
HE'LL BE CONTACTIN' US LATER.

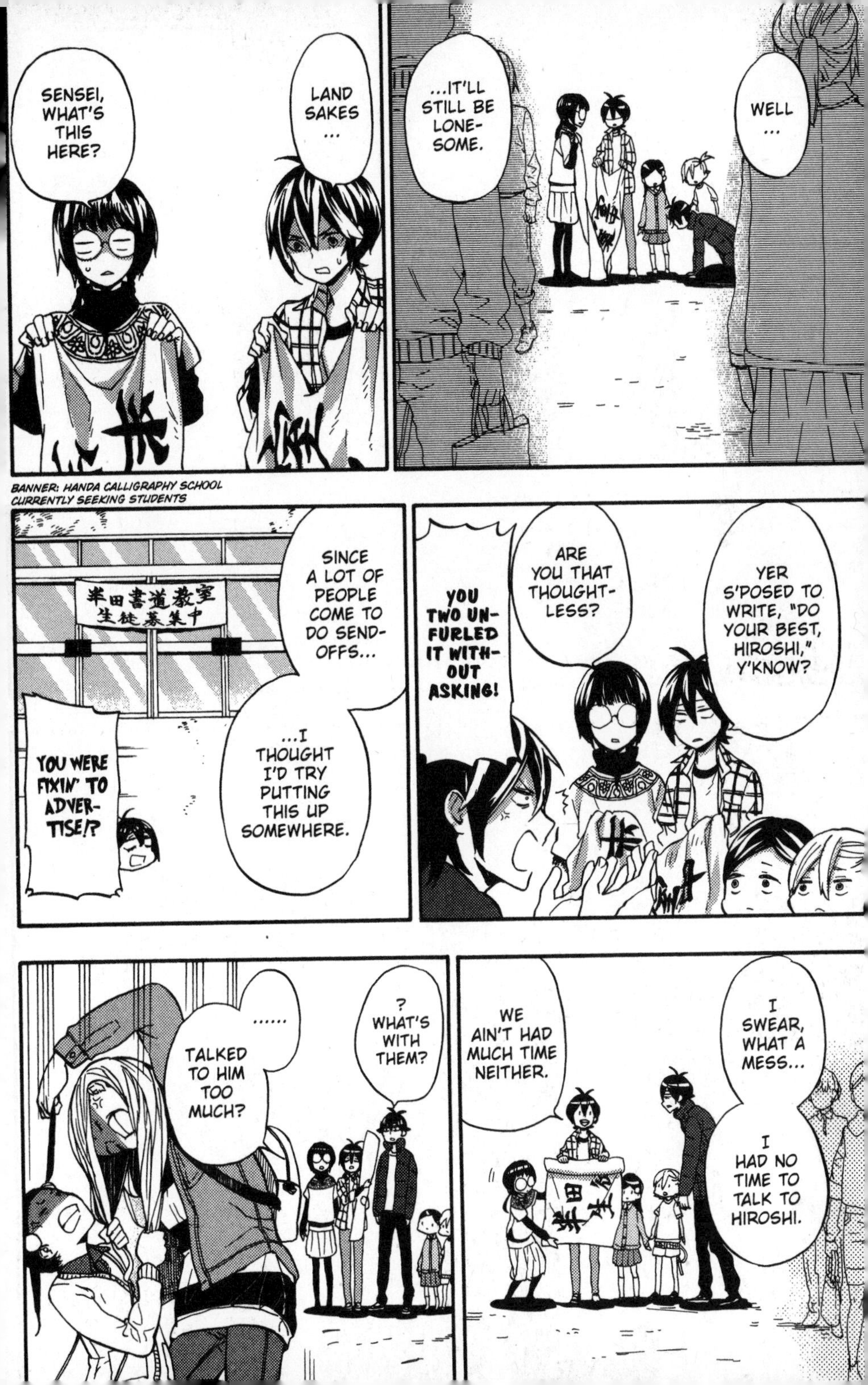
WELL...
...IT'LL STILL BE LONESOME.
LAND SAKES...
SENSEI, WHAT'S THIS HERE?
YER S'POSED TO WRITE, "DO YOUR BEST, HIROSHI," Y'KNOW?
ARE YOU THAT THOUGHTLESS?
YOU TWO UNFURLED IT WITHOUT ASKING!
SINCE A LOT OF PEOPLE COME TO DO SEND-OFFS...
...I THOUGHT I'D TRY PUTTING THIS UP SOMEWHERE.
YOU WERE FIXIN' TO ADVERTISE!?
半田書道教室
生徒募集中
BANNER: HANDA CALLIGRAPHY SCHOOL CURRENTLY SEEKING STUDENTS
I SWEAR, WHAT A MESS...
I HAD NO TIME TO TALK TO HIROSHI.
WE AIN'T HAD MUCH TIME NEITHER.
? WHAT'S WITH THEM?
......
TALKED TO HIM TOO MUCH?

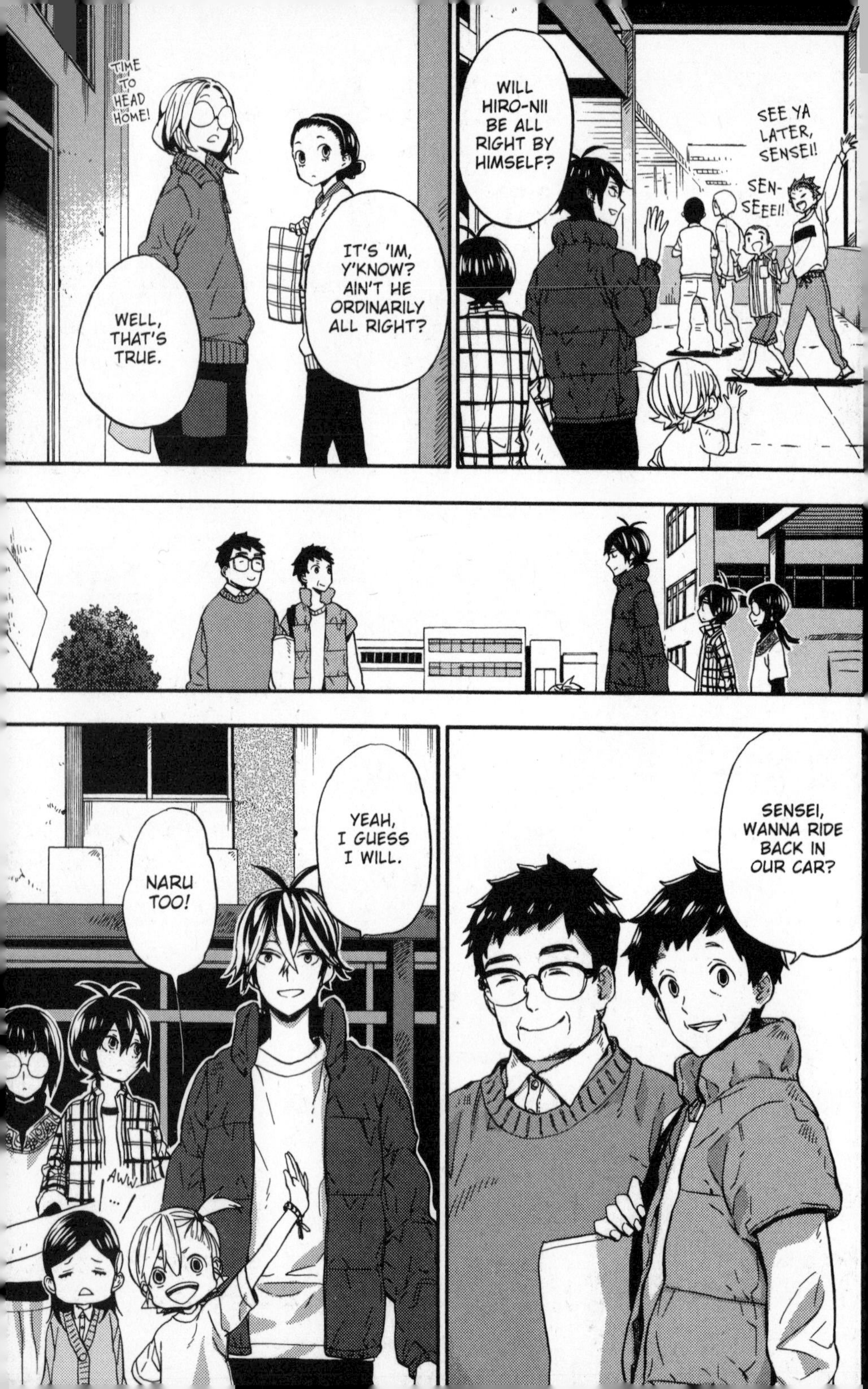

SEE YA LATER, SENSEI!
SEN-SEEEI!
WILL HIRO-NII BE ALL RIGHT BY HIMSELF?
TIME TO HEAD HOME!
IT'S 'IM, Y'KNOW? AIN'T HE ORDINARILY ALL RIGHT?
WELL, THAT'S TRUE.
SENSEI, WANNA RIDE BACK IN OUR CAR?
YEAH, I GUESS I WILL.
NARU TOO!
AWW
...

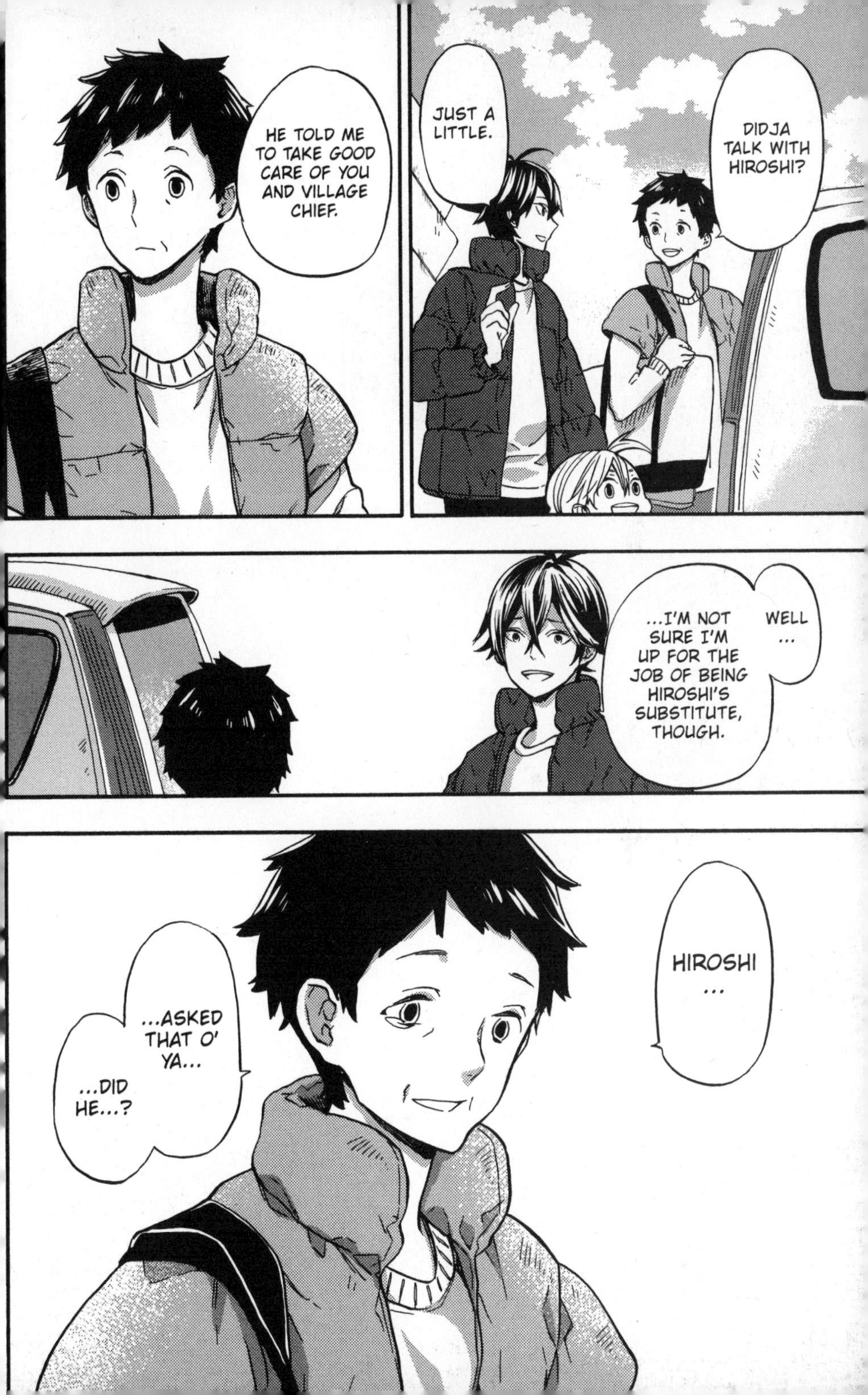
DIDJA TALK WITH HIROSHI?
JUST A LITTLE.
HE TOLD ME TO TAKE GOOD CARE OF YOU AND VILLAGE CHIEF.
WELL ...
...I'M NOT SURE I'M UP FOR THE JOB OF BEING HIROSHI'S SUBSTITUTE, THOUGH.
HIROSHI ...
...ASKED THAT O' YA...
...DID HE...?

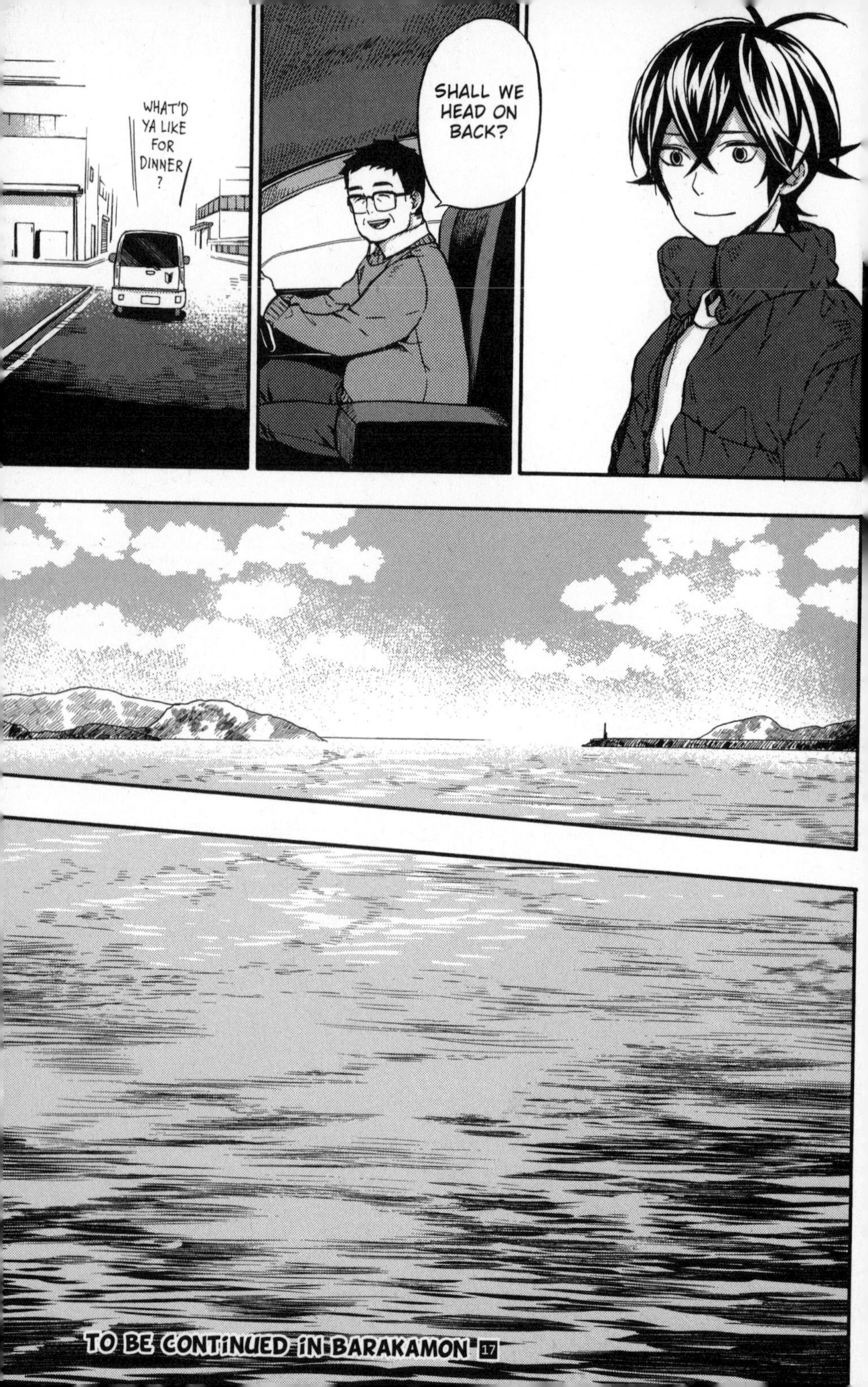
SHALL WE HEAD ON BACK?
WHAT'D YA LIKE FOR DINNER?
TO BE CONTINUED IN BARAKAMON 17

BONUS: DANPO THE 16TH
(Translation: Pond)

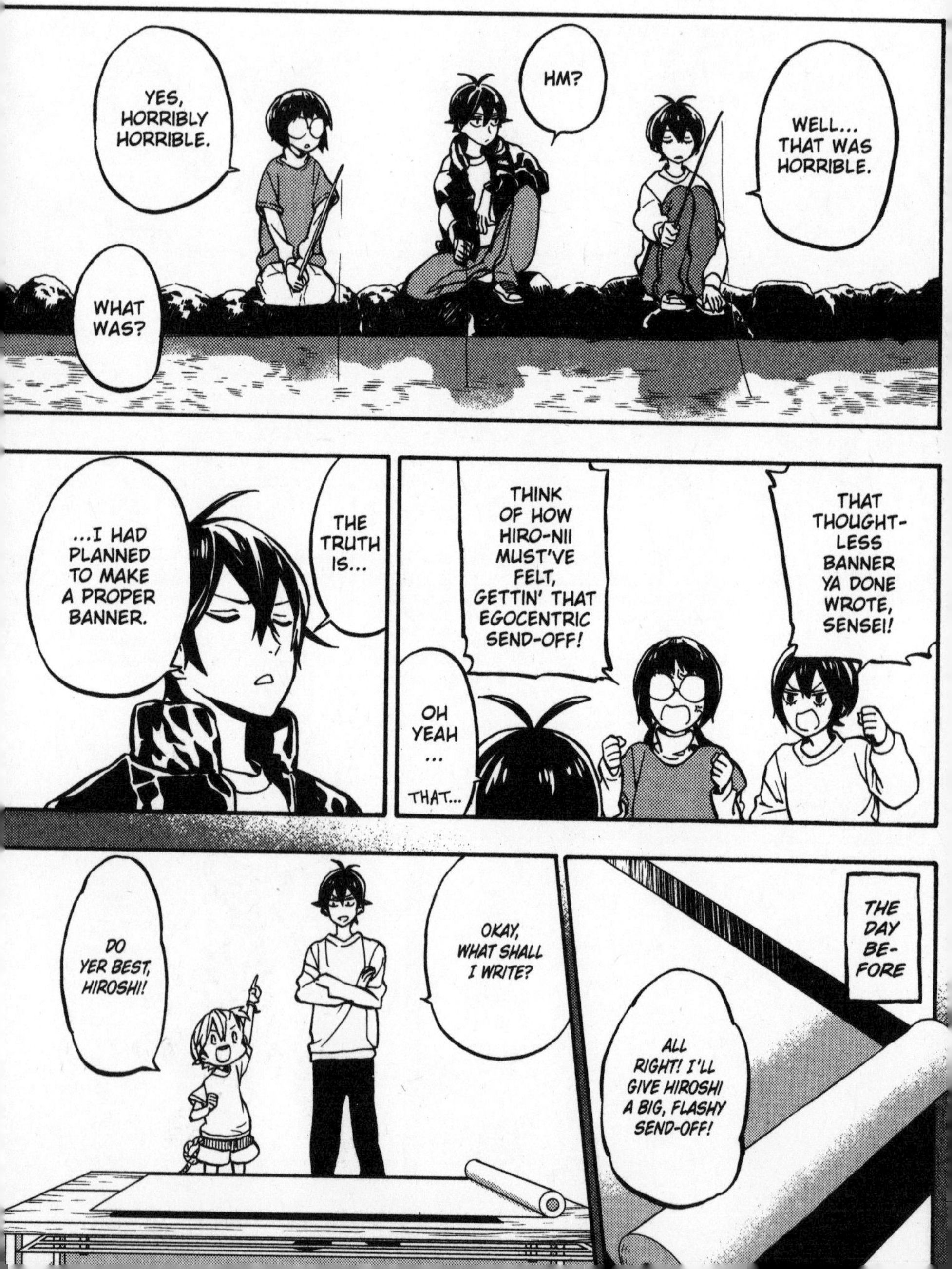
WELL... THAT WAS HORRIBLE.
HM?
YES, HORRIBLY HORRIBLE.
WHAT WAS?
THAT THOUGHT-LESS BANNER YA DONE WROTE, SENSEI!
THINK OF HOW HIRO-NII MUST'VE FELT, GETTIN' THAT EGOCENTRIC SEND-OFF!
OH YEAH ...
THAT...
THE TRUTH IS...
...I HAD PLANNED TO MAKE A PROPER BANNER.
THE DAY BE-FORE
ALL RIGHT! I'LL GIVE HIROSHI A BIG, FLASHY SEND-OFF!
OKAY, WHAT SHALL I WRITE?
DO YER BEST, HIROSHI!

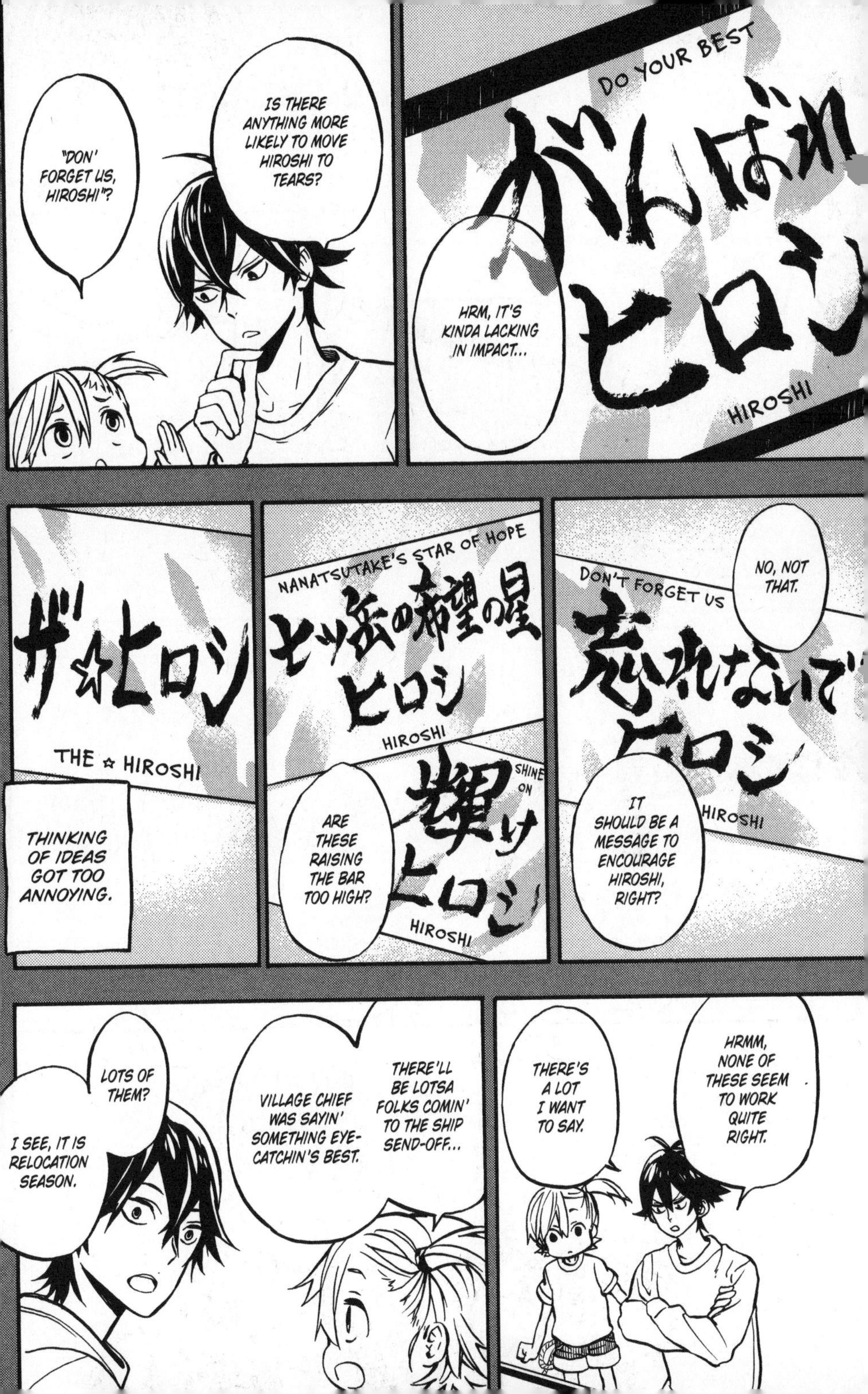
DO YOUR BEST
がんばれヒロシ
HIROSHI
HRM, IT'S KINDA LACKING IN IMPACT...
IS THERE ANYTHING MORE LIKELY TO MOVE HIROSHI TO TEARS?
"DON' FORGET US, HIROSHI"?
NO, NOT THAT.
DON'T FORGET US
忘れないで
HIROSHI
IT SHOULD BE A MESSAGE TO ENCOURAGE HIROSHI, RIGHT?
NANATSUTAKE'S STAR OF HOPE
七ツ岳の希望の星ヒロシ
HIROSHI
SHINE ON
輝けヒロシ
HIROSHI
ARE THESE RAISING THE BAR TOO HIGH?
ザ☆ヒロシ
THE ☆ HIROSHI
THINKING OF IDEAS GOT TOO ANNOYING.
HRMM, NONE OF THESE SEEM TO WORK QUITE RIGHT.
THERE'S A LOT I WANT TO SAY.
THERE'LL BE LOTSA FOLKS COMIN' TO THE SHIP SEND-OFF...
VILLAGE CHIEF WAS SAYIN' SOMETHING EYE-CATCHIN'S BEST.
LOTS OF THEM?
I SEE, IT IS RELOCATION SEASON.

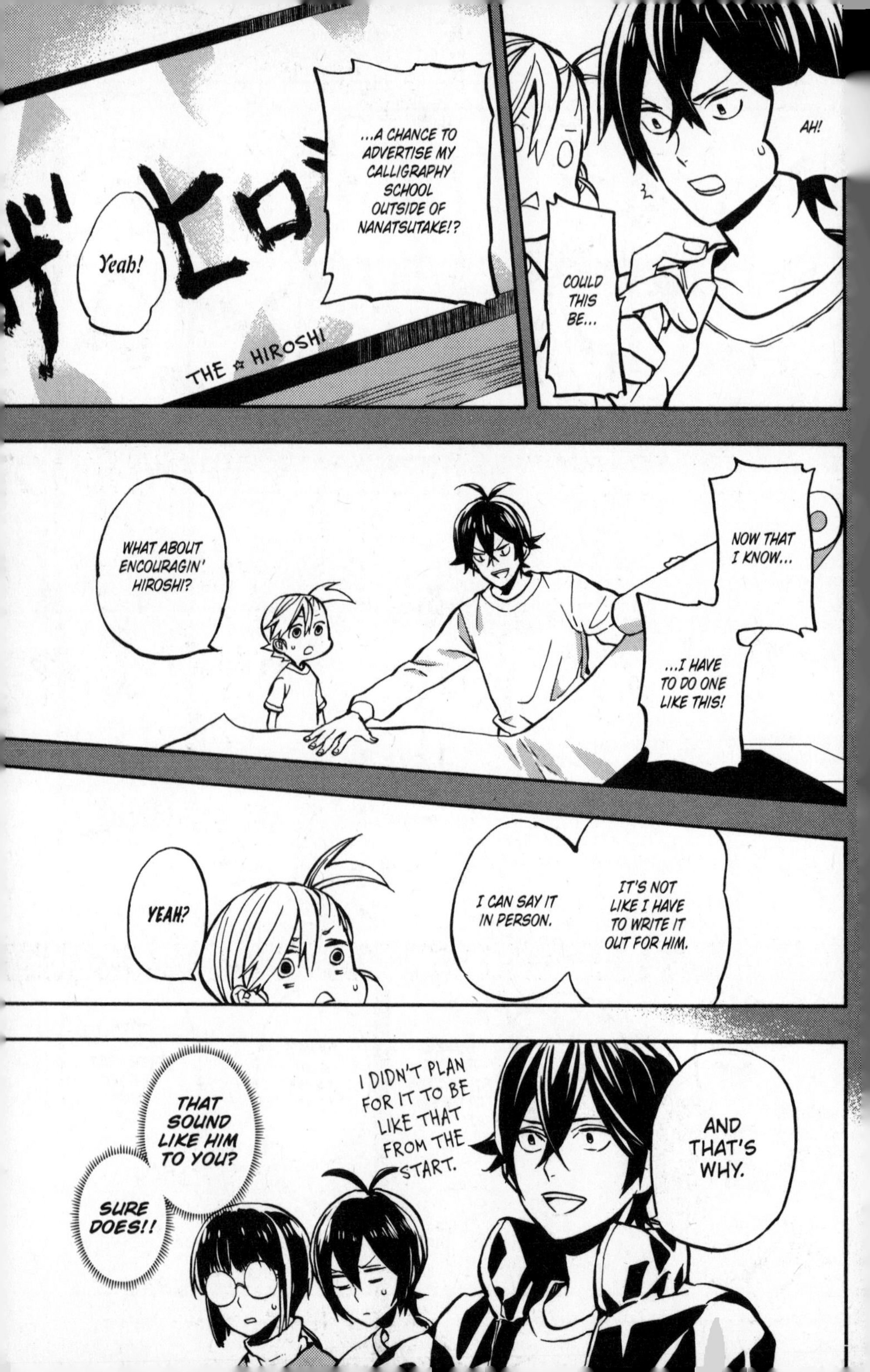
AH!
COULD THIS BE...
...A CHANCE TO ADVERTISE MY CALLIGRAPHY SCHOOL OUTSIDE OF NANATSUTAKE!?
Yeah!
THE ☆ HIROSHI
NOW THAT I KNOW...
...I HAVE TO DO ONE LIKE THIS!
WHAT ABOUT ENCOURAGIN' HIROSHI?
IT'S NOT LIKE I HAVE TO WRITE IT OUT FOR HIM.
I CAN SAY IT IN PERSON.
YEAH?
AND THAT'S WHY.
I DIDN'T PLAN FOR IT TO BE LIKE THAT FROM THE START.
THAT SOUND LIKE HIM TO YOU?
SURE DOES!!

BARAKAMON NEWS

Vol.510

Drama CD #3 Is Planned for Production!!

Included with *BARAKAMON* 17 First-Press Limited Edition

:veryone, thank you very much for buying Volume 16 of *BARAKAMON*! 'hanks to your warm support(ive reservations), they've decided to produce sequel *BARAKAMON* drama CD! For drama CD #2, currently on sale, we ad the participation of Hiroshi Kamiya-san (Kazuma Higashino), Atsushi Abe Dash Higashino), and a wonderful new cast, but what sort of drama CD will his next one turn out to be...!? Production updates will be made public as occa-ion calls in *Monthly Shonen Gangan*, on sale the twelfth of each month, and in *iangan ONLINE*, so please look forward to them!

t's now Volume 16, where Hiroshi finally sets out on his journey to Tokyo. Vhat sort of spring awaits everyone left behind? May we meet again next time 1 Volume 17.

Monthly Shonen Gangan January Issue Now on Sale!!

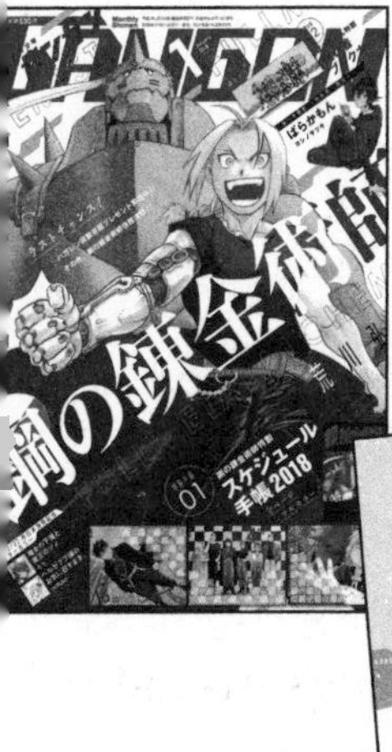

YOU CAN READ THE VERY NEXT CHAPTER OF THE SERIES IN LEAD POSITION WITH COLOR PAGES!!

Deluxe Pack-in
Specially Drawn Book Cover

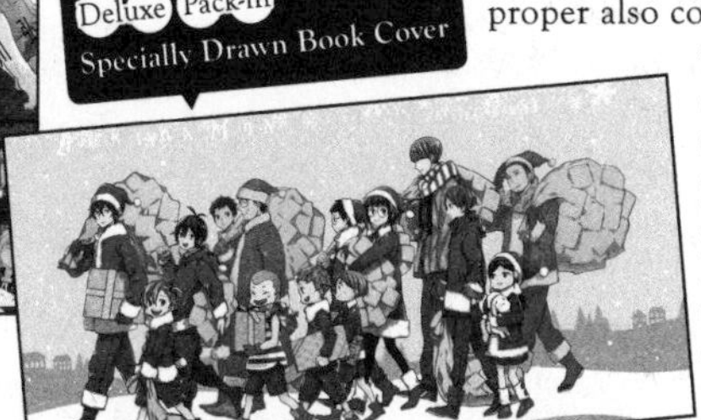

The January issue of *Monthly Shonen Gangan*, currently on sale, includes a book cover specially drawn by Yoshino-sensei that you can use over this book volume! The issue proper also contains the very next chapter of the series in lead position with color pages! Please be sure to check it out!

Please note the items on this page were only available in Japan.

COMMON HONORIFICS

no honorific: Indicates familiarity or closeness; if used without permission or reason, addressing someone in this manner would constitute an insult.

-san: The Japanese equivalent of Mr./Mrs./Miss. If a situation calls for politeness, this is the fail-safe honorific.

-sama: Conveys great respect; may also indicate that the social status of the speaker is lower than that of the addressee.

-kun: Used most often when referring to boys, this indicates affection or familiarity. Occasionally used by older men among their peers, but it may also be used by anyone referring to a person of lower standing.

-chan: An affectionate honorific indicating familiarity used mostly in reference to girls; also used in reference to cute persons or animals of either gender.

-sensei: A Japanese term of respect commonly used for teachers, but can also refer to doctors, writers, and artists.

Calligraphy: Japanese calligraphy has a long history and tradition, with roots stemming from ancient China. One of the traditions carried over was the Chinese expression of the "Four Treasures," which refers to the brush, ink, paper, and inkstone used in calligraphy. Traditionally, an inkstick — solidified ink — is ground against an inkstone filled with water in order to produce ink with which to write. This time-consuming process helped to teach patience, which is important in the art of calligraphy. However, modern advances have developed a bottled liquid ink, commonly used by beginners and within the Japanese school system.

Gotou Dialect: Many of the villagers, especially the elderly ones, are actually speaking the local Gotou dialect in the original Japanese. This dialect is reflected in the English translation with some of the grammar elements of older Southern American English to give it a more rustic, rural coastal feel without making it too hard to read. (It's not meant to replicate any particular American accent exactly.) This approach is similar to how dialect is made accessible in Japanese media, including *Barakamon*, because a complete dialect with all of its different vocabulary would be practically incomprehensible to most Tokyo residents.

Yen: 100 yen is roughly equal to one US dollar.

PAGE 3
The song the students are singing at graduation is "*Tabidachi no Hi ni*" (On the Day of Departure), a relatively new graduation song that was written in 1991 by staff at Kagemori Public Middle School in Chichibu, Saitama Prefecture.

PAGE 6
Con-kana Kingdom is a Gotou winery and resort, located near Onidake Hot Springs.

PAGE 15
second button: It's a semi-tradition, at schools that use blazers in their uniforms, to ask the boy you like for their second blazer button (from the top) at graduation.

PAGE 40
"payback time": The second graduation-type event Handa mentioned in Japanese was *o-rei-mairi*, which typically means "go back to a shrine to give thanks for a good result." But in a graduation context, it's more an unwelcome settling of scores in regard to disputes held during one's time as a student.

PAGE 48
The **Chinese character** Handa is holding up is *ei*, meaning "permanence." Traditionally, it's been widely used for beginning calligraphy students, since it has eight different common strokes in a single character.

PAGE 58
Rose Class: Kindergarten classes in Japan are often named after flowers instead of being numbered like for most grades.

PAGE 94
1,000-fungo drill: *Senbon-nokku* is a Japanese baseball term for fielding one thousand balls in a row in practice, and "fungo" is the English baseball term for fielding practice.

PAGE 98
"turned 'path' into 'dad'": The Japanese words sound very similar: *michi* ("path") versus *chichi* ("my father").

PAGE 100
The word **Mijoka** on Iku's basketball-team sweatshirt is the Gotou dialect word for "cute."

PAGE 110
Myoujou SS Kaioumaru: *Myoujou* means "morning star," and *Kaiou* means "King of the Sea"; *maru* is a common ending used for Japanese ship names, and "SS" is the English abbreviation for "steamship."

PAGE 115
Rishirifuji is another name for Mount Rishiri, which is an extinct volcano with a shape similar to Mount Fuji. It is one of Japan's famous hundred mountains and is located on its own island off the northwest coast of Hokkaido, the large island in the far north of the Japanese archipelago.

PAGE 121
Zunda mochi is a local specialty of Sendai, a city on the eastern coast of northern Japan. It is a filled rice cake, where the filling is a paste made from lightly sweetened *edamame* (green soybeans).

PAGE 141
"someone who can help drive": The Japanese term for the front passenger seat is *joshuseki*, which literally means "assistant driver's seat."

PAGE 142
Osezaki Lighthouse is on a list made in 1998 of Japan's top fifty lighthouses (to celebrate the fiftieth annual Lighthouse Day), so it's pretty famous. The first lighthouse on the site was built in 1876, and the current one is from 1971. It's located on a peninsula at the southwestern end of Fukue Island, so it's still a bit of a drive even if it's the same island they live on. (Still, it's much more accessible than the other Gotou entry, Meshima Lighthouse, located on remote Me Island, roughly fifty miles southwest of Fukue!) Additionally, while the Osezaki Observatory is technically around three hundred feet away from the lighthouse, following the path means walking closer to three thousand feet!

PAGE 145
"sympathy barf": The Japanese word *morai-gero* refers to someone vomiting due to seeing or smelling someone else's vomit.

PAGE 151
The rice ball Naru's eating contains kombu, a type of seaweed.

PAGE 165
The foods Handa yells out are mostly home-cooking type dishes he's enjoyed on the island, some of which you may remember from earlier volumes:
Nikujaga: Beef and potato stew made using Japanese seasonings.
Kakuzushi: Sushi rice put into a rectangular mold with at least one topping (many possibilities), then pressed into shape.
Karaage: Meat, usually chicken, marinated in Japanese seasonings, then deep-fried.
Champon: *Ramen* noodles and various ingredients, such as seafood and vegetables, cooked together in broth.

PAGE 180
Wasshoi is a word yelled at Japanese festivals by the group carrying the portable shrine at shoulder height and sometimes tossing it lightly into the air, much like what they're doing to Hiroshi. Its origins aren't completely clear, but it's commonly thought to be derived from *wa o seou*, meaning, "carry peace on your shoulders."

PAGE 181
"Senpai's kouhai!": *Kouhai* is the opposite of *senpai*, i.e., someone who started at a school, club, or job after you did. In this case, he means Miwa and Tama, who were born in the village after Hiroshi.

DAD AND GRADE-SCHOOL HIROSHI

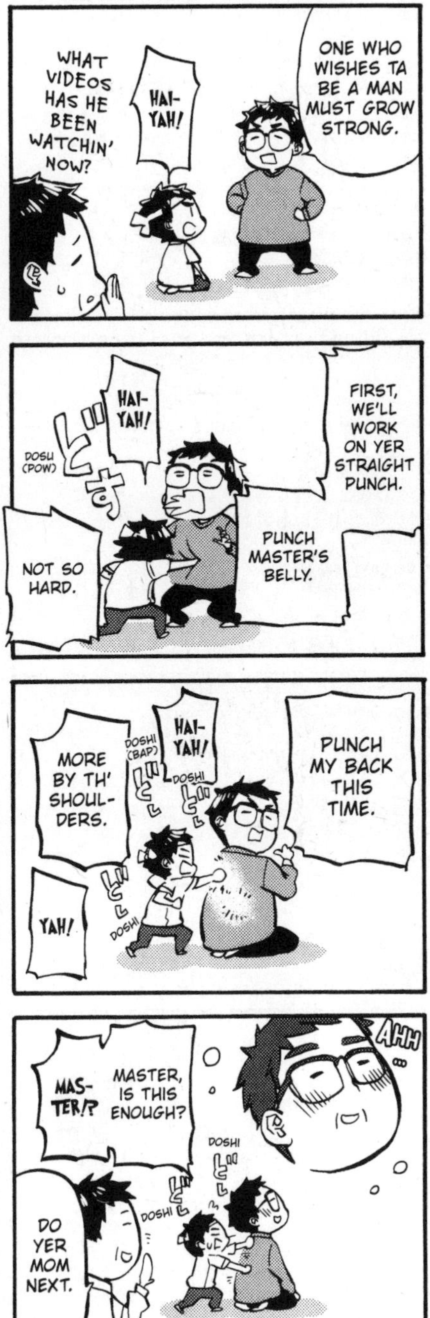

ONE WHO WISHES TA BE A MAN MUST GROW STRONG.
HAI-YAH!
WHAT VIDEOS HAS HE BEEN WATCHIN' NOW?
FIRST, WE'LL WORK ON YER STRAIGHT PUNCH.
HAI-YAH!
どす
DOSU (POW)
PUNCH MASTER'S BELLY.
NOT SO HARD.
PUNCH MY BACK THIS TIME.
HAI-YAH!
DOSHI (BAP)
DOSHI
MORE BY TH' SHOULDERS.
DOSHI
YAH!
AHH
MASTER, IS THIS ENOUGH?
MAS-TER!?
DOSHI
DOSHI
DO YER MOM NEXT.

DAD AND GRADE-SCHOOL HIROSHI

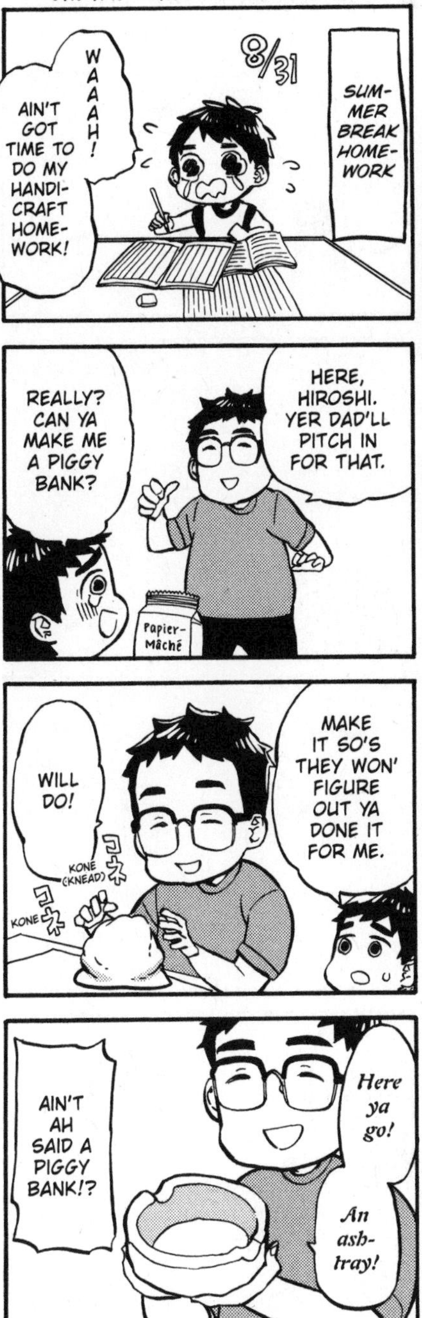

SUM-MER BREAK HOME-WORK
8/31
WAAAAH!
AIN'T GOT TIME TO DO MY HANDI-CRAFT HOME-WORK!
HERE, HIROSHI. YER DAD'LL PITCH IN FOR THAT.
REALLY? CAN YA MAKE ME A PIGGY BANK?
Papier-Mâché
MAKE IT SO'S THEY WON' FIGURE OUT YA DONE IT FOR ME.
KONE (KNEAD)
KONE
WILL DO!
Here ya go!
An ash-tray!
AIN'T AH SAID A PIGGY BANK!?

MOM AND GRADE-SCHOOL HIROSHI

HIROSHI, AH BOUGHT YA SOME PANTS.
TRY 'EM ON.
SURE!
OH.
DEAR ME, THEY'RE A MITE LONG...
LET'S TRY SHORT-ENIN' 'EM UP.
SURE.
AH'LL MAKE YA SOME RIGHT COOL-LOOKIN' PANTS!
SORRY... HIROSHI ...
YER MOM DONE WENT OVER-BOARD.

MOM AND GRADE-SCHOOL HIROSHI

PETA (SPREAD)
PETA
HEY, MOM ...
... WHAT'S THAT?
AH DO THIS GROOMIN' EV'RY DAY...
...TA KEEP MY SKIN FROM AGIN'!
HUH ...
TOO BAD YA AIN'T STARTED IT YOUNGER.
GYUUU (TUG)
OW, OW, OW!
OW, OW, OW!
HIROSHI LEARNED A VALU-ABLE LESSON.

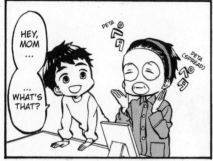

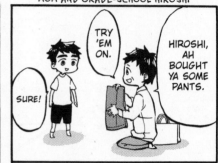

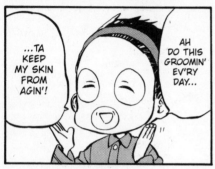

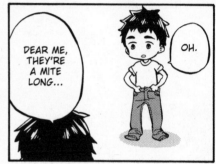

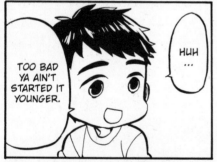

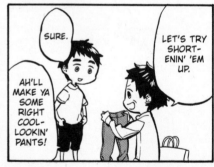

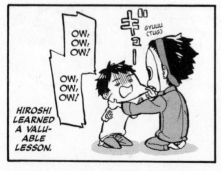

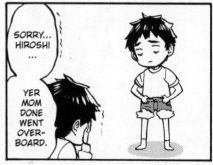

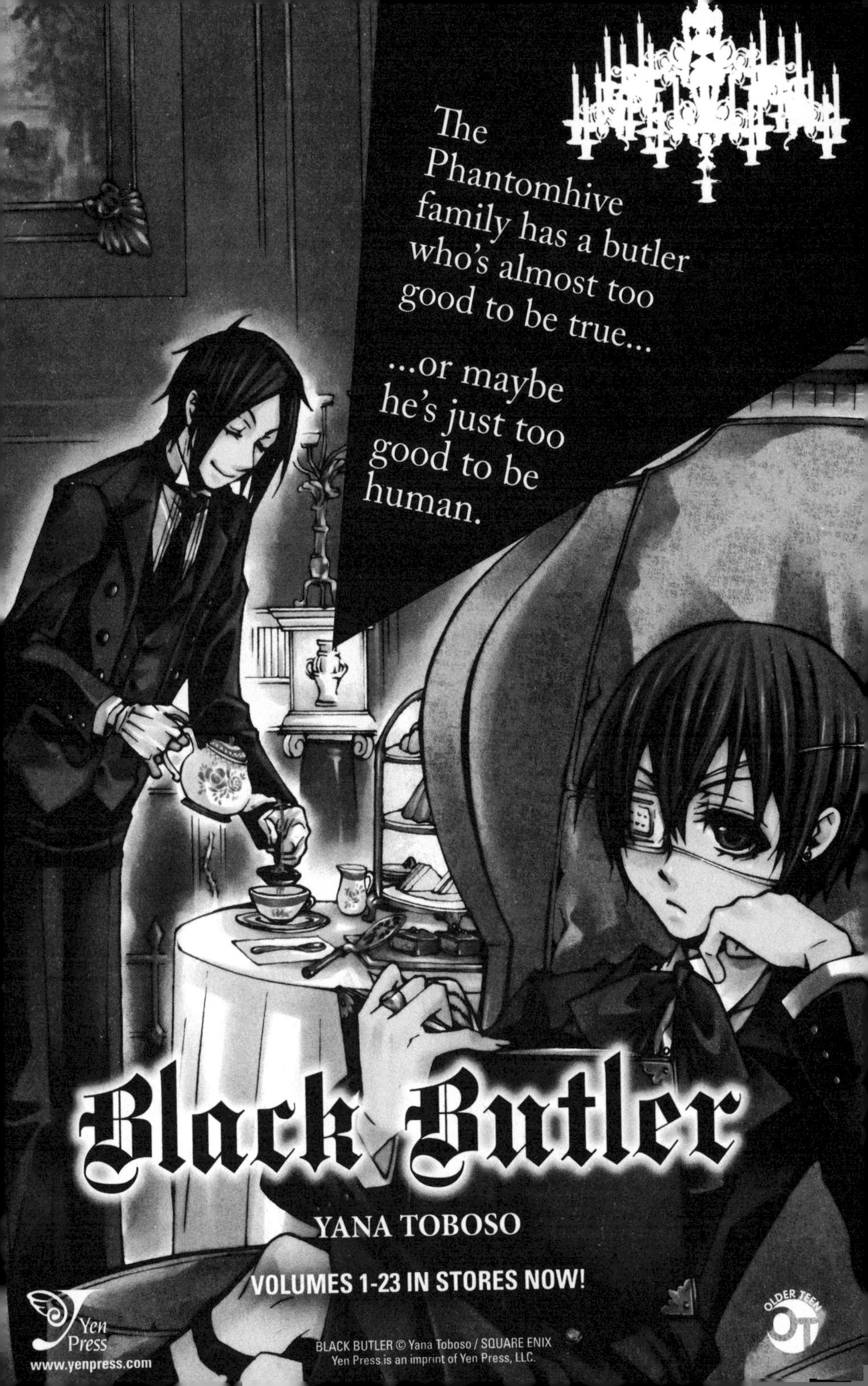
The Phantomhive family has a butler who's almost too good to be true...
...or maybe he's just too good to be human.
Black Butler
YANA TOBOSO
VOLUMES 1-23 IN STORES NOW!
Yen Press
www.yenpress.com
BLACK BUTLER © Yana Toboso / SQUARE ENIX
Yen Press is an imprint of Yen Press, LLC.
OLDER TEEN
OT

HE DOES NOT LET ANYONE ROLL THE DICE.

A young Priestess joins her first adventuring party, but blind to the dangers, they almost immediately find themselves in trouble. It's Goblin Slayer who comes to their rescue—a man who has dedicated his life to the extermination of all goblins by any means necessary. A dangerous, dirty, and thankless job, but he does it better than anyone. And when rumors of his feats begin to circulate, there's no telling who might come calling next...

Light Novel V. 1-2 Available Now!

Check out the simul-pub manga chapters every month!

Yen Press YEN ON
www.yenpress.com

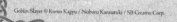

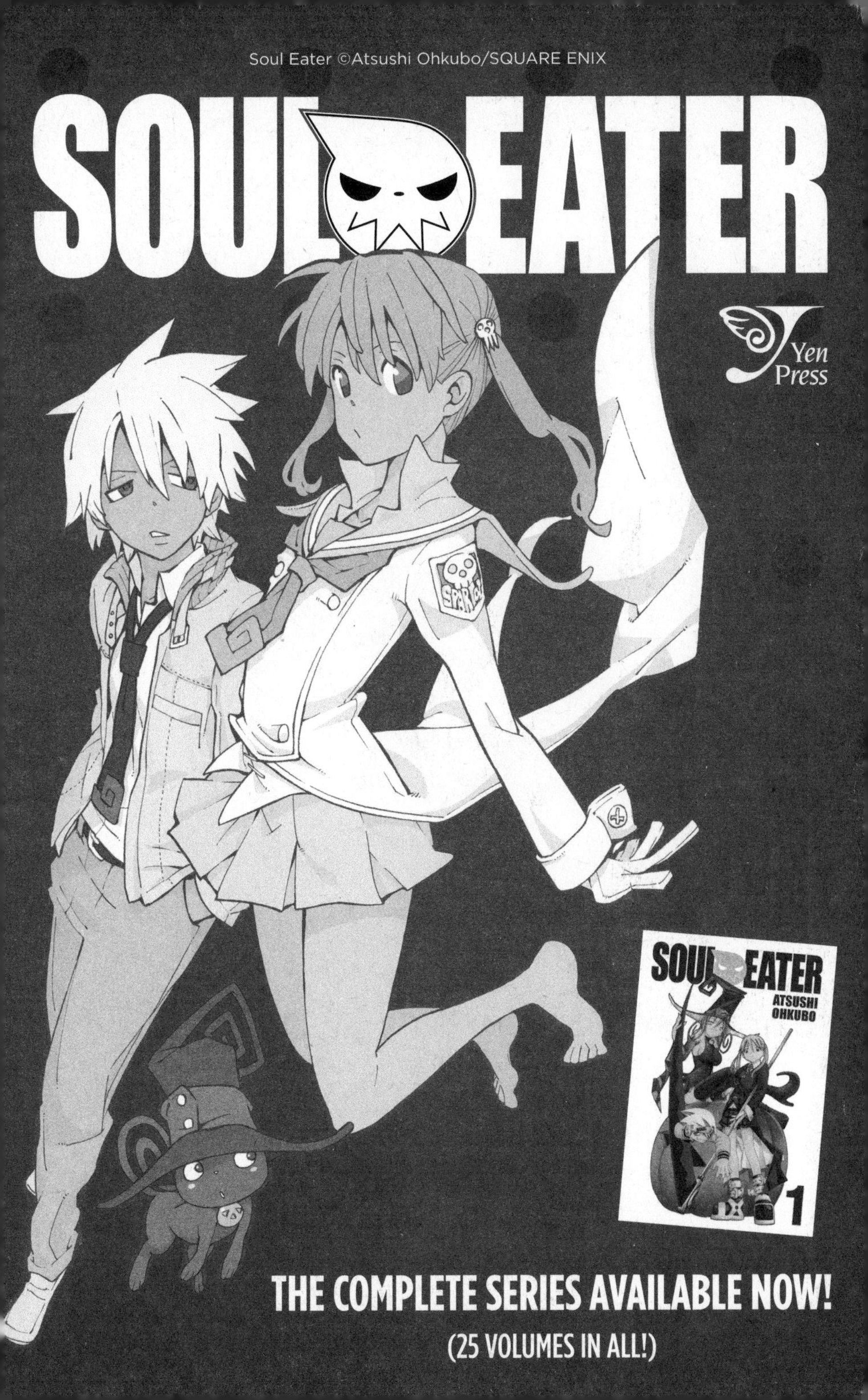
Soul Eater ©Atsushi Ohkubo/SQUARE ENIX
SOUL EATER
Yen Press
SOUL EATER
ATSUSHI OHKUBO
1
THE COMPLETE SERIES AVAILABLE NOW!
(25 VOLUMES IN ALL!)

ON 16

Satsuki Yoshino

Translation/Adaptation: Krista Shipley, Karie Shipley
Lettering: Lys Blakeslee

Barakamon Vol. 16 © 2017 Satsuki Yoshino SQUARE ENIX CO., LTD. First published in Japan in 2017 by SQUARE ENIX CO., LTD. English translation rights arranged with SQUARE ENIX CO., LTD. and Yen Press, LLC through Tuttle-Mori Agency, Inc.

English translation © 2018 by SQUARE ENIX CO., LTD.

Yen Press
1290 Avenue of the Americas
New York, NY 10104

Visit us at yenpress.com
facebook.com/yenpress
twitter.com/yenpress
yenpress.tumblr.com
instagram.com/yenpress

First Yen Press Edition: September 2018

Yen Press is an imprint of Yen Press, LLC.
The Yen Press name and logo are trademarks of Yen Press, LLC.

Library of Congress Control Number: 2015296448

ISBNs: 978-1-9753-0169-9 (paperback)
       978-1-9753-0170-5 (ebook)

10 9 8 7 6 5 4 3 2 1

WOR

Printed in the United States of America